PROSPERITY
AND
DEPRESSION

PROSPERITY
AND
DEPRESSION
A Theoretical Analysis of Cyclical Movements

Gottfried Haberler

With a new introduction by Joseph T. Salerno

Routledge
Taylor & Francis Group

LONDON AND NEW YORK

First published 2011 by Transaction Publishers

Published 2017 by Routledge
2 Park Square, Milton Park, Abingdon, Oxon OX14 4RN
711 Third Avenue, New York, NY 10017, USA

Routledge is an imprint of the Taylor & Francis Group, an informa business

Library of Congress Catalog Number: 2011015177

Library of Congress Cataloging-in-Publication Data

Haberler, Gottfried, 1900-
    Prosperity and depression : a theoretical analysis of cyclical move-
    ments / Gottfried Haberler ; with a new introduction by Joseph T.
    Salerno.
        p. cm.
    Includes bibliographical references and index.
    ISBN 978-1-4128-4220-4 (acid-free paper) 1. Business cycles.
    2. Economics. I. Title.
HB3711.H17 2011
338.5'42--dc22
                                                                2011015177

ISBN 13: 978-1-4128-4220-4 (pbk)

INTRODUCTION TO THE TRANSACTION EDITION

Gottfried Haberler (1901-1995) has been all but forgotten by contemporary economists despite the fact that he remained a productive scholar well into the 1980s and passed away less than twenty years ago. Under these circumstances it is not out of place to begin this introduction to the reissue of what many consider his *magnum opus* with a brief résumé of Haberler's career and work. This will set the stage for a discussion of the relevance of this great work to the current macroeconomic scene.

Haberler was born in Austria and immigrated to the United States in 1936 to join the faculty of Harvard University as professor of economics. From 1971, when he retired from Harvard, until his death, Haberler was a resident scholar at the American Enterprise Institute for Public Policy Research, a centrist-Republican think tank in Washington, D.C.

Haberler was one of the first economists to make a rigorous theoretical case for the superior productivity and universal benefits of "free," or politically unrestricted, international trade in terms of the modern subjective theory of value. He also developed an approach to analyzing cyclical booms and busts based on a synthesis of pre-Keynesian business-cycle theories and heavily emphasized the causal role of political manipulations of the money supply.

As a world-renowned and influential expert in these areas, Haberler almost always firmly and actively opposed the protectionist and inflationist programs and policies advocated by many of his fellow economists and adopted by the governments of both less-developed countries and Western mixed economies in the postwar period.

While residing in Austria during the 1920s and 1930s, Haberler was a member of the famous *Mises-Kreis*, the distinguished circle of economists, sociologists, and philosophers who regularly participated in the private seminar organized by Austrian economist Ludwig von

Mises. The formative influence of Mises and the Austrian school has always been strongly evident in Haberler's theoretical work as well as his prolific policy writings, although this influence has at times been obscured by his vigorous rejection of some aspects of the Austrian theory of the business cycle and his opposition, in later writings, to the international gold standard. Thus, in terms of economic worldview, Haberler is often, though not very accurately, characterized as a monetarist or even a "right-wing Keynesian," and the Austrian connection is altogether ignored.

One of Haberler's most important contributions to economic theory was in the area of international trade. He was the first to present, in 1933, a modern reformulation of the classical argument that free trade and the international division of labor maximizes social productivity and the standard of living for all participating nations (Haberler 1968; Haberler 1985, 3-19). Haberler's reformulation was based on the Austrian approach to value and price theory. This approach, which can be traced back to Carl Menger and his student Eugen von Böhm-Bawerk, rejected the classical labor theory of value. It rigorously established the crucial link between the subjective values of consumers and the objective market prices used by entrepreneurs in their cost and profit calculations, emphasizing the dynamic interdependence of all economic phenomena.

In the early 1950s, Haberler repudiated his earlier support for an international gold standard featuring national currency units rigidly defined as specific weights of gold. He began to campaign for a regime of national fiat currencies linked to one another by flexible exchange rates, a campaign in which Milton Friedman and other monetarist economists were especially prominent (Baldwin 1982, 166). In addressing the problem of stagflation, which became pandemic in Western mixed economies under the flexible exchange-rate regime in the early 1970s, Haberler (1974, 99-116; 1985, 349-62) broke with the monetarists and identified the relentless pressure by labor unions for wage rates in excess of market-clearing levels as the initiating factor of inflationary recession.

Haberler did not hold the naïve view that wage increases themselves were a direct cause of inflation. Rather, he argued, the excessive wage settlements gained by monopolistic labor unions created a politically intolerable level of unemployment that induced the monetary authorities to increase the volume of money and bank credit. The resulting price inflation was intended to alleviate the situation by surreptitiously reducing real wage rates back toward market-clearing levels. But this only mitigated the problem in the short run, because unions quickly caught on to the erosion of their real wages and increased their wage demands. This would ratchet up unemployment and stimulate yet another round of accommodative monetary policy. In the long run, Haberler contended, inflationary monetary policy invariably produced an unsustainable combination of high unemployment and inflation.

In sharp contrast to Keynesian economists, who advocated "incomes policies" such as wage and price "guidelines" as the remedy for "cost-push" inflation, Haberler (1974, 117-38; 1985, 267-310) fully accepted the proposition that a persistent rise in general prices cannot occur without an increase in the money supply, and he stood staunchly against any alleged remedy involving political intervention into the market, which distorted its pricing and resource-allocation process. Instead, Haberler prescribed a policy of strict restraint in the growth of the money supply combined with free market-oriented microeconomic policies aimed at radically reducing or eliminating the monopoly power of labor unions as well as of business organizations. These latter policies included further liberalization of international trade, deregulation of domestic industries, abolition of the minimum wage, the abrogation of "prevailing wage" laws mandating that government buy only from firms paying union wages, the termination of welfare and unemployment subsidies to striking workers, and the abolition of special legal privileges and immunities enjoyed by labor unions.

In the present book, which was sponsored and originally published in 1937 by the League of Nations, Haberler (1937) undertook a comprehensive analysis of the extant literature on business-cycle theory and formulated his own "synthetic" explanation of the causes and nature of cyclical phenomena. Although Haberler was by that time no longer a proponent of Austrian business cycle theory, his analysis involved a broadly Austrian emphasis on the causal role of changes in the supplies of money and credit in conjunction with price and, especially, wage-rate rigidities imposed by political interventions into the market process.

Haberler essentially completed the writing of *Prosperity and Depression* by May 1936. The book therefore contains only passing references in footnotes to John Maynard Keynes's *General Theory of Employment, Interest, and Money* published earlier the same year and yet to create the revolutionary impact that it eventually would. But this fortuitous circumstance means that Haberler's study marked the culmination of the remarkably rich and deep literature on business cycle theory that grew up during the interwar era prior to the Keynesian Revolution. This literature in turn embodied and systematized insights from more than a century's thinking, writing, and disputing about the causes of cyclical fluctuations that began with the British bullionist debates during the first two decades of the nineteenth century.

Unfortunately, many of the important insights and analyses of interwar cycle theory contained in Haberler's book have long lay deeply buried under the "Keynesian Avalanche." A few of these contributions were arduously rediscovered after old-style Keynesianism fell into disrepute during the stagflation-racked decade of the 1970s. Yet many more were never recovered, and even those that were did not strike deep roots in modern macroeconomics. As a result, even the modest progress made by the macroeconomics profession since the 1980s in repudiating the grosser fine-tuning dogmas of the Keynesian era was swiftly reversed by the recent financial crisis. Without a firm grounding in the sophisticated analytical insights and truths contained in Haberler's great synthesis, contemporary macroeconomists were totally confounded by the collapse of the real estate bubble and the pandemic financial meltdown that ensued. Having lost their intellectual bearings, many macroeconomists beat a headlong retreat back toward primitive Keynesianism in a vain search for explanations and solutions. Long-discredited doctrines like the "liquidity trap," the "savings glut," and the "zero interest rate bound" on expansionary monetary policy made their reappearance in academic writings. Never was the question even raised, except by a handful of contemporary Austrians, whether the tremendous expansion of money and credit during the first half of the last decade might have been at fault for the asset bubbles and financial crisis in the first place.

This confusion of thought among macroeconomists, not least of all Federal Reserve Chairman Ben Bernanke, has led to the adoption of policies that can only be described as Keynesian in the most primitive sense. These policies include trillion-dollar Federal deficits, zero short-term interest rates, and two rounds of "quantitative easing" that have flooded the economy with cheap credit while massively expanding the Fed's balance sheet and the monetary base. After more than two years of such policies, unemployment remains stubbornly high and real output growth staggers along at an exceedingly weak pace by the standards of past U.S. economic recoveries. Yet, despite the malaise in the real economy, signs of price inflation and renewed asset bubbles abound. Commodity prices have skyrocketed over the past year, land prices in the Midwest farm belt are rising at double-digit annual rates, the stock market is booming, and junk bond issues exceed last year's pace.

The reprinting of Haberler's treatise thus comes at a particularly auspicious moment—a moment of crisis in both macroeconomic thought and policy. As Keynesian stimulus policies fail yet again to bring about a sustainable, noninflationary recovery and the global economy is threatened by the devastation of another asset bubble, macroeconomists may finally be compelled to rediscover the grand tradition of pre-Keynesian business cycle theory. There is no better place to start than with *Prosperity and Depression*.

—Joseph Salerno, 2011

Bibliography

Baldwin, Robert E. 1982. "Gottfried Haberler's Contributions to International Trade Theory and Policy." *Quarterly Journal of Economics* 97 (February): 141-48.

Gillis, Malcolm. 1982. "Gottfried Haberler: Contributions upon Entering His Ninth Decade." *Quarterly Journal of Economics* 97 (February): 139-40.

Haberler, Gottfried. 1937. *Prosperity and Depression: A Theoretical Analysis of Cyclical Movements*. Geneva: League of Nations.

———. 1968. *The Theory of International Trade: With Its Applications to Commercial Policy*. Trans. Alfred Stonier and Frederick Benham. New York: Augustus M. Kelley Publishers.

———. 1974. *Economic Growth and Stability: An Analysis of Economic Change and Policies*. Los Angeles: Nash Publishing.

———. 1985. *Essays of Gottfried Haberler*. Ed. Anthony Y. C. Koo. Cambridge, MA: The MIT Press.

———. 1993 *The Liberal Economic Order*. Ed. Anthony W.C. Koo. London: Edward Elgar.

———. 1985. *The Problem of Stagflation: Reflection on the Microfoundation of Macroeconomic Theory and Policy*. Washington, DC: American Enterprise Institute for Public Policy Research.

———. "Price Economics versus Welfare Economics," *American Economic Review*, Vol. 10 (September 1920): 483-486.

Officer, Lawrence H. 1982. "Prosperity and Depression--and Beyond." *Quarterly Journal of Economics* 97 (February): 149-59.

Willett, Thomas D. 1982., "Gottfried Haberler on Inflation, Unemployment, and International Monetary Economics: An Appreciation." *Quarterly Journal of Economics* 97 (February): 161-69.

FOREWORD (1964)[1]

WHY DEPRESSIONS ARE EXTINCT

The business cycle has often been declared dead. To cite but one recent example, there was much confidence among economists of the 1920's that a new era of perpetual prosperity had dawned, securely based on better knowledge and skilful policies. Their optimism was rudely shattered by the Great Depression of the 1930's.

I do not say that the business cycle is dead. I do say that deep and long depressions are a thing of the past. I believe that the majority of economists—including many professional critics of the free enterprise system—would agree with this statement today, though not 10 years ago.

What, then, is a business cycle? At the time of this writing, January 1962, the American economy found itself in the midst of what economists call a "business cycle upswing." This upswing, or expansion, started in February 1961, which marked the lowest point of the preceding business cycle downswing, or recession. (Other synonymous expressions, also widely used, are " depression " and " contraction." There is no sharp dividing line between depression and recession; recession simply denotes a mild depression.)

Since the end of World War II, the American economy has passed through four mild recessions:

Postwar Business Cycle Calendar

Expansions	Recessions
Oct. 1945 — Nov. 1948	Nov. 1948 — Oct. 1949
(37 months)	(11 months)

[1] First published in *Think* Magazine (issued by IBM 1962).

Oct. 1949 — July 1953	July 1953 — Aug. 1954
(45 months)	(13 months)
Aug. 1954 — July 1957	July 1957 — Apr. 1958
(35 months)	(9 months)
Apr. 1958 — May 1960	May 1960 — Feb. 1961
(25 months)	(9 months)
Feb. 1961 —	

These ups and downs, the alterations of expansions and contractions around a rising trend, are business cycles. They have been observed in all developed industrial countries which organize their economies chiefly on the free enterprise principle. Naturally, business cycles have somewhat changed their outer appearance over the last century, and especially during the last 30 years. But their fundamental characteristics are still the same.

The basic feature of the business cycle is its pervasiveness. It affects almost all phases of economic life and is clearly reflected by all the broad measures of economic activity: Gross National Product (GNP), the Federal Reserve Index of Industrial Production, non-agricultural employment and unemployment. A very significant fact is that the wholesale price level almost always rises during the upswing and falls during the downswing of a cycle, and the money values—payrolls, aggregate profits, etc. —always go with the cycle. This proves that changes in effective demand, rather than changes in supply, are the proximate cause of the cyclical movement in real output and employment.

This view is generally accepted, explicitly or implicity, by all business cycle analysts, although their views about the forces that produce the swings in total monetary demand or expenditures differ widely.

Cycles in general, and depressions in particular, have varied greatly in length and intensity. Some recent recessions have been so mild that they might have gone unnoticed if we hadn't been equipped with so much statistical information. On the other hand, there is the Great Depression of the 1930's, which lasted 43 months (August 1929 to March 1933) and was a major catastrophe with tremendous economic and political repercussions. The rise of Hitler, and hence World War II, can be traced directly to the immense misery and suffering of the Depression years.

All four post-war recessions were mild and short. Their average length was 10 months, compared with 20 months for the average of 22 peacetime contractions from 1854 to 1961. The average length of post-war upswings was 36 months, compared with an average of 30 months for the 1854-1961 period. The mildness of post-war recessions is understood by the fact that GNP (in current dollars) declined by only about 2.5 per cent on the average, while it dropped by almost 50 per cent during the Great Depression and by 31.5 per 'cent during the short but exceptionally sharp depression from May 1937 to June 1938. This drop was even more catastrophic in view of the fact that it started from a very low base, since the economy had not recovered from the Great Depression.

Two related puzzles now arise: (1) Why are some depressions mild and why do others become malignant? Is it possible that the two types do not belong to the same species? (2) Why have post-war recessions been so benign? Have we our good luck to thank, or do they represent a trend due to a change in the structure of the economy or to good policy?

It is a fact that, at least in the U.S., depressions fall into one of two distinct groups; we can therefore distinguish unequivocally between deep-depression cycles and mild-depression cycles. Deep depressions were those of 1873–79, 1893–94, 1907–08, 1920–21, 1929–33 and 1937–38. The other 17 depressions since 1867 were of the mild variety. There is, however, no agreement among experts whether this sharp division is to be attributed to chance or whether there is a systematic reason for it, and if the latter view is adopted, what the reason is.

It is now fairly generally recognized that the exceptional severity of the Great Depression of the 1930's and that of 1873–79 was due to special circumstances—for the most part, to financial and monetary disturbances which can be definitely traced to the Civil War and World War I. In the 1930's, the great intensifiers of the Great Depression were: the failure of thousands of banks in the U.S. and other countries, the collapse of the international gold standards and gold exchange standards on the international level, and the massive destruction of bank money (deposits) and terrific deflation engendered by these events. Incredibly inept and timid anti-depression policies, on both the national and international level, must take much of the blame for the excessive length and severity of the Great Depression. It should be emphasized that anti-depression policies were timid and inept in the U.S. and elsewhere both by modern and old-fashioned standards. The deep depression of 1920–21 was clearly a financial aftermath of the war; and the deep depression of 1937–38 was part and parcel of the generally depressed period of the 1930's, which transcended the period of the Great Depression proper (1929–33) and came to an end only with the outbreak of World War II.

Deep depressions are thus due to special circumstances and are not essential features of the free enterprise, capitalist economy. I would therefore say that they belong to a category of their own.

Mild recessions, such as those of the post-war period, are more difficult to explain. Moreover, partly because their causes are not obvious, and for other reasons which will become clear later, it is hardly possible to avoid or cure these mild swings altogether —at least within the framework of a free enterprise system.

Why have depressions been so mild during the post-war period? My answer is this is the result of a profound and lasting change in economic institutions and policy, and is not due to a possibly ephemeral constellation of favourable circumstances.

A repetition of the catastrophe of the Great Depression today is practically impossible because of several reasons.

The U.S. financial structure has been greatly strengthened. Bank deposits are now insured. (Federal insurance of bank deposits by the Federal Deposit Insurance Corporation, which became effective in 1934, was the most important monetary reform since the establishment of the Federal Reserve System. It has virtually removed the danger of a run on banks by depositors fearful of losing their money.)

And finally, no wholesale failure of banks and protracted deflation would be tolerated anywhere, not even in the most capitalistic countries.

The scope of governmental activities has greatly increased since 1930. Then U.S. Government expenditure on goods and services amounted roughly to 10 per cent of GNP; now it is more than 20 per cent. And so-called " transfer payments "—for interest, subsidies, social security payments, unemployment benefits and the like—have gone up even more sharply. This expansion of the public sector one may deplore on some grounds, but it cannot be denied that it is a stabilizing factor, both by itself and because it provides greater leverage for the so-called " automatic stabilizers " and for " discretionary " anti-depression policies.

Let me illustrate this by two figures. If in 1933, at the bottom of the Great Depression, a one-year holiday of all Federal income and profit taxes had been declared, it would have added less than $1,000,000 to private incomes and would hardly have made a dent in the Depression. In 1960, such a tax holiday would have amounted to $67 billion and turned even a severe depression into runaway inflation.

Automatic or built-in stabilizers are the automatic increase in Government spending (for unemployment benefits, old age pensions and the like), and the automatic decrease in Government revenue (because of lower tax receipts under a pay-as-you go system of tax collection during a depression when GNP declines). These stabilizers automatically create a deficit in the Government budget in a depression and cushion the impact of a drop in output on disposable incomes and spending by preventing the spending power of the unemployed, the taxpayer, etc., from falling as much as it otherwise would. This has proved to be a very powerful brake on deflationary spirals and has been a major factor in keeping depressions mild.

Discretionary anti-depression policy consists of fiscal and monetary measures.

Fiscal measures consist of increasing Government spending by special public works, or by speeding up and advancing expenditures which would have been made anyway, on the one hand, and of reducing Government revenue by lowering tax rates, on the other hand, so as to counteract the decline of private spending in a recession. Little conscious and deliberate use has been made so far of the tax remission method to counteract recessions. There are, however, two instances on the post-war record when tax reductions, which were made for other reasons, happened to come at the right time to help contain an incipient depression. This happened both in 1948 and in 1953.

Monetary policy is the other branch of discretionary anti-depression (or, more generally, stabilization) measures. It is controlled by the Federal Reserve System. During post-war recessions, money has been made easier and the cost of borrowing sharply reduced by the Federal Reserve banks. This was done through a reduction of discount rates and through purchases of Government securities in the open market. It is a fact that during the post-war period the weapons of monetary policy have been wielded by the Federal Reserve System with much greater energy and promptness than during the inter-war period; the contrast is especially sharp—and favourable—with the lack of vigour displayed during the Great Depression, when the Federal Reserve stood by while the money stock fell sharply (by about one third) and the economy underwent a disastrous deflation.

Compared with the automatic stabilizers, discretionary anti-depression policies suffer from a serious handicap: lags in the adoption and operation of discretionary policies.

These lags are of different natures. There is first what might be called the "diagnostic" lag. If anti-depression policies are to be adopted promptly, the minimum requirement is that the onset and the end of a depression be promptly diagnosed. This is by no means easy, and there are many cases on record in which the majority of experts failed to recognize a cyclical turning point until months after it had occurred—or else they took what turned out to be a temporary ripple for a true cyclical turn. Once the correct diagnosis has been made there is likely to be a 'policy' lag, for administrative and political reasons, before effective measures are taken. This is true especially of fiscal measures. For example, tax changes require an act of Congress, and it usually takes some time before money voted for public works is actually spent. The policy lag has been reduced, and it may be possible to reduce it further, but it still exists and will probably never be eliminated completely.

The policy lag is less important in the case of monetary policy. The Federal Reserve can act without delay and in recent times has often acted very promptly. But in this area there is still another lag, namely, an "operational" lag between the adoption of monetary measures (for example, an easy money policy) and the monetary measures on the volume of actual expenditures. Whether the lag is six months, a year or longer, and whether it is always about the same remains an open question.

Now, assuming first that these lags exist, it is easy to see that in case their combined length is almost the length of a recession, discretionary anti-recession policies will have their effect too late. Thus the policy becomes destabilizing rather than stabilizing. There have, in fact, been clear cases in recent years when anti-recession spending polices became effective only after the recession was over, fanning the fires of inflation instead of alleviating the recession.

If recessions were longer than they actually have been since the war, it would be easier to deal with them by discretionary anti-recession policies. But for the short recessions which we have experienced in recent times, our discretionary policy instruments are simply too crude.

Our powers of prompt diagnosis have been improved, although they are still far from being perfect, especially in view of the fact that the true cyclical situation is often obscured and distorted by outside disturbances such as a nation-wide steel strike or influences from other parts of the world. But even if the diagnostic lag could be eliminated and the policy lag greatly reduced, there would still remain the operational lag. It follows that in order to avoid destabilizing effects it would be necessary to apply the anti-recession measures well in advance of the cyclical turns. This requires forecasting.

Unfortunately, economists have not yet been successful in predicting business cycle turns. It is true that National Bureau of Economic Research experts have developed " leading indicators "—time series and combinations of such series that usually turn the cyclical corners well in advance of the turning points in general business. These indicators are now being published in the Department of Commerce monthly bulletin, *Business Cycle Developments*. But the method is still in an experimental stage. The lengths of the lead of the various series over the business cycle turning point differ from one another, and they are often quite long and change from one turning point to the other. While the development of the leading indicators constitutes a great advance in our knowledge of cyclical movements and has greatly improved our diagnostic powers, it cannot be regarded, and does not claim to be, a reliable method of forecasting business cycles. Moreover, if and when it yields reliable forecasts, and policies are based thereon, the pattern of leads and lags is likely to change and we would have to look for other indicators. The economic weather is not immune to forecasts of its future course if these forecasts become the basis for preventive policies of governments and of anticipatory actions of private business.

For these reasons, it does not seem to me probable that it will be possible to iron out, or to reduce much more than we have already done, the mild cyclical swings which our economy has experienced during the post-war years.

Nonetheless, the great readiness which today exists to step in with anti-depression fiscal and monetary policies has stabilizing effects in an indirect but very important manner. It is a safeguard against long and deep depressions, and that this safeguard has been more and more accepted as effective by the business community has created an atmosphere of long-run optimism which has made long-run investment plans fairly immune to short-run setbacks. In the post-war period, long-term investment plans have been affected less than previously by recessions because there is increasing confidence that no long and deep depression will develop. This has helped, along with the operation of the built-in stabilizers, to prevent recessions from snowballing into deeper depressions.

The decline in output during the post-war depressions has to a large extent been confined to a drop in inventories and was due to a smaller extent than in former cycles to a reduction in investment in plant and equipment. How quickly in an environment of gloom and pessimism a setback can spiral into a deep depression is shown by the very sharp and fast (though short) slump in output which occurred in 1937–38.

At this point, one may ask: Aren't there other measures, besides built-in stabilizers and discretionary fiscal and monetary policy, that would eliminate the business cycle altogether? Let me suggest, very briefly, an answer, although I cannot pretend that my views express the consensus of the great majority of economists. My answer is that it could be done—but only at the price of a degree of Government control of the economy greater than most responsible people, if they realise all the implications, would be prepared to recommend.

To suppress the cycle altogether, and maintain uninterrupted stability at full employment, we would need to keep the economy continuously under strong inflationary pressure; at the same time, we would have to prevent runaway inflation by a maze of controls over prices, wages, investments, foreign trade and payments, and relax those controls selectively when and where slack and unemployment threatened to appear. Such a system of "repressed inflation" could effectively suppress the cycle, although it could hardly prevent a gradual rise in prices and would surely be detrimental to long-run growth.

This is, indeed, the system of war economics which many European countries carried over into peacetime. But the longer the "high presssure system" has been continued in peacetime, the more it has been found inefficient, wasteful and distasteful. In one country after the other it has been abolished, the controls dismantled and the price mechanism and free markets restored. Those countries, such as Germany and Italy, which were fortunate enough to get rid of the high pressure system soon after the war, have consistently outproduced those that have hung onto the system of high pressure and controls. And with the disappearance of high pressure and controls, mild cyclical swings— milder than in the U.S. but essentially of the same nature—have reappeared in Europe.

It is true that in the last seven or eight years the U.S. has not outproduced continental Europe or Japan. On the contrary, the rate of growth of GNP has been less in the U.S. than in those areas, and there has been much dissatisfaction with the performance of the U.S. economy. The true nature and causes, and possible remedies, of this apparent slowdown are very complex, and I will discuss only one aspect which is closely connected with what has been said earlier.

I mentioned that we may have to pay a price for the high level of stability which was achieved during the post-war period. This is the gradual rise in price level. During business cycle upswings, the price level rose, and as soon as contraction started, built-in stabilizers and discretionary and anti-recession policies went to work so that the price level remained stable, or even continued to creep up slowly. During no period since the middle 1930's has there been a noticeable drop in the price level. This is a new phenomenon which has created a greater sensitivity on the part of the public to further price rises. It has caused—along with other developments—a serious weakening in the U.S. balance of payments, especially since 1957.

This has forced the adoption of more restrictive financial policies, or at any rate prevented the adoption of easier money policies. If this could be changed, growth surely would be faster and the unemployment percentage lower over the cycle.

There is an unusually wide agreement among economists to the effect that in recent years the basic reason for inflation has been the excessive push for wage increases. This continuous rise in labour costs, well in excess of what can be absorbed without a price rise by the gradual increase in productivity, puts a nasty dilemma before the monetary authorities: by monetary expansion, they can let prices rise, and the balance of payments deteriorate; or they can, by keeping money tight and interest rates high, resist the trend of rising costs and prices and thus permit to appear an amount of unemployment large enough to check pressure for higher wages. What they have been doing is, in fact, a policy of compromise, permitting some price rise and some unemployment and slowdown of growth. If there were a little more money wage discipline and money wage rose not more (or still better, a little less) than the overall rise in labour productivity, it would be much better all around: the price level would remain stable (or still better, decline a little bit), unemployment would be lower, GNP would rise faster, and the balance of payments could get back into equilibrium (barring adverse developments abroad). As a consequence, real incomes in general, and *real* wages in particular, would be higher and rise faster. The business cycle would still be with us, but its swings would play around a steeper rising trend, and if the fear were removed that a vigorous anti-recession policy will give a boost to creeping inflation, a better job could be done of counteracting and offsetting recessions.

PREFACE

The first edition of this book was written at the suggestion of Alexander Loveday, then Director of the Financial Section and Economic Intelligence Service of the League of Nations, during my stay in Geneva as a member of the Secretariat of the League. My work was part of a larger project, financed by a grant from the Rockefeller Foundation, on the causes and cures of depressions. A later part of that larger project was Professor Tinbergen's celebrated two volumes *Statistical Testing of Business Cycle Theories*.[1]

The first draft of *Prosperity and Depression* was finished in the Summer of 1936. In August of that year, I had the opportunity of submitting my manuscript to a conference of experts, among them O. Anderson, J. M. Clark, A. H. Hansen, O. Morgenstern, B. Ohlin, and J. Tinbergen. Their criticisms and suggestions led to extensive revisions. Prior to that conference, I had greatly profited from the criticism and suggestions of the late Folke Hilgerdt and Rifaat Tirana, of J. B. Condliffe, Marcus Fleming, Alexander Loveday, Ragnar Nurkse, and Luis Rasminsky. The first edition of the book appeared in 1937.

I should like to take this opportunity to pay my tribute to that remarkable group of economists at Geneva. Under the inspiring leadership of A. Loveday, supported by a very small budget (compared with the sums at the disposal of international agencies in the post-war period), that group produced a most impressive collection of analytical and statistical documents dealing with many problems of international trade, economic development, commercial, financial and monetary policies, while at the same time advising governments of many countries on their economic

[1] Vol. I and Vol. II, League of Nations, Economic Intelligence Service, 1939.

problems. The group also provided a highly stimulating atmosphere from which temporary members of the Secretariat like
myself, and countless visitors to Geneva were able to derive
immense profit.

The second extensively revized and enlarged edition of the
book appeared in 1939. In this edition I added Chapter VIII,
which contains a lengthy discussion of the Keynesian literature.
The first edition had been substantially finished before the appearance of Keynes' *General Theory*, and only a few references to it
could be made in footnotes.

A third edition appeared in 1941 still under the imprint of the
League of Nations. This edition reprinted Parts I and II of the
second edition without change and added Part III, which dealt
with some later developments, such as the foreign trade multiplier
and multiplier-acceleration models. In this form, the book was
later reprinted by the United Nations whom I have to thank for
their hospitality.

The book now appears for the first time under the imprint of a
private publisher. Unfortunately, it was not possible, at this time,
to undertake a major revision. It was therefore decided to make
no changes at all in Part I and Part II. Part III has been eliminated
and its place has been taken by three papers which had been
published elsewhere. In these papers I have tried to sketch and
evaluate some recent developments of business cycle theory.

In order to reduce the size of the book as much as possible,
the introductions of Mr. Loveday to the first three editions, as
well as Appendices I and II of the earlier editions, are not reproduced.

GOTTFRIED HABERLER.

Harvard University,
September 1957.

The present edition differs from that prepared in September 1957
in that what was Appendix I " Notes on the present state of
Business Cycle Theory " has been omitted. A new Foreword
has been added. This edition is now similar to that issued in a
pocket format by Atheneum Publishers, New York in 1963.

G.H.

CONTENTS

ANALYTICAL TABLE OF CONTENTS

Analytical Table of Contents

Part III

MONETARY FACTORS AFFECTING ECONOMIC STABILITY

Analytical Table of Contents

INTRODUCTION

Purpose of the book. As has been explained in the Preface, this book is a first step in a more extended enquiry undertaken by the Economic Intelligence Service of the Secretariat of the League of Nations into the causes of the recurrence of periods of economic depression.

The present study confines itself to the task of analysing existing theories of the business cycle and deriving therefrom a synthetic account of the nature and possible causes of economic fluctuations. However, the next stage in this investigation—the application, as far as possible, of quantitative tests to the various causal hypotheses—has largely influenced the manner in which the preliminary problem has been approached in the following pages. The reader is invited to keep in mind, while studying the present report, the fact that it is planned as but a part of a greater whole.

Analysis of theories. In view of the scope of the investigation as a whole, the purpose of the first part of this report—i.e., of the Systematic Analysis of the Theories of the Business Cycle—is not to present a history of the development of economic thought on this subject (although every attempt has been made to interpret as accurately as possible the meaning of the various writers whose theories are discussed), nor to give anything like an exhaustive bibliography of business-cycle theory. The purpose is rather to gather together various hypotheses of explanation, to test their logical consistency and their compatibility with one another and with accepted economic principles. It is intended to give a rounded picture of the possible explanations of economic fluctuations and it is hoped that, by theoretical reasoning, the number of these possibilities can be considerably reduced.

The second part of the present report—the " Syn-
Synthetic   thetic Exposition relating to the Nature and Causes
exposition of of Business Cycles"—contains the comprehensive
the nature of explanation which emerges from the analysis of
the cycle.   theories in the first part. As has been said, it does not
claim to be an entirely new theory, but a synthesis and
development of existing theories, so far as they can be synthesised.
What is presented there is furthermore not a closed and rigid system,
but a flexible and open one : there are many points where no definite
solution can be proposed, but where the existence of a number of
possibilities will be indicated. The choice between these can then be
made only on the basis of empirical investigations. In many cases,
theoretical reasoning supported only by such broad facts as one
happens to know without special statistical or historical investigations can put intelligent questions, but cannot definitely answer them.

That by analysing various theories it should be possible to give
an explanation of the business cycle which, while leaving some
questions open or offering in other cases alternative answers,
nevertheless clarifies a number of problems presupposes that the
difference between the theories analysed is not so radical as is
sometimes believed. In fact, the assumption is that the real
differences in opinion have been frequently exaggerated, and that,
for certain important questions, a much greater harmony between
writers of different schools can be established than the superficial
observer would believe or even than these same writers would
be willing to admit. It is a natural thing that most writers are
inclined rather to dwell on the controversial issues than to stress
the points of general agreement. Here the opposite principle
will be followed and, in the following sections, it will be shown
how theories which seem *prima facie* to contradict one another can
sometimes be reconciled.

Part I

SYSTEMATIC ANALYSIS OF THE
THEORIES OF THE BUSINESS CYCLE

CHAPTER 1

PRELIMINARY REMARKS

---

§ 1. THE EXPLANATION OF THE BUSINESS CYCLE

Before we begin the exposition of the various theories of the business cycle, some remarks may be advisable on the general logical nature of any explanation of the cycle, and on the mutual relation between various possible explanations (theories). The implications of these observations will be fully realised only in the light of subsequent pages where these formal principles are, so to speak, put to work. Nevertheless, it seems useful to touch upon these things at the beginning in order to avoid misunderstandings. The study of the various theories will be more fruitful if the following general remarks are kept in mind.

Plurality of causes. Such a complex phenomenon as the business cycle, which embraces almost all parts of the economic system, does not easily lend itself to explanation by any one factor. Even if we assume from the beginning that the same explanation of the business cycle holds good in the highly industrialised countries of Western Europe and America as well as in industrially less developed countries such as New Zealand or Roumania, and in the twentieth century as well as at the beginning of the nineteenth—neither of which assumptions is by any means self-evident—it is not easy to speak of *the* cause of the business cycle. Few writers have ventured to proclaim just one single factor as *the* cause of the business cycle or of depression in particular. In fact, explanations which run in terms of one single cause have been more and more discredited and should be regarded with suspicion. The majority of modern writers on the subject are careful to point out that a whole set of factors, and perhaps not always the same combination of factors, contribute towards producing an alternation of prosperity and depression. Frequently, the difference between various theorists is rather a difference in the emphasis laid upon the different factors than a difference in the enumeration of contributing causes and conditions.

Even those writers whose theory centres round one single factor which they make responsible for the business cycle—*e.g.*, crop variations, or inventions, or the acceleration of derived demand, or changes in demand, or waves of optimism and pessimism—are forced to admit that what they call *the* cause of the business cycle can produce its effect only in a certain economic institutional environment. They assume, explicitly or implicitly, a certain structure of the exchange economy, a certain rigidity of wages and contracts, a certain behaviour of investors, the presence or absence of a certain amount of knowledge and foresight amongst entrepreneurs, a certain monetary organisation, etc. The business cycle might well not appear (*a*) if those " active " forces (crop changes, inventions, changes in demand, etc.) were absent, or (*b*) if one or several of the significant features in the economic institutional framework were changed ; if, for example, wages and contracts were perfectly plastic, if entrepreneurs behaved in a different way, if they possessed perfect foresight or if the monetary organisation were different and monetary authorities took steps to prevent repercussions : in a word, if they were to behave differently from what they actually do.

It might therefore just as well be maintained that the rigidity of our economic system, or its financial or monetary organisation, or particular features of the latter, are the causes of the cycle as that inventions or crop changes or changes in demand are responsible.

Theories differ mainly as to emphasis. Normally, a complex phenomenon such as the business cycle is caused and conditioned by a large number of factors and circumstances. Even if the same theory holds good for all cycles, there is still room for a multitude of " different " explanations which need not all be logically exclusive and contradictory. Each of them stresses one or other of the relevant factors and conditions and calls it the " dominant " or

" causally relevant " one. The other factors are neglected, or it is assumed that they do not change or cannot be changed, or that it is for some reason not desirable to change or eliminate them (*e.g.*, inventions) or that their changes cannot be further explained (at least not by the economist) and that they must therefore be taken for granted. In particular, monetary and non-monetary explanations of the business cycle seem to be frequently reconcilable. The non-monetary theorist (who stresses, *e.g.*, the impact of inventions, or changes in demand with intensified changes in derived demand) often tacitly assumes—or ought logically to assume—the willingness and ability of the banking system to expand credit on existing terms, whereas the monetary theorist takes such disturbing events as inventions or changes in demand for granted and blames the monetary authorities for not adjusting the terms of credit.

Classification of causal factors. These considerations suggest that it is useful to distinguish certain types of causal factors. One may draw a distinction, for instance, between active and passive factors or, in other words, between causes and conditions or between conditions *per quam* and conditions *sine qua non*. Inventions, crop changes, changes in demand are active factors, while institutional circumstances such as are mentioned above should be classified as passive conditions. Sometimes this distinction may be useful; but frequently it is difficult or impossible to draw a sharp line between the two types of factors. How is it possible to decide whether any given action on the part of the banks, such as lowering the discount rate when reserves are running high or failure to raise the rate when the demand for credit rises (*i.e.*, when the " natural rate " has risen), is an " active " or a " passive " factor ? This is obviously a terminological question and it is fruitless to press for an answer in every single case.

The real distinction—in some cases—is between *controllable* and *uncontrollable* factors.[1] The weather, *e.g.*, is uncontrollable, while institutional factors are at least in theory controllable.

---

[1] *Cf.* J. M. Clark, *Strategic Factors in Business Cycles*, New York, 1935, pages 4-5 and *passim*.

Among factors, furthermore, which can in principle be controlled, there are those which one does not find it desirable, for one reason or another, to control or to eliminate altogether—*e.g.*, inventions, or the liberty of the recipient of income to spend his income or to save it, or to exercise freedom of choice in regard to his consumption or occupation. Needless to say, opinion as to what it is possible and desirable to control or influence varies from time to time and from person to person.

A more usual if less pragmatic classification is that of causes which originate within and causes which originate outside the economic system. Wars, inventions, crop changes (so far as they depend on the weather and are not economic adjustments to changes in demand, prices or cost), spontaneous changes in demand (so far as they are due to changes in taste and are not simply a reaction to changed supply conditions) are examples of outside causes. Changes in production due to changed demand conditions, price changes due to rise in cost, intensified demand for producers' goods due to changes in demand for consumers' goods are examples of economic causes. But what is to be called an *economic* and what a *non-economic* factor or circumstance is frequently rather a matter of convention than of argument.

Exogenous and endogenous theories. Closely connected with the distinction between economic and non-economic factors and causes is the distinction between " *exogenous* " and " *endogenous* " theories of the business cycle. Exogenous theories are those which assume external disturbances—*e.g.*, crop changes or inventions—in order to explain the business cycle. Endogenous theories rely exclusively on movements which can be explained economically. This distinction, too, is not always definite. Is the monetary theory, which explains the business cycle in the light of certain actions or a certain policy on the part of the banking authorities, to be regarded as exogenous or endogenous ? If the banks lower the rate of interest, thereby inducing a credit inflation, their action will presumably be regarded as an exogenous factor : but suppose they do not raise the rate sufficiently in face of a rising demand for credit (due, *e.g.*, to inventions) with the same result in the shape of a credit inflation—is that the operation of an exogenous factor ?

It has been attempted to give more precision to the distinction between exogenous and endogenous theories by saying that the former assume movements in the data, while the latter suppose the data to remain constant.[1] This distinction is precise enough once the general theoretical system on which a writer builds his theory of the business cycle has been determined and accepted; but it is not possible to lay down beforehand once and for all what phenomena are to be regarded as accepted data and what are magnitudes to be explained and determined in the light of those data. What the theory of yesterday accepted as data, we try to explain to-day; and the independent variables (data) on which we build to-day may become dependent variables to-morrow. All attempts to make a definite distinction between data and results lead back to the earlier conception which regards forces or movements of a " non-economic " nature or " external " to the economic system as the " data " of economic theory. But this distinction between " economic " and " non-economic " phenomena is a purely conventional one. There is no reason why forces or movements not to be classified as economic should not become " dependent " or " explained " variables of a general—as distinct from an economic—theory.

With very few exceptions, all serious explanations are neither purely exogenous nor purely endogenous. In almost all theories, both the " originating factors " and the " responses of the business system " (to use the expression of J. M. CLARK[2]) play a rôle. On the one hand, a purely exogenous theory is impossible. Even if one assumes a weather cycle, the peculiar response of the business system, which converts harvest variations into a general alternation of prosperity and depression, has still to be explained. On the other hand, a purely endogenous theory is hardly satisfactory. It is not likely that, without outside shocks, a cyclical movement would go on for ever : and, even if it did go on, its course would certainly be profoundly influenced by outside shocks—that is, by changes in the data (however these may be defined and delimited by economically explained variables).

---

[1] See especially Tinbergen : " Suggestions on Quantitative Business Cycle Theory " in *Econometrica*, Vol. III, No. 3, July 1935, page 241.
[2] See his book : *Strategic Factors in the Business Cycle, passim.*

The interaction of exogenous and endogenous forces is intricate, and the logical possibilities of their mutual impacts are numerous. We shall not, however, discuss these problems in the abstract here at the beginning. They will find their solution as we proceed in our theoretical enquiry, especially in Part II of the present report.

Inherent instability in the economic system. One methodological rule of thumb may be suggested at this point, however, although it will find its full justification only later. For various reasons, it seems desirable, in the explanation of the business cycle, to attach as little importance as possible to the influence of external disturbances. In the first place, large swings in the direction of prosperity and depression as we find them in real life are difficult to explain solely by exogenous forces; and this difficulty becomes an impossibility when the alleged " disturbances " do not themselves show a wavelike movement. Even if a periodic character is assumed (*e.g.*, in the case of crops or inventions), the hypothesis is full of difficulty. The responses of the business system seem *prima facie* more important in shaping the business cycle than external shocks. Secondly, historical experience seems to demonstrate that the cyclical movement has a strong tendency to persist, even where there are no outstanding extraneous influences at work which can plausibly be held responsible.[1] This suggests that there is an inherent instability in our economic system, a tendency to move in one direction or the other. If it is possible (as we believe) to demonstrate that such a tendency exists and to indicate the conditions under which it works, it will be comparatively easy to fit all kinds of external perturbations, including all State interventions, into the scheme. Exogenous forces will then figure as the originators or disturbers of endogenous processes, with power to accelerate, retard, interrupt or reverse the endogenous movement of the economic system.[2]

---

[1] What is to be regarded as "outstanding" and "plausible" is, of course, a matter of dispute. As there is always something happening somewhere, it is always possible to find some external events which can be made the basis of a tentative explanation.

[2] For this reason, anything like perfect regularity in respect of the amplitude, length, intensity and concomitant symptoms of the cyclical movement is *a priori* improbable.

Mechanical analogy. A frequently used analogy may be adduced, not to prove anything, but to make the meaning of what has been said clearer. We can compare the economic system with a pendulum or with a rocking-chair. A rocking-chair may be made to perform fairly regular swings by quite irregular impulses (shocks) from the outside. (Besides it may conceivably have a mechanism installed which makes it swing without outside forces operating on it.) In the explanation of the movement of the chair we must now distinguish two factors : the structure of the chair and the impulses from the outside—endogenous and exogenous factors. The structure of the chair is responsible for the fact that irregular shocks are transformed into fairly regular swings. An ordinary chair would ordinarily respond quite differently, although some particular kinds of impulses are thinkable (regular pushes and pulls) which would make it move in regular swings.

Naturally, the structure of the rocking-chair—and hence the nature of the swings produced by external shocks—may be very different in detail. The system might be so constructed that incessant regular swings are produced if, after having been pushed, the system is left to itself. Or else the swings may gradually disappear—that would be the case with an ordinary rocking-chair; we speak in that case of " damped oscillations " and may distinguish various degrees of dampening. The opposite may be true, the swings may become more and more violent; the fluctuations are then said to be " explosive " or " antidamped ", or the system is in an unstable equilibrium.

The methodological suggestion made above then comes to this. We tentatively assume that, for the explanation of the fairly regular swings of the economic system (just as for those, of the rocking-chair), it is more important to study the peculiar structure of the system and hence its responses to outside shocks than to look for regularities in the occurrence of these shocks. This hypothesis is, of course, subject to subsequent confirmation or rejection.

If, therefore, in many of the following sections, not much is said about such external influences (and in particular about the various forms of intervention in the economic process by the State or other public bodies, which figure so prominently in the daily comments of economists, politicians and economic journals on contemporary events), this must not be taken to imply that, in our opinion, or in the opinion of the writers whose theories are reviewed, these factors do not influence the economic situation. Our object is in the first instance to isolate the responses of the economic system, in order to stage the scene and to describe the environment in which the external influences have play.

§ 2. METHOD OF THE FOLLOWING ANALYSIS

Principles of selection. The scope of the following analysis of theories has been defined in the Introduction (page 1).[1] The method followed in the exposition is thereby largely determined. No attempt has been made to present the various theories in chronological order or to picture the theoretical and sociological background of the various writers (except in so far as it may have been necessary in order to elucidate their doctrines). It has been preferred to present the theories in a systematic order, beginning (so far as possible) with the less complicated and proceeding thereafter to the more complicated. Frequently it happens that the latter cover all the factors on which the former lay stress, while drawing attention to others which the former have overlooked or treated as irrelevant or put aside by means of a convenient simplifying assumption (*e.g.*, by a *ceteris paribus* clause).

It has been necessary to select certain authors or certain works as illustrative of the various lines of thought. Preference has been given, where there was no reason to the contrary, to the more recent and more accessible works. No attempt has been made to trace every thought or hypothesis back to its origin in the history of economic doctrines.

---

[1] This special purpose explains the difference between the following exposition and the classification of theories and theorists given in such works as A. H. Hansen : *Business Cycle Theories*, Boston, 1927 ; W. M. Persons : " Theories of Business Fluctuations " (*Quarterly Journal of Economics*, Vol. 41, reprinted in *Forecasting Business Cycles*, New York, 1931) ; F. A. Hayek : *Monetary Theory and the Trade Cycle*, London, 1933 ; Macfie : *Theories of the Trade Cycle*, London, 1934.

Naturally, the work of those writers who have themselves attempted a synthesis of theories—such as MITCHELL, PIGOU, ROBERTSON—had to be mentioned at several points in connection with the various lines of thought which they have incorporated in their systems. Mention is not made, however, at every point of all the writers who have made useful contributions to the problem in hand. The method followed has been dictated by the purpose of the present enquiry : it does not pretend to do justice to the originality and importance of different writers' contributions. It is not intended to be an appraisal of the merits of various writers, but a review and analysis of explanatory hypotheses.

Heads of analysis. The various theories under review have been examined, as far as possible, under the following heads :

General characteristics.
Explanation of the upswing (prosperity).
„   „   „   upper turning-point (crisis).
„   „   „   downswing (depression).
„   „   „   lower turning-point (revival).
Reasons given for recurrence, periodicity, etc.
International complications.

CHAPTER 2

THE PURELY MONETARY THEORY

─────────

§ 1. PRELIMINARY REMARKS

Cyclical fluctuations of MV. Money and credit occupy such a central position in our economic system that it is almost certain that they play an important rôle in bringing about the business cycle, either as an impelling force or as a conditioning factor. During the upswing, the physical volume of production and of transactions grows while prices rise or, in some rather exceptional cases, remain constant.[1] This means that the money volume of transactions rises. During depression, the money volume of transactions falls. In other words, the work which money must and does perform rises and falls with the ups and downs of the business cycle.[2] It follows, then, that the product (MV) of the quantity of money (M) and its velocity of circulation (V) rises and falls. This does not necessarily mean that the rise and fall of M and/or V is in all cases the active cause of changes in business activity : it may equally well be a passive condition or even a mere symptom. It is conceivable that MV may adjust itself automatically to changes in the volume of business without exerting any influence by itself. But, in any case, the analysis of a theory which puts the monetary factor at the centre of its scheme of causation will almost certainly reveal

─────────

[1] The outstanding example of a boom without a rise in prices is the American boom of 1926-1929. The stability of prices was, however, confined to the wholesale-price level. A more general price index (as constructed by Mr. Carl Snyder) shows a marked rise.

[2] It should be noted that this is not implied by the definition of prosperity and depression. It is conceivable that the rise and fall of the volume of production might be accompanied by an opposite movement of prices, so that the money value of the volume of production or of transactions in general would remain constant or even vary inversely with the physical volume.

important features of the business cycle which no adequate synthesis can afford to neglect.

§ 2. THE THEORY OF MR. R. G. HAWTREY:
GENERAL CHARACTERISTICS

Importance of consumers' outlay. The purely monetary explanation of the business cycle has been most fully and most uncompromisingly set out by Mr. R. G. HAWTREY.[1] For him the trade cycle is "a purely monetary phenomenon" in the sense that changes in "the flow of money" are the sole and sufficient cause of changes in economic activity, of the alternation of prosperity and depression, of good and bad trade. When the demand for goods in terms of money (that is, the flow of money) grows, trade becomes brisk, production rises and prices go up. When demand falls off, trade slackens, production shrinks and prices sag. The flow of money—*i.e.*, the demand for goods in terms of money—is proximately determined by "consumers' outlay", that is, by expenditure out of income.[2] Consumers' outlay comprises, however, not only expenditure on consumers' goods, but also expenditure on new investment goods—that is to say, that part of consumers' income that is saved and invested. (For consumers' outlay, one can substitute MV, if one defines "V" as "income velocity", in contradistinction to "transaction

---

[1] See *Good and Bad Trade*, London, 1913 ; *Monetary Reconstruction,* 1923, 2nd ed., 1926 ; *Currency and Credit*, 1919, 1923, 1928 ; *Trade and Credit*, 1928 ; *Trade Depression and the Way out*, 1931, 1933 ; *The Art of Central Banking*, 1932 ; *The Gold Standard in Theory and Practice*, 3rd ed., 1933 ; *Capital and Employment*, 1937.

[2] See, especially, *The Art of Central Banking*, London, 1932, Chapter III. Independently, very similar ideas have been expressed by Professor Albert Hahn in his earlier writings. See his *Volkswirtschaftliche Theorie des Bankkredits*, 1st ed., 1924 (3rd ed., 1930). Since then he has, however, changed his view considerably.

Many of the propositions advanced by Mr. Hawtrey and reviewed in the following pages, especially those on the relation between interest rates and prices, have had a long history and were given an early expression in A. Marshall's evidence before the Gold and Silver Commission, 1887. (See *Official Papers* of A. Marshall, 1926, pages 52 and 131, reproduced and elaborated in his *Money, Credit and Commerce*, pages 75-76 and 254-257.)

velocity " as it figures in IRVING FISHER's famous equation of exchange. But, V being thus defined as the ratio of consumers' outlay to the quantity of money, the two magnitudes—MV and consumers' outlay—are by definition the same; and not much is gained by the substitution of one expression for the other.)

Non-monetary factors such as earthquakes, wars, strikes, crop failures, etc., may produce a general impoverishment : others, such as harvest changes, over-development of certain industries (*e.g.*, over-investment in constructional industries), may produce a *partial* depression in particular branches of industry. But a general depression in the sense of the trade cycle—*i.e.*, a situation in which unused resources and unemployment are general—cannot be induced by non-monetary forces or events except in so far as they give rise to a fall in consumers' outlay—*i.e.*, in the flow of money.

Instability of money and credit. Changes in consumers' outlay are principally due to changes in the quantity of money. Everyone agrees that a sudden diminution in the quantity of money, an outright deflation, has a depressing influence on economic activities, and that an increase of the circulating medium, an inflation, has a stimulating influence.

If the quantity of money diminishes, demand falls off, and producers who have produced in anticipation of the usual demand will find that they cannot sell the usual output at the anticipated prices. Stocks will accumulate; losses will be incurred; production will fall; unemployment will be rife; and a painful process in which wages and other incomes are reduced will be necessary before equilibrium can be restored.

Inflation has the opposite effect. Demand exceeds anticipations, stocks decrease, dealers give larger orders to producers, and prices rise. Production increases and unemployed factors of production are gradually absorbed.

This is the familiar picture of a " Government deflation or inflation ". According to Mr. HAWTREY, the trade cycle is nothing but a replica, on a small scale, of an outright money inflation and deflation. Depression is induced by a fall in consumers' outlay due to a shrinkage of the circulating medium, and is intensified by a decline in the rapidity of the circulation of money. The prosperity phase of the cycle, on the other hand, is dominated by an inflationary process.

If the flow of money could be stabilised, the fluctuations in economic activity would disappear. But stabilisation of the flow of money is no easy task, because our modern money and credit system is inherently unstable. Any small deviation from equilibrium in one direction or the other tends to be magnified.

Mr. HAWTREY starts with the assumption that, in the modern world, bank credit is the principal means of payment. The circulating medium consists primarily of bank credit, and legal tender money is only subsidiary. It is the banking system which creates credit and regulates its quantity. The means of regulation are the discount rate and open-market purchases and sales of securities. The power to expand credit is not, of course, vested in each individual bank, but in the banking system as a whole. A single bank cannot go very far in expanding credit on its own account; but the banking system as a whole can, and there is a tendency to make the whole system move along step by step in the same direction. If one bank or group of banks expands credit, other banks will find their reserves strengthened and will be induced, sometimes almost forced, to expand too. In this way a single bank or group of banks may carry with it the whole system.

(These are familiar propositions of modern banking theory. It does not seem necessary at this point to work them out in detail with all necessary qualifications.)[1]

§ 3. THE UPSWING

Driving force of bank expansion. The upswing of the trade cycle is brought about by an expansion of credit and lasts so long as the credit expansion goes on or, at least, is not followed by a credit contraction.

A credit expansion is brought about by the banks through the easing of conditions under which loans are

---

[1] *Cf., e.g.,* the exposition in Keynes' *Treatise on Money.* The history of thought on this subject has been written in great detail by V. Wagner, *Geschichte der Kredittheorien,* Vienna, 1936, and A. W. Marget, *The Theory of Prices : A Re-examination of the Central Problems of Monetary Theory,* Vol. I., New York, 1938.

granted to the customer. Borrowing may be encouraged in various ways. The banks can apply a less severe standard to security offered; they can increase the maximum period for which they are willing to lend; they can refrain from discriminating as to the purpose for which the borrower wants the loan. But the principal instrument of expansion is a reduction of the discount rate; and each of the other measures is equivalent in some way to a reduction in the costs of credit.

The strategic position of the merchant. Mr. HAWTREY is aware of the objection, which has been raised very frequently, that a reduction of 1 or 2% in the interest on bank advances is too unimportant an item in the profit-and-loss account of the average business-man to induce him to expand his business and to borrow more. His answer to this objection is that there exists one class of business-men which is very sensitive even to small changes of the rate of interest—namely, the merchants. The merchant buys and sells large quantities of goods compared with his own capital, and he adds to what he buys the relatively small value which represents the dealer's profit. To him, a change in interest charges of 1 or 2% is not negligible, as it is perhaps to the manufacturer. It is not denied, of course, that there are other considerations besides the rate of interest which might induce a merchant to borrow more (or less) and to increase (or reduce) his stocks of goods. If prices are expected to rise, or if a fall is anticipated, a reduction in the interest rate may be unnecessary or insufficient. But a general rise or fall in prices sufficient to induce the majority of merchants to increase or decrease their borrowing, irrespective of minor changes in the rate of interest, is unlikely to occur except as a consequence of an expansion or contraction of credit and will be discussed later.

Thus, according to Mr. HAWTREY, the merchant is in a strategic position. If the rate of interest is sufficiently reduced—and in ordinary circumstances a slight reduction is sufficient—merchants are induced to increase their stocks. They give larger orders to the producer. Increased production leads to an enlargement of consumers' income and outlay. This " means increased demand for goods in general, and traders find their stocks diminishing. There result further orders to producers, a further increase in productive activity, in consumers' income and outlay, and in demand, and a further depletion of stocks. Increased activity means increased demand, and increased demand means increased activity. A vicious circle is set up, a cumulative expansion of productive activity ",[1] which is fed and propelled by a continuous expansion of credit.

Effects of rising prices.   " Productive activity cannot grow without limit. As the cumulative process carries one industry after another to the limit of productive capacity, producers begin to quote higher and higher prices ."[1] When prices rise, dealers have a further inducement to borrow. Rising prices operate in the same way as falling interest charges : profits are increased and traders stimulated to hold larger stocks in order to gain from a further rise in prices. In the same way, the producer is stimulated to expand production and to borrow more freely in order to finance the increased production. The cumulative process of expansion is accelerated by a cumulative rise in prices.

Instability of the velocity of circulation.   There is yet another accelerating element. In addition to the expansion of the circulating medium, there is an increase in its velocity of circulation. When prices rise and trade is brisk, merchants and producers not only borrow more : they use up any idle balances which may be at their disposal. Idle balances are the inheritance of the previous depression. If they exist to a large extent, " it may be that an enlargement of the consumers' income and outlay is brought about with little or no expansion of the outstanding bank credit ".

" Thus there is a principle of the instability of velocity of circulation, which is quite distinct from the principle of the instability of credit, but is very apt to aggravate its effect."[2]

To sum up, expansion is a cumulative process—that is to say, once started, it proceeds by its own momentum. No further encouragement from the banks is required. On the contrary,

---

[1] *The Art of Central Banking*, page 167.
[2] *Op. cit.*, page 171.

banks have then to be careful not to let the expansion get out of hand and degenerate into wild inflation. They should raise the rate of interest drastically : slight increases will not deter people from borrowing if prices rise and are expected to rise further. That is what is meant in saying that the process has gained momentum. A discount rate which would have sufficed to nip the expansion in the bud would later be much too low to stop it.

§ 4. THE UPPER TURNING-POINT

Credit restriction responsible. Prosperity comes to an end when credit expansion is discontinued. Since the process of expansion, after it has been allowed to gain a certain speed, can be stopped only by a jolt, there is always the danger that expansion will be not merely stopped but reversed, and will be followed by a process of contraction which is itself cumulative. (There are other reasons for this, which will be discussed presently.)

" If the restriction of credit did not occur, the active phase of the trade cycle could be indefinitely prolonged, at the cost, no doubt, of an indefinite rise of prices and an abandonment of the gold standard." [1]

The wage-lag, the cash drain and the gold standard. Man-made limitations on the amount of the circulation—that is, limitations imposed by law and custom—constitute the barrier which prevents our present economic system from getting rid of its cyclical movement with all its bad consequences. So long as there is a gold standard, or other restriction in the supply of legal tender money (*e.g.*, that involved in the attempt to stabilise the exchange rate *vis-à-vis* another country which does not itself expand credit), the banks are sooner or later forced to stop expansion and even to contract.

Cash—*i.e.*, legal tender money—is predominantly used for small and retail transactions, because for these purposes credit has no

---

[1] *Trade and Credit*, London, 1928, page 98.

greater convenience to compensate for its inferior security. The amount of cash which passes into circulation depends largely on the incomes, expenditures and hoards of working-men. An expansion leads sooner or later to a drain of cash out of the holdings of the banks while, as earnings and wage rates rise, an increasing amount will be retained in cash balances. This, however, is a slow process, because the rise in wages lags considerably behind the expansion of credit and the rise in prices and profits. Meanwhile, the central bank, in its anxiety to maintain exchange stability, declines to supply cash to the commercial banks indefinitely. The latter are therefore forced to put the brake on and to stop the expansion. When they start to do this, the cash holdings of the working population still continue to increase—by reason of their lag behind the credit expansion—and go on rising after the expansion has come to an end. This induces the banks, not merely to stop expanding, but actually to contract; and so the depression is given its start.

§ 5. THE DOWNSWING

The reverse of the upswing. The process of contraction is cumulative no less than the process of expansion. " When credit has definitely turned the corner, and a contraction has succeeded to an expansion, the downward tendency of prices is sufficient to maintain the process of contraction, even though the rate of interest is no longer, according to the ordinary standards, high." [1]

The process is cumulative for the following reason. When prices are falling, merchants expect them to fall further. They try accordingly to reduce stocks, and give smaller orders, or no orders at all, to producers. Consumers' income and outlay decrease; demand flags; stocks accumulate in spite of endeavours to reduce them; borrowing is reduced further—and so on in a long and painful process. All the factors which tended to stimulate the upswing conspire now to push contraction further and

---

[1] *Currency and Credit*, 3rd ed., London, 1928, page 153.

further. The vicious spiral downward is in all respects the negative counterpart of the vicious spiral upward. The details need not be repeated.

§ 6. REVIVAL

Sufficiency of credit expansion. During a depression, loans are liquidated and gradually money flows back from circulation into the reserves of the banks. The reserve ratio becomes normal, and reserves above normal are slowly built up. Interest is by this time fallen to an abnormally low level; but, with prices sagging and with a prevalence of pessimism, it may be that even an exceedingly low level of interest rates will not stimulate people to borrow. According to Mr. HAWTREY, however, there are almost always some people who are willing to increase their borrowing; and this should enable the banks to get over the dead point. But if, as happens in abnormally deep depressions, pessimism is so widespread that no rate above zero will induce an expansion, the central bank has another weapon for overcoming the reluctance of the business community to make use of existing credit facilities—and that is the purchase of securities in the open market.

When the central bank buys securities in the open market, cash is pumped into the banks and their liquidity increases. For a time, the new money may be used to repay debts to the banks, so that the only result is a change in the composition of the assets of the banks (cash increases, loans decrease). But Mr. HAWTREY is confident that eventually, if only the purchases of securities are carried far enough, the new money will find an outlet into circulation, consumers' income and outlay will begin to rise, and a self-reinforcing process of expansion will be started. Mr. HAWTREY believes that the ordinary measures of banking policy—discount policy and open-market operations—may be trusted to bring about a revival and that it is therefore not necessary to have recourse to more drastic methods (such as public works) to start an expansion. This attitude of his is closely connected with his theory that changes in the rate of interest must operate through influencing working capital rather than through stimulating investment in fixed capital. We shall have to come back to this proposition because it conflicts sharply with the theories of many other writers, with which we shall have to deal.

A credit deadlock. In his earlier writings Mr. HAWTREY had already mentioned the theoretical possibility of a complete credit deadlock arising. That is a situation where even exceedingly low interest rates fail to evoke a new demand for credit. In such a situation, the ordinary means of bank policy prove wholly ineffective. In his *Good and Bad Trade*[1] he ascribes this phenomenon to the fact that " the rate of depreciation of prices " may be so rapid that " nothing that the bankers can do will make borrowing sufficiently attractive " to lead to a revival in the flow of money.

In more recent publications, under the impression of the slump of the nineteen-thirties, Mr. HAWTREY has modified his views to some extent.[2] He now doubts whether it can be legitimately assumed that " the expectation of falling prices is (always) the result of a preceding experience of a prolonged actual fall "[3] and that such a condition of stagnation is not possible except in the course of a reaction from a riot of inflation.[4]

He still believes that " a failure of cheap money to stimulate revival " is " a rare occurrence ", but he admits that " since 1930, it has come to plague the world and has confronted us with problems which have threatened the fabric of civilisation with destruction ".[5]

These admissions and qualifications go a long way to meet the objections of those who do not share Mr. HAWTREY's unshakable optimism regarding the efficacy of the traditional methods of banking policy for bringing about a revival.

---

[1] 1913, page 186.
[2] *Cf.* his *Trade Depression and the Way Out*, 2nd ed., pages 29-31 and 133-135, *Capital and Employment*, pages 85-87, " A Credit Deadlock " ; and his contribution to *The Lessons of Monetary Experience* (edited by A. D. Gayer), " The Credit Deadlock ", pages 129-145.
[3] *The Lessons of Monetary Experience*, page 131.
[4] *Ibid.*, page 131, and *Monetary Reconstruction*, page 133.
[5] *Capital and Employment*, page 86.

Apart, however, from such a contingency, and
Wage-lag and for a typical trade cycle under the gold standard
bank policy. before the war, Mr. HAWTREY describes the transition from depression to prosperity in the following way. During the depression, money begins to flow back to the banks. But, again, there is that lag of the flow of cash behind the movement of credit. As the outflow of cash does not at once follow the expansion of credit, the inflow of cash lags behind the contraction. The consequence is that, when the banks come to the conclusion that they can stop contracting, because their reserves have reached the desirable level, the process of inflow of cash has not yet come to an end. People's cash balances respond slowly. Cash continues to flow in for a considerable time after contraction of credit has been arrested. Surplus reserves accumulate, and these excessive reserves tempt the banks later on to over-expand and so begin another cycle.

§ 7. RHYTHM AND PERIODICITY

Mr. HAWTREY's theory explains why there are not
Rigid reserve merely small oscillations around the equilibrium, but
proportions. big swings of the pendulum in the one or the other direction. The reason is the cumulative, self-sustaining nature of the process of expansion and contraction. The equilibrium line is like a razor's edge. The slightest deviation involves the risk of further movement away from equilibrium.

But even so, Mr. HAWTREY thinks, the recurrence of the breakdown is not inevitable. The expansion could go on indefinitely, if there were no limits to the increase in the quantity of money. The gold standard is, in the last resort, responsible for the recurrence of economic breakdowns. Under the gold standard, it is the slow response of people's cash balances which prevents the banks from stopping expansion or contraction in time. " If an increase or decrease of credit money promptly brought with it a proportionate increase or decrease in the demand for cash, the banks would no longer either drift into a state of inflation or be led to carry the corresponding process of contraction unnecessarily far." Given, however, this slow response of the people's cash balances, "so long as credit is regulated with reference to reserve proportions, the trade cycle is bound to recur ".[1]

Under the automatic working of the gold standard, "the length of the cycle was determined by the rate of progress of the processes on which the cycle depended, the absorption of currency during the period of expansion and its return during the period of contraction ".[2]

No trade cycle since the war. Since 1914, the automatically working gold standard has ceased to exist. After the war and post-war inflations, the gold standard—a managed gold standard—was once more restored; but the first major shock upset it. Therefore, according to Mr. HAWTREY, the former marked regularity and periodicity in the alternation of periods of prosperity and depression, of expansion and contraction, can no longer be expected and do not, in fact, any longer exist. "For the time being there is no trade cycle " if by " cycle " is meant a periodic movement of marked regularity. There are, of course, periods of prosperity and depression; for the credit system is still inherently unstable and there are forces more powerful than ever, the operation of which makes for expansion or contraction. But the intricate mechanism which produced the former regularity in the alternation of expansion and contraction is completely dislocated.

Periodicity is not, however, essential for the purposes of Mr. HAWTREY's theory. On the contrary, he is entitled to claim for his theory that it does not postulate exclusively movements of a definite length and regularity. The regular cycle can always be interrupted by non-cyclic forces. It must be admitted that an explanation which is flexible in this respect is preferable—if it is tenable in other respects—to a more rigid one.

---

[1] *Monetary Reconstruction*, 2nd ed., London, 1926, page 135.
[2] *Currency and Credit*, 3rd ed., page 155.

§ 8.   SPECIAL FEATURES OF THE THEORY

Fluctuations in investment in fixed capital.   As has been mentioned, Mr. HAWTREY's theory stands in contradiction to many other related theories in that it contends that a change in the rate of interest influences the economic system, not through a direct influence on investment in fixed capital, but through the provision of working capital and particularly stocks of goods.   The alternative view will be discussed later.   Here it must be asked how Mr. HAWTREY's theory can account for the undoubted fact that the instrumental industries experience greater cyclical fluctuations than the consumption industries.   The explanation offered is that activity brings a more than proportional increase in profits; and, as profits (whether reinvested by corporations or distributed to shareholders) are the principal source of savings, the funds available from savings for capital outlay are similarly increased.   The disproportionate fluctuations in the instrumental industries are therefore a consequence of changes in consumers' income and outlay, and are not due (as many writers believe) to any repercussions which credit expansion may have—directly, or indirectly through changes in long-term-interest rates—on investment in fixed capital.   That credit expansion has a certain effect on investment in fixed capital is not altogether denied by Mr. HAWTREY; but he holds it to be unimportant as compared with the direct influence on the merchant and on working capital.

Implications for policy.   To complete the picture of Mr. HAWTREY's theory, a word must be said as to the policy banks should pursue in order to eliminate the credit cycle, and with it the trade cycle.   The banks, and especially the leaders of the banking system, the central banks, should not watch the reserve proportions so much as the flow of purchasing power.   The demand for goods, the flow of money, is the important thing—not the outstanding aggregate of money units.   The aim of banking policy should be to keep the consumer's outlay constant, including (as has been pointed out) outlay for new investment.   But account should be taken of changes in the factors of production—not merely the growth of population, but also the growth of capital—and allowance ought to be made for the proportion of skilled labour of varying grades and for the appropriate amount of economic rent. In other words, the aim should be to stabilise, not the price level of commodities, but the price level of the factors of production.[1]

§ 9. INTERNATIONAL COMPLICATIONS

With the purely monetary explanation of the business cycle, it is comparatively easy to account for various kinds of international complications. The analysis of any given international constellation involving two or more countries must invariably turn on the question of how the money supply in each of these countries is likely to be affected. This analysis has not yet been worked out systematically from the standpoint of the explanation of the business cycle. But the instruments of the analysis are ready to hand. The theory of the international money mechanism under different monetary standards is one of the most fully elaborated chapters of economic science.[2]

§ 10. CONCLUDING REMARKS

A feature of particular interest in Mr. HAWTREY's monetary theory of the business cycle is the demonstration and analysis of the cumulative nature of the process of expansion and contraction. In this respect, there is, as we shall see, much agreement between theorists of different schools of thought. Mr. HAWTREY's propositions on this point, largely taken over from MARSHALL and the Cambridge tradition, have found a place in the theory of a great number of writers.[3]

Other features of Mr. HAWTREY's theory are more questionable. His contention that the reason for the breakdown of the boom is

---

[1] See his paper " Money and Index-Numbers " in *Journal of the Royal Statistical Society*, 1930, reprinted in *The Art of Central Banking*, pages 303-332.

[2] See below Ch. 3, §§ 8, 16, and Part II, Ch. 11.

[3] No attempt has been made to establish priorities or to trace the various lines of thought to their historical origins.

always a monetary one and that prosperity could be prolonged and depression staved off indefinitely, if the money supply were inexhaustible, would certainly be challenged by most economists.

These and other features of the purely monetary explanation of the cycle will be referred to, explicitly or implicitly, in connection with the discussion of the non-monetary theories.

———————

CHAPTER 3

THE OVER-INVESTMENT THEORIES

---

§ I. GENERAL CHARACTERISTICS

Maladjustments, *vertical and* *horizontal.* In this section, it is proposed to analyse some closely related theories of a great number of writers, which may be labelled generically " over-investment theories ".

The central theme of all these theories is the over-development of industries which produce producers' goods or capital goods in relation to industries producing consumers' goods. They all start from the universally admitted fact that the capital-goods industries are much more severely affected by the business cycle than industries which produce for current consumption. During the upward phase of the cycle the output of producers' goods rises much more, and during the downward phase is much more curtailed, than the output of perishable consumers' goods. Durable consumers' goods, such as houses and automobiles, are in a special position approximating to that of capital goods.

According to the over-investment theorists, this phenomenon is the symptom of a serious maladjustment which develops during the upswing. The capital-goods industries, it is argued, are relatively over-developed : the production of capital goods as compared with the production of consumer's goods is pushed farther than the underlying situation can permanently tolerate. Thus it is a real maladjustment in the structure of production that causes the breakdown of the boom, and not a mere shortage of money due to an insufficiency of bank reserves. It follows that, after the boom has once been allowed to develop, the setback cannot be staved off indefinitely by monetary measures.

The situation as it develops during the boom, according to the over-investment school, may be described as a " *vertical* disequilibrium or maladjustment " in contradistinction to a " horizontal disequilibrium or maladjustment " in the structure of production. The distinction between vertical and horizontal maladjustments can be formulated as follows. Supposing that by some means the aggregate money flow is kept constant, equilibrium in the structure of production will be preserved, if the allocation of the factors of production to various employments corresponds to the distribution of the money flow—*i.e.*, the monetary demand for the products of the different branches of industry. This distribution is, broadly speaking, determined by (1) the decisions of the population as to spending and saving, (2) the decisions of consumers as to the distribution of expenditure between various lines of consumption goods, and (3) the decisions of producers at every stage as to the distribution of their cost expenditure between different forms of input. If the structure of production does not correspond to the first set of decisions, we have a *vertical* maladjustment—vertical because the industries which are not harmoniously developed are related to each other in a " vertical " order, as cost and product. One may also speak of " higher " and " lower ", or " earlier " and " later " stages of production—in which case " lower " and " later " mean " nearer to consumption ". If the structure of production does not correspond to the second or third set of decisions, we have a *horizontal* disproportion—a disproportion between industries of the same "rank" as measured by distance from consumption.

We have seen that Mr. HAWTREY also recognises *Money and the structure of production.* the fact that the cyclical movement is much more violent in the capital-goods industries. But in his view, this is merely the consequence of fluctuations in the flow of money (consumers' income and outlay). It is not an evil in itself. According to the over-investment theories, fluctuation in investment is the cause of the business cycle, and the forces which bring about expansion (being to a large extent of a monetary nature) have a direct effect on investment—viz. (mainly) on investment in fixed capital. Fluctuations in investment generate fluctuations in consumers' income rather than the other way round.

Thus, according to these theories, the business cycle is not a purely monetary phenomenon. But that does not preclude the possibility of money's playing a decisive rôle in bringing about the cycle and causing periodically a real maladjustment. Some members of the over-investment school consider monetary forces to be the *impelling* factor disturbing the equilibrium. Others believe that certain monetary arrangements are *conditioning* factors, which do not actively disturb the equilibrium but are the instruments through which the active forces of a non-monetary nature operate.

We can distinguish three sub-groups with a still *The schools of* greater variety in detail.[1]
over-investment theorists.   (A) Writers who believe that monetary forces operating under a particular form of credit organisation (banking system) produce the disequilibrium between the lower and higher stages of production.

This type of theory, which is frequently called the "Neo-Wicksellian" school, may perhaps be included amongst the monetary explanations of the business cycle, inasmuch as the active cause which disturbs the equilibrium is a monetary one. But the business cycle is for these writers more than a purely monetary phenomenon. Monetary forces produce a real maladjustment,

---

[1] Naturally, other groupings are possible, but that selected seems to be the most natural and useful.

the consequence of which is the breakdown of the boom. Crisis and depression cannot be explained purely by contraction of the circulating medium, although deflation may come in as a secondary and intensifying element. Among the writers whose theories fall within this group are HAYEK, MACHLUP, MISES, ROBBINS, RÖPKE and STRIGL. WICKSELL has provided the theoretical basis for this theory, but belongs himself rather to the following group (group (B)), while ROBERTSON holds an intermediate position between group (A) and group (B).

(B) This group consists of writers whose theories do not run in terms of money. They stress factors in the sphere of production such as inventions, discoveries, the opening of new markets, etc.—that is, circumstances which provide new investment opportunities. Some of them refer to the money factor only incidentally or incline to minimise it. But it can be shown— and is indeed frequently recognised by the writers in question— that certain monetary forces are indispensable for the active factors on which they lay stress to produce the effect postulated. CASSEL, HANSEN, SPIETHOFF and WICKSELL are prominent in this group. ROBERTSON has been already mentioned. PIGOU'S and SCHUMPETER'S analyses go parallel for a long way with the theories of these writers.

(C) There is a third view which adds much to the force of the over-investment theory—namely, the theory that changes in the production of consumers' goods give rise, for technological reasons, to much more violent fluctuations in the production of producers' goods in general and fixed capital equipment in particular. This so-called principle of "the acceleration and magnification of derived demand" has been elaborated by AFTALION, BICKERDIKE, CARVER and PIGOU. In recent years, J. M. CLARK and R. G. HARROD have laid great stress upon it in their explanation of the business cycle. MITCHELL, ROBERTSON and SPIETHOFF mention it as a factor which intensifies the cyclical movement. The principle can also be used, as we shall see, in support of a special type of the under-consumption theory of the business cycle.

A. The Monetary Over-investment Theories

§ 2. GENERAL CHARACTERISTICS AND THEORETICAL FOUNDATION

Banking system and money supply. The theories of the following writers will now be examined : F. A. HAYEK,[1] F. MACHLUP,[2] L. MISES,[3] L. ROBBINS,[4] W. RÖPKE[5] and R. STRIGL.[6] The explanation given by these writers of the upswing and of the down-turn (crisis) is fundamentally the same. Such differences as exist are mainly in respect of amplifications in the later publications. Serious conflicts of opinion are to be found, on the other hand, in respect of the description and explanation of the downswing and the up-turn (revival). Professor RÖPKE, in particular, dissents strongly from the opinion of the other writers named in the interpretation of the later phases of such prolonged depressions as that of 1929-1936. The writers of this group have this in common with the purely monetary theory of Mr. HAWTREY, that they assume an elastic money supply. They argue that the circulating medium consists under modern conditions primarily of bank money (deposits), and that the banking system regulates the quantity of money by changing the discount rate and by conducting open-market operations. It has long been recognised that there is a complicated functional relationship between the interest rate, changes in the quantity of money and the price level.

---

[1] *Monetary Theory and the Trade Cycle*, London, 1933 (translated from the German). *Prices and Production*, London, 1931, enlarged edition, 1934. See also his latest exposition, "Preiserwartungen, monetäre Schwankungen und Fehlinvestitionen" in *Nationalokonomisk Tidskrift*, 1935 (translated into French : "Prévision de prix, perturbations monétaires et faux investissements" in *Revue des Sciences économiques*, 1936).

[2] *Börsenkredit, Industriekredit und Kapitalbildung*, Vienna, 1931.

[3] *The Theory of Money and Credit*, London, 1934 (translated from the German). *Geldwertstabilisierung und Konjunkturpolitik*, Jena, 1928.

[4] *The Great Depression*, London, 1934.

[5] *Crises and Cycles*, London, 1936 (translated from the German). "Trends in German Business Cycle Policy", *Economic Journal*, September 1933.

[6] *Kapital und Produktion*, Vienna, 1934.

These relationships have been expounded systematically by KNUT WICKSELL ; his theory, outlined below, is the basis of the explanation of the business cycle which follows.[1] It should be added that, in what follows, we shall leave international complications for the moment out of account and disregard the fact that a change in the interest rate in one country will influence the flow of credit from and to other countries. These complications can easily be introduced into the picture later. For the present, we presuppose a closed economy.

Natural rate WICKSELL distinguishes between the "money *and money rate* rate" or actual "market rate of interest" as *of interest.* influenced by the policy of the banks (and other monetary factors) on the one hand and the " natural rate of interest " on the other. The latter is .defined by WICKSELL as "that rate at which the demand for loan capital just equals the supply of savings ".[2] If the banks lower the market rate below this natural or, as it should perhaps more correctly be called, equilibrium rate, the demand for credit will rise and exceed the available amount of savings, and the supply of credit must be supplemented by bank credit created *ad hoc*—that is, by inflation. If, on the other hand, the rate is raised above the equilibrium level, the demand for credit will fall, some portion of the total saving will not be used, and credit will be liquidated

---

[1] *Interest and Prices*, London, 1936, translated from the German, *Geldzins und Güterpreise*, Jena, 1898 ; *Lectures on Political Economy*, London, 1934, Vol. II, translated from the Swedish ; "The Influence of the Rate of Interest on Prices", *Economic Journal*, June 1907. On the evolution of Wicksell's theory, see the excellent introduction by Professor B. Ohlin to *Interest and Prices*. Compare also the elaboration of Wicksell's theory by recent Swedish writers as summarised in Professor G. Myrdal's paper "Der Gleichgewichtsbegriff als Instrument der geld-theoretischen Analyse " in *Beiträge zur Geldtheorie*, ed. by Hayek, 1933, and E. Lundberg, *Studies in the Theory of Economic Expansion*, London, 1937. Some aspects of the theory and their history have been discussed at great length by A. W. Marget, *The Theory of Prices*, Vol. I, Ch. VII-X. In Vol. II, which has not yet appeared, the discussion will be continued.

[2] *Vorlesungen über Nationalökonomie*, Vol. II, page 220. It is possible to trace in Wicksell's writings an alternative definition of the natural rate—viz., as that rate which would prevail in a barter economy where loans are made *in natura*. This conception presents, however, great theoretical difficulties. We shall therefore disregard it.

or deflated.[1] WICKSELL goes on to argue that, if the market rate is below the natural rate, prices will rise : if it is above, prices will tend to fall.

Two meanings of the concept "natural rate". There is, however, a fallacy in this last proposition, as was pointed out for the first time by the Swedish economist DAVIDSON.[2] In a progressive economy, where the volume of production and transactions rises, the flow of money must be increased in order to keep the price level stable. Therefore, the rate of interest must be kept at a level low enough to induce a net inflow of money into circulation. The rate which stabilises the price level is below the rate " at which the demand for loan capital just equals the supply of savings ".

Making allowance for this discrepancy, we may formulate the theorem as follows. If the banks lower the interest rate, *ceteris paribus* the flow of money incomes will expand or, if it was shrinking,

---

[1] Inasmuch as money loaned out is supposed to be used for productive purposes (that is to say, is invested), we can also say that the equilibrium rate is that rate at which savings—voluntary savings as distinct from "forced savings"—become equal to investment. If the market rate is below the equilibrium rate, investments exceed savings : if it is above, investments fall short of savings. Saving, in this context, has not to be interpreted according to the unusual definition adopted by Mr. Keynes in the *Treatise on Money*, and later discarded by him in the *General Theory of Employment, Interest and Money.* Mr. Keynes now employs a definition of saving according to which aggregate saving is only another aspect of aggregate investment, both being defined as the difference between the money value of output and expenditure on consumption. This is not the sense, however, in which saving is used by the authors now under consideration. For them, additions to the value of current output do not *immediately* constitute disposable income ; and it is thus open to them to regard saving as something different from investment. When they say that investment exceeds saving, they mean that there is in progress an inflationary increase in the money value of output which is not immediately translated into increased incomes. When they say that investment falls short of current saving, they mean that there is in progress a process of hoarding, a deflationary decrease in the money value of output. Which terminology is the more convenient—whether it is better to regard saving as necessarily equal to investment or not—is at present still an open question which will be discussed at some length in Chapter 8, below:

[2] *Cf.* Brinley Thomas, "The Monetary Doctrines of Professor Davidson " in *Economic Journal*, Vol. 45, 1935, pages 36 *et seq.*, and F. A. Hayek, *Monetary Theory and the Trade Cycle, passim.*

the process of contraction will be stopped or slowed down : prices will rise or, if they were falling, the fall will be arrested or mitigated. If the banks raise the interest rate, *ceteris paribus* the flow of money incomes will contract or, if it was expanding, the expansion will be stopped or slowed down : prices will fall or, if they were rising, the rise will be arrested or mitigated. Under given conditions, there is one rate which keeps the price level constant and another which keeps the flow of money incomes constant. The two coincide only in a stationary economy. In a progressive economy, the rate which stabilises the price level is below the rate which keeps the flow of money incomes constant.

Which of these two rates is called the " natural " or " equilibrium rate " will depend on which is thought the likelier to maintain the equilibrium of the economic system. We shall see that those writers of the group under review, whose analysis takes account of the difference, reserve the adjective " natural " for the rate which keeps the flow of money incomes constant. But for the moment we shall ignore this distinction, which the writers in question themselves are by no means consistent in respecting.[1]

§ 3.   THE UPSWING

Interest rates and prices. According to the theory with which we are dealing, the boom is brought about by a discrepancy between the natural and the money rate of interest. How this discrepancy is produced, and whether there is any reason why it should recur again and again in a more or less regular fashion, will be discussed later. If the money rate stands below the equilibrium rate, a credit expansion will ensue. As soon as prices begin to rise, the process tends to become cumulative for the reason that there is a twofold causal connection between interest rates and the

---

[1] Independently from Wicksell, Mr. Hawtrey introduced the notion of the "natural rate" (which he distinguished from the "profit rate") in his first book *Good and Bad Trade* (London, 1913). But, since he did not use this concept in any of his later writings, we have made no reference to it in the summary of his theory. The concept of a "natural rate" (and even the term) can be found in earlier English economic writings.

price level. A low interest level tends to raise prices and a high level to depress them ; but, on the other hand, rising prices tend to raise interest rates and falling prices to reduce them. If prices rise and people expect them to continue to rise, they become more eager to borrow and the demand for credit becomes stronger. Falling prices have the contrary effect. Rising prices are equivalent to a premium for borrowers, falling prices are a tax on borrowers. Professor IRVING FISHER distinguishes between the " nominal or money rate of interest " and the " real rate of interest ".[1] The first is the rate as we find it in the market : the second is the money rate corrected for changes in the value of money in terms of goods and services. Thus, if prices rise by 3% during the year, a nominal rate of 5% is equivalent to a real rate of (approximately) 2%, because the purchasing power of the capital sum falls by 3%. If prices rise by (say) 10% a year, a nominal rate of less than 10% becomes equivalent to a negative real rate, because the creditor loses, in terms of real purchasing power, more on the capital than he receives as interest. If prices fall by (say) 10% annually, a money rate of 5% becomes equivalent to a real rate of about 15%.

Mr. HAWTREY proposes the term " profit rate " for true profits of business, which he describes as being the ratio of labour saved per annum by the capital actually in use to labour expended on first cost, corrected for price changes.[2]

Demand and supply of loanable funds. The most convenient way of approach to the understanding of these rather complicated inter-relationships is to conceive of the situation in terms of the supply of, and demand for, credit. The supply is furnished by the savings of individuals and corporations, supplemented by inflationary bank credits. The ability of the banks to create credit makes the total supply more elastic than it would otherwise

---

[1] See the latest version of his theory in *The Theory of Interest*, New York, 1930, Chapter II. The first version was contained in his *Appreciation and Interest* (1896). *Cf.* also Adarkar, " Fisher's Real Rate Doctrine " in *Economic Journal*, Vol. 44, 1934, page 337, and Professor D. H. Robertson, " Industrial Fluctuations and the Natural Rate of Interest ", *ibid.*, pages 650 *et seq.*

[2] As Professor Hansen has pointed out, many of these concepts must be interpreted as referring to "expected'' rather than to "contemporary''

be. A considerable increase in the demand will be met without much rise in the interest rate, though the supply of voluntary saving may have increased only a little or not at all. The demand for credit is a very complex and volatile phenomenon. We shall see later on, in connection with the analysis of other theories, that it is exposed to sudden influences from various sides and is subject to rapid changes. To elucidate the theories here under review it is sufficient to assume that, at any given moment of time, there is a negatively inclined demand schedule. The lower in such case the price of credit—*i.e.*, the interest rate—the larger the amount of credit demanded.

We start from a situation where the banks maintain a level of interest rates at which the demand for, and supply of, credit exceeds the supply of savings. A credit expansion ensues, prices rise, and the rise in prices raises profits. The demand for credit rises : at each rate of interest, more is demanded than before. But the monetary expansion does not expand savings to the same extent, and the equilibrium rate of interest rises. Consequently, if the banks persist in maintaining the same rate of interest, the gap between the equilibrium rate and the market rate will be even wider than before, and the amount of credit expansion required even greater. Prices rise higher still, profits are raised, and the vicious spiral of inflation continues. After the movement has gathered momentum, it can only be stopped by a considerable rise in the rate of interest being enforced by the banks.

The process need not be discussed in greater detail, because so far the monetary over-investment theory runs parallel with the purely monetary theory.[1] The only difference is a difference of terminology—namely, the introduction of the terms " natural or

---

magnitude. It is the "expected" profit or yield from capital investment which must be set against the money rate of interest. Fairness to the older writers demands this interpretation, even if they frequently failed to emphasise "expectations" to the extent which has since become fashionable.

[1] It should be remembered that the present theory has been developed independently of Mr. Hawtrey's. Whether and to what extent they have historically a common origin in the Marshallian tradition and earlier English and Continental writers will not be discussed here.

equilibrium rate of interest " for a concept which is equally implicit in Mr. HAWTREY's analysis.

The capitalistic structure of production. So much for the monetary aspect of the upswing. But, according to the theory under review, it has its complement in a distortion in the structure of production, a maldistribution of economic resources. This "real" aspect it is now proposed to consider.

The rate of interest has not only the function of regulating the quantity of money. Like every other price, it has, in an individualistic economy, the more fundamental function of serving as a guide to the allocation of the factors of production to the different branches in the production process. It is the vertical structure, more specifically, which is governed by the rate of interest. In order to explain this part of the price mechanism, it is necessary to go somewhat deeper into the theory of capitalistic production.

At any given moment, the available means of production are in some way apportioned between the various stages of production. Some of them are at work in the industries which produce consumers' goods; others in the industries just before the last stage ; others are applied to produce half-finished goods, raw materials, tools and machinery.

The apportionment of the factors of production devoted to the production of consumers' goods and to the earlier stages of production respectively can, of course, be modified and is being modified continuously. Economic progress has to a large extent been conditioned by the fact that an ever-increasing proportion of the available productive resources has been devoted to earlier stages of production. New stages have been added or interpolated, with the result that the vertical structure of production has been elongated. In other words, the methods of production have become more indirect, more " roundabout " and more " capitalistic ", in the sense that a greater amount of capital, intermediate goods such as machinery and raw materials and half-finished products, is used per unit of output of consumable goods.[1] The

---

[1] Intermediate goods and consumers' goods are measured in value units. Since we are concerned with a proportion of values, we are not bothered by the objection that there can be no common measure for

ultimate aim of the accumulation of capital is naturally an increase in the output of consumers' goods. But the percentage increase in capital stock piled up behind the consumption industries is greater than the percentage increase in the rate of flow of consumers' goods.

The force which determines the lengthening of the process of production is, broadly speaking, the rate of saving. The signals for the entrepreneurs' to elongate the process are the availability of new capital and the lowness of the rate of interest.

Saving and interest.
If a part of current income is being saved—*i.e.*, if not all income is devoted to buying consumers' goods—the demand for consumers' goods falls off and factors of production are made available.[1] If the money saved is not withdrawn from circulation, but is offered in some way in the capital market, the rate of interest will fall and this will induce entrepreneurs to make new investments. There are always opportunities for investment which cannot be undertaken for want of capital. Labour-saving machinery can be installed (which involves the creation of a new stage in the process of production), railways can be electrified and in a hundred other ways the process of production can profitably be lengthened —if only the rate of interest is low enough and the necessary amount of capital available. It is the function of the rate of interest to select among the great number of existing opportunities for investment those extensions of the production process which can be undertaken with the existing supply of capital (savings). The rate of interest distinguishes those of the new roundabout methods of production which are permissible from those which are not.

---

valuations at different time points. The problem of the "time-dimension" of capital has given rise to endless disputes, especially in recent years. We shall, however, refrain from going more closely into the matter, since the theories at present under discussion can be analysed without a final decision on this point. (*Cf.* Nicholas Kaldor : " Annual Survey of Economic Theory : The Recent Controversy on the Theory of Capital " in *Econometrica*, Vol. V, 1937, page 201 *et seq*, the reply by F. H. Knight and rejoinder by N. Kaldor, *loc. cit.*, Vol. VI, 1938. See also Hugh Gaitskell : " Notes on the Period of Production ", *Zeitschrift für Nationalökonomie*, Vol. 7, 1936, and Vol. 9, 1938.)

[1] *Cf.*, *e.g.*, Bresciani-Turroni : " The Theory of Saving ", in *Economica* (New Series), Vol. 3, 1936, pages 1 *et seq.*, and 162 *et seq.*

If a certain plan of investment, which from the technological point of view seems to be productive and useful, cannot be realised for the sole reason that the expected yield would not justify the investment at the existing rate of interest—*i.e.*, because the profit rate is lower than the prevailing rate of interest—that by no means proves the imperfection of our present pricing system, but simply shows that there exist other opportunities for improving the productive process which hold out a higher rate of return and should rationally, therefore, be undertaken first.

If the rate of interest falls because of increased savings, the demand for capital can be satisfied to a greater extent and the equilibrium point moves down along the curve of demand for capital. Investments which were extra-marginal under the higher rate now become permissible. Factors of production are shifted from the lower to the higher stages of production. The production process is lengthened and eventually the output of consumers' goods per unit of input (in terms of " original factors " of production) is raised.[1]

" Artificial " lowering of the interest rate.   From the point of view of the entrepreneur who wants to embark on new schemes of investment, the situation is not changed if the lowering of the rate of interest is due to capital's having been made more plentiful, not by an increase in voluntary saving, but by an expansion of bank credit. Such an artificial cheapening of capital will also lead to a lengthening of the process

---

[1] It has been questioned whether this process of saving and investment runs smoothly. A great number of writers believe that the process of saving is likely to produce serious disturbances (*a*) because saving produces depression in the consumption industries which then spreads to the higher stages, (*b*) because money which is saved frequently disappears on the way and is not invested (deflation), (*c*) because increased investments eventually bring about an increase in the production of consumers' goods, which cannot be sold at the prevailing prices unless the flow of money is increased. But it is not with these alleged frictions and disturbances that we are here concerned. They will have to be discussed at a later stage of our enquiry. The theorists now under review believe that ordinarily the process of saving and investment runs smoothly. According to them, troubles arise only if voluntary saving is supplemented from " inflationary sources ", that is, by new bank credit or by expenditure from money hoards (which is equivalent to by a rise in the velocity of circulation of money).

of production. If we start from an equilibrium position of full employment with no excess capacity—we shall see later that the argument can also be adapted to apply to a situation with unemployment and unused plant—means of production will be drawn away from the consumption-goods industries. These industries will have to contract and the higher stages of production will expand.

This comes about in the following way. Entrepreneurs who want to invest are provided with purchasing power by the banks and compete for capital goods and labour. Prices will rise or be prevented from falling—this last case we shall discuss in detail later—and consumers' goods industries (the demand for the product of which has not risen, or not risen so much as the demand for capital goods, which is swollen by the newly created purchasing power) will be unable to retain at the enhanced prices all the factors of production which they used to employ. They will be compelled, therefore, to release means of production for use in the higher stages of production—that is, for the production of additional capital goods.[1]

---

[1] The concept "forced saving" has a long history (*cf.* F. A. Hayek, "A Note on the Development of the Doctrine of Forced Saving" in *Quarterly Journal of Economics*, Vol. 47, page 123). In addition to the writers of the present group, Professor Schumpeter has given it a prominent place in his account of the upward phase of the cycle. (See his *Theory of Economic Development*, English translation from the last German edition, 1934. First German edition, 1911.) Unlike the monetary over-investment theorists, however, he does not use the alleged peculiarities of forced saving to explain the crisis. This point will be taken up later (*cf.* Ch. 5, § 3). Recently the doctrine of forced saving has been attacked by Mr. Keynes (*The General Theory of Employment, Interest and Money*, pages 79-81, 183). But, as Professor Robertson has pointed out (*cf.* "Some Notes on Mr. Keynes' General Theory of Employment" in *Quarterly Journal of Economics*, Vol. 51, 1936, page 178), Mr. Keynes' objections are purely verbal. He banishes the word, but is forced to recognise the thing which the word denotes, though in another dress, when he says that, under the pressure of investment which is imperfectly foreseen, there may occur a "temporary reduction of the marginal propensity to consume" (*loc. cit.*, pages 123 and 124).

Obviously, the necessary condition is that the
Credit expan- demand for consumers' goods does not rise *pari*
sion and *passu* with the creation of credit and the rise in
" *forced* demand for capital goods. Either there will be a
saving ". lag in the rise of aggregate incomes, or—what is
probably the same thing from another angle—the
increment of income will not at once be available (owing to discon-
tinuities in the receipt of it) for expenditure purposes. Prices
will thus rise quicker than disposable income, and consumption
will be curtailed. In addition, the rigidity of certain contract
incomes such as rents, pensions, salaries, etc., may have the effect
of modifying the distribution of income in favour of classes who
are more disposed to save and have greater incentives to do so,
with the result that consumption will tend to be still further
reduced. People are to some extent forced, and to some extent
induced, to save more; and this " forced saving " has the same
result as is usually brought abou tby voluntary saving—viz., a
restriction of consumption and the release of productive resources
for the production of additional capital goods. In other words,
the real capital which is needed for the increased investment is
extorted from the consuming public by means of rising prices.

Treatment of these theories is complicated by the fact that there
is as yet no agreement as to the exact use of the expression " forced
saving ". It has been used to indicate the extra saving created by
the transfer of resources and incomes from creditor to debtor,
from rentier to State, from wage-earner (at least temporarily) to
employer, as the result of inflation. Professor STRIGL has objected
to this theory of forced saving[1] that, if those with relatively
fixed incomes get less and are obliged to restrict consumption,
others expand their incomes to a corresponding amount and,
unless they refrain voluntarily from expanding consumption to
the required extent, there cannot be a net increase in capital formation. In other words, there is no forced saving, but only ordinary,
voluntary saving.

---

[1] *Kapital und Produktion*, Vienna, 1934, page 195, and " Die Produktion unter dem Einfluss einer Kreditexpansion ", in *Schriften des Vereins
für Sozialpolitik*, Vol. 173, 1928.

Apart, however, from the increase of saving as a result of what Professor PIGOU styles a " doctoring of past contracts ", there is a more direct channel whereby additional bank credits may increase investment. This is the process which Professor ROBERTSON discusses at length in *Banking Policy and the Price Level* under the head of " Automatic Stinting ". Either dishoarding or the expenditure of newly created money, he says, " brings on to the market an additional daily stream of money which competes with the main daily stream of money for the daily stream of marketable goods, secures a part of the latter for those from whom the additional stream of money flows, and thus deprives the residue of the public of consumption which they would otherwise have enjoyed ".[1] As PIGOU argues in the particular case of the expansion of bank credits : " What in substance has happened is that the bankers have transferred to business-men purchasing power and, through purchasing power, real stuff in the form of wage goods and so on, formerly belonging to other people. They have done this by giving new money titles to business-men while leaving the money titles in other people's hands untouched in exactly the same way as they would have done had they taken money titles from other people and handed them to business-men."[2]

Neither Professor PIGOU nor Professor ROBERTSON seems to have in mind a reduction in *total* consumption, but only a re-distribution of consumption in favour of wage-earners, an augmentation of the real-wages bill, which, according to Professor PIGOU, brings with it an augmentation of capital. But this is the same type of mechanism envisaged by Professor HAYEK and Professor MISES as the instrument by which investment is financed in excess of voluntary saving in the case where an increase in capital involves a diminution of the flow of goods available for consumption. In the latter case, however, it is implied that the incomes created by the additional investment do not immediately become available to be spent or saved.

Professor Francesco VITO uses the expression " forced savings " for what is usually called "corporate saving". If a business firm or company fails to distribute its entire profits to the shareholders,

---

[1] *Banking Policy and the Price Level*, 1932 ed., page 48.
[2] *Industrial Fluctuations*, 1929, page 141.

this may mean that the latter have been " forced " to save (against their will) by the directors of the corporation. Professor VITO believes that this type of forced saving is likely to cause the same troubles as the type envisaged by Professor HAYEK.[1]

§ 4. THE DOWN-TURN (CRISIS)

Why must this process of monetary expansion and heavy investment always end in a collapse ?. Why does it not go on indefinitely or tail off into a more stable situation ?

Abandonment According to the over-investment theory, this is *of over-* impossible, because, by the artificial lowering of the *capitalistic* interest rate, the economy is lured into long round-*processes.* about methods of production which cannot be maintained permanently. The structure of production becomes, so to speak, top-heavy. Forces are set up which tend to restore the old arrangement. For some time, increasing advances by the banks enable entrepreneurs to carry on construction by the new roundabout methods. But sooner or later—and the later it happens the worse the result—it becomes clear that the newly initiated extensions of the structure of production cannot be completed, and the work on the new but incomplete roundabout processes must be discontinued. The investment boom collapses and a large part of the invested capital is lost.

Before discussing in detail how this comes about and what the external symptoms are, it will be useful to make the broad lines of the argument clearer by comparison with a centralised communistic economy.

The Russian Five-year Plan was a supreme effort to increase the " roundaboutness " of production and thereby the future production of consumers' goods. Instead of producing consumers' goods with the existing rather primitive methods, they curtailed production for immediate consumption to the indispensable minimum. Instead of food, shoes, clothes, houses, etc., they

---

[1] See F. Vito : " Il Risparmio forzato e la teoria di cicli economici " in *Revista internazionale di scienze sociali,* 1934, and " Die Bedeutung des Zwang-sparens für die Konjunkturtheorie " in *Beiträge zur Konjunkturlehre,* 1936.

produced power-plants and steel works : they sought to improve the transportation system : in a word, they built up a productive apparatus which could turn out consumption goods only after a considerable period of time.

But suppose it had become impossible to carry through this ambitious plan. Suppose the Government had come to the conclusion half-way that the population could not stand the enormous strain and had decided to change the policy. In such a case, they would have been forced to give up the newly started round-about methods of production and produce consumers' goods as quickly as possible. They would have had to interrupt the construction of power-plants, steel works and tractor factories and try instead to produce as quickly as possible simple implements and tools to increase the output of food and shoes and houses. That would have involved an enormous loss of capital, sunk in the abandoned construction works.[1]

Exactly the same thing happens, according to the monetary over-investment theory, in our individualistic exchange economy at the turning-point from prosperity to depression during the ordinary business cycle. The only difference is this : what in a communistic society is done upon a decision of the supreme economic council is in our individualistic economy brought about as the net effect of the independent actions of individuals and carried out by the price and interest mechanism.

It is not so easy to trace this process in detail, step by step, as it is to convey the general meaning of the argument : and, at this crucial point, the reasoning of our authors is not always altogether clear and consistent. It should be kept in mind that we are still concerned with what happens at the end of the boom and with the nature of the maladjustment which necessarily emerges and leads to the collapse. What happens after the turn will be discussed later. We shall see that, once the depression has started,

---

[1] Since the appearance of the first edition of this book, a very lucid analysis, also in " real " terms but much more elaborate than the above, has come to the author's notice : *Autour de la crise américaine de 1907, ou Capitaux-réels et Capitaux-apparents*, by Marcel Labordère (enlarged reprint from the *Revue de Paris* of February 1st, 1908), Paris, 1908. This important study has been entirely overlooked by the whole literature on the subject.

the whole economic scene is completely changed and quite different arguments apply.

Shortage of investible funds. The proximate cause for the breakdown of the boom is almost invariably the inability or unwillingness of the banking system to continue the expansion. Furthermore, it can be shown that a mere stoppage of expansion without actual contraction is very likely to lead to serious trouble. The process of expansion and investment involves the banking system in heavy commitments for the future, not in the legal but in the economic sense. The newly started roundabout methods of production can be completed only if a flow of capital is available over a considerable period. If this flow is not forthcoming, the completion of the new schemes is impossible. This must not be interpreted in too narrow a sense. What is meant is not merely that the construction of an indivisible piece of investment, a railway line or a power-plant or a new Cunarder, may have to be interrupted.[1] A much more important case is where a higher stage in the structure of production has been so much developed that it can work with full capacity only if the lower stages are adding to their equipment. If the steel industry, for example, has been developed to satisfy the needs of a rapid expansion in the building or automobile industry, it may suffer a contraction as soon as the building or automobile industry— without actually contracting—stops expanding and no longer adds to its equipment. This proposition will be discussed in greater detail in connection with the so-called " acceleration principle ". It explains or helps to explain why the transition from expansion to a stationary state is so difficult.

As has already been said, the fact that banks are forced to stop expansion for monetary reasons is the proximate cause of the boom's coming to an end. Shortage of capital causes the collapse; but the term " shortage of capital " is provisional and has to be used with great care. In the first instance, it may be interpreted in the monetary sense as equivalent to a shortage of investible funds.

---

[1] Such an over-narrow interpretation of the " Austrian " theory seems to be implied in Professor D. H. Robertson's article : " Industrial Fluctuations and the Natural Rate of Interest " in *Economic Journal*, Vol. 44, 1934, page 653.

The whole over-investment school, however, deny that the difficulty is a purely monetary one. They deny that monetary measures could avert the crisis, and contend that they could only postpone it. If all legal and customary limitations were removed and the necessary funds provided, the monetary expansion could go on, but prices would inevitably rise. There would be no end to this rise of prices, which would proceed with increasing rapidity like the German inflation in 1921-1923; and, if the credit expansion were not stopped, it would be brought to an end by a complete collapse of the monetary system—that is to say, the public would eventually abandon and repudiate the 'rapidly depreciating currency, as the German public started to do with the German Mark in 1923.

Hayek's theory of capital shortage. Great pains have been taken to explain this process in terms of relative prices and of supply and demand for particular types of goods. To Professor HAYEK we owe the most elaborate analysis. It runs as follows :

The whole stream of money or flow of purchasing power—that is, the demand for goods in terms of money per unit of time—is at any given point of time divided between producers' goods and consumers' goods. Since the productive process is split up into numerous successive stages—or, in other words, since the original factors of production (whatever that may mean) have to undergo numerous successive transformations before they are ready for final consumption—the money volume of transactions in producers' goods per unit of time is a multiple of transactions in consumers' goods. Much more money is spent per unit of time on producers' goods in all stages than on consumers' goods. If a part of income is saved and invested, *ceteris paribus*[1] the proportion between the demand for consumers' goods and the demand for producers' goods is modified in favour of the latter; and it

---

[1] This qualification is necessary, because there are other facts which influence the proportion mentioned in the text. If, for example, two or more successive stages of production are merged and run by a single firm instead of by two independent firms, the transfer of the intermediate goods from the former to the latter will from that time on be accomplished without the help of money. The amount of money required in the business sphere is reduced by such an act of integration.

must be permanently modified because, by the act of saving, the stock of capital, as well as the volume of transactions in capital goods, has been permanently increased.

An analogous change in the proportion between money spent for consumers' and producers' goods may be induced by injections of bank credits for production purposes. But in that case, in contradistinction to the case of voluntary saving, there is a strong probability that individuals will tend to restore the old proportion. " Now, the sacrifice is not voluntary and is not made by those who will reap the benefit from the new investments. It is made by consumers in general who, because of the increased competition from the entrepreneurs who have received the additional money, are forced to forgo part of what they used to consume . . . There can be no doubt that, *if* their money receipts should rise again, they would immediately attempt to expand consumption to the usual proportion. "[1]   And receipts will rise sooner or later, for the new money is spent partly to hire labourers, partly to buy capital goods of all sorts; and in both cases the money, partly at once, partly after a while, becomes additional income in the hands of the owners of the factors of production.

Faulty bookkeeping practices.   There is another factor which tends to swell the demand for consumers' goods. Bookkeeping is more or less based on the assumption of a constant value of money. Periods of major inflations have shown that this tradition is very deeply rooted and that long and disagreeable experiences are necessary to change the habit. One of the consequences is that durable means of production—such as machines and factory buildings—figure in cost accounts at the actual cost of acquisition, and are written off on that basis. If prices rise, this procedure is illegitimate. The enhanced replacement cost should be substituted for the original cost of acquisition. This, however, is not done, or is done only to an insufficient extent and only after prices have risen considerably. The consequence is that too little is written off, paper profits appear,[2] and the entrepreneur is tempted to increase his

---

[1] Hayek : *Prices and Production*, 2nd ed., London, 1934, page 57.

[2] These paper profits are also likely to add to the cumulative force of the upswing, because they stimulate borrowers and lenders to borrow

consumption. Capital in such case is treated as income.[1] In other words, consumption exceeds current production.

The onset of the depression. If the demand for consumers' goods rises relatively to the demand for producers' goods, consumers' goods industries become relatively profitable, and factors of production are enticed away from the higher stages of production and employed in the lower stages. The price of labour (wages) and of other mobile means of production, which can be used in various stages and can be transferred from the higher to the lower stages, rises. This involves a rise in money cost, which affects both lower and higher stages of production. But, while in the lower stages demand has risen, this is not true of the higher stages. Hence losses and a curtailment of production in the higher stages. The collapse of the boom has begun.

It sounds perhaps paradoxical that a general increase in demand for consumers' goods should have an adverse influence on the production of capital goods in general, which derive their economic value from the consumers' goods which they help to produce. The paradox has puzzled many writers, but it is not difficult to explain.[2] It should be borne in mind in the first place that

and lend more. They foster the optimistic spirit prevailing during the upswing, and so the credit expansion is likely to be accelerated. This phenomenon has its exact counterpart during the downswing of the cycle. See the excellent analysis of this phenomenon by E. Schiff, *Kapitalbildung und Kapitalaufzehrung im Konjunkturverlauf* (1933), esp. Ch. IV, pages 113-134 ; also Fr. Schmidt, *Die Industriekonjunktur—ein Rechenfehler* (1927), who has tried to build a complete theory of the cycle on this factor.

[1] In so far as entrepreneurs repay loans to the banks, they find themselves in possession of a real surplus, since their obligations have remained unchanged, while their receipts, etc., have risen owing to the rise in prices. This surplus may, and probably will, to a certain extent be utilised for increased consumption. Professor Robertson has drawn attention to this consideration : see his *Banking Policy and the Price Level*, 2nd ed., London, 1932, page 73. A further factor which operates in the direction of increasing demand for consumers' goods is the fact that, with rising prices, the consuming public is likely to dishoard and "to hurry on with the purchase of goods (such as clothes and motor-cars) of which the exact moment of purchase can be varied within pretty wide limits" (Robertson, *op. cit.*, page 75).

[2] A. H. Hansen and H. Tout, in "Investment and Saving in Business Cycle Theory," *Econometrica*, April 1933, have pointed out the underlying assumptions.

the proposition holds good only if all factors of production are reasonably well employed or if at least some of the factors attracted to consumers' goods trades would otherwise have been employed elsewhere.   In other words, under full employment, the production of consumers' good or that of producers' goods are alternatives.[1] [2] At the end of the boom, the condition of reasonably full employment can as a rule be assumed to be true.   Secondly, it is assumed that the demand for consumers' goods rises *relatively* to the demand for producers' goods.   This second assumption excludes the possibility of a compensatory expansion of credit, since, if credit for the purpose of acquiring producers' goods could be expanded *pari passu* with the increased demand for consumers' goods, it would no longer be true that the proportion between demand for consumers' goods and producers' goods has changed.[3]   The change involves a rise in interest rates; for prosperity in consumers' goods ·industries holds out good prospects of profits in the higher stages of production.   Producers in the higher stages of production will be eager to continue lengthening the productive structure and will try to raise the necessary funds by borrowing from the banks. Demand for credit rises; but supply is unchanged, or not sufficiently changed—for it is assumed that credit ceases to expand, or does not expand sufficiently.   This entails a rise in interest rates; and such a rise, as Professor HAYEK has shown, falls more heavily on production costs in the higher than in the lower stages of production.   The situation is now, therefore, that money cost has

---

[1] If competition in the labour market and the mobility of labour are imperfect, the condition of full employment can, of course, be relaxed.

[2] The fact that the production of consumers' goods can be expanded only at the expense of a reduction in the production of producers' goods and *vice versa* does not, of course, hold if there are idle factors of production available.   Furthermore, it does not preclude the possibility that, besides this physical connection between the production of the two categories of goods, there may be connections of another nature—*e.g.*, an increase in the production of consumers' goods may tend to stimulate the production of producers' goods, as postulated by the " acceleration principle " (see below, § 17 *et seq.* of this chapter), or there may be a causal connection in the opposite direction as postulated by the so-called " multiplier " (see below, *passim*).

[3] The proposition therefore does not apply during depression when there are unemployment, unused plant in almost all branches of industry, and a plentiful supply of credit.

risen, but demand has not risen (or not sufficiently risen), because the necessary funds are no longer forthcoming.

This is the exact and full interpretation of what is loosely called a " shortage of capital "; and it is a shortage of capital in this well-defined sense that is supposed to be the real cause of the breakdown. " Shortage of capital " in this sense is equivalent to under-saving and over-consumption. If people could be induced to save more—that is, to spend a smaller part of their income on consumers' goods and devote a larger part (through the intermediary of the capital market) to the purchase of capital goods—the flow of money and the structure of production would be brought into harmony and the breakdown avoided.

The fruits of the boom lost in the crisis. If this cannot be achieved—and the chances that it will be achieved are almost nil—the new extensions to the structure of production are doomed to collapse. With some slight exceptions which are introduced as after-thoughts and treated as theoretical curiosities of no practical importance, the authors of the monetary over-investment school conclude that every credit expansion must lead to over-investment and to a breakdown. It is asserted over and over again with great emphasis that it is impossible to bring about a lasting increase in the capital stock of society as a whole by means of forced saving and that no permanent extension of the structure of production can be accomplished with the help of an inflationary credit expansion. What is thus built up during the upswing will inevitably be destroyed in the breakdown.[1]

In the specific case of the American boom of 1925-1929, the authors are emphatic that the same thing applies to an expansion which does not lead to a rise in prices, but is just enough to prevent a fall in prices that would otherwise have taken place because of

---

[1] The durable means of production constructed during the upswing outlast, of course, the boom. But the contention is that they are lost economically. They are not used at all or are used in such a way that their marginal product does not cover the cost of reproduction. It should, however, be noted that important qualifications are called for in respect of permanent goods or instruments where the cost of maintenance is negligible compared with production cost.

Compare H. S. Ellis, *German Monetary Theory* 1905-1933 (1934), pages 425-431, on other views on "The 'Productivity' of Bank Credit".

a continuous increase in the volume of production. For reasons which will be expounded in the subsequent pages, it seems, however, that the undertaking to prove this latter point rigorously has not been made good.

                        In his *Prices and Production*,[1] Professor HAYEK
Neisser's argues that, even where the extension of the
criticism. structure of production which entrepreneurs were
                        induced to undertake by the artificial cheapening of credit is completed, the old arrangement tends to be restored later on for the reason that consumers will " attempt to expand consumption to the usual proportion "[2] and " the money stream will be re-distributed between consumptive and productive uses "[3] in the same, or nearly the same, proportion as it was distributed before such proportion was artificially distorted from the normal by the injection of money.

But, as Professor NEISSER[4] has shown, there is no reason to expect this return to the old arrangement, if the new roundabout methods of production have been brought to completion. When they are completed, the flow of consumers' goods which was temporarily reduced will rise again, and will even reach a higher level than that from which the expansion started, so that consumers can safely expand their consumption. Forced saving will cease to be necessary when the new processes of production are completed. When they are completed, all that is required to maintain them is that the entrepreneurs—not the consumers—should refrain from " disinvestments ", that is, from consuming capital or from spending amortisation quotas on consumption. There is no reason why the old proportion between money spent for consumers' and for producers' goods should be restored. It is not true that the whole of newly injected money becomes income either at once or after a while. Part of it must be retained by the entrepreneurs in order to pay for intermediate goods (in

---

[1] 2nd ed., pages 55 *et seq.*
[2] *Ibid.*, page 57.
[3] *Ibid.*, page 58.
[4] "Monetary Expansion and the Structure of Production" in *Social Research*, Vol. I, New York, November 1934, pages 434 *et seq.* Similar objections had been raised by Piero Sraffa, *Economic Journal*, March 1932.

contradistinction to payments for the original factors of production). In other words, only a part of the new money becomes income. Another part remains permanently in the business sphere. It is only if entrepreneurs "dissave"—*i.e.*, if they eat up their capital and refrain from investing that part of their gross receipts which is not net income (working capital and amortisation quotas)—that the pre-inflation arrangement is restored.

We may conclude that the theory under review is bound either to assume that the former proportions between capital and income will be restored by actual capital consumption or that the expansion must be discontinued before the new processes have been completed —or rather before *all* the new processes have been completed. This latter qualification seems to be called for, and is important, because it sheds doubt on the contention that no permanent extension of the process of production can be effected by a credit expansion. It is a plausible assumption that, when the expansion comes to an end, there will always be *some* new processes in an incomplete state. But there is no reason why others should not have been completed. The latter can be retained when the former have to be scrapped. This cessation of work is the essence of the crisis.

But why must there be any incomplete processes at all when the expansion has to end ? Professor HAYEK admits the possibility of the expansion's tailing-off gradually, in such a way that the started processes are completed but no new ones are inaugurated (except where voluntary savings are available). But, evidently, he does not believe that this possibility has any practical importance. Much seems to depend on the intensity of the expansion and on certain "indivisibilities", on which Professor ROBERTSON lays so much stress. But the writers of the group under review have not discussed this point in detail. We shall have occasion to deal with it in another connection.

Why need the expansion end ? It is evident that no collapse would occur if the credit expansion could go on indefinitely. It follows—the point is made by Professor HAYEK himself—that a crisis is equally inevitable in the case of voluntary saving if the flow of saving is suddenly reduced. It is, however, asserted—although the reasons given are not always quite convincing—that sudden changes are not likely to occur in respect of voluntary saving, while forced saving must come to an end abruptly. It is therefore very important to ask why should the expansion of credit stop. The answer is that in a closed economy, leaving out of account purely monetary and institutional factors (inability of the banking system to continue expansion within the limits fixed by the gold standard or some other legal or customary rules), the continuance of the expansion will involve a progressive rise in prices. A progressive rise in prices and the danger of a complete collapse of the monetary system is the only insurmountable barrier which prevents an indefinite continuation of the expansion.[1]

It seems to follow that the present theory does not prove, as it claims to do, that a credit expansion which does not lead to a rise in prices but only prevents a fall in prices must have the same evil effect as the more violent type which brings about a rise in the absolute price level. In a progressive economy, where the output of goods in general grows continually and prices tend therefore to fall, there is scope for a continuous expansion of credit at a steady rate.

Necessity of quantitative assumptions. Against this objection, the following argument has been advanced.[2] It is true, in an economy where the output, owing to improvements in the methods of production, grows at a constant rate, that a steady expansion in terms of money may be made : that is to say, per unit of time a constant amount of new money may be put into circulation.[3] But even if this is just enough to keep the

---

[1] Hayek : "Capital and Industrial Fluctuations" in *Econometrica*, Vol. II, April 1934, page 161. Reprinted as Appendix to 2nd ed. of *Prices and Production*. See also E. F. M. Durbin : *Purchasing Power and Trade Depression*, London, 1933, pages 153-155. The latter concludes that the crisis is a purely monetary phenomenon, brought about by the refusal of the banks to continue the expansion of credit.

[2] Hayek, *op. cit.*, pages 160 and 161.

[3] Mr. Durbin argued that if the rate of increase of production is constant (say 10% per year) an increasing amount of money can be put into circulation without raising prices, because the absolute increase in output per unit of time increases (the 10% is reckoned from an are ever-increasing total). Evidently, different quantitative assumptions can be made, and it is impossible to say which one corresponds best to reality. For further comments on the failure of the writers of the present school to make their assumptions quantitatively precise, see the following paragraph.

price level of finished goods constant, prices of factors of production will rise continuously. Hence, successive additions to the money stock will only be able to buy successively diminishing amounts of the factors of production. But, to render the completion of the newly initiated processes of production possible, the entrepreneurs in the upper stages must be enabled to absorb factors of production at a constant rate ; and, as the prices of factors of production rise, a credit expansion at an increasing rate will be necessary to enable them to do so. The conclusion is that a relative inflation, such as can be made within the limits of a constant price level, is not sufficient to allow of the completion of the new roundabout methods of production which have been initiated under the stimulus of the expansion. Either the rate of expansion of credit will be sufficiently increased and prices will be driven up and the inevitable breakdown will be postponed, or the boom will collapse at once owing to an insufficiency in the capital supply.

Incomplete assumptions. This reasoning is, however, not convincing. The result will depend on a complicated quantitative relationship between certain factors—namely :

(*a*) the rate of progress of the economy : that is, the rate of increase in efficiency or output which determines the rate of credit expansion that can be made without raising the price level; (*b*) the supply of capital which is required in successive periods to make possible the completion of productive processes which have been started in the past. In respect to both factors, Professor HAYEK's argument makes implicitly certain assumptions, the bearing of which is not quite clear. The problem has not been either clearly visualised or explicitly stated. The concrete circumstances by which the magnitude of the two factors is determined are left vague. It is open to grave doubt whether generalisations can be made on this point without extensive factual investigations.

In any case, the theory in its fully developed form seems to make the emergence of a serious disequilibrium dependent upon relatively small fluctuations in the rate of forced saving. This being so, the question arises whether fluctuations of this order of magnitude are not equally likely to occur in the flow of voluntary savings.[1]   If they do occur, evil consequences must be expected, even in the absence of credit inflation.   (We shall see, in connection with the discussion of other theories, that there are numerous other disturbances possible which may interrupt the upswing and start a vicious spiral downward—disturbances which are probably of the same, or even of a higher, order of magnitude than the fluctuations in the rate of forced or voluntary saving discussed above.)

To sum up, we may say that the theory has not proved rigorously that a stabilisation of prices in a progressive economy must always lead to over-production, crisis and depression.[2]   The practical importance of this conclusion is considerable in view of the American prosperity in the twenties, a notable feature of which was the fact that wholesale prices did not rise.

§ 5.   THE DOWNSWING

The depression as a period of readjustment.   The theory of the depression is not nearly so fully elaborated by the authors of the monetary over-investment school as the theory of the boom. The depression was originally conceived of by them as a process of adjustment of the structure of production, and was explained in non-monetary terms. During the boom, they argued, the process of production is unduly elongated.   This elongation has accordingly to be removed and the structure of production has to be shortened or, alternatively, expenditure on consumers' goods must be reduced (by retrenchment of wages and other incomes which are likely to be spent

---

[1] *Cf.* C. Bresciani-Turroni, "The Theory of Saving" in *Economica*, 1936, pages 165 *et seq.*

[2] The following statement of a prominent adherent of the monetary over-investment theory is significant : "This theory does not make the pretence of being the only explanation of all cycles and crises that have ever occurred, nor does it pretend that it states unconditional necessities" (F. Machlup, "Professor Knight and the 'Period of Production'" in *Journal of Political Economy*, Vol. 43, October 1935, page 622.

wholly or mainly on consumers' goods) sufficiently to make the new structure of production possible. This involves a lengthy and painful process of rearrangement. Workers are thrown out of work in the higher stages, and it takes time to absorb them in the lower stages of production. In modern times especially, with inflexible wage systems and the various other obstructions represented by all kinds of State intervention, this process of shifting labour and other means of production is drawn out much longer than is necessary for purely technological reasons.[1]

The secondary deflation.

This non-monetary explanation of the depression is, however, admittedly incomplete and unsatisfactory. The majority of the authors of the group under review were at first very reluctant to recognise that there is a cumulative process of contraction corresponding to the cumulative process of expansion. But eventually it was admitted that, in addition to the difficulties which must arise from the fact that the structure of production does not correspond to the flow of money (in other words, the disturbances which result from the deflection of the money stream from the higher to the lower stages of production), there must be a deflation—that is, a shrinkage in the aggregate flow of money. The difficulties which result from this general shrinkage in the flow of money are superimposed on the disturbances involved in the necessary readjustment in the structure of production. Without assuming a general deflation, it is impossible to explain why the depression spreads to *all* stages and branches of industry, why it is not confined only to those industries which are over-developed and must therefore eventually contract (the higher stages), but extends also to those which are under-developed and must therefore eventually expand (the lower stages). It has become customary to speak of " secondary deflation ", by which it is intended to convey that the deflation does not come about independently, but is induced by the maladjustment in the structure of production which has led to the breakdown. Without the latter, it is believed, the deflation would not start at all.

---

[1] See especially L. Robbins : *The Great Depression*, London, 1934.

The mechanism of secondary deflation has not been analysed very closely by the members of the school under review. Broadly speaking, there are two views.

(*a*) Professor RÖPKE has studied the question in various publications[1] and has come to the conclusion that the process of deflation has a tendency to become cumulative and self-perpetuating. Genetically, it is true, it is connected with the extravagances of the preceding boom and the real maladjustment which the boom has produced. But the intensity of the deflation by no means necessarily corresponds to the extent of the over-investment. It is also untrue, he believes, that the deflation contributes (as is more or less vaguely suggested by the other authors of the monetary over-investment school) to bringing about the necessary adjustment (shortening) in the process of production. Once started, the deflation is propelled by its own momentum and by a number of institutional factors. What these factors are and how they work, we shall discuss at greater length in another connection. HAWTREY, KEYNES, PIGOU and ROBERTSON have contributed most towards the understanding of this phenomenon.[2]

Those who believe that the deflation has a life of its own, so to speak, which is largely independent of the disequilibrium bred out of the preceding boom, are naturally inclined to assume that it can be directly counteracted, even if the boom has been allowed to give rise to a maladjustment in the structure of production.

(*b*) The other group, in which we may reckon HAYEK, MACHLUP, MISES, ROBBINS, STRIGL, is, or was, of the opinion that the deflation is the necessary consequence of the boom. If once the boom has been allowed to develop and to give rise to maladjustments, the

---

[1] See : *Crises and Cycles*, London, 1936 (translated from the German). "Geldtheorie und Weltkrise" in *Deutscher Volkswirt* of September 25th, 1931. "Praktische Konjunkturpolitik" in *Weltwirtschaftliches Archiv*, 34. Band, 1931. "Trends in German Business Cycle Policy" in *Economic Journal*, September 1933.

[2] See, in particular : Keynes : *A Treatise on Money*, London, 1930. Robertson : *Banking Policy and the Price Level*, and the controversy in *Economic Journal* of the following dates : Robertson, "Mr. Keynes' Theory of Money", September 1931 ; Keynes, "A Rejoinder to Mr. Robertson", September 1931 ; Robertson, "Saving and Hoarding", September 1933, and three notes on "Saving and Hoarding", by Keynes, Hawtrey and Robertson, December 1933.

price has to be paid in the shape of a process of deflation. It is admitted by some that, at a certain point in the contraction process, an injection of money may help to shorten the contraction. But they warn us at once that the medicine is very dangerous, that it has to be given in careful doses, and can be useful only at a certain stage of the process and must be administered in a certain way, and will do harm if any one of these conditions is not strictly complied with. As this is too much to expect from the monetary authorities, the only practical policy is to let the deflation run its course and avoid interventions which would only make things worse.

The struggle for liquidity. The most coherent theory of the depression along these lines is that of Professor STRIGL.[1] He admits that the breakdown of the boom induces a process of hoarding and deflation. After the breakdown of the boom, the banks will not merely stop expansion : they will contract credit in order to increase their liquidity. Under the influence of the general feeling of insecurity and pessimism, industrial firms will also seek to strengthen their cash reserves, and amortisation quotas will be kept in liquid form instead of being invested. This general struggle for liquidity involves hoarding. It means that money, whose function it is to be the vehicle of investment of real capital, fails to fulfil this function and is sterilised for the time being in swollen cash reserves or, in the case of bank money (deposits), annihilated altogether. The general price fall which ensues operates as a further deterrent to investment. The profit rate falls below the money rate. Perhaps the most important external symptom of this process is the intense liquidity and the extremely low rates on the money market which develop during the depression. The low money rates are caused by the fact that the overflow of funds from the money market to the capital market is impeded by an invisible barrier of distrust and pessimism.

It goes without saying that the writers of the group not only admit, but even stress, the fact that the pressure of deflation is intensified and prolonged by all kinds of ill-advised intervention by the State and other public bodies, such as the competitive raising of tariffs, the scramble for gold in order to liquidate existing

---

[1] *Kapital und Produktion*, Vienna, 1934, pages 208 *et seq.*

gold-exchange standards, and all similar measures designed to keep up prices and incomes.[1]

§ 6. THE UPTURN (REVIVAL)

The effective quantity of money.

If left to itself, the economic system would gradually return to equilibrium with reasonably full employment of all productive resources. The equilibrium could be maintained, if only the banks would refrain from a new credit expansion—in other words, if the money rate of interest were kept on the equilibrium level. The equilibrium rate is implicitly or explicitly defined as that which keeps the effective quantity of money (MV) constant.

The concept " effective quantity of money " is very complicated. It is not easily defined in theory and is hopelessly difficult to measure statistically. The difficulty comes in principally through the factor " V ". The velocity of circulation meant is not the transaction velocity, nor is it the income velocity. One might perhaps call it trade velocity, the term being understood to cover all transactions which involve an exchange of goods in all stages of production, but to exclude financial transactions (*e.g.*, on the stock exchange). If the quantity and the transaction velocity of money remain constant, but at the same time the requirements of the financial circulation rise, the result will be a decrease in the effective quantity of money as defined above. But these qualifications are not yet sufficient. Allowance must also be made for integration and disintegration of the process of production. If two or more successive stages in a particular line of industry (such as spinning and weaving), which are carried out by independent firms, are integrated by the formation of a vertical trust, the transfer of the intermediate product from the higher to the lower stage, which formerly gave rise to monetary transactions, may in future be effected by mere entries in the books of the new firm. Thus the merger may set free a certain amount of money. The trade velocity of money need not be changed, but the supply of money ought to

---

[1] See especially L. Robbins : *The Great Depression*, London, 1934.

be restricted; otherwise inflationary consequences will ensue.[1]

From these considerations, it follows that the prescription to " keep the effective quantity of money constant " is by no means an easy one to follow.

Recovery in demand for credit. The writers of the group under review are, however, well aware of the great danger that the discrepancy between the money rate and the equilibrium rate of interest, which prevailed during the depression, will at once be succeeded by a discrepancy in the opposite direction. In view of the falling prices and the state of pessimism and discouragement, the money rate during the downswing stands above the natural rate. When the fall of prices comes to an end and pessimism gives way to a more optimistic outlook, the current money rates, without being changed, will soon stand below the equilibrium rate. In other words, the equilibrium rate is likely to rise above the money rate.[2] In terms of

---

[1] On this subject, compare M. W. Holtrop : *De Omloopssnelheid van het geld*, Amsterdam, 1928, and " Die Umlaufsgeschwindigkeit des Geldes " in *Beiträge zur Geldtheorie*, ed. by Hayek, Vienna, 1933, pages 115-211. Compare further J. Marschak : "Volksvermögen und Kassenbedarf " in *Archiv für Sozialwissenschaft u. Sozialpolitik*, Vol. 68, 1932, pages 385-419, and " Vom Grössensystem der Geldwirtschaft," *loc. cit.*, Vol. 69, 1933, pages 492-504. H. Neisser : *Der Tauschwert des Geldes*, Jena, 1928. " Der Kreislauf des Geldes " in *Weltwirtschaftliches Archiv*, 1931, Vol. 33, pages 365-408. " Volksvermögen und Kassenbedarf " in *Archiv für Sozialwissenschaft u. Sozialpolitik*, Vol. 69, 1933, pages 484-492. A. W. Marget : " A Further Note on Holtrop's Formula for the 'Coefficient of Differentiation' and Related Concepts " in *Journal of Political Economy*, Vol. 41, pages 237-241 and " The Relation between the Velocity of Circulation of Money and the Velocity of Circulation of Goods ", *loc. cit.*, Vol. 40, 1932, pages 289-313 and 477-512. J. Schumpeter : " Das Sozialprodukt und die Rechenpfennige " in *Archiv für Sozialwissenschaft u. Sozialpolitik*, Vol. 44, pages 627-715. The whole literature on this subject is well reviewed and summarised by Professor H. S. Ellis, *German Monetary Theory* 1905-1933 (Cambridge, Mass., 1934), Part II, and by A. W. Marget, *The Theory of Prices. A Re-examination of the Central Problems of Monetary Theory*, Vol. I, New York, 1938, *passim*.

[2] In the earlier versions of the theory, the assumption was made, more or less explicitly, that the discrepancy between the equilibrium rate and money rate of interest is always brought about by a lowering of the money rate—that is, from the supply side. It is now pretty generally accepted that the situation is more complex and that the equilibrium rate is likely to move upward under the influence of psychological forces, price changes, inventions and discoveries, etc.

supply and demand, this can be expressed by saying that the credit demand curve will move to the right or, loosely speaking, that demand will rise. At the same time, the banks will be in a liquid position, and there is every reason to expect that they will liberally comply with the increased demand for credit. The barrier between the money market and the capital market is broken down, and the funds accumulated behind the barrier flow into the investment market.[1]

Thus a new upswing starts smoothly—at first, almost imperceptibly—out of the ashes of the last boom. No special stimulus from outside is required in the shape of inventions, crop changes, discoveries, etc. We shall see, however, that the writers of the next group believe that such an incentive from outside is necessary. In this respect the present theory is the more "endogenous" in the previously defined sense. But it would seem to be difficult and not very helpful to lay down hard-and-fast rules as to whether the upswing must be assumed to be brought about by forces "internal" or "external" to the economic system.

Expansion from a position of partial employment. It is convenient at this point to introduce the question of the existence of unused productive resources of all kinds. The explanation given by the writers of the school under review for the upswing, or rather for the boom, almost invariably starts from an equilibrium position with full employment of the means of production.[2] But the argument can easily be adapted to the other case. If there are unemployed resources, evidently the expansion of credit may go on much longer than when all resources are employed. There need, then, be no shift of factors from the lower to the higher stages,

---

[1] Strigl, *op. cit.*, Anhang I. It may be added that, owing to the existence of the various reserves which will have been accumulated during the depression, the expansion can go far with little or no help from the banks.

[2] Professor Hayek in particular has laid down the methodological rule that the analysis of the cyclical movement should never start on the assumption of existing unemployment, because that would beg the question of why unemployment can exist at all. This postulate would seem to narrow down unduly and quite unnecessarily the scope of such analyses.

but only the absorption of unused resources predominantly in those stages of production which are especially stimulated by the expansion—namely, in the upper stages (capital goods industries). Arguing along the lines of the theory under review, one has to assume that the unemployed resources are mainly put to work in the higher stages (capital-goods industries). But, so long as there is a reserve of unemployed resources, the reaction from excess investment, which consists (as we have seen) of a comparative rise in the demand for consumers' goods, will not produce a breakdown, since there is no necessity to detach factors of production from the higher stages. Prices need not rise much. The expansion of credit can go on.

This process has never been analysed so closely as the process of expansion starting from a position of full employment.[1] But, applying the same type of reasoning, the conclusion seems to be as follows : A disequilibrium between the higher and the lower stages is produced by the fact that the unemployed resources are not distributed among the different stages of production in the way they ought to be if ultimate equilibrium is to emerge. A larger amount is absorbed into the higher stages than can in the long run be employed there with the given rate of voluntary saving. Thus the recovery from the depth of the depression has a wrong twist from the beginning.

§ 7. RHYTHM AND PERIODICITY

The ideological basis of inflation. Professor MISES gives the following answer to the question why the cycle of prosperity and depression recurs again and again.[2] The behaviour of the banks is responsible for the occurrence of the business cycle. If the banks did not push the money rate below the natural rate by expanding credit, equilibrium would not be disturbed. But why do the banks make the same mistake again and again ? " The answer must be : because the

---

[1] See, however, Bresciani-Turroni, " The Theory of Saving " in *Economica*, May 1936, pages 172-174.

[2] *Geldwertstabilisierung und Konjunkturpolitik*, Jena, 1928, pages 56-61.

prevailing ideology among business-men and politicians looks on the reduction of the rate of interest as an important aim of economic policy, and because they consider an inflationary expansion of credit the best means to attain that objective " (page 58). " The root cause of the phenomenon that one business cycle follows the other is thus of an ideological nature " (page 60).

Professor MISES believes, furthermore, that the commercial banks alone without the support of the central bank can never produce a dangerous credit inflation, because they would immediately lose cash and become insolvent. It is only with the backing of the central bank that it is possible to expand credit sufficiently to produce a dangerous boom. The ability of the central banks to increase the circulation is due to the monopoly which they hold of the issue of bank-notes. If the issue of notes were not a monopoly, if competition were restored in this field of the central banks' activities—that is to say, if every bank had the right to issue notes, convertible into legal tender money (gold)—a dangerous expansion of credit and reduction of the interest rate would be impossible. The unsound banks would quickly be eliminated, and the sound banks would learn by experience that expansion is punished by bankruptcy.[1]

What banking policy will eliminate the cycle ? All the other members of this group of writers believe that the solution of the problem of the rhythmic nature of the cycle is not so simple as the above. They would all probably agree that there must exist some form of banking policy by following which the business cycle would be eliminated. But they have become more and more conscious of the difficulties of giving precise criteria for the ideal policy. It is not a sufficient explanation to say that from time to time banks lower the rate too much. As has been pointed out above, it is rather the rise in the equilibrium rate than the fall in the money rate which creates the discrepancy between the two.

It follows that it is impossible to define the policy which the banks should pursue in negative terms by saying that the banks should refrain from lowering the rate of interest. It must be stated in

---

[1] Compare Professor H. Neisser's criticism in his article : " Notenbankfreiheit ?" in *Weltwirtschaftliches Archiv*, Vol. 32, pages 446-461, and Vera Smith, *The Rationale of Central Banking*, London, 1936.

positive terms that they should vary the rate in such a way that no credit expansion or contraction ensues in the face of changing demand for credit. But this, again, seems simple and exact only on a superficial view. It has been pointed out above how difficult it is, even in theory, to define exactly what is meant by saying that the effective quantity of money should be kept constant. In addition to the theoretical difficulty of giving exact criteria, there is the extremely difficult task of applying these criteria in concrete cases.

Professor HAYEK has pointed out that, for the individual banker, it is impossible to distinguish between deposits which have been created by voluntary saving and deposits which have an inflationary origin. The velocity of circulation of money, especially of bank money (deposits), may change without affecting the reserves of the banks. Neither bank reserves nor reserve ratios nor the price level are an unfailing criterion of the correct credit policy from the standpoint of the theory under review. Expansion may take place without any action on the part of the banks.

Cyclical implications of seasonal variations in credit. Professor MACHLUP[1] has called attention to one factor which helps to explain the recurrence of the cycle and throws into relief the passive rôle of the banks, at any rate during the first phase of the upswing. It is this. A considerable portion of the payments which have to be made during a given period, say a year, are not evenly distributed, but are concentrated at certain dates, some of them at the end of each month and others at the end of each quarter. Therefore, even with the most elaborate clearing and compensation arrangements, no complete continuous offsetting of the debts and liabilities of each firm is possible. At the critical dates, at the end of the month and of the quarter, there is therefore always a strong demand for short-term credit and a resultant strain on the money market. If the banks were not able and willing to relieve this monthly and quarterly tightness of money by granting temporary credits, individual firms would be compelled to provide for their requirements at the critical dates by accumulating cash during

---

[1] See his book, *Börsenkredit, Industriekredit und Kapitalbildung*, Vienna, 1931, pages 161-178.

the intervals between them. But, as the banks lend money to overcome these difficulties—credit expansion for such a temporary stringency being generally regarded as perfectly legitimate and safe—it is not necessary to accumulate cash, and the sums involved can be invested instead.

It is clear that we have here a source of inflation; and the inflation, according to Professor MACHLUP, will not be confined to the single occasion of the first introduction of these " ultimo loans ", but will tend to recur cyclically. " While the utilisation of temporary surplus cash together with (inflationary) bank credit created the possibility of initiating illicitly long processes of production, the depression, after the elimination of the untenable enterprises, will release these sums again " (pages 175 and 176). During the depression, the investment of these sums is impossible, and they accumulate on the money market; but, as soon as the spirit of enterprise revives, they can be utilised for financing the boom for a long time without any, or with very little, additional bank credit.[1]

Summary. We may conclude that the question why one cycle follows another without interruption cannot be answered, on the basis of the theory under review, by a simple formula. The inevitability of the sequence " forced saving—breakdown—depression " has been somewhat whittled down. The severity of the decline is no longer believed to vary rigidly with the degree of the structural maladjustments which gave rise to it. There is no longer the same confidence in the inevitability or the curative function of the depression. Above all, it has been realised to be impossible to fix the sole responsibility for the boom on the expansionary propensities of the banking system. Even in a purely cash economy, movements of hoarding and dishoarding might be induced, with the result that waves of expansion and contraction of economic activity would take place. It thus seems impossible to reduce to a few simple rules the problem of what ought to be done to eliminate the cycle. The high expectations which were originally entertained in this respect have given way to a much more cautious and much more sceptical attitude.

---

[1] Whilst there can be little doubt that we have here a possible source of inflation (whatever its quantitative importance), it is difficult to see in this factor any independent *cyclical* significance.

§ 8.   INTERNATIONAL COMPLICATIONS

Guiding
principles.
A systematic account of the international aspect of the business cycle on the basis of the theory hitherto under consideration has never been attempted. With the help of the theory of the international money mechanism, it is, however, possible to trace out the way in which (if one accepts the monetary over-investment theory) the course of the cycle in a particular country must be influenced by its position in the international economy, and the manner in which the cyclical movement in such country is likely to react on the country's international trade and on the internal situation of other countries.

As in the case of the purely monetary explanation of the business cycle, the first questions to be asked are : How does a given change in the international situation of a country influence the expansion or contraction of credit ? Is it likely to facilitate and prolong, or retard, an expansion already under way ? How is a contraction in process influenced by a given change in other countries ? It is impossible to enumerate and systematise at this point all the conceivable contingencies. But a few principles may be laid down and some illustrations be given.

Influences
through the
balance of
payments.
Any improvement in the balance of payments —that is to say, any increase in the demand for the means of payment of a given country in terms of the money of other countries—will have an expansionist influence. This improvement may be due to a great variety of circumstances—changes in the demand for particular commodities, crop changes, capital movements, etc. The erection of new tariff walls by an individual country, if not followed by compensatory action on the part of other countries, will have a favourable influence on the international monetary situation of the country which has raised its tariffs. In other words, it will enable the latter to expand its circulation without a deterioration of its exchange rate. Thus, the immediate influence of protectionist measures may be a stimulation of prosperity or an alleviation of depression. But the conditions

in which this is true must be borne in mind. If many countries pursue this policy at the same time, the stimulating influence is lost. In the long run, the raising of tariff walls impairs the national dividends of all the countries involved.[1] Indirect effects (*e.g.*, on capital movements) may prevent even the immediate stimulation afforded by protectionist measures. Finally, an improvement in the balance of payments can always be utilised as a means of increasing the gold and foreign-exchange reserve in lieu of expanding the circulation.

While international influences are capable of stimulating of retarding a process of expansion or contraction, they may also arrest and reverse it—that is to say, international forces may start a revival or precipitate a crisis and depression in a country.

The gold standard. Under the gold standard, the monetary authorities are obliged, if the country is losing gold, to put the brake on expansion. Gold may flow out either because the country has expanded more rapidly than other countries and prices are getting out of line with those in the rest of the world, or because other countries have started to contract or because there is a movement of capital (which may have been brought about by a great variety of causes), or because of a crop failure which necessitates increased imports or reduces exports, etc. Instead of contracting, a country may choose to leave the gold standard. If this is not thought safe, as being likely to lead to a flight of capital, resort may be had to exchange control. Thus, innumerable possibilities may arise, which cannot all be worked out at this point: but they can easily be analysed in the way indicated, although it may be extremely difficult to foresee in any given case the outcome of the many forces and reactions involved.

The fact that a crisis and depression or a revival is brought about in one way or another by " international forces " in no way, therefore, invalidates the theory of the business cycle, even though the theory has been elaborated without taking into account these international complications.

---

[1] Therefore, the statement made in the text is perfectly compatible with the free-trade argument. The qualifications made should be sufficient to exclude protectionist measures from the arsenal of a rational depression policy.

In arguing on the basis of the over-investment *International* theory, special attention must be paid to international *capital* capital movements.[1] They not only affect the *movements.* purely monetary situation by stimulating or retarding the expansion or contraction of credit : they have also a bearing on the structure of production. An individual country may finance a boom, wholly or partly, by capital imports from other countries instead of by an internal expansion of credit and forced saving. So long as this is possible, the reaction which the theory under review holds responsible for the breakdown— namely, a corresponding rise in the demand for consumers' goods —may be staved off. Thus, in so far as a particular country is concerned, the boom may be prolonged. On the other hand, international capital movements are subject to risks and disturbances which are absent in the case of an internal expansion.

An interesting question is how the composition *The* of exports and imports of a country changes during *composition* the different phases of the cycle. It might be sup- *of exports* posed that capital imports during the upswing are *and imports.* bound to be effected through the import of capital goods. As a general statement, this would, however, be wrong. In any given situation in respect of tariffs or otherwise, what a country imports will depend on the comparative cost situation or, in other words, on the comparative facilities of the various countries for the production of different types of goods. It is conceivable that capital for investment purposes may be imported, not in the shape of capital goods (raw materials, machinery, electrical equipment, etc.), but in the shape of consumers' goods. This will be the case in a country where capital-goods industries and the production of raw materials are well developed, while consumers' goods industries are less so.[2]

---

[1] See especially R. Nurkse : *Internationale Kapitalbewegungen*, Vienna, 1935, Ch. V, pages 187-211.

[2] We need not go into the causes which give a country an advantage in the production of this or that type of goods. They range from climatic conditions and the quality of the soil to the structure of the tariff and social legislation. *Cf.* B. Ohlin, *Interregional and International Trade, passim*, Cambridge, Mass. (U.S.A.), 1933.

It is difficult to find concrete examples which illustrate this proposition, since in actual fact the situation is usually very complex. Countries do not usually specialise solely in the production of consumers' goods, capital equipment, or raw materials, etc. Still, the economic equipment is usually deficient in various directions, though protectionist policy has done much to diversify national production and lessen international specialisation. On the whole, industrial countries are at the same time exporters of capital. Therefore, it is natural that capital movement should take place chiefly through the shipment of machinery, railroad and electrical equipment, etc. The outstanding example of capital movements taking place through the import of foodstuffs, other articles of consumption and raw materials is Germany in the post-war and post-inflation period—that is, from 1924 to 1928.

It is hoped that these remarks give an idea of the almost endless multiformity of the international complications, and at the same time of the possibility of analysing each of these innumerable cases with the help of a few principles, and of understanding them as special cases which can be brought under the general doctrine.

§ 9. CONCLUDING REMARKS

The most valuable and original contributions of the monetary over-investment theory are (1) the analysis of the maladjustment in the structure of production brought about by the credit expansion during the prosperity phase of the cycle and (2) the explanation of the breakdown as consequent on that maladjustment. But our analysis has also shown that the theory is not in all respects complete. The claim to exclusive validity is open to doubt. It is a little difficult, for example, to understand why the transition to a more roundabout process of production should be associated with prosperity and the return to a less roundabout process a synonym for depression. Why should not the original inflationary expansion of investment cause as much dislocation in the production of consumers' goods as the subsequent rise in consumers' demand is said to cause in the production of investment goods ?[1]

---

[1] *Cf.* Durbin : *The Problem of Credit Policy*, 1935 ; Bresciani-Turroni, " The Theory of Saving " in *Economica*, May 1936, pages 175 and 176.

As to the explanation of the depression, especially the later phases of the depression, there is not a high measure of agreement between the various members of the school. So far as the existence of a vicious spiral of deflation is admitted, the analysis of the deflation is, on broad lines, not dissimilar from the analysis given by writers of other schools.

B. The Non-monetary Over-investment Theories

§ 10. GENERAL CHARACTERISTICS

Principal authors. The most prominent writers in this group are Professors A. SPIETHOFF[1] and G. CASSEL.[2] In the writings of these two authors (of SPIETHOFF especially), we find the culmination of a very important line of thought which can be traced back to MARX. Spiethoff's immediate forerunner was the well-known Russian author TUGAN-BARANOWSKI.[3] Both SPIETHOFF and CASSEL have had a great influence on business cycle theory, particularly in Germany,[4] but also in the Scandinavian and Anglo-Saxon countries. WICKSELL himself adopted SPIETHOFF's explanation of the cycle.

With regard to Professor CASSEL, it must be remarked that we are here dealing primarily with the theory as expounded in the earlier editions of his *Theory of Social Economy*. In his later books and especially in his popular writings, he has more or less

---

[1] See "Vorbemerkungen zu einer Theorie der Ueberproduktion" in *Jahrbuch für Gesetzgebung, Verwaltung und Volkswirtschaft*, 1902. "Krisen" in *Handwörterbuch der Staatswissenschaften*, 1925.

[2] See *Theory of Social Economy*, revised ed., London, 1932, Vol. II (translated from the German).

[3] See *Les Crises industrielles en Angleterre*, Paris, 1913 (translated from the Russian). For further references, see A. H. Hansen, *Business Cycle Theory*, 1927, Ch. IV.

[4] *Cf.*, *e.g.*, the highly interesting analysis of the cyclical movement on the basis of the Cassel-Spiethoff theory by Professor Georg Halm in his article "Das Zinsproblem am Geld- und Kapitalmarkt" in *Jahrbücher für Nationalökonomie und Statistik*, Vol. 125, 1926, pages 1-34 and 97-121.

accepted a purely monetary explanation, at least so far as the 1929-1936 depression is concerned.[1]

It is significant that Professor SPIETHOFF, with his quite different theoretical background, has reached, so far as concerns the interpretation of the later phases of the upswing and of the situation which leads to the collapse, substantially the same result as the writers of the monetary over-investment school and Professor CASSEL.

Stress on production of capital goods. The difference between the monetary and non-monetary over-investment theories concerns, as the names suggest, the rôle of money and monetary factors and institutions in bringing about the boom and the over-investment which leads to the collapse and depression. The theory of the writers of this group does not run in monetary terms; they mention monetary forces, but relegate them to a relatively subordinate rôle. It can, however, be shown that they are compelled to assume an elastic currency or credit supply in order to prove what they wish to demonstrate. But monetary factors are for them passive conditions which can be taken for granted rather than impelling forces.

Both Professors SPIETHOFF and CASSEL emphatically assert that the business cycle is characterised by changes in the production of capital goods, especially of fixed capital equipment. The production of consumers' goods does not exhibit the same regularity of change during the business cycle. Professor SPIETHOFF makes the point that upswings have occurred during which consumption has actually fallen. This was the case, according to him, in Germany in the years 1845-1847/48, when the economic situation of the working classes positively deteriorated because of rising food prices due to a series of crop failures.[2] But, even if no account is taken of changes in agricultural production, which are only remotely connected with the ups and downs of industrial production, " the

---

[1] See, *e.g.*, *The Downfall of the Gold Standard*, Oxford, 1936. Like Mr. Hawtrey, he believes that " the economic development of post-war times has been so strikingly dominated by great monetary disturbances that trade cycles of the earlier kind are no longer applicable " (*The Theory of Social Economy*, Vol. II, page 538).

[2] See Spiethoff's article "Krisen" in the *Handwörterbuch der Staatswissenschaften*, Vol. VI, 4th ed., Jena, 1925, page 49.

production of consumption goods shows no marked dependence on trade cycles. This means that the alternation between periods of boom and slump is fundamentally a variation in the production of fixed capital, but has no direct connection with the rest of production. "[1]

§ 11. THE UPSWING

Cumulative expansion process. Professor SPIETHOFF describes the mechanism of the cumulative and self-sustaining process of expansion, which begins to work after the dead point of the depression has been overcome, in approximately the same way as the monetary over-investment school. (In respect to this particular problem, indeed, there is now much agreement even outside the schools which we have analysed so far.) The revival of investment activity generates income and purchasing power. Demand rises, first for capital goods and investment materials (iron, steel, cement, lumber, bricks) and later also for consumption goods. Prices rise, mainly prices of capital goods and investment materials. This stimulates further investment. Profits are made which swell the funds available for investment and provide an important psychological stimulus for further expansion. Thus, like a snowball, prosperity increases rapidly as it proceeds.

The monetary side of this process is not closely analysed. But Professor SPIETHOFF admits that " credit is an indispensable means to the upswing ".[2] Professor CASSEL is less explicit in this respect. But it can be inferred from various remarks which he lets fall that he realises the necessity for an elastic currency supply. Both writers seem to believe that monetary funds are accumulated during the depression, on which the producers can draw during the upswing to finance the expansion. It follows that no positive steps need be taken by the banking system, at any rate during the first phases of the upswing. It is, however, not denied that, after a certain point, support by the banks is required to carry on.

---

[1] G. Cassel : *The Theory of Social Economy*, revised ed., London, 1932, page 552.

[2] *Op. cit.*, page 74.

These monetary conditions and the monetary mechanism of credit expansion have been more thoroughly explored by the monetary school. In the writings of Professor ROBERTSON, Mr. KEYNES and Professor PIGOU (all of whom have much in common with SPIETHOFF and CASSEL) will be found the best synthesis of the monetary and non-monetary aspects of the process.

§ 12. THE DOWN-TURN (CRISIS)

Shortage of capital. The non-monetary over-investment school offers its most valuable contribution to the theory of the business cycle in connection with the explanation of the breakdown of the boom. The upswing cannot go on indefinitely; but how, precisely, is it brought to an end ?

Professor SPIETHOFF rejects all under-consumption theories which assume that the collapse is due to a shrinkage of the demand for consumers' goods, or to its failure to rise (owing to the lag in the rise of wages behind the rise of prices and profits), or to the fact that too much is being saved by individuals and corporations. He believes, on the contrary, that it is an actual shortage of capital that brings about the crisis; and he is at great pains to point out that capital shortage does not mean simply a deficiency of monetary funds, but is the symptom of a serious disproportion in the production of certain well-defined types of goods. Therefore, monetary measures can never prevent the crisis. It is not over-saving but under-saving which is responsible for the collapse ; it is not under-consumption but, in a sense, over-consumption which leads to a scarcity of capital and brings about the end of the boom.

In order to show this in detail, Professor SPIETHOFF distinguishes four categories of goods : (1) goods for current consumption (food, clothing, etc.); (2) durable and semi-durable consumption goods such as residential buildings, water supply, electric light installations, gas plants and other public utilities (furniture and motor-cars occupy an intermediate position between (1) and (2)); (3) durable capital goods (fixed capital) such as mines, ironworks, brick and cement factories, textile plants, machine factories, railroads, power plants, etc.; (4) materials required for

the construction of durable goods (" goods for indirect or repro-
ductive consumption "), such as iron, steel, cement, lumber, bricks.

It is between the production of these categories of goods, he
says, that a disproportion regularly develops during the boom.
The result is a situation in which there is shortage and plenty
at the same time. As these categories of goods are complementary,
a shortage of one category means *ipso facto* over-production of the
other. It is as if one glove of a pair were lost. The one that
remains constitutes a useless and unsaleable surplus stock; the
missing one represents an actual deficiency.

Over-production of durable goods. Over-production occurs regularly in the case of
durable capital goods, and also in the case of durable
consumption goods. This necessarily involves a
decrease in demand and over-production of constructional material such as iron, steel, cement, etc.

This discrepancy between demand for, and supply
of, durable instruments has its causes on the supply side as well as
on the side of the demand. Additions to the capital equipment
are paid for out of " capital " (" Erwerbskapital "). Therefore,
the production and marketing of durable capital goods (and to a
certain extent also of durable consumption goods) must depend
on the amount of " capital " which seeks investment. (To-day
we should rather say that the demand for such goods is constituted
by savings out of income, plus supplements to the flow of saving
arising out of various inflationary sources—additional bank credits
and hoards of all kinds.) According to Professor SPIETHOFF, the
formation of monetary capital (" Erwerbskapital ") tends usually
to diminish at the end of the boom for various reasons. Wages
rise—which has an adverse effect on the rate of saving; and the
increased production encourages the adoption of wasteful methods
and leads to losses. Thus the demand for capital equipment
falls off.

More important, however, than the decrease in demand is the
increase in production and supply. A large proportion of the new
capital equipment constructed during the boom is used to produce
materials which are required for the further production of such
new equipment. So the supply rises progressively in face of a
constant or falling demand.

This over-production has been greatly facilitated—or rather, perhaps, made possible—by the development of modern methods of production, which have rendered the production of fixed capital goods largely independent of organic growth. Professor SPIETHOFF refers especially to the substitution of iron, steel and cement for lumber, of mineral coal for charcoal, etc. Contributing factors are furthermore the long interval between the beginning of the construction of plant and factory and the point at which they begin to turn out their products, and the durability of these instruments. (These latter circumstances will be discussed more fully in connection with other theories of the cycle in which they are pivotal.)

Shortage of Thus there develops an over-production of
labour producers' goods and durable consumers' goods.
and means These are the remaining glove. But where is the
of subsistence. missing one? Is not the missing one a purely
monetary phenomenon—namely, investible funds
which could be supplied by the printing press?
No, answers Professor SPIETHOFF. The lack of monetary funds available for investment represents a shortage of physical goods of a certain kind. It becomes impossible to utilise the whole supply of raw material and equipment destined for the construction of more capital equipment and durable consumption goods, for the simple reason that they alone cannot do the job. They could do it only in collaboration with labour and incidentally with means of subsistence for the labourers. A lack of investible funds simply means that these complementary goods are not available. There we have the missing glove. It consists of labour and consumers' goods.

From this proposition we must draw the conclusion (although Professor SPIETHOFF does not do so himself) that, if the rate of saving did increase—*i.e.*, if some people did refrain from consuming their whole income—the complementary goods would be forthcoming and the boom could continue.

If we have correctly interpreted Professor SPIETHOFFS' theory,[1] his diagnosis of the disequilibrium at the end of the boom is substantially the same as that given by the monetary over-investment school. The allocation of factors of production to

---

[1] See the penetrating critical analysis by Professor G. Halm (*loc. cit.*, pages 30-34).

the various stages of production does not correspond to the flow of money. The lower stages in the structure of production are under-developed; the higher stages which produce capital goods are over-developed.

Consumers' It might sound paradoxical that a " lack " of
goods consumers' goods should be the cause of the
and capital- breakdown in the capital-goods industries. If
goods there is such a shortage, consumers' goods indus-
industries. tries must flourish. But should not that be a cause
for rejoicing rather than for despair to the capital-
goods industries ? Professor SPIETHOFF does not analyse this objection explicitly. But, obviously, the question must be answered in the same way as it was answered by the monetary over-investment school. If the necessary credit is available and the rate of interest remains low, the prosperity of the consumers' goods industries will automatically spread to the higher stages, because the latter will then be in a position to compete successfully for the factors of production with the former. If unused factors of production (unemployed labourers, surplus stocks and idle plant) are available and if there are no special causes (*e.g.*, lack of confidence due to political risks) which deter people from investment in spite of profitable opportunities, an all-round increase in production will follow with no rise, or only a slight rise, in prices. If this, however, is not the case, if additional credit is not available and all factors are reasonably well employed, as is the case at the end of the boom, the rate of interest will rise and the capital-goods industries will not be able to retain all the factors which they used to employ : they will be depressed although, or even *because*, the consumers' goods industries prosper. (It is not denied that the prosperity of the latter also will soon come to an end, because the difficulties in the capital-goods industries will lead to a destruction of purchasing power and a fall in the demand for consumers' goods.)

Such a situation is clearly possible, although it looks superficially paradoxical. The phenomenon (alleged to be frequent)[1]

---

[1] Recent statistical studies have made it very doubtful whether such a lag actually exists. Compare, *e.g.*, Professor J. Tinbergen in *Statistical Testing of Business-Cycle Theories II. Business cycles in the United States, 1919-1937.* In preparation.

of consumers' goods industries feeling the setback of the depression much later than the capital-goods industry is regarded as a verification of the theory. Another question, which will be raised in connection with the discussion of rival theories, is whether this is the only possible outcome of the boom, or whether there is not another cause of the breakdown just as conceivable as a shortage of capital in the sense of a relative over-development of producers' goods industries, which is again equivalent to undersaving or over-consumption.

The Cassel variant. Professor CASSEL's explanation of the collapse of the typical investment boom is much the same as SPIETHOFF's, although couched in different language and not so fully developed in terms of goods.

In the first phase of the upswing, he says, the increase in production runs parallel to, or is even caused and encouraged by, a corresponding shift in the flow of money. That is to say, there is a strong tendency towards an acceleration of the formation of capital—*i.e.*, an increase in the flow of savings. In the later phases, capital accumulation in this sense slows down, while the production of fixed capital equipment increases. The discrepancy between the flow of money and the trend of production eventually brings about the crisis. " The typical modern trade boom does not mean over-production, or an over-estimate of the demands of the consumers or the needs of the community for the services of fixed capital, but an over-estimate of the supply of capital, or of the amount of savings available for taking over the real capital produced. What is really over-estimated is the capacity of the capitalists to provide savings in sufficient quantity."[1]

§ 13. THE DOWNSWING (DEPRESSION)

Psychological elements. Professor SPIETHOFF lays great emphasis on the psychological reaction which is bound to come after the excesses of the boom. Pessimism and reluctance to invest and to embark on new enterprises prevail during the depression. The severity and

---

[1] *The Theory of Social Economy*, Vol. II, page 649.

length of the depression depend very much on whether the boom has collapsed with the great detonation of a crisis, financial panic and numerous bankruptcies, or whether it has come to an end gradually, without thunder and lightning—a point much stressed also by Professor PIGOU. Much depends also on the international situation of the country. If the boom was financed from abroad, the consequences of the cessation of capital investments, according to Professor SPIETHOFF, will probably be less severe, because in that case the capital-exporting country has to bear its share of the difficulties and the capital-importing country is to that extent relieved.

The process of contraction also has a cumulative nature. Pessimism and reluctance to invest cause a shrinkage in the volume of purchasing power. Money is hoarded or used to finance losses instead of being invested and spent on producers' goods. Since savings are not invested, everything that increases the rate of saving (*e.g.*, inequality in the distribution of income) has a depressing influence. (During the upswing the influence is quite the reverse.) Prices fall and this intensifies the prevailing pessimism. There are many other intensifying factors of an institutional nature—*e.g.*, reluctance to reduce prices, especially on the part of industries that are cartellised, and rigidity of wages.

The analysis of these factors, which intensify the depression, has, however, been carried much farther in recent years, especially by English writers belonging to various schools such as KEYNES, PIGOU, ROBBINS, ROBERTSON. At this point of SPIETHOFF's description the monetary aspects are somewhat neglected.

§ 14. THE UPTURN (REVIVAL)

Cost adjustments and new investment opportunities. According to Professors SPIETHOFF and CASSEL, the revival is never brought about by an increase in the demand for consumers' goods, but always through increased investment. New investments are stimulated by the lowering of construction cost of capital equipment which ensues during the depression as a result of reduction of wages, fall in the price of raw materials, reduction of interest charges, adoption of improved methods of production, etc. Professor CASSEL lays stress on the fall of the rate of interest as exercising an immediate and powerful influence on the value of fixed capital equipment. But on the whole, according to Professor SPIETHOFF—Professor CASSEL is less pessimistic in this respect—these adjustments, which are automatically made during the depression, are not of themselves sufficient to revive the spirit of enterprise and overcome the dead point of the depression. Stronger incentives must come from outside, such as new inventions or discoveries of new markets or good harvests—factors which open out new opportunities for investment and raise the prospective rate of profit. There is now agreement among a great number of students of the subject that the cycles of the nineteenth century were ushered in by discoveries and inventions. In the terminology of the monetary school, it may be said that the discrepancy between the money rate of interest and the profit rate was brought about by a rise in the profit rate rather than by a fall in the money rate.

It would appear that in this respect no hard-and-fast rule can be laid down. If the rate of interest is low and credit plentiful and easily available, the expansion will come sooner or later ; but, if a special stimulus appears in the shape of an invention, the opening-up of new territories or the like, the expansion will come earlier and will gather momentum more quickly.

Schumpeter and the rôle of the business pioneer. Many further details can be, and have been, added to the picture. Psychological and sociological factors can be adduced which may play a rôle in bringing about an acceleration or retardation in the response of entrepreneurs to existing opportunities for profitable investment. The psychological factors will be analysed separately. At this point, however, we may mention the explanation which Professor SCHUMPETER has offered for the fact that innovations appear *en masse*.[1] One must distinguish,

---

[1] See *The Theory of Economic Development*, Cambridge, Mass., 1934. (Translated from the German. The first German edition was published in 1911.) It must, however, be noted that Professor Schumpeter puts forward this theory, not as an explanation of the lower turning-point, but of the movement of the system away from equilibrium. He believes that it is possible to divide the upswing as well as the downswing in two sharply

he says, between additions to our technological knowledge (that is, inventions which create the possibility of innovations in the productive processes actually employed) on the one hand and the practical introduction of the new methods on the other hand. What matters is not the discovery in the laboratory of a new process but the actual application of a new technique—it may be, a technique the feasibility of which was discovered a long time ago. There is no reason why inventions should not be distributed more or less evenly in time; but there are good reasons for believing that, in practice, new methods come into use in a mass. Only a few business-men have the imaginative power and energy successfully to introduce innovations such as new productive processes for the production of goods already on the market or the introduction of new types of goods, opening-up of new markets, improved methods of marketing and the like. But, while only a few are able to take the lead, many can follow. Once someone has gone ahead and demonstrated the profitability of a " new combination of the factors of production " (as Professor SCHUMPETER puts it), others can easily imitate him. Thus, whenever a few successful innovations appear, immediately a host

---

distinguishable phases : a movement towards equilibrium called revival and recession respectively, and a movement away from equilibrium, prosperity (or boom) and depression. Revival and prosperity constitute the upswing, recession and depression the downswing. The recuperative forces of adjustment inherent in the economic system are sufficient, so Professor Schumpeter believes, to lift output and employment from the subnormal level to which it has been reduced by the vicious spiral of deflation during the depression phase ; no special incentives are needed to explain the lower turning-point. Professor Schumpeter's " genial entrepreneur " and the crowd of imitators who follow him come in later during the upswing and prevent the system from settling down for any length of time at an equilibrium position.

Serious objections can be raised against this view. But the idea that the system passes through an equilibrium, or at least approaches a normal position, somewhere between the upper and the lower turning-point seems to have been vaguely envisaged by many writers. It will be clearly elaborated in Professor Schumpeter's forthcoming volume on the business cycle. It may be added that the fact that Professor Hayek starts his analysis from an equilibrium position seems to indicate rather a methodological principle than the proposition that the system actually passes through an equilibrium position on its way from the lower to the upper turning-point.

of others follow them. (While Professor SCHUMPETER's account of the revival and the description of the cumulative process of expansion fits in perfectly well with Professor SPIETHOFF's theory, his story of the upper turning-point is quite different and will be considered later.)

§ 15. RHYTHM AND PERIODICITY

Business mechanism likened to steam-engine. We may well start the discussion of this section with a famous metaphor from Professor SPIETHOFF's forerunner—Michael TUGAN-BARANOWSKI.[1] TUGAN-BARANOWSKI likens the working of the business-cycle mechanism to that of a steam-engine. " The accumulation of free, loanable capital plays the role of the steam in the cylinder; when the pressure of the steam on the piston attains a certain force, the resistance of the piston is overcome, the piston is set in motion and moves to the end of the cylinder; an opening appears for the steam and the piston recedes to its old position. In the same manner the accumulating free loan capital, after having attained a certain pressure, forces its way into industry, which it sets in motion; it is spent and industry returns to its earlier position. "[2]

Now the question arises : What corresponds in the business system to the fuel of the steam-engine ? Why is it that the cyclical movement goes on and on and never comes to an end ? Why do these waves of economic activity not gradually die down like the movement of the steam-engine when no fresh fuel is added ? Professor SPIETHOFF's answer to these questions must be inferred from his theory in general, because he does not put the question explicitly.

Inevitability of the cycle. The fact that oscillations are large is to be explained by the cumulative nature of the expansion and contraction process, which again is largely due to psychological reactions. Expansion creates optimism which stimulates investment and intensifies expansion. Contraction creates pessimism, which increases contraction.

---

[1] *Studien für Geschichte der Handelskrisen in England,* Jena, 1901.
[2] *Loc. cit.,* page 251.

Expansion comes to an end because it is almost impossible to estimate correctly the supply of savings and capital. The construction of capital goods must be undertaken in anticipation of demand, which in turn is constituted by saving and cannot be foreseen correctly. The durability of instruments on the one hand and the length of the construction period on the other make it difficult for supply and demand to keep pace.

The state of depression is interrupted (*a*) because it creates automatically a situation favourable to the revival of investment, (*b*) because pessimism disappears with the lapse of time, and (*c*) because of the introduction of stimuli from outside. Professor SPIETHOFF would probably subscribe to Professor PIGOU's theory of the mutual generation of errors of optimism and pessimism (which will be discussed later on[1]).

Professor CASSEL says explicitly that the cyclical movement would gradually die down, if no stimuli were provided from time to time from the outside in the shape of inventions and discoveries.

On the whole, it may be said that the question has not been systematically discussed or satisfactorily answered by the writers of the school under review. But the tenor of the theory suggests an answer in terms of both endogenous and exogenous forces— *i.e.*, of responses of the economic system to shocks from without.

Re-investment cycles. There is, however, an idea vaguely indicated at various points in Professor SPIETHOFF's writings which can be used for the explanation of the regular recurrence of cycles of prosperity and depression. I mean the idea that the massing of the construction of fixed capital equipment at certain dates or during certain short periods of time gives rise to the recurrence of such outbursts of investment, or rather re-investment, in the future, owing to the fact that machinery and other durable equipment installed around a certain date will come up for replacement massed, although probably less densely, around a certain date in the future. This idea that, given an initial boom in capital construction, replacement tends to assume a cyclical pattern, that re-investment moves in cycles, can be traced back to Karl MARX. It has been fully elaborated with all necessary

---

[1] See Chapter 6, § 2, page 148 below.

qualifications by Dr. Johan EINARSEN, who has also written its history and has applied the principle to a concrete case with the help of modern statistical devices in his admirable study, *Reinvestment Cycles and their Manifestation in the Norwegian Shipping Industry*.[1]

§ 16.   INTERNATIONAL COMPLICATIONS

The question of international complications has not been exhaustively and systematically treated by the theorists of the present group; but it is in principle not very difficult to imagine how the cyclical movement in one country must be assumed, from the point of view of the non-monetary over-investment theory, to influence other countries and to be influenced by international trade conditions.   What has been said in this respect in connection with the *monetary* over-investment theory applies also to the *non-monetary* version of the over-investment school.   It has been mentioned already that the opening of investment opportunities in new territories is considered to have been one of the most potent incentives for the revival of investment during the 19th century.[2]

C.   Over-investment resulting from Changes in the Demand for Finished Goods : The Principle of Acceleration and Magnification of Derived Demand

§ 17.   INTRODUCTION

Influence of consumers' demand on investment.   The monetary over-investment theory starts from the discrepancy between the natural and the money rate of interest, and holds monetary factors responsible for the recurrence of over-investment and disequilibrium.   The non-monetary branch of the over-investment school emphasises non-monetary factors, technological changes, innovations and discoveries.   The difference between the two types of over-investment

---

[1] Published by the University Institute of Economics, Oslo, 1938. See also article by the same author, " Reinvestment Cycles " in the *Review of Economic Statistics*, Vol. 20, February 1938.

[2] This idea is fundamental to the Neo-Marxian theory of Imperialism of such writers as Rosa Luxemburg, *Akkumulation des Kapitals*, and

theories is not very great : there are intermediate positions, and the two types shade off into each other. They are at one in the belief that the impetus which sets the process of expansion in motion comes from the side of investment and not from that of consumption. Demand for consumers' goods is, however, affected indirectly by changes in investment; and variations in the demand for consumers' goods are an important link in the cumulative processes of expansion and contraction. But it has not been sufficiently investigated how changes in consumers' demand react back on investment.

We have now to discuss an explanation of the business cycle, given by a number of writers, which assigns a leading rôle to changes in the demand for consumers' goods. It is the proposition that, for technological reasons, slight changes in the demand for consumers' goods produce much more violent variations in the demand for producers' goods. This proposition alone does not furnish a complete theory of the business cycle. It must be combined with other relationships between economic variables, and there are various possible schemes into which it can be fitted. It does not necessarily lead to the over-investment theory; and, in fact, the explanations which are built on the acceleration principle are not as a rule classified as over-investment theories. But we shall see that it can easily be combined with the over-investment explanation. The acceleration principle and the over-investment theory as discussed in the preceding pages are in reality not alternative but complementary explanations. The proposition that changes in demand for consumers' goods are transmitted with increasing intensity to the higher stages of production serves, in conjunction with other factors which have already been mentioned, as an explanation of the cumulative force and self-sustaining nature of the upward movement. It adds an important touch to the picture of the typical business cycle as painted by the over-investment theoreticians. The matter is of the greatest practical importance for the reason that much light is shed on the fact, which in the last few years has been more and more recognised and

---

Fritz Sternberg, *Imperialismus* (1928). For a brief review, criticism and references to this literature compare H. Neisser, *Some International Aspects of the Business Cycle*, Philadelphia, 1936, pages 161-172.

emphasised, that it is the production of *durable* goods, of consumers' goods as well as of capital goods, which fluctuates most violently during the business cycle.

The following authors have developed the acceleration principle —Albert AFTALION,[1] BICKERDIKE,[2] Mentor BOUNIATIAN,[3] T. N. CARVER,[4] and MARCO FANNO.[5] In recent years, it has been expounded most fully by J. M. CLARK,[6] SIMON KUZNETS,[7] A. C. PIGOU[8] and R. F. HARROD.[9] W. C. MITCHELL,[10] D. H. ROBERTSON,[11] and A. SPIETHOFF[12] have incorporated it into their account of the cycle as a contributory factor.[13] Mr. HARROD has, without much reference to the previous literature, rechristened the principle as " the Relation ".[14]

The discussion will proceed in two stages. First, the economic-technological principle will be expounded with the necessary

---

[1] *Les crises périodiques de surproduction*, Paris, 1913.

[2] "A Non-monetary Cause of Fluctuations in Employment" in *Economic Journal*, September 1914.

[3] *Les crises économiques*, Paris, 1922 ; 2nd ed., 1930.

[4] "A Suggestion for a Theory of Industrial Depressions " in *Quarterly Journal of Economics*, May 1903.

[5] *Beiträge zur Geldtheorie*, ed. by Hayek.

[6] " Business Acceleration and the Law of Demand " in *Journal of Political Economy*, March 1917. *Economics of Overhead Costs*, Chicago, U.S.A., 1923. Controversy with Ragnar Frisch in *Journal of Political Economy*, October and December 1931, April 1932. *Strategic Factors in Business Cycles*, New York, 1934, pages 33 *et seq.*

[7] " Relations between Capital Goods and Finished Products in the Business Cycle " in *Economic Essays in Honour of Wesley Clair Mitchell*, New York, 1935.

[8] *Industrial Fluctuations*, 2nd ed., 1929, Ch. IX.

[9] *The Trade Cycle*, Oxford, 1936, Ch. II.

[10] *Business Cycles*, 1913.

[11] *A Study of Industrial Fluctuation*, London, 1915, Part I, Ch. 2. *Banking Policy and the Price Level*, 3rd improved ed., London, 1932, Ch. 2.

[12] " Krisen " in *Handwörterbuch der Staatswissenschaften*, 1925.

[13] Compare also the critical discussion of the principle by J. Tinbergen, " Statistical Evidence on the Acceleration Principle " in *Economica*, Vol. V (New Series), May 1938, pages 164-176. Professor Tinbergen does not find much statistical evidence, but this is not surprising in view of the many qualifications which must be made (see below in the text).

[14] This would not seem to be a fortunate terminology, because, apart from the relation between consumption and investment which is postulated by the acceleration principle, there are relations between the two magnitudes of another kind (see below).

qualifications and amplifications; and secondly the way in which it can be used, within the framework of the over-investment theory, for the explanation of the business cycle will be examined.

§ 18.   STATEMENT OF THE PRINCIPLE

Changes in demand for, and production of, finished goods and services tend to give rise to much greater changes in the demand for, and production of, those producers' goods which are used for their production. " Finished goods " need not be interpreted in the narrow sense as consumers' goods, but in a broader sense : goods at any stage are " finished " relatively to the preceding stage of production. The acceleration principle holds, not only for consumers' goods in respect to the preceding stage, but for all intermediate goods with regard to their respective preceding stages of production. Slight changes in the demand for consumers' goods may thus be converted into violent changes in demand for goods of a higher order; and, as this intensification tends to work through all stages of production, it is quite natural that fluctuations should be most violent in those stages of production which are farthest removed from the sphere of consumption. It may even happen that a slackening in the rate of growth of demand in one stage is converted into an actual decline in demand for the product of the preceding stage.

We can distinguish three cases of the working of *Demand for* the acceleration principle which, as we shall see, can *durable goods* be easily brought under a single formula.

and commodity   (a) *Durable producers' goods.*—The intensification *stocks.*   runs here from changes in demand for the finished goods (which may be durable or perishable) to changes in demand for durable producers' goods (machines, buildings, etc.) required for the production of the finished article.

(b) *Durable and semi-durable consumption goods* such as apartment-houses, automobiles, wireless apparatus, etc. Here the intensification runs from changes in demand for the service (apartments) to changes in demand for the instrument which provides the service (houses).

(c) *Commodity stocks.*—Even if there are no individually durable producers' goods (such as machines), there may be an intensification running from changes in demand for the product to changes in demand for the various goods in process, in cases where a certain stock of these various goods has to be held, the amount of which is relatively fixed in proportion to the magnitude of the output. Such necessary stocks can be regarded as durable *in toto*, although the parts which constitute the whole are perishable individually.

Monetary aspects. In order to illustrate the working of the principle, we assume a change in demand for a particular finished article—say for shoes, hats, automobiles—and investigate the influence of this change on derived demand for producers' goods in the preceding stage. Two very important questions which come at once to the mind will be discussed later, viz. : (1) Where does this first increase in demand originate—*i.e.*, is it due to a switch-over of purchasing power from other uses so that, as the demand for commodity A increases, there is a corresponding decrease in the demand for B, or does it constitute a net increase in aggregate demand out of inflationary sources ? Again, (2) How is the induced change in the demand for, and production of, producers' goods financed ? By an expansion of credit or by current savings ? Obviously, these problems are closely connected with the problem of the place of the acceleration principle in the theory of the cycle. They will be discussed later. For the moment we shall assume that there *is* an increase in the demand for particular commodities—wherever this increase comes from—and shall endeavour to explain why the derived demand changes more violently.

§ 19. ACCELERATION OF DERIVED DEMAND DUE TO THE EXISTENCE OF DURABLE PRODUCERS' GOODS

Preliminary statement of the principle. Take the following—static—situation. The value of the yearly output of (say) shoes is 100. The original and replacement cost of the fixed capital equipment—that is, of durable means of production which we shall call " machines "—required for this output is 500, 10% of which must be replaced each year, because the machinery wears out at that rate. In other words, the lifetime of such a machine is ten years. Under this assumption, new machines at the cost of 50 must be constructed each year for replacement.[1] Now suppose the demand for shoes rises, so that, if it is to be satisfied, production must be increased by 10%, to 110 a year. If there is no excess capacity and if methods of production are not changed, this increase necessitates an increase of 10% in the stock of fixed capital—that is, an additional production of machinery of 50, which brings the total production of machines from 50 to 100. So an increase of 10% in the demand for, and production of, finished goods necessitates an increase of 100% in the annual production of equipment. The absolute magnification of the change in demand is from 10 to 50 ; an increase in current production of 10 requires new investment of 50.[2]

But this increased volume of production of machines can be maintained only if the demand for consumers' goods goes on rising by the same annual amount of 10. If, in the second year, the increase in demand for shoes slows down to (say) 5, so that the demand for shoes in the second year is 115, the demand for machines will be 75 (50 for replacement and 25 for additional machines). Derived demand has therefore fallen absolutely in consequence of a mere decrease in the rate of increase of the demand for the finished product. Assuming replacement demand constant, derived demand for durable producers' goods changes with the rate

---

[1] A continuous replacement presupposes, of course, that the existing capital stock has been constructed in a continuous series of instalments. If that is not the case, replacement will be also discontinuous. " Replacement waves " may ensue, if the construction of the capital stock proceeds by fits and starts.

[2] This statement is somewhat simplified for purposes of exposition. It is here tacitly assumed that the demand for, and supply of, the finished product jumps suddenly at the beginning of a new year to the extent of 10 per annum. Simultaneously, new machines must be available to the extent of 50, which, added to the replacement output of 50 per annum, brings the total machine output for the year to 100. It would be more realistic perhaps to suppose that the rise in demand comes about gradually and evenly in the course of the year. In this case the machine output would, as before, be 100 (*i.e.* an increase of 50 over the year before the expansion began) ; but the augmentation of the output of the finished product would amount only to $10/2 = 5$. It is further assumed that machines retain their productive efficiency unimpaired throughout their lifetime.

of change—and not with the *direction* of the absolute change of the final demand; it does not, in other words, depend on whether final demand is rising or falling in an absolute sense.

The assumption that replacement demand is *Replacement* constant calls for a quantitative qualification to which *demand.* Professor FRISCH[1] has drawn attention. If capital equipment is being continuously increased by equal amounts per unit of time, the demand for replacement must rise after a while to a new level. In our numerical example, this point would be reached after ten years, when the 50 additional machines of the first year are worn out and must be replaced. If at this point the demand for the finished product ceases to rise, the disappearance of the demand for additional machines will be compensated by the increase in replacement demand. Hence it is not quite correct to say that a decrease in the rate of increase of demand for the finished product must always lead to an actual decrease in the derived demand. It is worthy of note, however, that in each situation (under the conditions assumed) there is one, and only one, state of demand for finished goods—sometimes a rising or falling, sometimes a constant, demand—which will preserve stability in the demand for machines. The exact relationship between the various magnitudes involved could be formulated mathematically.[2] We shall see later that a number of restricting and modifying qualifications must be made : it seems hardly worth while therefore at this point to attempt an absolute precision which cannot in any case be maintained in applying the theorem.

One point should, however, be clearly realised : *Influence of* and that is the circumstance that the degree of *degree of* magnification of derived demand depends *ceteris* *durability.* *paribus* upon the durability of the machines. If we assume the service life of the machine to be twice as long—viz., twenty years—the replacement demand for a stock

---

[1] "The Inter-relation between Capital Production and Consumer Taking" in *Journal of Political Economy*, Vol. 39, October 1931, page 646. See also the subsequent discussion between Frisch and J. M. Clark in Vols. 39 and 40 of *Journal of Political Economy*. Pigou has already made sufficient allowance for this quantitative qualification in his formulation of the acceleration principle in his *Industrial Fluctuations*, Ch. IX.

[2] See the above-mentioned article by Frisch.

of 500 is only 25 per year. But, if an increase in demand of 10 % for the finished goods supervenes and requires an increase in the stock of equipment of 10%, the total production of machines jumps from 25 to 75—*i.e.*, it is trebled, instead of doubled as in the previous case of a service life of ten years. To go to the other extreme : suppose the service life is zero ; that is to say, suppose that there are no durable means of production but only materials and labour. Then, in a static situation in regard to production, there being no permanent stocks, the whole supply of materials must at once be replaced. If the output of the finished article (shoes) is 100, and the material (leather) used for this is 50, the whole amount must be replaced. If the demand for shoes then rises by 10 % to 110, the production of leather must rise also by 10 % to 55. There is no magnification at all.

The qualifications of the principle which are implicit in our assumptions should be kept in mind. The existence of unused capacity is excluded, and a fixed relationship between output and capital equipment is assumed. These and other qualifications have their counterpart in the other two cases set forth in § 20 and § 21 below, and will be discussed in connection with the combined statement of all three cases.

§ 20. ACCELERATION OF DERIVED DEMAND IN THE CASE OF DURABLE CONSUMPTION GOODS

Analogy with previous case. The case of durable consumption goods is perhaps the most important of the three. As an example, take apartment-houses. The situation is exactly analogous to the case of the production of shoes analysed in § 19. We have only to substitute " annual service of the house " for " annual production of shoes ", and " apartment-houses " for " machines used for the production of shoes ". In other words, we can conceive of the durable consumption goods as producing a stream of services.

We start again from a static situation. The annual production of the service (housing accommodation as measured, say, by apartment rent) is 100. The stock of durable goods—that is, of houses—from which this stream of services originates is (say) 1,000, of which 100 (10%) must be replaced each year, corresponding to a durability of ten years. If there is an increase in the demand for apartments of 10%, the number of houses, or rather the amount of dwelling-space, must also be increased by 10%—which means a doubing of the construction of new houses, 100 for replacement and 100 as addition to the existing stock. Thus, an addition to the annual flow of services of 10 necessitates an investment of 100.

The further analysis is exactly the same as in the case of the shoes. The case of less durable goods such as motor-cars may also be analysed in the same way by distinguishing between the flow of services and the durable instrument whose value is a multiple of the value of its annual service. (There is, of course, this important institutional difference that, in the case of dwelling-houses, the ownership of the instrument is usually or frequently divorced from the use of the services, while the consumer of the services of an automobile is, as a rule, the owner of the instrument. The technological principle is not altered by this circumstance; but it has other consequences which will be discussed later.)

Depreciation and running cost. One important quantitative peculiarity of certain types of durable consumers' goods may be pointed out at this point. The cost of the final service (annual rent of an apartment) consists of two parts —viz., the contribution of the durable instrument and the running expenses (heating, water, maintenance, etc.). If demand for the service rises, the acceleration principle becomes effective in respect of the first part. The quantitative effect—that is, the absolute magnification of derived demand—depends, other things (especially the durability of the instrument) being equal, upon the relative importance of the two parts. In the case of the dwelling-space, the contribution of the durable instrument (the house) is probably relatively large, say four-fifths of the cost of the total output. In our example of the shoe factory, we assumed that the total output was 100, of which only one half consisted of the contribution of the durable instruments, the other half consisting of materials and labour. Under these assumptions, other things being equal, the absolute magnification of derived demand is much greater in the case of an increase in the demand for apartments than in the case of an equal increase in the demand for shoes.

If the demand for shoes rises from 100 to 110, the demand for machines rises from 50 to 100. If the demand for apartments rises from 100 to 110, the demand for houses rises from 80 to 160.

§ 21. ACCELERATION OF DERIVED DEMAND
AS A RESULT OF THE EXISTENCE OF PERMANENT STOCKS OF GOODS

Analogy with previous cases. Even if there are no durable means of production, there may be a certain magnification of derived demand, if distributors and producers hold stocks in a fixed (or relatively fixed) proportion to the rate of sales or production. The assumption that the stock bears a fixed proportion to the rate of sales or to output is the counterpart of the assumption that there is a fixed relationship between output and machines.

Let us start again with a static situation, say, with a monthly sale of 100,000 pairs of shoes. Suppose that dealers usually hold permanent stocks equal in magnitude to the sales of one month and that demand and sales rise to 110,000 and the increase is believed to be lasting. Dealers will then increase their orders with producers by more than their sales have gone up in order to bring their stocks up to the usual ratio to sales. They will order 120,000 pairs; but the larger orders will be maintained only if sales go on rising. If the increase in sales ceases at the end of one month, even though there is no decrease, stocks will no longer be augmented and orders for producers will fall to 110,000 (although not to the original level of 100,000).

The principle works, however, in the other direction as well. If the demand for shoes falls off, dealers will reduce stocks and their orders will therefore fall by more than the amount by which their sales have decreased. Derived demand fluctuates more violently.

Some qualifications. Although from the formal mathematical point of view the parallelism between the case of stocks and the case of fixed capital is complete, the case of the stocks presents some quantitative peculiarities, the consequence of which is to imply much more drastic qualifications and reservations in the application of the principle. (1) The assumption of a comparatively fixed relationship between sales and stocks is much more precarious, and subject to more serious and frequent exceptions, than the corresponding assumption as to the fixity of the ratio between output and capital equipment. Stocks can be easily diminished or increased : they can be consumed rapidly, and are therefore subject to speculative changes. (2) The durability is smaller than in the case of fixed equipment. Hence replacement demand responds much more rapidly to an increase in output and sales in the case of stocks than in the case of machines. If new machinery with a service life of ten years is installed, its installation does not affect replacement demand until after ten years. If sales go up and stocks are increased correspondingly, replacement demand rises in the succeeding period.

For these reasons, the stocks factor is less likely to exhibit clearly the acceleration of derived demand than the fixed capital factor.

§ 22. GENERALISED STATEMENT OF THE PRINCIPLE

In all three cases which have been distinguished, the relevant circumstance is that, in order to increase the rate of output, it is usually necessary to make heavy immediate investments in the shape of stocks or—what is in practice much more important—in fixed capital, the fruits of which investments mature only in the more or less distant future.

The same thing can be put in another way. The durability of instruments makes it necessary to provide all at once for future demand over a considerable period. The supply required to satisfy the demand for any given period to come must be produced immediately and stored up in the shape of stocks and durable instruments.

If we assume that there is a periodic up-and-down movement in the demand for a finished article as represented by a sine curve, the movement in the requirements for the capital equipment has to be represented by a steeper curve of the same type. This derived curve, which represents the effect, will usually show a lead *vis-à-vis* its cause. It will reach the high points and low points *before* the causal curve. This is a rather paradoxical situation, because one would expect the cause to precede the effect and not the effect the cause. But the dominant factor is, with certain qualifications which have been made above (§ 19), not the *direction* of the change (the mere fact that demand for the finished product is rising or falling absolutely), but the *rate* of change, or changes in the rate of change, in the demand for the finished product.

§ 23. QUALIFICATIONS

Limited application in negative sense.   We spoke of changes in " the requirements for capital equipment ". If we want to substitute for this " demand " for, or " production " of, capital goods, we must consider that demand and production cannot become negative.[1] As soon as the production of capital goods falls to zero—the demand for the finished product continuing to decline—excess capacity will develop; and, when demand for the finished product rises again, the production of capital goods will not be resumed until after the accumulated surplus has been absorbed. So long as there is unused capacity (or dealers are overstocked),[2] the acceleration principle of derived demand will not come into play.

Variable proportions of factors.   Excess capacity has been excluded by the assumption that there is a constant ratio between rate of output on the one hand and capital equipment and stocks on the other. In reality, this ratio is not constant, even apart from inventions and improvements in the technique of production which allow an increase in output per unit of capital equipment. Existing capital equipment

---

[1] This point has been well put by Professor J. Tinbergen. In the article mentioned on page 87, he says :

" In its more rigorous form, the acceleration principle can only be true if the following conditions are fulfilled.

" (*a*) Very strong decreases in consumers' goods production must not occur. If the principle were right, they would lead to a corresponding disinvestment and this can only take place to the extent of replacement. If annual replacement amounts to 10% of the stock of capital goods, then a larger decrease in this stock than 10% per annum is impossible. A decrease in consumers' goods production of 15% could not lead to a 15% decrease in physical capital as the acceleration principle would require. It is interesting that this limit is the sharper the greater the duration of life of the capital goods considered."

[2] The term "unused capacity" must be interpreted with great care. There is always some inferior capacity which can handle an increase of demand.

may be utilised more or less intensively. Overtime can be worked or more hands can be engaged. Nor is this all. If demand for the product rises and new machinery has to be installed, the durability of the new equipment may be different. Whether more or less durable machines are employed, whether more or less fixed capital is combined with a given amount of labour and circulating capital, depends among many other things on the rate of interest and the rate of wages and on the general outlook, that is the expectations entertained by producers about the future development of wages, interest and other cost items on the one hand and the future state of demand on the other.

This raises very fundamental questions, and it might be well to reflect once more on the essential nature of the principle.

In its more rigorous form, it postulates a certain quantitative relationship between the production of finished goods and that of their means of production. In a less ambitious form, taking all qualifications into consideration, it simply says that an increase in demand for, and production of, consumers' goods tends to stimulate investment and that a fall in the former tends to affect the latter adversely.

Various interrelations between consumption and investment. In this less ambitious sense, its validity can hardly be doubted. It should, however, be noted that this does not preclude the possibility of (*a*) there being causal connections between the production of consumers' goods and investment of a different sort than the one postulated by our principle and even operating in the opposite direction in certain cases,[1] and (*b*) the production of capital goods (investment) being influenced, not only by changes in the demand for consumers' goods, but by other factors as well. It may perhaps be said that any investment, directly or indirectly, is looking forward to, and is made in the expectation of, a future demand for consumers' goods. But, as Professor HANSEN has pointed out,[2] there are

---

[1] Compare *e.g.*, § 4 of this chapter, page 45 above.

[2] See his criticism of Harrod's rather unqualified utilisation of the acceleration principle in *The Quarterly Journal of Economics*, Vol. 51, May 1937, pages 509 *et seq.* (now reprinted in *Full Recovery or Stagnation*, New York, 1938).

types of investment which look forward for their utilisation to a very distant future—*e.g.*, the opening up of a new region by the construction of a railroad. In such cases, the connection between the investment and the present state and recent movement of the demand for consumers' goods is very slender. Long-run expectations determine investment decisions of this sort, and the influence of the current output of finished goods on these expectations can hardly be assumed to follow a uniformly defined quantitative pattern.[1]

Besides these adventurous kinds of investments, there are other investments, in working and fixed capital, which follow more or less closely the ups and downs of consumers' demand—routine investments one might call them. It is with these that the acceleration principle in its more rigorous form is concerned.

§ 24. THE CONTRIBUTION OF THE PRINCIPLE OF DERIVED DEMAND TO THE EXPLANATION OF THE GENERAL BUSINESS CYCLE

Reciprocal action of consumers' demand and capital production. It has sometimes been assumed that, in order to utilise the acceleration principle for the explanation of the general business cycle, one has to presuppose a cyclical alternation of expansion and contraction in consumers' demand.[2] The acceleration principle then serves to explain the larger fluctuations in the capital-goods industries. The situation is, however, much more involved, because consumers' demand and capital production (investment) interact on one another.

In order to throw light on this inter-relation, the two questions which have been raised above and reserved for later discussion must now be dealt with.

---

[1] This has also been well put by Professor D. H. Robertson. " ... Some of the principal forms of investment in the modern world—the instruments of power-production, of transport, of office activity—are, after all, very loosely geared to the visible demand for particular types of consumption goods and depend rather on fairly vague estimates of the future progress of whole areas and populations. (See his review of Harrod's *The Trade Cycle* in *The Canadian Journal of Economics and Political Science*, Vol. III, 1937, page 126.)

[2] Criticism by C. O. Hardy before the American Statistical Association, December 1931. Quoted by J. M. Clark in *Journal of Political Economy*, October 1932, page 693.

Nature of the
initial
impulse.
Where does the increase in the demand for the finished product come from? Two cases have to be distinguished, viz. : (*a*) the case of a net increase in aggregate demand due to a monetary change, an increase in the quantity of money, dishoarding or an increase in the velocity of circulation; and (*b*) the case of a mere shift in demand from one commodity or group of commodities to another.

Ad (*a*). If an (inflationary) increase in the aggregate demand for finished goods in terms of money takes place, the acceleration principle is sufficient explanation of the marked stimulation experienced in the higher stages of production. Demand for capital goods rises, and this involves a rise in demand for bank credit. The profit rate rises, and our principle reveals an important factor which makes for progressive expansion and adds to the cumulative force of the upswing.

Ad (*b*). The situation is rather different where there has been no rise in aggregate income, but only a shift in demand from commodity A to commodity B. Demand for capital goods derived from A falls, demand derived from B rises. Do not these two changes cancel each other out, so that, on balance, activities in industries producing producers' goods will not be stimulated? The answer is that they may cancel out, but that there is not only no necessity for them to do so but even a probability against it. It is likely that in many cases a net increase in demand for producers' goods will result.

Factors
affecting
the outcome.
The outcome will mainly depend on three circumstances : first, on the relative importance and durability of fixed capital in the production of A and B; secondly, on the existence or non-existence of unused capacity and on the relative magnitude of the same in the two industries; thirdly, on whether and to what extent the machinery used for the production of A can also be used for the production of B.

If, in the production of B (say automobiles), the demand for which has risen, fixed capital plays a more important rôle, and a more durable equipment is needed than in the production of A (say textiles) where demand has fallen, then this shift in demand for finished goods will induce a considerable increase in the demand for capital goods.

But, even if the proportion of fixed to working capital and the durability of the former is the same for A and B, it is quite possible that the shift in demand from A to B will create a net increase in demand for fixed capital (provided the machinery producing A is such that it cannot be used for the production of B). The principle of acceleration of derived demand works in both directions, as we know. But, in the downward direction, its operation is limited by the fact that production cannot fall below zero. If, therefore, in the case of a shift of demand from A to B, the demand for machinery producing A falls to zero, this loss may very well be more than compensated by an increase in the demand for new equipment producing B.[1]

The net result of a shift in the demand for finished products on the demand for capital goods will be lessened, if machinery producing A can be used without alteration, or with only slight alterations, for the production of B. It is very likely that, in some higher stage, the two streams of production, traced backward from A and B, coincide. The steel industry, for example, is common to a number of industries besides A and B—*e.g.*, railway construction and the building industry. Obviously, it makes a great difference whether the production processes of A and B coincide in (say) the second, or only in the fifth, stage of production. If the two commodities A and B are far removed from one another in the sphere of production, only a small part of the fixed capital devoted to the production of A can be used for the production of B; and so in the event of a shift of demand from A to B, any increase in the demand for new equipment and for the materials needed to construct it will be comparatively strong.

---

[1] It follows that the expansionary effect of a shift in the demand is more likely to be great if it occurs during a period when the demand for equipment in both industries is at a relatively low level. If it takes place while a general expansion is in progress, the acceleration principle has free play to operate in both directions and the effects on industry A and B are therefore more likely to compensate each other.

Method of financing the new investment. Two alternatives are open for discussion. The new investments can be financed (*a*) by means of current savings or (*b*) by way of inflation through the creation of new bank credit and/or more intensive utilisation of existing means of payment. In other words, the increased investment may or may not be consistent with the maintenance of the stability of the monetary circulation—*i.e.*, of *MV*.

Ad (*a*). Suppose that, with the working of the acceleration principle, a shift or an increase in the aggregate demand for finished goods affords new investment opportunities, but that the supply of capital in terms of money is not increased by way of inflation. There is no elastic credit supply, and no hoards of any sort which producers can draw on. The consequence will be a rise in the rate of interest. This will produce a retrenchment of investment—of reinvestment or new investment, as the case may be—in different branches of industry, offsetting the increased investment in industries in which the demand for the finished product has risen. The *aggregate* demand for producers' goods cannot therefore rise.

Ad (*b*). It is of course recognised by the leading exponent of the acceleration principle, Professor J. M. CLARK, that the principle cannot serve as an explanation of the business cycle, nor even as an incomplete and partial explanation, except in conjunction with an elastic credit supply. Unless it entails a credit expansion, an increase in investment in particular branches of industry cannot produce a general up-turn in business activity. If there has been an increase in the circulating medium, income and demand for finished goods will rise; this will further stimulate investment, and so a cumulative process of expansion will be started.

The acceleration principle is thus assimilated by the over-investment theory, and adds an important feature to the picture of the cycle as drawn in the preceding sections.

Further considerations. Closer analysis reveals further points of connection between the acceleration principle and the over-investment theory.

The fact that durable instruments are required in order to satisfy current demand for finished goods or services may be characterised, in the terminology of the monetary over-investment theory, as an incentive to the initiation of roundabout methods of production. The more durable the instrument, the longer the roundabout methods of production.

It has been mentioned already that the durability of the instruments, and the amount invested in them in response to an increase in demand for a finished product, cannot be taken as economic constants, determined solely and rigidly by the state of technological knowledge. As a rule, there are various methods of production to choose between; and more or less durable equipment can be installed, the more durable varieties being more costly. (Less durable instruments which cost as much as their more durable rivals are, of course, ruled out as uneconomical from the beginning.) The choice between these depends mainly on the rate of interest. The lower the rate the more durable the instrument and the longer the roundabout process of production. There is, furthermore, the risk factor. In an atmosphere of optimism and confidence, people will be more inclined to undertake heavy investments than in a state of uncertainty and fear. Also the rapidity of replacement of existing equipment, and therefore the length of its service life, will be influenced by these factors.

The production of durable consumers' goods may give rise to credit expansion no less than the production of durable producers' goods. If demand for apartments rises, the construction of houses may be undertaken with the help of inflationary bank credit. In the case of semi-durable goods, such as automobiles, where it is usually the instrument (and not only the service) that is bought by the last consumer out of his income, an instalment purchase scheme may enable consumers to extend their current purchases beyond their current income. Thus a slight increase in the income which allows its recipient to increase current consumption may bring about a much larger increase in demand in general.

Naturally, not only an *actual*, but also an *anticipated*, increase in demand for a finished product may bring about an increase in investment many times as large as the expected annual increase in demand for the finished product.

All these considerations bring out the importance of the rôle played by the acceleration principle in the mechanism of expansion as described by over-investment theorists.

After the upward movement has been started, the acceleration principle explains the rapid absorption of unused factors of production in the upper stages of production. Naturally, the principle cannot work unobstructed after all the factors, or particular types of the factors, of production have become fully employed. But these questions have been discussed above in connection with the monetary over-investment school.

Causes of the breakdown. The nature of the cumulative process of expansion having been thus explained, there remain various possibilities of explaining the collapse of the boom. One explanation is that sooner or later a shortage of capital in the previously defined sense arises.

It has been pointed out above that a decrease in the rate of increase of demand for a finished product (say railway lines) need not entail an actual decrease in demand for, and production of, producers' goods (say steel). It is possible that the decrease in new demand will be compensated by an increase in replacement demand. If the construction of new railway lines decreases only after a long period, the steel industry need not experience any decline at all. Whether this condition can be fulfilled depends to a large extent (but not wholly) on the availability of capital. If a shortage of capital develops, railway construction must be curtailed and the steel industry will suffer a decline in demand. We observe here again a close interrelation between the over-investment theory and the acceleration principle.

But shortage of capital is not the only conceivable explanation of the breakdown. Professor AFTALION, who is amongst the exponents of the acceleration principle, has put forward the theory that the turning-point comes, not because the new investments cannot be completed owing to a shortage of capital, but, on the contrary, after the new roundabout processes of production (construction of durable instruments) have been completed and begin to pour out consumers' goods. Prices fall; consumers' goods industries become depressed; and this depression is transmitted with increasing violence to the higher stages of production.

This line of thought will be discussed again in connection with under-consumption theories.

A somewhat different standpoint in this matter is taken up by Professor RÖPKE, who has recently laid great stress on the acceleration principle as affording an explanation of why a serious breakdown is unavoidable after a period of rapid expansion.[1] His analysis of the rôle of the acceleration principle in the mechanism of expansion is the same as that which is given above. He does not, however, explain the ensuing breakdown by the emergence of capital shortage or of an insufficiency of consumers' demand : nor does he believe that the breakdown can be avoided by more saving (as the capital shortage theorists do) or by more spending (as the under-consumption theorists do). He believes that, owing to the operation of the acceleration principle, a situation in the structure of production is bound to develop which can under no circumstances be maintained—either by less saving on the part of the public or by more—so that a serious breakdown is inescapable. According to him, this type of maladjustment is unavoidable after a period of rapid capital accumulation, even in a planned socialist economy of the Russian type.

But how, it may be asked, does he describe this maladjustment from which there is no escape except through a more or less severe crisis ? " It is the steep rise of the absolute amount of investments which matters, not the fact that our economic system must rely on credit expansion to make this rise possible."[2] And again : " The scale of investment grows, and so long as the rate at which it grows remains constant, or even increases, the boom has the power to last. Eventually, however, the moment must come when investment is not suddenly broken off certainly, but ceases to grow at the previous rate. We cannot always be building and ' rationalising ' further, always constructing new electricity works, etc.—especially as the power of the credit system to go on continually financing this investment delirium is finally exhausted. At this point, the boom must come

---

[1] *Crises and Cycles* (1936), pages 102 *et seq.* See also his article "Socialism, Planning and the Business Cycle" in *Journal of Political Economy*, Vol. 44, June 1936. A similar analysis is to be found in R. G. Harrod, *The Trade Cycle*, Oxford (1936), page 165 and *passim*.

[2] *Crises and Cycles*, page 110.

to an end, since the shrinkage of the capital goods industries is unavoidable." [1]

These quotations do not make the situation envisaged by our author perfectly clear; [2] but it is the nearest we can get to his meaning. In the second part of this book (see § 5 of Chapter 11) it is proposed to work out a situation which perhaps covers what Professor RÖPKE really has in mind.

---

[1] *Crises and Cycles,* page 102.

[2] It is not clear whether he has visualised the theoretical possibility of replacement demand's stepping into the shoes of new investment in such wise as to bring about a smooth transition to a stationary equilibrium.

CHAPTER 4

CHANGES IN COST, HORIZONTAL MALADJUSTMENTS
AND OVER-INDEBTEDNESS AS CAUSES OF CRISES
AND DEPRESSIONS

---

§ 1. INTRODUCTION

In this chapter we shall discuss certain factors which have
sometimes been put forward as *the* causes of the periodic recurrence
of crises and depressions. The argument, however, goes too
far. It is not in this case a question of elaborate theories embody-
ing a full explanation of the business cycle comparable to the
monetary explanation or the over-investment theory, but of
certain particular factors which contribute something to the
explanation of certain phases of the cycle. To recognise that
these factors may sometimes, or frequently, play a rôle in shaping
the course of the cycle is by no means incompatible with acceptance
of the monetary or over-investment theory of the cycle, though
of course all members of these two schools would not attribute
much importance to the factors in question.

§ 2. CHANGES IN COST OF PRODUCTION AND EFFICIENCY
OF LABOUR AND PLANT

In a competitive business economy, the statement that a restriction in industrial activity is due to the fact that production cost has
risen above selling price does not add much to the mere statement
that industrial activity has been reduced—at any rate, if " price "
is interpreted (as it obviously should be) as the expected future
price and " cost " as marginal cost at the expected volume of activity. This statement is compatible with any explanation of the crisis

and depression. Whether a series of crop failures, over-investment, monetary deflation, under-consumption or anything else is ultimately responsible for the breakdown of the boom and for the depression, the proximate cause of the reduction in industrial output is the fact that expected prices do not cover production cost. All these factors must finally find their expression somewhere in a disappearance of the profit margin. (There are other formulæ which are as vague and unhelpful as the cost-of-production formula—*e.g.*, the assertion that the breakdown is due to the fact that demand has fallen short of supply, to a disequilibrium between production and consumption, or to over-production in certain lines of industry and so on.)[1]

Mitchell on the cyclical movements of production cost. The rise of production cost during the prosperity phase and the reduction of production cost during the depression play a prominent rôle in the explanation of the cycle by Professor W. C. MITCHELL. The following is his description of the process : " The decline in overhead cost per unit of output (which was brought about by the first increase in production after the trough of the depression) ceases when enterprises have once secured all the business they can handle with their standard equipment, and a slow increase of these costs begins when the expiration of the old contracts makes necessary renewals at the high rates of interest, rent and salaries which prevail in prosperity. Meanwhile, the operating costs rise at a relatively rapid rate. Equipment which is antiquated and plants which are ill located or otherwise work at some disadvantage are again brought into operation. The price of labour rises, not only because the standard rates of wages go up, but also because of the prevalence of higher pay for overtime. Still more serious is the fact that the efficiency of labour declines, because overtime brings weariness, because of the employment of ' undesirables ', and because crews cannot be driven at top speed when jobs are more numerous than men to fill them. The prices of raw materials continue to rise faster, on the average, than the selling prices of products. Finally, the numerous small wastes

---

[1] Compare L. Robbins, *The Great Depression* (1934), Chapter II.

incident to the conduct of business enterprises creep up when managers are hurried by a press of orders demanding prompt delivery."[1]

A corresponding process of cost reduction is going on during the depression and prepares the ground for a revival.

Elements contained in other theories.
In the passage quoted, the operation of a number of factors is very luminously described. But, analytically, the various forces making for higher unit cost, partly in real terms, partly only in terms of money, are very different in nature.

That cost of production in terms of labour rises because inefficient workers and undesirables must be employed and because antiquated equipment must be brought into operation when production is expanded is quite natural. This is simply a way of expressing the law of decreasing returns. The supply price rises, and this " obviously limits the extent to which production expands in response to a given rise in demand; and, since the whole process takes time, it is natural that we should find expansion carried forward continuously up to a point, and then stopped ".[2] This does not, however, explain why expansion is followed by a breakdown and depression.

That money wages rise during the upswing (and fall during the downswing) has been shown in connection with the theories reviewed earlier in this book. This rise (and fall) in wages is a consequence of credit expansion (and contraction). It does not explain anything, unless it is possible to show why efficiency wages must rise, or are likely to rise (or fall) more (or less) rapidly than prices—that is to say, if a time-lag can be established between the movement of wages and prices.

The rise in interest rates is, as the monetary over-investment theory has shown, a symptom of a vertical maladjustment in the structure of production. It works out in an increase in money costs, but affects the higher stages of production more severely. As a link in the analysis of the over-investment theory or a purely

---

[1] See " Business Cycles " in *Business Cycles and Unemployment*, New York, 1923, pages 10 and 11. A similar description is to be found in other writings by Mitchell on the subject.

[2] Pigou, *Industrial Fluctuations*, 2nd ed., London, 1929, page 228.

monetary theory *à la* HAWTREY which explains the breakdown by an act of hoarding or credit-restriction, the rise in interest rates adds something to the explanation of the business cycle; but it is not very helpful if regarded only as contributing to the increase of the money cost of production.

A new point, not so far mentioned in our analysis, *Movements* is the argument that efficiency tends to fall during *in efficiency.* the upswing, because waste crops up everywhere (and efficiency tends to increase during the downswing because of the elimination of waste). Since money wages generally rise during the upswing (and fall during the downswing), this is equivalent to saying that efficiency wages rise faster than money wages during the upswing (and fall faster during the downswing). This is probably a factor which affects all branches and all stages of production alike; or, if it does not, the differences .are due to accidental circumstances, and there is no tendency for higher and lower stages—*i.e.*, the production of durable capital goods and of perishable consumers' goods—to be affected in a different.degree.

This tendency of efficiency wages to rise during the upswing— the reader will easily make the necessary adjustments for the application of the argument to the downswing—is surely a factor which must unfavourably affect the whole situation. Other things being equal, the breakdown would at least be postponed if this lowering of efficiency could be avoided. But the avoidance of waste and the maintenance of the level of efficiency attained during the depression would not in themselves mean the avoidance of vertical and horizontal maladjustments in the structure of production. If, on the other hand, there is no horizontal or vertical misdirection of investments, the influence of an all-round lowering of efficiency may be compensated by an increase in prices or a reduction of money wages.

It cannot, however, be denied that, theoretically, a heavy fall in efficiency, unaccompanied by a corresponding fall in money wages and not compensated by a rise in prices, may produce a general depression.

The same effect may perhaps be brought about by a rise in money wages, induced from the supply side, unaccompanied by a rise in efficiency or a general increase of prices. There are reasons to believe that something of this sort happens during the later phase of the upswing of an ordinary business cycle. The decrease in efficiency alone, on the other hand, is probably not of the same order of magnitude as the rise in general prices.

But this involves a quantitative estimate and calls for statistical investigation; and it is not easy to find a statistical measure for the changes in the efficiency of labour. The well-established fact that, in a number of industries, output per head of the employed labourers rises sharply during the depression and falls during the upswing of the cycle is not a sufficient proof, because it may be entirely due to the fact that antiquated plants, etc., are put into operation during the upswing and are closed down during the downswing, and that less efficient workers are engaged during the upswing and discharged during the downswing. In technical parlance, the change of efficiency which we have in mind must be represented by a shift of the productivity curve, while the statistically observed changes in the output per head of the labour employed may be due —and to a certain but unknown degree undoubtedly are due— to a movement along the curve.

§ 3. HORIZONTAL MALADJUSTMENTS

Capable of explaining a general depression. The distinction between " horizontal " and " vertical " maladjustments in the structure of production was explained above. We have seen that, according to the over-investment theory, a vertical maladjustment is normally the cause of the collapse of the boom; and the exponents of the monetary form of the over-investment theory especially seek to show that such a vertical maladjustment (of which the outstanding symptom is capital shortage and a sharp rise in the interest rate) does not arise by pure chance, but develops as the natural and necessary consequence of the inflationary forces which are at work during the upswing, falsifying certain essential price relationships by distorting the rate of interest.

Even if one accepts this theory as fundamentally correct, it does not follow that horizontal maladjustments are not equally likely to arise, or in certain cases to be responsible for the breakdown.

It is true, a horizontal maladjustment alone (that is to say, an over-development of a particular branch of industry) can explain only a partial—as opposed to a general—depression for the reason that, if industry A is over-developed, there must be an industry B which is under-developed and, if A is depressed, B must prosper. But the same is true, as we have seen, of a vertical maldistribution of the factors of production.

In order to explain a *general* depression, it is necessary to recognise that a deflationary cumulative process can be set in motion by partial dislocation of the productive process. If this is accepted, there is no difficulty in assuming that such a vicious spiral of contraction may be started by a horizontal, as well as by a vertical, maladjustment in the structure of production.

"*Error theories.*"

Such horizontal maladjustments can be brought about by a great number of circumstances which may be classified as (1) shifts in demand and (2) shifts in supply.

It is here that the "error theories" of the business cycle, or rather of the crisis, have their proper place. These theories stress the great complexity of our economic system, the lack of knowledge, the difficulties in foreseeing correctly the future demand for various products. One producer does not know what the other is doing. A given demand cannot be satisfied by producer A : producers B, C, D, etc., are accordingly called upon to satisfy it, and this creates an exaggerated impression of its volume and urgency. This leads to competitive duplication of plant and equipment, involving errors in the estimation of future wants. The circumstances conducive to bringing about such mistakes have been most fully described and analysed by Professors F. W. TAUSSIG,[1] A. C. PIGOU,[2] Sir WILLIAM BEVERIDGE[3] and T. W. MITCHELL.[4]

---

[1] *Principles of Economics*, 3rd ed., 1925, Vol. 1, pages 388 *et seq.*

[2] *Industrial Fluctuations*, Chapter VI ("The Structure of Modern Industry and Opportunities for Errors of Forecast ").

[3] *Unemployment*, new ed., London, 1930.

[4] "Competitive Illusion as a Cause of Business Cycles" in *Quarterly Journal of Economics*, Vol. 38, August 1924, pages 631 *et seq.*

Clearly, mistakes which lead to a misdirection of productive resources can be made at any time. But there are good reasons for the view that they are specially likely to arise during the upswing. The prosperity phase of the cycle is characterised by heavy investments for the reason that, in many lines of industry, provisions are made for satisfying future needs of the ultimate consumer as well as of producers in the intermediate stages of production. Evidently, the longer ahead demand has to be estimated the greater the risk of serious errors. If the estimate has to be made in a period of rapid changes in the economic system in general, and if new methods of production and the production of new types of goods are involved, the risk becomes still greater. Indivisibility and durability of instruments and the complicated relation between changes in the demand for finished goods and the demand for durable producers' goods (as postulated by the acceleration principle) combine to make a smooth adjustment of cost and supply to changes in demand extremely difficult.

"Horizontal" The border-line between horizontal and vertical maladjustments is sometimes very difficult to draw. *and* But since the two are not mutually exclusive, since *"vertical"* they can, and probably frequently do, coexist and *maladjust-* reinforce one another, the fact that classification is *ments.* sometimes difficult in concrete cases does not weigh too heavily in the balance.

To illustrate the close relationship between horizontal and vertical maladjustment, take again the case where a demand for a capital good (say constructional steel) drops violently as a result of a decrease or cessation of growth of demand for the product (say houses or motor-cars). It has been argued (as already stated)[1] that this is in reality the consequence of a shortage of capital—in other words, of a *vertical* maladjustment in the structure of production—and that, if the necessary capital were forthcoming, the building activity and motor-car production could continue until the replacement demand for houses and cars was such that the steel mills could use their whole capacity to satisfy it.

This may be so : but it is just as possible, and a good deal more probable, that the decrease in demand for new houses and motor-

---

[1] By Professor Hayek.

cars is due to the demand situation—*i.e.*, that the demand for houses and cars has been well satisfied for the time being relatively to other needs, and that savings are therefore invested in other directions, where no steel, or not so much steel, is needed. In this case, we have a *horizontal* maladjustment in the structure of production. So far as the deterioration of the steel industry and the repercussion which this might have on tributary industries and on the volume of the circulating medium are concerned, the consequences of a horizontal and a vertical maladjustment are exactly the same.

§ 4.   OVER-INDEBTEDNESS

Introductory. Professor IRVING FISHER[1] thinks that there are two main causes of the recurrence of economic depressions, namely " over-indebtedness " and " deflation ". These two factors, he thinks, tend to produce and to reinforce one another. Deflation swells the burden of debts, and over-indebtedness leads to debt liquidation, which engenders a shrinkage of the money stream and a fall in prices.

Professor FISHER'S debt-deflation theory is embedded in a general view about the trade cycle which sounds *prima facie* somewhat strange. He likes to call " *the* " business cycle a myth. But a closer examination shows that he deprecates only the use of the term " cycle " in the sense of a strictly periodic and regular movement. He stresses the differences in the appearance, amplitude and length of the various " cycles "—that is, in the alternations of good and bad years—which we find in the economic history of the last hundred years. He admits and even emphasises the fact that the economic system is liable to deteriorate in a cumulative process—that there is a vicious spiral of contraction and another vicious spiral of expansion. But how far expansion or contraction goes depends (he maintains) on innumerable circumstances, which differ from case to case.

---

[1] *Cf.* his article "The Debt-deflation Theory of Great Depressions" in *Econometrica*, Vol. 1, No. 4, October 1933, pages 337 *et seq.*, and his book *Booms and Depressions*, London, 1933.

This difficulty cleared away, it is comparatively easy to determine the place of the debt-deflation theory in our system of explanations of the cycle, and to distinguish those elements which add something new from those which have been already discussed in connection with other theories.

The description of the vicious spiral downward, which comes into play after the depression has once been started, is substantially the same as we found it in the writings of the monetary and over-investment schools. A fall in demand leads to a fall in prices, to the disappearance of the profit margin, to a reduction in production, to a decrease in the velocity of money, and so to a contraction of credit, a further drop in demand, pessimism, hoarding, etc.

What, then, is the rôle of debts and over-indebtedness? They influence the course of the cycle in two respects. In the first place, the existence of large debts expressed in terms of money tends to intensify the deflation, and in the second place a state of over-indebtedness may be the cause which precipitates the crisis. Professor FISHER does not distinguish the two cases in these words, but the distinction is clearly implied by his analysis.

Debts intensify deflation. 1. The existence of large debts in terms of money is certainly a most potent factor (although not the only factor) tending to aggravate the depression. The burden of debts becomes heavier with the fall in prices; and this leads to distress selling, which depresses prices further. Thus, directly and indirectly, a liquidation of bank credits is induced, which means a shrinkage in the volume of the circulating medium and of the demand for goods in general.

It would seem that the intensifying influence of money debts on the contraction process is an important corollary of the theory of the deflation as elaborated by the writers previously reviewed. Deflation would cause depression and the process of contraction would be cumulative, even if (as it is conceivable) the upswing were financed by shares and not by bonds, and by the producers' own capital instead of by borrowed money; but the depression would be milder if the amount of debts was smaller. (To this problem we shall return presently.)

Over-indebted- 2. A much more precarious proposition is that
ness may which regards the state of " over-indebtedness "
cause the as the normal cause of the collapse of the boom
downturn. What is meant by over-indebtedness ? " Over
indebtedness means simply that debts are out-of-line,
are too big relatively to other economic factors."
How is over-indebtedness brought about ? " It may be started
by many causes, of which the most common appears to be *new
opportunities to invest at a big prospective profit*, . . . such as through
new inventions, new industries, development of new resources,
opening of new lands or new markets. Easy money is the great
cause of over-borrowing."[2]

It seems clear that in these cases over-indebtedness is closely
connected with over-investment. To say that the cause of the
breakdown is over-investment is the same thing as saying that
investments have been made which later turn out to be unprofitable : that is, in other words, sales proceeds do not cover cost, and
one important cost item is interest on fixed and working capital. The
over-investment theory tries to show why this is the necessary consequence of any inflationary boom, and how entrepreneurs are lured
into too heavy investments. Professor Irving FISHER, on the other
hand, stresses the fact that these over-investments have been made
with borrowed money. But clearly over-investment, rather than
over-indebtedness, is the primary cause of the breakdown. If the
investments are excessive (in the sense that the structure of production is not in equilibrium), then these enterprises will suffer
losses, whether they are financed with shares or with bonds, with
borrowed capital or with the entrepreneur's own capital. Further
investment will be stopped and deflation is likely to ensue. If, on
the other hand, the structure of production is in equilibrium, there
is no reason why the indebtedness of the new enterprises should
cause trouble. It may, however, readily be admitted that the
repercussions of the breakdown of the investment boom are likely
to be much more severe where the investments have been financed
with borrowed money.

---

[1] *Booms and Depressions*, page 11.
[2] " The Debt-deflation Theory," *loc. cit.*, page 348. Italics in the
original.

We may thus conclude that the " debt-factor " plays an independent rôle as intensifier of the depression, but can hardly be regarded as an independent cause of the breakdown.[1]

§ 5. FINANCIAL ORGANISATION AND THE SEVERITY
OF THE DEPRESSION

Rigid money contracts intensify deflation. Mr. A. LOVEDAY has called attention to certain features of our present financial organisation which tend to aggravate the consequences of a fall in the price-level. " We may not—we do not—know", he says, " the causes of the recurrence of periods of depression; but we do know many of the factors that contribute to their severity."[2] " When prices and the national income expressed in money values diminish, the money claims represented by the contracts remain unchanged; the contractors who have received a money claim obtain a greater share of the national dividend and others obtain less. When contracts are for short periods, . . . the shift in the distribution of income may be nugatory or nil. They can be changed as rapidly or almost as rapidly as the prices of commodities move. But when they stretch over a period of years, or when rapid change is in practice difficult, they must affect the distribution of income and thus of purchasing power. . . .

" . . . The point which I desire to throw into relief is that, in a financial organisation such that claims on national income vary less readily than do prices of goods, the rigidity of those claims itself constitutes a contributory cause of further price declines. The greater the proportion of monetary fixed claims in society as a whole the greater the danger.

" In the international field, the effects of such fixed claims are still more serious, because the transfer of wealth from debtor to

---

[1] There are other factors of which Fisher seems also to think when he talks of over-indebtedness, *e.g.*, war debts and reparation payments. It may, of course, be readily conceded that, if such political debts are excessive and if the countries concerned do not pursue an appropriate policy, the existence of such debts may lead to contraction and depression.

[2] " Financial Organisation and the Price Level " in *Economic Essays in Honour of Gustav Cassel*, London, 1933, page 409.

creditor that has to be made is not within the country. It is not the distribution of a national income that is affected directly, but its amount. A larger slice must be cut off the national income of the debtor State and handed over to the foreign creditor." [1]

Bonds versus equities. Mr. LOVEDAY then points out that for various reasons these financial rigidities have increased. "In recent years, the joint-stock system, under names varying with the law in different countries, has replaced to a constantly increasing extent the more personal enterprise. . . . Gradually with the growth of the big industrial concern, with the extension of the multiple shop . . . a greater and greater proportion of the population has been thrust out of positions of direct, independent control into the mass of wage-earning and salaried classes. Such persons can no longer invest in themselves; to the extent that they play for safety or apparent safety, and give preference to fixed-interest-bearing obligations over profit-sharing equities, they inevitably add to the rigidity of the financial system. Many forces have induced them to prefer safety to profit "[2]—that is, fixed-interest bonds to shares and participations.

The rising importance of the small investor as compared with the large capitalist has increased the preference for bonds, since the small capitalist has not the means of a large investor to spread his risk, and is not in a position to form a rational judgment about the chances of investments in equities. Therefore, he prefers savings deposits and fixed-interest obligations. To an increasing extent, moreover, international investments have taken the form of fixed-interest-bearing obligations in preference to shares.

There can be no doubt that these circumstances have played an important part in aggravating the depression of 1923 to 1933. These factors must therefore be incorporated in a fully elaborated theory of the business cycle : but they can find a place in any theory which recognises the deflationary nature of the depression.

---

[1] *Op. cit.*, pages 410 and 411.
[2] *Op. cit.*, page 412.

CHAPTER 5

UNDER-CONSUMPTION THEORIES

§ 1. INTRODUCTION

Historical background. The under-consumption theories have a long history. In fact, they are almost as old as the science of economics itself. Lord LAUDERDALE, MALTHUS and SISMONDI are prominent among the early adherents of this school of thought. The authors who have done most in recent times to re-state and propagate the under-consumption theory in a scientific way are Mr. J. A. HOBSON[1] in England, Messrs. W. T. FOSTER and W. CATCHINGS[2] in the United States, and Professor Emil LEDERER[3] in Germany.[4] The cruder versions of the theory, which exist in innumerable varieties in all countries, will not be considered here, as their fallacy has been clearly demonstrated on various occasions.[5]

---

[1] See *The Industrial System*, London, 1909, 1910 ; *Economics of Unemployment*, 1922 ; *Rationalisation and Unemployment*, London, 1930.

[2] See *Money*, Boston, 1923 ; *Profits*, Boston, 1925 ; *The Road to Plenty*, Boston, 1928.

[3] "Konjunktur und Krisen" in *Grundriss der Sozialökonomie*, Tübingen, 1925 ; *Technischer Fortschritt und Arbeitslosigkeit*, Tübingen, 1931.

[4] While not himself primarily an advocate of the underconsumption thesis, Mr. Keynes has laid great stress on the deflationary character of acts of saving. In the *General Theory of Employment, Interest and Money*, London, 1936, he has forged, in the concept of the " propensity to consume" an instrument apt for the purposes of the underconsumption theory. The implications of this concept have been more fully developed by Mr. Harrod in his work, *The Trade Cycle*, Oxford, 1936.

[5] For example, by E. F. M. Durbin's *Purchasing Power and Trade Depression*, London, 1931, and H. Gaitskell's contribution to *What Everybody wants to know about Money*, ed. by G. D. H. Cole, London, 1933, pages 348 *et seq.*

It is difficult to summarise these theories because, with some notable exceptions, their scientific standard is lower than the standard of those reviewed earlier in this volume. They cannot be reviewed as systematically as the over-investment and monetary explanations, for it is only in regard to certain phases of the cycle that these theories have anything original to contribute. The under-consumption theory is a theory of the crisis and depression rather than a theory of the cycle. Those members of the school who attempt to explain the cycle as a whole and deal with all its phases (*e.g.*, Professor E. LEDERER) have taken over many features from—or have much in common with—the monetary and over-investment theories.

The following pages will therefore be not so much a review of a theoretical system totally different from the theories reviewed in the preceding pages as a selection of certain hypotheses which admit of consideration in conjunction with parts of the theories examined earlier. It is possible, as we shall see, to find a logically tenable alternative to the explanation of the crisis given by the over-investment theory; and the new explanation of this particular phase of the cycle seems to be quite compatible with the monetary and over-investment theories' account of the nature of the upswing and the downswing.

§ 2. DIFFERENT TYPES OF UNDER-CONSUMPTION THEORIES

Various senses of under-consumption. Another reason why it is difficult to summarise the views of the under-consumption theorists is that under-consumption is not a clear-cut, well-established concept, but covers a great variety of phenomena. It is true that all under-consumption theories are concerned with the alleged insufficiency either of money incomes or of expenditure on consumers' goods out of those incomes; but the variations between the different theories are very great. We shall now consider briefly the different ways in which under-consumption in one sense or another has been held responsible for the recurrence of economic depressions. Two versions of the theory will finally emerge which seem to merit closer examination.

1. The unqualified statement that, owing to technological improvements and inventions and to the accumulation of capital, there is a tendency for production to outgrow the capacity for consumption—this is the under-consumption theory in its crudest form—can be dismissed offhand as wholly unfounded.

2. Very frequently, "under-consumption" is used to mean the process by which purchasing power is in some way lost to the economic system, and therefore fails to become income and to appear as demand in the market for consumers' goods. Money disappears or is hoarded, and the income-velocity of money diminishes. In this sense, under-consumption is just another word for deflation. Deflation is, of course, a possible cause of the breakdown of the boom and the main cause of the depression; but, as such, it is covered by the monetary explanation of the business cycle.

3. The under-consumption theory is frequently *Under-* put forward in the following form. There is, it is *consumption* said, a secular tendency for the volume of production *and the secular* to grow. The population increases. Inventions *fall of prices.* and improvements raise the output of goods. Additions are made to the stock of capital—that is, to tools and implements. Commodity prices must therefore fall and depression ensue, unless the quantity of money is continuously increased so as to create the consuming power necessary to absorb the increasing output of goods at stable prices. This is certainly too sweeping a statement to be of much value in explaining the course of the cycle. The various factors which make for an increase in the volume of production must be treated separately. In particular, a distinction must be made between growth factors which involve a decrease in the unit cost of production and those which do not. Technological improvements reduce the unit cost of production. Most authorities conclude, therefore, that an increase in production which is due to such improvements does not call for an increase in the quantity of money. In that case, a fall in prices is not harmful, because it goes parallel with a fall in cost and does not involve a fall in money wages and incomes in general. On the contrary, in the face of falling cost, a price-stabilising policy would create a

profit inflation and lead to a dangerous boom and later on inevitably to a collapse and depression. To this proposition we shall return later.

In the case of a growing population, the situation is different. Here most authorities (with the notable exception of Professor HAYEK) would agree that the quantity of money ought to increase. Otherwise all prices, including the prices of the factors of production, principally wages, must fall. It goes without saying that this is not a satisfactory arrangement, if only because of the rigidity of wages.[1]

More difficulties are presented in the case of a growing capital stock. Should the quantity of money be increased in such a way that prices remain stable ? And which prices : commodity prices or factor prices ?

These problems, which cannot be dealt with exhaustively at this juncture, have been much discussed, principally by monetary writers (in recent times, for example, by Mr. HAWTREY and Professor ROBERTSON).[2] They occur in the writings of the under-consumption theorists intermingled with other arguments which will be discussed presently. (It is for this reason that they have been touched upon here, although they do not constitute the heart of the under-consumption theory.)

But what is the bearing of these considerations on the explanation of the business cycle ? The growth of population, the enlargement of the capital stock, the improvements in the technical

---

[1] This Professor Hayek too would admit. But he thinks that the injection of money necessary to prevent the fall in wages would create a vertical maladjustment in the structure of production, of the kind that we have discussed in the section on the monetary over-investment theory. See *Prices and Production*, 2nd ed., 1934, page 161.

[2] Compare also G. Haberler, *The Different Meanings attached to the Term " Fluctuations in the Purchasing Power of Gold " and the Best Instrument or Instruments for measuring such Fluctuations* (Memorandum submitted to the Gold Delegation of the League of Nations, 1931). A German translation appeared under the title : " Die Kaufkraft des Geldes und die Stabilität der Wirtschaft, " in *Schmoller's Jahrbuch*, Vol. 55, 1932. See also W. Egle, *Das neutrale Geld*, Jena, 1933, and J. G. Koopmans, " Zum Problem des neutralen Geldes, " in *Beitrage zur Geldtheorie*, Vienna, 1933. The older literature is well reviewed in C. M. Wash, *The Fundamental Problem in Monetary Science*, New York, 1903.

processes of production, are all secular movements. Therefore, the proposition that the supply of money does not keep pace with the growth of production cannot, *per se*, explain a cyclical movement. It is hopeless to explain the business cycle without taking account of the cumulative nature of the "short-run" processes of expansion and contraction. The considerations in question do not show why these processes are cumulative. Nor do they explain why those processes come to an end sooner or later and give rise at once to a cumulative process in the opposite direction. Their value is rather as a means of determining the trend, a deviation from which, in the one or the other direction, is liable to start a cumulative process of expansion or contraction.

There remains the possibility that the growth of production or the increase in the supply of money moves in cycles. The volume of production shows, of course, a cyclical movement. But this is exactly the phenomenon which is to be explained : it cannot be taken as an independent cause.[1] The second assumption that the supply of the circulating medium changes cyclically is the essence of the purely monetary explanation of the business cycle.

We conclude that these arguments put forward under the name " under-consumption " theory are partly irrelevant for the explanation of the short cycle and partly covered by other theories.

Over-saving theory. 4. In its best-reasoned form (*e.g.*, in the writings of Messrs. J. A. HOBSON and FOSTER and CATCHINGS), the under-consumption theory uses " under-consumption " to mean " over-saving ". Depressions are caused by the fact that too large a proportion of current income is being saved and too small a proportion spent on consumers' goods. It is the process of voluntary saving by individuals and corporations which upsets the equilibrium between production and sales.

---

[1] By an "independent cause" is meant a change produced by outside factors which can be taken for granted by the economist, such as changes in agricultural production, due to weather conditions. Nothing of this sort is to be found in industrial production.

The next step in Mr. HOBSON's analysis is the contention that the cause of over-saving is to be found in the unequal distribution of income. It is principally the recipients of large incomes who are responsible for most of the saving.[1] If the wage level could be raised and the national dividend more equally distributed, the proportion of savings would no longer be dangerous. The demand for equalisation of income as a means of reducing cyclical fluctuations, which is very popular in certain quarters, has one of its roots here.

We shall leave this part of the argument on one side, however, and concentrate on the fundamental proposition that over-saving is the cause of the evil.

The activity of saving may conceivably exert an adverse influence on the economic situation in three different ways.

Saving and hoarding.   (*a*) Saving may lead to depression because savings do not find an outlet in investment. There may be an excess of savings over new investment which will be intensified by every additional act of saving, at any rate where saving extends beyond a certain limit. In other words, saving produces a deflation, a decrease in aggregate demand for goods, because the sums saved are used to liquidate bank credit or are accumulated and hoarded in the shape of cash or idle deposits. There is the further possibility that savings are spent, not in financing new investments, but in buying property and titles to property sold by people who are forced to sell because they have suffered losses. During the depression, when the spirit of enterprise runs low and pessimism prevails, it is probably true to a large extent that saving engenders deflation rather than new investments, and that the slump is to that extent prolonged and intensified. But the breakdown of the boom can hardly be explained in this way. There is no evidence that an absorption of savings occurs during the boom or before the crisis : on the contrary, there invariably exists a brisk demand for new capital, signalised by high interest rates. There is an excess of investment over saving and not the contrary.[2] The situation changes, of course, completely

---

[1] Statistical evidence is to be found, *e.g.*, in *America's Capacity to Consume*, edited by the Brookings Institution, Washington, 1934.

[2] It should be noted that the terms "savings" and "investment" are used here in the ordinary meaning of the two words. Mr. Keynes, in

after the turning-point, when the depression has set in. Then there is an excess of savings over investment.

But this analysis is no special contribution of the under-consumptionists : it is the common ground of the monetary and over-investment theorists (especially Professor ROBERTSON).

Now we come to the heart of the under-consumption or over-saving theory.

Saving

decreases   (*b*) Savings lead on the one hand to a fall in the *demand for,* demand for consumers' goods, because the money *and increases* saved is not spent on consumption.

supply of,   (*c*) On the other hand, savings are, as a rule, *consumption* invested productively. The sums saved are used *goods.* to add to the capital equipment of the community.

Factories, railways, power-plants and machines are constructed. The ultimate aim of all this is to increase the •production of goods for final consumption.

Thus the demand for consumers' goods is reduced, their supply is increased and their prices must fall. The market for consumption goods holds the central position in the economic system. So long as all goes well there, the whole productive apparatus, which is piled up behind the consumers' market and is there only to serve it, will run smoothly : when the equilibrium is disturbed there, the whole economic system will suffer.

To this theory there are serious objections. To *Criticism.* say that the situation in the earlier stages of production depends *exclusively* on the state of affairs in the consumption industry—that, if the latter flourishes, the former will prosper and that, if production falls or stagnates in the latter, the former will necessarily decline or stagnate too—is, in this general and categorical form, certainly wrong. We have already had occasion to discuss a case where a general increase in demand for consumers' goods and a consequent tendency of the consumption

---

his *Treatise on Money,* has given them a very peculiar definition, according to which an excess of savings over investment does not imply deflation but is, by definition, equal to losses, and an excess of investment over savings equal to profits. An extensive discussion of the problem of defining saving, investment and hoarding is to be found in Chapter 8, below.

industries to expand production are not only not a sufficient condition of prosperity in the higher stages of production, but, on the contrary, the cause of its collapse. The monetary over-investment theory has shown the possibility that, when at the end of the boom the demand for consumers' goods rises and their production tends to increase, this upsets the equilibrium between costs and prices in the higher stages, because there are then no idle factors of production which can be drawn into employment in the higher stages, and there are not the necessary funds (capital supply in terms of money) to retain employed factors of production against the competition of the consumption industries.

According to the over-saving (under-consumption) theory, the equilibrium is upset by the opposite course of events—that is, by a decrease in the demand for consumers' goods. The criticisms to which the theories of Messrs. FOSTER AND CATCHINGS (who have elaborated the over-saving theory most fully) have been subjected by Messrs. DURBIN, HANSEN, HAYEK, ROBERTSON and others,[1] have at least shown that, in spite of a high rate of saving, there is always an equilibrium position *possible* with full employment of the factors of production. This is true in the first instance (that is, during the period of construction of the new capital) as well as in the long run (after the new capital equipment has been put into operation).

The function   Looking at the problem broadly, it is clear that the social function of saving is to release resources *of saving.*   from the production of goods for immediate consumption for the production of producers' goods.[2] Temporarily, the production of consumers' goods is curtailed in order to permit of increased production at a later point with the help of capital goods which have been constructed in the meantime. The fall in the demand for consumers' goods has therefore its function. The monetary incentive for the entrepreneur

[1] See Durbin : *Purchasing Power and Trade Depression*, London, 1933 ; Hansen : *Business Cycle Theory*, 1928, Chapter III : Hayek : " The Paradox of Saving " in *Economica*, May 1931 ; D. H. Robertson : " The Monetary Doctrines of Messrs. Foster and Catchings " in *Economic Essays and Addresses of Pigou and Robertson*, London, 1931.

[2] Compare especially C. Bresciani-Turroni, " The Theory of Saving, " in *Economica*, 1936.

to undertake the construction of new capital equipment, in spite of decreased demand for consumers' goods, is provided by a fall in the rate of interest, which permits a lowering of unit cost through the utilisation of roundabout methods of production of superior productivity. The cruder versions of the under-consumption theory do not offer an adequate analysis of these essentials of the capitalistic method of production. They therefore do not deal with the possibility of a smooth adjustment of the production process to saving. But it must be admitted that, while their opponents have shown the theoretical *possibility* of a smooth absorption of savings in new investments, they have not shown its *necessity*. Entrepreneurs may make no use of the possibility of extending the structure of production. The consumers' goods industries and the immediately preceding stages will thereupon curtail production; and this may lead to a destruction of purchasing power. This in turn may deter producers in the higher stages from embarking on new investments, in spite of the incentive provided by the fall in the interest rate. All depends on their psychological reactions, on their anticipations. If the money saved is not invested, a cumulative process of deflation will start and saving may thus defeat its own end.

Thus we are back at case (*a*) discussed above. Much will depend on whether there is a continuous flow or a gradual increase of savings, whether there are violent changes, and whether there is a brisk and continuous demand for new credit (capital) so that an increasing supply is readily absorbed at slightly falling interest rates.[1]

Let us now apply this analysis to the broad facts of the business cycle. During the depression, demand for new capital is at a low level and inelastic. There is therefore a great danger of new savings running to waste instead of being invested. During the upswing, demand is brisk and new savings easily find an outlet in new investment. Can the over-saving doctrine contribute anything to the explanation of the crisis, the down-turn from prosperity to depression?

There is no evidence for the assumption that the rate of saving rises at the end of the boom and so creates serious difficulties.

---

[1] Bresciani-Turroni, *loc. cit.*

On the contrary, for reasons which have been touched upon in an earlier passage, it would seem rather that the rate of saving falls in the later phase of the boom.

Valuable aspects of the under-consumption theory. 5. But it has been argued by many writers— and the argument may be said to represent a new version of the under-consumption theory—that the end of the boom comes when the fruits of the new processes which have been initiated with the help of voluntary and forced saving during the upswing begin to emerge. The crisis is brought about, not by a sudden rise in the rate of saving (*i.e.*, a fall in the *demand* for consumers' goods) but by a rapid rise in the rate of output (*i.e.*, in the *supply* of consumers' goods). This theory, which is the direct opposite of the shortage-of-capital explanation of the breakdown, merits close examination and will be discussed in the next section.

6. Another valuable version of the under-consumption theory is the doctrine that the failure of wages to rise rapidly enough during the upswing—more explicitly, the lag of wages behind prices—is the cause of excessive profits, which in turn entail a dangerous credit inflation and eventually engender serious disturbance of existing relations culminating in a crisis. This theory will be discussed in § 4 of this chapter.

§ 3. INSUFFICIENCY OF CONSUMERS' DEMAND VERSUS SHORTAGE OF CAPITAL AS THE CAUSE OF THE COLLAPSE OF THE BOOM

Capital shortage versus insufficiency of consumers' demand. So far we have encountered, and discussed, the following answers to the question why the cumulative process of expansion always comes to a more or less abrupt end : Disturbances from outside the economic system; insufficiency of the money supply; shortage of capital in the sense of a vertical maladjustment of the structure of production; horizontal maladjustments; a general rise in " cost " and decline of efficiency.

The hypothesis with which we have now to deal is the exact counterpart of the shortage-of-capital theorem. It is important to make the issue and the two answers quite clear. The problem is this : Is the turn from prosperity to depression brought about by a shortage of capital or by an insufficiency of the demand for consumers' goods ? Does the investment boom collapse because the supply of capital becomes too small to complete the new roundabout methods of production, or because consumers' demand is insufficient to sustain the increased productive capacity ?

The argument of the under-consumptionists is this. During the upswing of the cycle, society develops its productive apparatus. But it takes some time before the production of consumers' goods begins to increase. In the meantime, their supply is deficient; prices rise; and there is therefore a constant stimulus in the direction of further investment. But as soon as the new roundabout methods of production are completed, the new investments are finished, consumers' goods begin to be poured out; the markets for consumers' goods are glutted : and this reacts with increasing intensity on the higher stages of production.

According to the other view, exactly the opposite is true. The trouble is due, not to a deficiency of consumers' demand, but to the contrary tendency. The demand for consumers' goods tends to rise because the newly created purchasing power, which has been placed at the disposal of entrepreneurs, becomes income in the hands of the owners of the factors of production and is spent on consumers' goods before the supply of these goods can be sufficiently increased. The demand for consumers' goods is thus too large rather than too small. There is not enough " waiting ", not enough " lacking " in the terminology of Professor ROBERTSON, or, in ordinary words, not enough saving to complete the investments initiated. The consequence is that the rate of interest tends to rise, and the banks are called upon to provide the necessary amounts of capital. Sooner or later, however, the inflation must be stopped; the flow of new credit comes to an end; and the completion of a great number of new investments becomes impossible. They are consequently abandoned, and this is the break which sets in motion the downward spiral of contraction.

Both theories contemplate what we have called a *vertical* maladjustment in the structure of production; but these vertical maladjustments are not of the same order. As we shall see at once, the

" top " of the structure of production according to the one theory, the " bottom " according to the other, is over-developed in relation to the flow of money. In a sense, both theories can be described as over-investment theories. In the one case, new investments are excessive in relation to the supply of saving; in the other case, they are excessive in relation to the demand for the product. That the distinction is important may be seen from the fact that the conclusions drawn as to the appropriate policy to follow in order to avert, mitigate or postpone the breakdown are diametrically opposed. According to the one view, every measure that tends to increase consumers' demand and to reduce saving is helpful. According to the other view, exactly the opposite policy is called for. (But such policy, it should be noted, holds only for the later phase of the boom. As soon as the downward movement has got under way and the spiral of deflation has been started, the position changes completely and quite different considerations come into play.)

We must try to make the distinction still clearer and to distinguish these two cases from horizontal maladjustments and from a purely monetary insufficiency. This is not always easy : it is sometimes difficult to ascertain which case a writer has in mind.

The structure of production and the flow of money. The best method of finding out the exact meaning and implications of the different theories is to ask what are the appropriate measures called for, and to what extent the crisis can be averted by the public changing its habits of saving and spending and the mode of spending (without considering whether in practice this change can or cannot be brought about by State intervention). If an insufficiency of the supply of money, a credit contraction pure and simple, is the sole cause of the termination of prosperity, the situation can be remedied by purely monetary measures—viz., by an increase in the money or credit supply by means of a reduction of interest rates. With a very few exceptions (among whom Mr. HAWTREY is prominent), most writers would agree that in most cases this is impossible.[1] The down-turn and

---

[1] See A. Amonn: " Zur gegenwärtigen Krisenlage und inflationistischen Krisenpolitik " in *Zeitschrift für Nationalökonomie,* Vol. V, 1934, page 1 and *passim.*

the depression can be postponed, but not averted, by a cheap-money policy.   The reason is that the difficulties do not arise, or do not solely arise, from an insufficiency of the flow of money in general so much as from the fact that the structure of production—*i.e.*, the allocation of the factors of production to different stages and branches of industry—does not correspond to the flow of money as determined by the distribution of individual money incomes between saving and spending and the different branches of spending.   Such a discrepancy cannot be remedied by a simple expansion of credit.   The authorities may perhaps determine where the new money is to be spent at first.   They can, that is to say, choose the point of injection of the new money into the economic system; but they cannot hope—at any rate without drastic reorganisation of the whole economic system (*i.e.*, without abandoning the existing individualistic organisation of the system) —to control how the money is spent by the successive recipients. But suppose it *were* feasible to change at will the people's habit as to saving and spending, what changes would be best calculated to forestall serious trouble ?   Obviously, if we rule out an insufficiency in *total* demand, there must be such a distribution of the national income as will make the flow of money correspond to the flow of goods.

The capital-shortage theory replies that all trouble could be avoided if people would consume less and save more, and thus supply the necessary funds for completing the uncompleted roundabout processes of production.   The reply of the pure under-consumptionist is the contrary.   If people will expand consumption and save less, he says, the breakdown can be averted. That is very well, if the difficulty is due to the too early completion of the new roundabout processes of production.   The situation is that people intend to save more, to wait longer.   This implies that they are not yet prepared to take over an increased output of consumers' goods.   Over-investment is not a correct descrip-tion of such a situation.   Under-investment would be a better description, since the crisis can be avoided, for the time being at least, by undertaking longer roundabout processes of produc-tion—*i.e.*, more ambitious investment schemes which would postpone the appearance of consumable goods on the market.

Saving and investment ex-ante and ex-post. These two situations can be well described with the help of the terminological apparatus developed by some Swedish writers.[1] These writers distinguish in respect of saving, investment, income and similar concepts between an *ex-ante* and an *ex-post* sense in which these concepts can be used. On the one hand, it is necessary, for the practical business man as well as for the theoretical economist, to find out *ex-post* what actually happened during a certain period. There must be a system of bookkeeping which " answers the question what has happened during a past period. It is an account *ex-post* " (OHLIN, *loc. cit.*, page 58).

" This, however, explains nothing, for it does not describe the causal or functional relations. As economic events depend on man's actions, one has to investigate what determines these actions. They always refer to a more or less distant future. Hence, one must study those expectations about the future which govern actions . . . This analysis of the forward-looking type can be called *ex-ante*, using MYRDAL's convenient expressions " (OHLIN, *loc. cit.*, page 58-59).

With the help of these concepts, we can now formulate as follows an equilibrium condition which is implicit in the two rival theories under discussion : *Ex-ante* saving should be equal to *ex-ante* investment. In other words, the investment plans of entrepreneurs should correspond to the intended savings of the public. If the two do not coincide, some producers will be disappointed and the equilibrium will be disrupted.

The situation envisaged by the capital shortage theorists can now be described as an excess of *ex-ante* investment over *ex-ante* saving, which must lead to a disappointment and losses of producers of capital goods (in the higher stages of production), as analysed in detail by Professor HAYEK.

---

[1] Compare especially G. Myrdal, " Der Gleichgewichtsbegriff als Instrument der geldtheoretischen Analyse " in *Beiträge zur Geldtheorie*, edited by Hayek, 1933, and B. Ohlin, " Some Notes on the Stockholm Theory of Savings and Investment " in *Economic Journal*, Vol. 47, 1937, pages 53 *et seq*, and pages 221 *et seq*. For further details of this approach, see Chapter 8.

On the other hand, the situation which, according to the under-consumption theorists, typically arises at the end of the boom, can be described as an excess of *ex-ante* saving over *ex-ante* investment, which must lead to disappointment and losses on the part of producers of consumers' goods.[1]

Both kinds of maladjustment could be avoided by an appropriate change in the saving and spending plans of the public.

If horizontal maladjustments are involved, a shift in the distribution of income between saving and expenditure on consumers' goods cannot remedy the situation. Changes in consumption habits will then be necessary to restore equilibrium. For example, if the motor-car industry is over-developed, people must be made to buy more motor-cars instead of something else.

It is clear that shortage of capital and insufficiency of consumers' demand are alternative explanations. The public cannot be reproached at the same time for saving too little and saving too much. But, as Professor ROBERTSON has pointed out,[2] it is quite conceivable that, if in a given situation capital shortage was " the actual spear-head of relapse ", insufficiency of consumers' demand in presence of an increase in output would have brought about the crisis somewhat later.

Difficulty in distinguishing vertical and horizontal maladjustments. Vertical maladjustments of each type on the one hand and horizontal maladjustments and insufficiency of total demand (insufficiency of money supply) on the other are quite compatible. To a certain extent they probably always go together and are frequently difficult to distinguish. Since many writers do not carefully distinguish these cases, it is often difficult to know which they have in mind. The reason for this ambiguity is perhaps to be found in the fact that, in all these cases, the proximate cause of the breakdown is an insufficiency of demand as compared with the supply coming on the market. This is true alike in the case of a horizontal

---

[1] Certain differences, fundamentally of a terminological kind, between the Swedish analysis and the analysis used by the writers dealt with in the text will be discussed more thoroughly in Chapter 8 below.

[2] In " Industrial Fluctuations and the Natural Rate of Interest," *Economic Journal*, December 1934.

maladjustment or an insufficiency of demand for consumers' goods, and in the case of a capital shortage, which finds its expression in an insufficiency of demand for producers' goods and "machines" in particular, since possible purchasers cannot get hold of enough "capital" to purchase them (SPIETHOFF). Furthermore, as Professor LEDERER[1] has remarked, the fact that the breakdown begins in the producers' goods industries need not mean that capital shortage is the real cause of the trouble. It is conceivable that the consumption industries may quickly become aware of the limitations of their further expansion in view of the insufficiency of consumers' demand. If that is the case, they will restrict their orders, and by so doing may precipitate a crisis in the higher stages of production without having themselves got into trouble. This can only be made clear by putting and answering the question with which we started : How should the flow of money between saving and spending and between the various branches of spending be modified in order to restore equilibrium ?

Lederer's theory.   Professor LEDERER explains the breakdown of the boom chiefly by insufficiency of consumers' demand. (How he explains the genesis of this insufficiency will be seen in the next section.) He says that equilibrium could be easily restored if wages were increased and profits lowered [2]—that is to say, the rate of saving (he says, of "accumulation") must be reduced and the rate of consumption increased. This is brought about eventually during the crisis and depression.[3] But he makes an important qualification. He says that, so far as "the crisis originates from a disproportion in the sphere of production" (in contradistinction to a disproportion in incomes), it cannot be cured by a rise in wages. He seems to be thinking of what we call horizontal maladjustments in the structure of

---

[1] " Konjunktur und Krisen " in *Grundriss der Sozialökonomie*, IV. Abteilung, I. Teil, Tübingen, 1925, page 394.

[2] *Op. cit.*, page 401.

[3] *Op. cit.*, page 394. He seems to overlook the alternative possibility of the breakdown being caused by capital shortage—that is, by under-saving and over-consumption. Speaking about Spiethoff's theory, he says : "An over-production in the earlier stages of production, in the coal-mines, iron-and-steel works, etc., obviously means only that the demand for finished goods cannot rise to that extent which would correspond to the actual production of producers' goods " (page 386).

production, and (later on) of the deflation during the depression. If the value of money which was lowered during the boom is gradually restored during the depression, wages must fall. But he insists that wages should fall less than prices. If they fall more rapidly than prices, the crisis is intensified.

A monetary under-consumption theory. Professor Hans NEISSER has worked out a theory which could be described as a "monetary under-consumption theory".[1] He explains the breakdown of the boom by under-consumption in the sense defined above and analyses carefully how the difficulties in the consumers' goods industries are likely to entail deflation and so spread the trouble to all parts of the system. He is not exclusively an under-consumption theorist; he points out that other reasons for the collapse of the boom, such as under-saving (the opposite of under-consumption), are not at all inconceivable and have actually brought a number of cycles to an end. He believes, however, that the situation is especially serious if the trouble first arises in the consumption industries, for this constitutes, so to speak, an "endogenous" cause of deflation. When consumption industries suffer losses, investment will at once be curtailed and recession will spread immediately to the upper stages of production while, according to him, a difficulty which arises in the capital goods industries is in itself no sufficient reason for a decline of production in consumers' goods industries.

Importance of construction period in the upswing. An influential sponsor of the view that the breakdown of the boom is brought about, not by a shortage of capital, but by insufficiency of demand in face of a rapid increase in the output of consumers' goods is Professor Albert AFTALION.[2]

Professor AFTALION builds his theory largely on the acceleration principle. Moderate increases or reductions in

---

[1] " General Over-production. A Study of Say's Law of Markets " in *Journal of Political Economy*, Vol. 42, 1934, pages 433-465. *Cf.* also his book : *Some International Aspects of the Business Cycle*, Philadelphia, 1936.

[2] *Les crises périodiques de surproduction*, Paris, 1913. See also his article " The Theory of Economic Cycles based on the Capitalistic Technique of Production " in the *Review of Economic Statistics*, October 1927, pages 165 *et seq.* Only part of Aftalion's theory will be examined

the production of consumers' goods give rise to relatively large fluctuations in the production of capital equipment. The boom is stimulated by a deficiency of consumers' goods; and this leads to an increase in the production of capital goods. But the modern capitalistic process of production is time-consuming. The construction of capital goods which must precede the production of consumers' goods takes months or even years. Therefore, the output of consumers' goods does not rise at once, or at any rate does not at once rise sufficiently. Prices of consumers' goods remain high, the profit margin persists, and there is a constant stimulus to produce capital equipment. This phase of capitalistic production, in which capital goods are being created, is the period of prosperity. It is the capitalistic technique of production, the fact that a long time must elapse before the output of consumers' goods can be increased, which prolongs the prosperity period, over-stimulates the construction of capital goods, and leads finally to a disruption of economic equilibrium.

The breakdown comes when the roundabout processes of production which have been started during the upswing are completed and consumers' goods begin to pour out. It is of course true that the duration of the processes of production is not uniform for all types of goods. Therefore, the processes of production which have been initiated will not all be completed at the same time. The prosperity does not terminate when a single process is finished; it ends only when a great quantity of capital in the majority of industries is set to work turning out consumers' goods.

Professor AFTALION compares the time required for the manufacture of means of production to the time which elapses between the moment of rekindling a fire and the moment at which it begins to give off heat. "If one rekindles the fire in the hearth in order to warm up a room, one has to wait a while before one has the desired temperature. As the cold continues, and the thermometer

---

here. On the whole, his theory cannot be classified as an under-consumption theory : but his explanation of the crisis as reviewed in the text is the same as that of the under-consumptionists. His explanation of the cycle as a whole suffers from the inadequacy of the analysis of the monetary factor. Compare the criticism by D. H. Robertson in *Economic Journal*, Vol. 24, 1914, page 81, and A. H. Hansen's review in *Business Cycle Theory*, pages 104-111.

continues to record it, one might be led, if one had not the lessons of experience, to throw more coal on the fire. One would continue to throw coal, even though the quantity already in the grate is such as will give off an intolerable heat, when once it is all alight. To allow oneself to be guided by the present sense of cold and the indications of the thermometer to that effect is fatally to overheat the room." [1]

The idea that the length of the prosperity phase of the cycle depends on the duration of the new productive processes (which is, in the main, the period of construction of new capital equipment) has been widely re-echoed. Professors Pigou and Robertson attribute to what they call the *gestation period* of capital goods, [2] which is substantially equivalent to the period of construction, an important rôle in determining the length of the upswing. It is also part of Professor Schumpeter's theory that the boom is terminated when the new productive processes are completed and an additional flow of finished goods appears in the market.

The view of these writers is that the upswing is usually concentrated in one or two leading industries—railway construction in the third quarter of the nineteenth century and, later, electrical machinery and automobiles.

It must be admitted that the exact classification of these theories is not easy. It is not always apparent whether all these writers are thinking of over-saving in the strict sense in which we have defined it above, when they say that the consumers' demand is insufficient to absorb the swollen stream of goods flowing into the market. It is not always quite clear whether they are not thinking also of horizontal maladjustments or some other maladjustments which may have no place in this conspectus of the position. The " gestation period " of durable goods may also be interpreted as meaning that the capital supply (*i.e.*, the flow of saving) is

---

[1] Substantially the same theory is advanced by F. W. Taussig, *Principles of Economics*, 3rd ed., Vol. I, pages 391 and 392. This idea has been frequently used for the explanation of cycles in particular industries—*i.e.* the " hog cycle ", " shipbuilding cycle ", etc.

[2] This is also stressed by F. Lavington : *The Trade Cycle, an Account of the Causes producing Rhythmical Changes in the Activity of Business*, London, 1922, page 72.

insufficient to absorb the new capital goods as they are completed. The obscurity will remain in the absence of answers to the initial question as to what changes in the flow of money from saving to spending, from spending to saving, or from one branch of spending to another, are capable of restoring equilibrium or forestalling disturbance.[1]

Unfortunately, explicit answers to this question are few and far between.   But, since we are interested rather in possible theories (that is, in hypothetical explanations) than in theorists and their doctrines, we may leave the matter there.

§ 4. THE FAILURE OF WAGES TO RISE SUFFICIENTLY AS THE CAUSE OF THE EXCESSES OF THE BOOM

Lag in wage-rise stimulates investment. In its bare outline, the argument is this. The prosperity phase of the cycle is characterised by a great increase in the production of capital goods. The breakdown is caused by " over-investment ". (As will be seen later, it is not always clear exactly what the authors whose theories are discussed in this section mean by over-investment.) The necessary stimulus and the necessary funds for these investments are derived, in part at any rate, from the excessive profits of entrepreneurs.   This profit-inflation can and must arise because wages and certain other incomes fail to advance in harmony with rising prices or falling costs due to rapid technical progress.

This theory has been used to explain the business cycle in general by E. LEDERER[2] and E. PREISER.[3]   In recent writings, it has frequently been advanced as an explanation *ad hoc* of the last American boom.[4]

It is obviously closely connected with the monetary over-investment theory. A certain lag of wages or other income

---

[1] Cases are of course conceivable in which no such change would be sufficient to restore equilibrium.

[2] Lederer, *op. cit.*, pages 393 and 394.

[3] Preiser : *Grundzüge der Konjunkturtheorie*, 1933.

[4] *Cf.* A. D. Gayer : *Monetary Policy and Economic Stabilisation*, pages 113-131, 1935, and A. B. Adams : *Our Economic Revolution*, pages 1-15, 1934.

(especially, of the relatively inflexible incomes such as those of State officials, pensioners, rentiers, the holders of fixed-income-bearing securities, and the like) is a normal and important corollary of forced saving—that is, of the formation of capital by means of an inflationary expansion of credit. If wages and all other incomes were to rise automatically with, and to the same extent as, prices with each injection of new money, there would be little scope for forced saving.

As we have seen, the monetary over-investment theory runs mainly in terms of the rate of interest. According to it, the expansion is brought about by the fact that the rate of interest is too low, either because the money rate of interest has been lowered or because the natural rate has risen. It is obviously compatible with this view that the movement of wages and other incomes should also have a determining influence. If wages, etc., fail to rise, profits swell; and this provides a strong stimulus for further expansion of credit and investment. In the terminology of the over-investment school, the profit rate rises; hence the demand for credit goes up and credit inflation ensues. Thus the lag of wages and other income is an important factor in the reinforcement of the cumulative expansion process. It follows that the boom could be stopped by a sufficient rise of wage rates as well as of interest rates.

So far, this type of under-consumption theory[1] and the monetary over-investment theory are in no way contradictory, but are rather complementary to each other. There seems also to be agreement that credit expansion is a necessary feature of the picture.

---

[1] It may, of course, be argued that this type of theory is not properly an "under-consumption" theory, since it stresses the cost aspect of wages, etc., rather than the fact that they constitute demand for consumers' goods. There is also a certain contradiction, at least on the surface, in that the same writers who see in a lag of wages a stimulating factor for the boom are nearly all of the opinion that a fall in wages intensifies depression. That is to say, they advocate a rise in wages in order to check the boom and to combat the depression. It would, however, seem possible to reconcile these two propositions by special assumptions about the monetary situation. During the depression, a fall in wages may conceivably lead to the liquidation of bank credit, while a failure of nominal wages to rise during the upswing does not have the same deflationary or anti-inflationary effect.

The difference between the two groups arises over *Wage-lag as* the question, why exactly does the boom eventually *viewed by* collapse ?   What is the nature of the disequilibrium, *over-investment* and which factor does the mischief ?

theorists and According to the over-investment theory, the *by under-* credit expansion is the villain of the piece. Excessive *consump-* profits due to the lag in wages and other inflexible *tionists.* incomes are harmful only in so far as they are responsible for inflationary credits, which in turn lead to over-investment in the sense defined above.

To the under-consumptionist group, the danger *Excessive* in the excessive profits is not that they induce a *profits* credit inflation, but that they are the source of *as source* excessive saving.   It is a widely held belief, accepted *of saving.* by socialists and liberals, under-consumptionists and over-investment theorists [1] alike, that the bulk of a nation's savings comes from the higher income strata.   The profit-recipients and not the wage-earners provide the funds for investment.   Therefore, when profits rise relatively to wages and other incomes, the flow of savings grows.   Thus far the monetary over-investment theorist is in agreement.   In fact, he welcomes the idea as a useful addition to his picture of the boom. The expansion of capital-goods industries relatively to consumption trades is financed, not only by inflationary credits (flowing from various sources) and ordinary voluntary savings, but also by new additions to voluntary savings out of the big profits realised during the boom.[2]   These profits are supposed to be very substantial, and the sums set aside for investment purposes are excessive.   Too much is invested; and this leads eventually to the collapse of the

---

[1] The one group draws the conclusion that an unequal distribution of income is a good thing, the other that it is a bad thing.

[2] This is also Mr. Hawtrey's view. He does not believe that these voluntary savings are supplemented to any considerable extent by inflationary bank credit placed at the disposal of producers. According to him, additional bank credit enters the economic system rather by way of the dealer—that is, near the consumers' end of the structure of production—than by direct stimulation of investment in fixed capital and in the higher stages of production as the monetary over-investment theory would have it.

boom. The breakdown could be avoided, if the profit-recipients would choose to expand their consumption instead of investing.

The process as pictured by the under-consumptionists can also be described as over-investment. But a closer analysis shows that, by over-investment, they mean the contrary of what the monetary over-investment theorists mean by over-investment. For the writers with whom this section is concerned, investments are excessive in respect to consumers' demand and not in respect to capital supply. Over-investment is equivalent to insufficiency of consumers' demand and not to insufficiency of the flow of savings. "The failure of the income of the final consumer in the end checked the process" of expansion in America in 1929.[1] "Relatively to the means of the ultimate consumer, the vast expansion of capacity in durable-goods industries and the huge volume of domestic and factory buildings erected were altogether excessive."[2] "This lopsided growth in the division or distribution of the national money income brought about a rapid development of industry, ending in our present condition, which is marked by excessive productive power and a deficiency of consumers' money income."[3] This seems to be also the idea of Mr. PREISER.[4]

Thus, this version of the under-consumption theory turns out to be the same as that discussed in the previous section. But the conclusion was not inevitable from the first. If we start with the proposition that a lag of wages and other income during the upswing intensifies the boom, it is quite possible to pursue the argument along the lines of the monetary over-investment theory and to hold that the collapse is brought about by an insufficiency of capital supply (*i.e.*, of the flow of savings).

It would seem logical to conclude that an increase in the flow of investible funds which is due to a rise in profits (that is, to a rise and redistribution of income) has exactly the same influence and

---

[1] Gayer, *op. cit.*, page 127.
[2] *Ibid.*, page 128.
[3] Adams, *op. cit.*, page 9.
[4] *Op. cit.* : "The continuation of the production process finds its barrier, in every case, in the ultimate consumption" (page 106). "The recession comes, because the accumulation was excessive" (page 110). It is true, however, that there are other passages where he seems to be thinking of "horizontal disproportionalities"—*e.g.*, on pages 84 and 85.

consequences as an increase due to a rise in the rate of voluntary savings (without any change in the size and distribution of income). Hence, those writers who lay the blame on high profits should also take objection to any rise in the rate of savings.

" Auto-
nomous "
and " hetero-
nomous "
saving.

This conclusion is, however, expressly rejected by Mr. Preiser. He has the idea that a rise of investible funds due to higher profits (he calls this " heteronomous " saving) is a quite different phenomenon from an increase due to a rise in the rate of saving from an unchanged income (" auto- nomous " saving). While the first must lead to a collapse, he sees no reason why the second should not go on indefinitely. The difference is not only of degree, but also of kind. It arises from the alleged fact that the appearance of profits makes the misdirection of capital inevitable. In the case of autonomous saving, it is the rate of interest which guides the entrepreneur in his investment policy. The savings are directed over the capital market, which guarantees a rational distribution. When profits appear everywhere, the investor has to grope in the dark. He has lost connection, so to speak, with the demand of the ultimate consumer; for " heteronomous " savings do not flow through the capital market (pages 80 and 84). The passages quoted in an earlier footnote show that the author does not make it clear what he means by misdirection of capital; is there too much all round in relation to aggregate consumers' demand, or too much in parti- cular branches at the expense of others ?

CHAPTER 6

" PSYCHOLOGICAL THEORIES "

---

§ I. INTRODUCTION

Psychological and economic factors. It is in a way misleading to speak of " psychological " explanations of the trade cycle or of particular phases of it. Every economic fact has a psychological aspect. The subject-matter of economic science is human behaviour—chiefly conscious and deliberate behaviour—which can hardly be separated from its psychological basis. The psychology of human behaviour is therefore a constituent part of the subject-matter of economics. When we assume that an entrepreneur will increase his output if demand rises or cost is reduced, or that workmen will respond to changes in money wages but not so readily to changes in real wages, or that consumers will buy more of a given commodity if the price falls and less if they think it will fall further, or that people will hoard money if the value of money rises—all these assumptions are assumptions about human behaviour which presuppose a certain state of mind on the part of the human agents. Propositions about such actions may be considered as belonging to the sphere of applied psychology : but they also figure continually, whether implicit or expressed, in the economic theories of the cycle. What, then, distinguishes a " psychological " theory from an " economic " one ?

There is really no fundamental difference between the " economic " theories already reviewed in these pages and the so-called " psychological " theories. Both make assumptions as to economic behaviour in certain situations. The real difference is sometimes this. The " psychological " theories introduce certain assumptions about typical reactions, mainly on the part of the entrepreneur and the saver, in certain situations; and these reactions are conventionally called psychological, because of their (in a sense) indeterminate character.   But the distinction between the writers who give prominence to these "psychological" factors and the writers so far reviewed is, taken as a whole, a distinction of emphasis rather than of kind.   The "psychological" factors are put forward as supplemental to the monetary and other economic factors and not as alternative elements of causation, while on the other hand, though they may be assigned a less prominent place in the chain of causation, they are in no sense overlooked by the majority of writers of the other group.

§ 2.   ANALYSIS OF THE PSYCHOLOGICAL FACTOR
IN THE EXPLANATION OF THE BUSINESS CYCLE

Stress on expectations. The writers who have laid the greatest stress on "psychological" reactions in the explanation of the various phases of the cycle are KEYNES,[1] LAVINGTON,[2] PIGOU[3] and TAUSSIG.[4]
Of the writers whose theories have been analysed earlier in this report, MITCHELL, ROBERTSON, RÖPKE, SPIETHOFF all attach a certain importance in their system to "psychological" elements.

It remains to define more precisely the actions and reactions in connection with which the operation of "psychological" factors is postulated by these writers in their explanation of the cycle. "Psychological" factors come into consideration in economic theory in connection with anticipations and expectations. Static theory and those business-cycle theories which are in the main based on the static hypothesis—of which the most typical exponent is perhaps Professor HAYEK—picture the entrepreneur's decisions as to the volume, and alterations in the volume, of output and employment as being determined by a comparison of prices and costs—that is to say, the price of his product or products

---

[1] *General Theory of Employment, Interest and Money*, London, 1936, Chapter 22 (" Notes on the Trade Cycle ").
[2] *The Trade Cycle, an Account of the Causes producing Rhythmical Changes in the Activity of Business*, London, 1922.
[3] *Industrial Fluctuations*, 2nd ed., London, 1929.
[4] *Principles of Economics*, 3rd ed., Vol. I, page 393.

and the price of the means of production. "Price" and "cost" are economic terms : but what the economist is concerned with—in all but a few unimportant limiting cases—is *expected* future prices and cost. The prices, costs, profit margins, etc., by which the producer is guided in his decision, should be conceived of, in short, not simply as given factors, but as factors expected to rule in the future.[1] This is so even in the simplest case—the case which seems to underlie a large part of static theory—where the producer is guided in his decisions solely by current prices. *Prima facie*, it might seem that in this case no element of expectation is present. But this is not so : the expectation in this case is the hope or belief that current prices[2] will continue to dominate the future.

---

[1] In recent years, it has become fashionable to lay stress on the element of expectation. Keynes' *General Theory of Employment, Interest and Money* is conceived in terms of expectation ; and, at an earlier date, the concept of economic expectation was interpreted and developed by the Swedish school (especially E. Lindahl, G. Myrdal and B. Ohlin : see Myrdal's report on this Swedish literature in his article " Der Gleichgewichtsbegriff als Instrument der geldtheoretischen Analyse " in *Beiträge zur Geldtheorie*, edited by Hayek, Vienna, 1933 : see also a number of articles by J. R. Hicks, viz., "Gleichgewicht und Konjunktur" in *Zeitschrift für Nationalökonomie*, Vol. IV, No. 4, 1933, pages 441 *et seq.* ; "A Suggestion for simplifying the Theory of Money " in *Economica*, February 1935, page 1 ; and "Mr.Keynes' 'General Theory of Employment, Interest and Money'" in *Economic Journal*, Vol. XLVI, June 1936). It should not, however, be forgotten that even the theories of authors who do not usually refer explicitly to expectations and anticipations can, and should, be interpreted in terms of expectation, as the authors in question are themselves often well aware (*cf.*, for example, Hayek's article "Preiserwartungen, monetäre Störungen und Fehlinvestitionen " in *Nationaløkonomisk Tidsskrift*, Vol. 73, pages 176-191—French translation "Prévision de prix, perturbations monétaires et faux investissements " in *Revue des Sciences économiques*, 1935). Professor Morgenstern has a trenchant analysis of the problem of expectations and anticipations in his *Wirtschaftsprognose, eine Untersuchung ihrer Voraussetzungen und Möglichkeiten*, Vienna, 1928, and his article " Vollkommene Voraussicht und wirtschaftliches Gleichgewicht" in *Zeitschrift für Nationalökonomie*, Vol. VI, Vienna, 1935, pages 337-358.

[2] The reference in this case is to prices : but what is true of prices is equally true of other factors in economic decisions. In perfectly competitive circumstances, price is the only factor which the producer has to forecast. In monopolistic circumstances, it is rather the "demand" than the "price" with which he is concerned, since the price is not in such case independent of the action of the producer.

With the introduction of the element of expecta-
Expectations tion, uncertainty enters the field.   Future events
are uncertain. cannot be forecast with absolute precision; and the
farther they are distant in the future, the greater
the uncertainty, and the greater the possibility of unforeseen and
unforeseeable disturbances.   Every economic decision is part of
an economic plan which extends into the more or less distant
future.   ·In principle, there is therefore always an element of uncertainty in every activity.   There are, however, certain cases where
the element of uncertainty is especially great and conspicuous,
such as the case of investment of resources in long processes and
durable plant and the provision of funds for these purposes.   The
longer the processes in which capital is to be sunk, and the more
durable the instruments and equipment to be constructed, the
greater the element of uncertainty and risk of loss.

Naturally, economic actions and reactions in such cases are less
rigidly determined by observable facts than in other cases.   It is
therefore mainly here that the "psychological" theories make
their essential contribution.   Optimism and pessimism are introduced as additional determinants.   An attitude of optimism is an
attribute of the prosperity phase of the cycle, and an attitude of
pessimism an attribute of the depression; and the turning-points
are marked by a change from optimism to pessimism and *vice versa*.

What do these new elements add to the picture
Optimism   of the expansion and contraction process which has
and   emerged from the analysis of the "non-psycholo-
pessimism. gical" theories reviewed so far ?   If the psychological argument that during the upswing
people take a more optimistic, and during the downswing a more
pessimistic, view meant no more than that people invest more
freely during the upswing and are reluctant to invest during the
downswing, it would add nothing at all to the picture of the
upswing and downswing as drawn by the monetary over-investment theory.   But the psychological theories mean, of course,
more than that.   Optimism and pessimism are regarded as causal
factors which tend to induce or intensify the rise and fall of investment which are characteristic of the upswing and downswing
respectively.   But are optimism and pessimism really separate

factors definitely distinguishable from those analysed in the non-psychological theories of the cycle ? The factors and forces making for cumulative expansion may be defined, broadly speaking —as they are defined in these theories—as low interest rates and/or the appearance of new investment opportunities as a result of inventions, changes in demand, etc., which are themselves the consequences of growth of population, the need for replacement of outworn equipment and so on. An increase in investment, however brought about, leads to an inflow of new money into the circulation and so to a rise in the money demand for goods in general which in turn stimulates investment : the process is cumulative. An indispensable condition is of course an elastic money supply. What now is changed, if to this list of factors optimism and pessimism are added as intensifying elements ? If all that is meant is that a fall in the rate of interest, or the appearance of an invention requiring for its application a heavy investment of capital, or a rise in demand makes people anticipate better returns from particular investments, there is no new element in the mechanism as pictured by, say, the monetary over-investment theory, since to the latter too profits can only mean *expected* profits.

Entrepre-
neurs'
reactions are
indeterminate.

But the introduction of optimism and pessimism as additional factors signifies more than this. It implies that the connection between a fall in the interest rate and a change in the other objective factors, on the one hand, and the decision of the entrepreneur to invest more, on the other hand, is not so rigid as the " economic " theories sometimes maintain. If in a given situation the rate of interest falls, or demand increases, or there is a change in the technological situation (exploitation of an invention or introduction of an innovation), it is not possible on the basis of these data alone to predict the strength of the entrepreneurs' reactions or the extent to which they will increase investment. It is true, such phrases as " the degree of optimism " or " a change in optimism " are omnibus formulæ which conveniently cover a number of other factors such as the general political situation and other elements likely to influence the outcome, though to an unknown extent. It should be clearly recognised that, while it is true that developments are not determined wholly by the objective factors with which the non-psychological theories are concerned, the introduction of the determinants " optimism " and " pessimism " makes no positive contribution to the explanation of the cycle so long as the optimism and pessimism remain purely psychological phenomena—*i.e.*, states of mind of the entrepreneurs (or other members of the economic community with whose behaviour the theory is concerned). We cannot observe states of mind; but it is possible to make certain observations from which states of mind or changes of mind can be inferred. It is at this point that the " psychological " theories have a positive contribution to make.

" Irrational "   What observable factors are there (other than
influences   those which have already been taken into account
stressed by   by the " non-psychological " theories) that go to
" psycholo-   make people optimistic or pessimistic—*i.e.*, that
gical "   stimulate or discourage investment ? There is in
theorists.   the first place the fact that, in a period when demand
                and production are rising in many branches of
industry, producers in branches which have not yet felt an increase in demand are inclined to expect one. The connection between the objective factors (interest rate, etc.) with which the non-psychological theories are concerned and the volume of investment is, as it were, loosened. The response of total investment to changes in the objective factors becomes stronger than " rational " economic considerations would suggest. Professor PIGOU, in this connection, speaks of " errors of optimism ". LAVINGTON likens business-men who infect each other with confidence and optimism to skaters on a pond. " Indeed, the confidence of each skater in his own safety is likely to be reinforced rather than diminished by the presence of numbers of his fellows. . . . The rational judgment that the greater their numbers the greater will be the risk is likely to be submerged by the mere contagion of confidence which persuades him that the greater the numbers the more safely he himself may venture. "[1]

----

[1] *Op. cit.*, pages 32 and 33.

Another point to which the psychological theories direct attention is the fact that, when demand and prices have continued for a while to rise, people get into a habit of expecting more and more confidently a further rise of equal or approximately equal extent—that is to say, they project current experience too confidently into the future. All this leads them to an excessive valuation of capital assets. As Mr. KEYNES says : " It is an essential characteristic of the boom that investments which will in fact yield, say, 2% in conditions of full employment are made in the expectation of a yield of, say, 6%, and are valued accordingly."[1]

Errors of optimism create errors of pessimism. The theorists who stress the psychological factor, especially Professor PIGOU and Mr. KEYNES, point out, furthermore, that the discovery of errors of optimism gives birth to the opposite error of pessimism. Professor PIGOU speaks of " the mutual generation of errors of optimism and pessimism ".[2] The above passage from Mr. KEYNES continues : " When disillusion comes, this (optimistic) expectation is replaced by a contrary ' error of pessimism ', with the result that the investments which would in fact yield 2 % in conditions of full employment are expected to yield less than nothing; and the resulting collapse of new investment then leads to a state of unemployment in which the investment, which would have yielded 2% in conditions of full employment, in fact yields less than nothing."[3]

Professor PIGOU points out that " the extent of the revulsion towards pessimistic error, which follows when optimistic error is disclosed, depends, in part, upon the magnitude of the preceding optimistic error. . . But it is also affected by what one may call the detonation which accompanies the discovery of a given amount of optimistic error. The detonation is greater or less according to the number and scale of the legal bankruptcies into which the detected error explodes. "[4] If the enterprises which are making losses have been financed by the entrepreneurs with

---

[1] *Op. cit.*, page 321.
[2] *Industrial Fluctuations*, Chapter VII.
[3] *Op cit.*, page 322.
[4] *Op. cit.*, page 94.

their own money, the repercussions are less serious than in the case where they have been financed by borrowing, especially by borrowing from the banks.

§ 3.   SUMMARY

Compatibility with other theories.   We can now sum up our analysis of the contribution of the psychological explanation of the cycle and its relation to the non-psychological explanations.

The " psychological " theorists are writers who lay more stress on—or attribute more independent influence to—the " psychological ", as opposed to the " non-psychological ", factors than other theorists. The argument that optimism or pessimism is a contributory factor in the process of expansion or contraction simmers down to the proposition that, for a number of reasons, the reaction of investment to a change in the determinant objective economic factors (interest rate, flow of money, etc.) is likely to be stronger than the analysis of the purely " economic " theories would at first sight suggest.

Mr. HAWTREY, in his review of PIGOU's *Industrial Fluctuations*,[1] endeavours to make the point that optimism and pessimism are wholly dependent on the policy of the banks. People are optimistic, he says, so long as credit expands and consequently demand rises : they become pessimistic when credit is contracted and demand flags. On the whole, this is probably correct. But the fact remains that the reaction of activity (*i.e.*, mainly, of investment activity) to given changes in interest rates and in the demand for consumers' goods, etc., may be different under different circumstances. The " psychological " explanations seek to analyse certain of the more elusive circumstances on which the strength of the reaction depends. In terms of the demand-and-supply schematism of investible funds, we may say that the reference to the psychological factor or factors is to be represented by an accentuation of the shift of the demand curve to the left during the depression and to the right during the upswing of the cycle.

---

[1] *Trade and Credit*, page 168.

There is one other important point. The psychological theories as such are not concerned with specific assumptions as to the nature of the maladjustment which brings about the collapse of the boom. The result of the optimistic error with which the psychological theories are concerned may be shortage of capital, insufficiency of consumers' demand or horizontal misdirection of capital : the " psychological " theory is compatible with any or all of these hypotheses.[1]

---

[1] In the passage quoted, Mr. Keynes seems to suggest that no actual losses are needed to make a boom collapse—*i.e.*, that no maladjustment in the structure of production need occur (where by maladjustment is meant an arrangement of the productive structure which implies losses at least for some firms). A fall in profits, he seems to argue, may be sufficient to make the boom collapse, if, for example, it creates expectations of a further fall in profits to zero or less than zero. This interpretation of Mr. Keynes' theory presents, however, great difficulties, inasmuch as, in his *Treatise on Money*, he defines an entrepreneur making losses as one whose remuneration has fallen to such a level as to induce him to restrict output. The difficulty is perhaps purely verbal, due to a change in his definition of loss and profit. In any case, the idea is not sufficiently developed to admit of fruitful discussion.

CHAPTER 7

HARVEST THEORIES.
AGRICULTURE AND THE BUSINESS CYCLE

§ 1.   INTRODUCTION

Theories of periodic harvest variation.
    The relation between changes in the agricultural situation and industrial fluctuations is much more complicated than many people think. There exist a good many theories on the subject, which are not easy to reconcile though all are either based on, or backed by, statistical research. One group of theories, which includes the writings of W. S. Jevons,[1] H. S. Jevons,[2] and H. L. Moore,[3] seeks to account for the periodicity of business cycles by establishing the existence of a similar periodicity in agricultural output. The chain of causation runs from cosmic influences to weather conditions, from weather conditions to harvests, and from harvests to general business.

The authors of these theories are generally willing to admit that the effects of weather-induced harvest variations may be

---

[1] *The Solar Period and the Price of Corn*, 1875 ; *The Periodicity of Commercial Crises and its Physical Explanation*, 1878 ; and *Commercial Crises and Sun-spots*, 1879—all reprinted in *Investigations in Currency and Finance*, 2nd edition, London, 1909.

[2] *The Causes of Unemployment, The Sun's Heat and Trade Activity*, London, 1910 ; and " Trade Fluctuations and Solar Activity " in *Contemporary Review*, August 1909.

[3] *Economic Cycles : their Law and Cause*, New York, 1914, and *Generating Economic Cycles*, New York, 1923.

partially or totally offset by the effects of other causes, whether causes outside the economic system (wars, revolutions, inventions, currency depreciations and so forth) or causes inherent in the economic system. On the other hand, these factors may also operate to reinforce the harvest variations. W. S. JEVONS suggested on one occasion[1] that " if, then, the English money market is naturally fitted to swing or roll in periods of ten or eleven years, comparatively slight variations in the goodness of harvest repeated at like intervals would suffice to produce those alternations of depression, activity, excitement, and collapse which undoubtedly occur in marked succession ".

Professor H. S. JEVONS believes that the industrial system and the emotional outlook of the business community take longer to revolve than the period of a complete harvest cycle, and that the impulses liberated in two or more harvest cycles accumulate accordingly until a major business cycle is generated.

One consideration which tells against those theories is the absence of agreement as to the exact period of crop variations. W. S. JEVONS based his argument on a crop-cycle of ten and a-half years, Professor H. S. JEVONS on a period of three and a-half years, and Professor H. L. MOORE on an eight-year period. It is, however, conceivable that the same agricultural series may contain fluctuations, or tendencies to fluctuate at intervals of different lengths (*i.e.*, shorter cycles superimposed on longer ones) as also, for that matter, that general business should exhibit a similar tendency. Moreover, different branches of agricultural output show fluctuations of different periods. The crop-fluctuations which had the greatest effect on general business in the eighteenth and early nineteenth centuries may not be same as those which have had the greatest effect in succeeding epochs. The attempt to find an explanation of the changing periods of business cycles on lines consistent with their agricultural origin is not therefore hopeless.

---

[1] In a paper read to the British Association in 1875 on " The Solar Period and the Price of Corn " (in *Investigations in Currency and Finance*, page 185).

Other views
as to the
relation
between
agriculture
and business.

It is not necessary, in order to establish a causal connection between agricultural output and the business cycle, to assume a cyclical movement in agricultural output itself. Fluctuations in crop-yield or in the output of live-stock and animal products may be regarded as analogous to inventions, wars, earthquakes, etc., which appear at irregular intervals, and set in motion cumulative processes of expansion or contraction in the industrial system, or alternatively reinforce or retard a concurrent expansion or contraction. Harvest fluctuations which do not happen to coincide with a turning-point in the business cycle will tend rather to disturb the periodicity of the cycle than to determine it.

The above may be presumed to be the view taken by Professor PIGOU[1] and Professor ROBERTSON,[2] since, though they treat harvest variations as important potential causes operating to precipitate cumulative upward and downward movements, they attribute to these cumulative processes a life of their own with periods determined—in part—by psychological and other factors and in any case with no relation to the periods of crop-fluctuations. Professor SPIETHOFF,[3] for his part, speaks of good harvests and innovations as two amongst many possible initiating factors of industrial expansion. But none of these writers can be represented as putting forward an " agricultural theory " of the trade-cycle. They do not ignore the agricultural factors; but they combine them with other factors in integrated but flexible schemes, in which allowance is made for various processes of response—monetary, psychological and technical.

There is a third view, held mainly by American economists such as Professors A. HANSEN[4] and J. M. CLARK,[5] which denies that fluctuations in agricultural output are among the causes of the cyclical fluctuation of business. Agriculture, these writers say,

---

[1] *Industrial Fluctuations.*

[2] *A Study of Industrial Fluctuation* and *Banking Policy and the Price Level.*

[3] Article "Krisen" in "Handwörterbuch der Staatswissenschaften."

[4] "The Business Cycle in its Relation to Agriculture" in *Journal of Farm Economics*, 1932.

[5] *Strategic Factors in the Business Cycle.*

is not an active but a passive element. The very inelasticity of agricultural supply exposes the farming community to considerable instability of income as a result of changes in demand arising out of trade fluctuations brought about by internal forces of the business economy. In the words of Professor HANSEN, agriculture is the " football of business ".

Compatibility of different theories. These three points of view are not necessarily mutually exclusive. It is possible to reconcile a general lack of response on the part of agricultural output to changes in demand with occasional or periodic spontaneous variations which may have an effect on business. The writers of the second and third groups referred to are probably not so much at odds on the theory as on the statistical question whether the influence of agricultural fluctuations can in fact be traced in business indices.

It is a more serious shortcoming of these " agricultural " theories that they are not agreed on the important point as to whether plentiful harvests are correlated with prosperity and poor harvests with depression, or the other way round; and their divergence in this respect is symptomatic of a fundamental disagreement as to the channels by which the influence of agricultural fluctuations is brought to bear on other departments of economic life.

We have therefore, if we are to investigate the problem systematically, to consider the various possible ways in which (1) agricultural fluctuations can influence general business and (2) industrial fluctuations can influence agriculture.

§ 2. HOW AGRICULTURAL FLUCTUATIONS INFLUENCE INDUSTRY AND TRADE

Assumption of a closed economy. Here, as in so many departments of economic theory, it is necessary to begin with the consideration of a closed economic system. The world economy as a whole has to be brought under review before it is possible to discuss the relationship of parts of the whole (*e.g.*, single countries) with the rest of the world. The following enumeration of the repercussions (through all the different channels) of fluctuations in agricultural output relates, therefore, in the first instance (sections A to H) to a self-sufficient economic system.   In section I, the position is considered from the standpoint of the external trade relations of an individual country.

Professors PIGOU and ROBERTSON link up harvest
A.   "*Real*" variations and industrial fluctuations by arguments
elasticity   appropriate to an economic system without a
theories.   common medium of exchange (*i.e.*, a barter economy),
and then proceed to take account of the modifications introduced into the relationship by the fact that economic incentives present themselves in a money form.

The successive steps of the argument, as culled from various chapters of Professor PIGOU's *Industrial Fluctuations* and his *Theory of Unemployment*, seem to be as follows.

An exceptionally good harvest leads to a larger demand on the part of agriculturists in terms of agricultural produce for the products of industry.[1]

In so far as this raises the real income of the community, it will lead to an increase in the supply of new capital from savings, a downward tendency in interest rates and an increase in the demand for labour in terms of wage-goods.[2]

In so far as it involves an increase in the employers' expectations of the yield of labour in terms of goods in general, the rise in the agricultural demand for industrial products will increase the employers' demand for capital and *pro tanto*—whether the demand is satisfied out of stocks or savings—the demand for labour in terms of wage-goods.[3]   Whether the big harvest will in fact increase the employers' expectations of the " real " yield of labour depends, according to Professor PIGOU, on the "elasticity of the general demand for agricultural produce ".   He writes : " If the general demand for agricultural produce is highly inelastic—*i.e.*, has an elasticity less than unity—the enlarged amount of agricultural produce obtainable " for a unit of industrial output represents,

---

[1] *Industrial Fluctuations*, 2nd ed., Chapter IV, page 41.
[2] *Ibid.*, Chapter III, page 20.
[3] *Ibid.*, Chapters III and XI.

" not an enlarged, but a diminished amount of things in general ". In this case there will not be any increased willingness to save nor yet any increased expectation of yield to induce employers to borrow more for the purpose of increasing their real demand for labour.[1]

Supposing, however, that the general demand for agricultural products is elastic, the increase in the demand for labour in terms of wage-goods will lead to more employment for the reason that the supply-schedule of labour, thanks to the rigidity of wage rates, is highly elastic.[2]

So far, the analysis proceeds on the assumption of a purely barter economy. The following is Professor PIGOU's adaptation of the argument to a money economy.

The additional borrowing requirements of the employers, induced by their improved expectations of yield, are satisfied partly by the banks. The result is a monetary expansion of a cumulative nature which, in a variety of ways, enhances the demand for labour in terms of wage-goods and thus increases industrial output.[3]

Since workers under the influence of the " money illusion " are willing to accept lower real wages if they appear in the shape of rising prices, the rise in prices which results from monetary expansion has the effect of increasing the supply of labour available at a given real wage. Hence, industrial activity responds more sharply to an increase in the real demand of the agriculturists.[4]

Elasticity of demand in terms of money and of " effort ".
This argument is obscured by the ambiguity of the phrase " elasticity of the general demand for agricultural produce ". Normally, we think of an elasticity of demand in terms of money; but it might be translated into " real " terms as relating to the quantity of industrial produce, the use or consumption of which the industrial population as a whole is willing to forgo in exchange for varying quantities of agricultural produce, the total production of industrial produce remaining unchanged.

---

[1] *Industrial Fluctuations*, 2nd ed., page 41.
[2] *Ibid.*, Chapter II, page 20, and Chapter XX.
[3] *Ibid.*, Chapter III, page 33, Chapters XVI and XVII, etc.
[4] *Theory of Unemployment*, Part IV and Part V, Chapter IX.

This would seem the most natural interpretation of the phrase. But an examination of the footnote on page 42, and of the whole discussion in Chapter V, of PIGOU's *Industrial Fluctuations* shows that PIGOU supposes any increase or diminution in the amount of industrial goods offered for agricultural produce to represent an equivalent increase or diminution in the production of industrial goods. In this case, "elasticity of demand for agricultural produce" seems to relate to the total amount of effort or activity industrialists will undertake to produce goods for their own consumption and for exchange against varying quantities of agricultural produce. Thus, by assuming the elasticity of the industrialists for agricultural products in terms of effort as given, Professor PIGOU assumes a knowledge of how total industrial output changes in response to changes in the harvest. But it is this magnitude which the theory is concerned to discover. It is the unknown quantity. It must not be assumed in advance.

It is only when interpreted in the first sense mentioned above —viz., in terms of money (or its complement in real terms)—that the phrase "elasticity of demand" can play a useful rôle in the explanation of the repercussions on industry of agricultural fluctuations. But, a soon as "elasticity of demand" is thus interpreted, we are confronted with the difficulty that movements in the *money* demand for industrial labour vary in the contrary direction to the "*real*" demand in the sense in which the term "real" is employed by Professor PIGOU. He says that the increased supply of agricultural produce represents an increased "real" demand for industrial produce (and gives rise to an increased "real" demand for labour) only if the demand for agricultural produce is elastic. But these are the very circumstances in which the *money* demand for industrial output will diminish, since a greater proportion of expenditure goes in such case to agricultural produce : and, since wage-earners respond primarily to the money demand for labour, an *elastic* demand for agricultural produce in terms of money and of goods already produced means an *inelastic* demand in terms of effort and employment.

Similar difficulties and ambiguities are encountered in connection with Professor ROBERTSON's treatment of the problem in his *Banking Policy and the Price Level*. He enquires by what process, and with what price accompaniments, a given response in industrial output (represented by iron) to enhanced agricultural output (represented by wheat), such as would take place in barter conditions, will be reached under the operation of this or that policy on the part of the monetary authority. He realises, and expressly states, that " iron-makers " react more readily to increased money receipts than to falling prices in the objects of expenditure : but, for him, the money demand for iron depends only on the *effort*-elasticity of the demand for wheat and the general price-level as determined by monetary policy. He appears to overlook the fact that the buyer's elasticity of demand for wheat in terms of iron —in the absence of any change in the total money demand— influences the money demand for, and supply of, iron and *pro tanto* the effort-elasticity of the iron-makers' demand for wheat.

In a monetary economy, it is never possible to take the effort-elasticity of the demand for a particular commodity—or, generally, of the demand of industry as a whole for agricultural produce— as a psychological datum, as it is convenient to do in the case of the elasticities of buyers' demand for a single good. Producers are stimulated almost entirely by monetary incentives, so that a long process of analysis by progressive stages, coupled with assumptions as to the operation of the monetary factors throughout, is required if it is desired to arrive at conclusions as to the actual effort-elasticity of demand in any given case. It is not therefore permissible, in order to indicate the probable consequences on industry of agricultural fluctuations, to assume a particular effort-elasticity from the start; for this is equivalent to assuming the solution of the problem. Nor is it permissible to estimate the effort-elasticity of demand from actual experience of how industrial production has responded to agricultural fluctuations, and to proceed to treat the estimate as a relatively stable psychological function, independent of monetary conditions.

B. Influence on industries using agricultural raw materials. Changes in agricultural output of all sorts exercise a dominating influence over those industries which utilise agricultural raw material, such as the food and textile industries, as also the industries engaged in the handling and transportation of the crop or animal produce.

The nexus between an industry and its source of raw materials is necessarily very close.   In the absence of surplus stocks which can be drawn on, a short crop will restrict the activity of the industry which it serves.   A bumper crop will lower the price of the raw material in relation to that of the finished product, till either the manufacturers decide to absorb it all by increased output or the holders decide to keep the surplus in store.   In any case, the activity of the later stages will be increased, because the holding of stocks never completely offsets harvest fluctuations.

Transport concerns which are accustomed to handle agricultural produce are in much the same position *vis-à-vis* crop fluctuations as are the industries utilising the produce as raw material.

C. Influence on real wages.   In dealing with the " effort-elasticity " theories, it was pointed out that the supply of labour varied rather with the money demand for labour than with the demand in terms of goods and services.   But the " real " equivalent of the money wage is not something quite irrelevant to the incentive to work or to accept employment.   If, for example, food prices fall, it may be easier to reduce money wages or to prevent them from rising, and *vice versa* if food prices go up.   This is particularly likely to be the case where wage-scales are based on cost-of-living indices.   On the whole, however, this factor is probably of little practical importance in the short run.

D. Migration of labour between town and countryside.   There is another channel by which the industrial labour supply may conceivably be influenced by good and bad crops.   Most crops taken individually, and certainly agricultural production as a whole, have to face an inelastic demand (in terms of money) on the part of consumers who have the choice between agricultural and non-agricultural commodities.   Therefore, good crops mean low farm incomes. It is conceivable that a fall in agricultural incomes may give rise to an exodus of labour from agriculture to industry.   The process is known to work in the opposite direction in many countries, where the agricultural labour supply varies with industrial prosperity. The converse movement, though rarer, is not unknown.

The more contentious questions arise when we
E. *Effects on* come to deal with the effects of crop fluctuations
non-agricultu- on industries not utilising agricultural raw materials.
ral consumers' These may be divided for convenience into con-
goods sumers' goods industries and producers' goods
industries. industries, or again into industries serving the
agricultural population and industries serving the
nonagricultural population. It may fairly be assumed that, except
in advanced phases of expansion, the elasticity of supply of goods
in face of an increase in the money demand is considerable.

The effect of a big harvest on non-agricultural consumers' goods
industries will depend on whether the money demand for consumers' goods of agricultural origin is elastic or not. The *less*
elastic it is the *more* probable it is that the big harvest and the
consequent fall in the price of food will result in a diversion of
demand from food to non-agricultural goods, inducing a rise in
the supply of the latter, the extent of which depends on supply
conditions. The same is true, *mutatis mutandis*, of poor harvests.

While there may be a general tendency for crop
F. *Farmers'* changes to affect non-agricultural consumers' goods
purchasing industries as a whole in a given direction, a distinc-
power. tion must be made between those which supply the
agricultural population and those which supply the
non-agricultural population. It is often asserted that changes in
agricultural output affect general business by changing the purchasing power of the agriculturist. Good harvests either increase
or diminish the farmer's income, according as the elasticity of
demand is greater or less than unity, and so affect the prosperity
of the branches of industry which serve his needs. It is clear,
however, that this argument in itself proves nothing. For what
the farmer loses in purchasing power other people are bound to
gain, and *vice versa*. Business flags in the case of the industries
supplying the farmer, but is brisk in the case of the industries
supplying other people. The net result of this redistribution of
purchasing power will depend on the concrete situation,
the phase of the trade cycle, the credit situation in the
various countries and localities affected by the redistribution, and
so on.

G. *Effects on investment.*

It is important to consider the effect of crop fluctuations on investment both because of the initial effect on the activity of investment-goods industries and because of the indirect effect on monetary expansion or contraction in subsequent periods. Roughly speaking, the following may be expected to be the effects of a good harvest, for which the demand in money terms is inelastic :

(*a*) A fall in investment by agricultural producers;

(*b*) A rise in investment by industries transporting and utilising the crop;

(*c*) A rise in investment by consumers' goods industries not utilising agricultural materials, particularly those not serving the agricultural population;

(*d*) A change in the amount of investment in holding stocks of agricultural produce. This aspect has recently been stressed by Mr. KEYNES.[1] A distinction must be made between the initial effect occurring immediately after the harvest (which will probably be a fall in the value, as distinct from the physical quantity, of stocks held as compared with a normal year) and the subsequent effect (which may be an increase in the value of the carry-over).

Strictly speaking, these movements refer less to investments than to the " tendency to invest ", or the demand for investment funds. To what extent this demand will be satisfied, and the tendency to invest take the shape of actual investment, depends on the elasticity of the supply of investible funds in the various countries concerned. It is not impossible, for example, that a violent redistribution of incomes between agriculturists and others, accompanied by a flow of money from agricultural to non-agricultural countries, or *vice versa*, might ultimately result in a deflationary shock to the credit system, which would tend to neutralise any increased demand for investible funds that might be simultaneously engendered.

---

[1] *The General Theory of Employment, Interest and Money*, pages 329 *et seq.*

Before any conclusions can be drawn as to the
H. Effects further consequences of crop fluctuations on the
on saving. industrial economy by way of cumulative monetary
expansion or contraction, the effects on investment
must be compared with the effects on saving. An excess of
investment over saving would generate an expansion, while an
excess of saving over investment would cause a contraction.
Mr. J. H. KIRK[1] bases his conclusions as to the deflationary
effects of big harvests on the tendency of consumers to save a
part of the extra purchasing power accruing to them through
the fall in agricultural prices. Obviously, no conclusion as to
the net effect can be drawn *a priori* : but, in any concrete case,
the attempt must be made to strike a balance between all the
tendencies towards changes in investment and all the tendencies
towards changes in saving. As was pointed out, tendencies
towards increased investment, in conjunction with an elastic
credit-supply, engender monetary expansion, while tendencies
towards increased saving, if unaccompanied by increased
investment, engender monetary contraction.

We may now pass from the analysis of the effects
I. Inter- of fluctuations in the total crop of a self-sufficing
national economy on the industrial activity of that economy
aspects. as a whole to an examination of the effects of
fluctuations in the crop of a geographical subdivision of the total economy (a district or country) on the industrial
activity of that subdivision.

The elasticity of demand for the crops of a single country (in
terms of international money) is of course much greater than that
for the crops of the world as a whole : and the smaller the country,
and the more perfect the world market for the crops, the greater
the elasticity of the demand. It is greater, for example, in the
case of New Zealand than in the case of the United States of
America, and greater in the case of wheat than in the case of most
animal products. Thus, in many or most cases, an increase in
the crop of one country, unaccompanied by any change in the
crops of other countries, will result in an increase in the money

---

[1] *Agriculture and the Trade Cycle*, London, 1933.

receipts of the agriculturists in the country concerned. (If the elasticity of demand is less than unity, agriculturists elsewhere will lose to a more than equivalent extent.) Furthermore, a given increase in the money receipts of the agriculturists will mean an even greater increase in the money receipts of the country as a whole, since the home population will be spending less than before on farm products and (probably) more than before on home industrial products, so that both the agriculturists and industrialists will rejoice in increased receipts—and that increase can only come from outside.

This initial increase in the receipts and incomes of the country which has been blessed by a good crop will provide an inflationary stimulus to the industry of that country (though we must take account of the continual " leakage " of purchasing power abroad). It will be gathered from the new considerations thus introduced in the argument that conclusions as to the general effect on world industry of a net world crop variation cannot be drawn from a comparison between the agricultural fluctuations of any given country and the industrial activity of that country. In the case of countries like Australia, New Zealand, Roumania, Argentine, Canada, etc., this is obvious; but it is often lost sight of, particularly in the case of the United States.

Summary. It will be apparent that the channels through which fluctuations in agricultural output (good and bad harvests) exercise their effect upon the economic system in general and industrial activity in particular are no other than those with which we have become familiar in the perusal of the various theories discussed in the earlier sections of this work. The several processes of monetary expansion and contraction originating in the varying demand for capital, of over-saving resulting from plenty, and of the dependence of investment on consumers' demand—to each of which a varying degree of importance is attached by the different schools of thought—are all relevant to the problem. There can be no " agriculture theory " of the cycle in the sense of an alternative to, say, the monetary theory or the over-investment theory any more than there can be an " invention theory " or an " earthquake theory ". All that can be attempted in this direction is to bring out the importance of agricultural fluctuations as one amongst other potential stimuli in the economic system. What has been said of agriculture and the trade cycle might be said with scarcely any modification of inventions and the trade cycle, or even of earthquakes or wars and the trade cycle.

It will be observed that no attempt has been made to strike a balance between the arguments for and against the proposition that good harvests are good for trade and bad harvests bad. On the whole, the arguments in favour of the proposition that good harvests have a stimulating effect dominate the literature on the subject, though the opposite view is not without support. There is of course very little doubt that a good harvest in a particular country tends to stimulate the business life of that country. The problem only becomes obscure when a completely closed economy is the object of study.

A priori, analysis cannot settle the question, because forces are released which pull in opposite directions; and only estimates of the quantitative importance of the different factors—effect on investment, effect on saving, effect on the credit structure, etc.— can supply a basis for judgment as to which tendency will prevail. Much probably depends on the phase of the business cycle in which the disturbance occurs. It is conceivable that a good harvest may exercise now a stimulating and now a depressing influence according to the phase of the cycle and the portions of the earth's surface and the world's population affected. Nor must it be too readily assumed that a good wheat crop and a good cotton crop have the same kind of effect. After it has been decided in all the different possible cases whether the influence of crop-fluctuations on general business is positive or negative and whether that influence is important enough to outweigh other influences operating simultaneously, it will still remain to consider to what degree crop fluctuations are cyclical and, if they are cyclical, to what degree they are spontaneous and independent of the general business cycle.

§ 3.   INFLUENCE OF THE BUSINESS CYCLE ON AGRICULTURE

Inelasticity of farm output.
As each part of the economic system is to some degree sensitive to developments in all other parts, industrial fluctuations are bound to exercise a certain influence on agriculture.   This influence operates through the demand for, and price of, agricultural produce on the incomes of the agricultural classes.   If there was a fairly immediate and substantial reaction on the part of agricultural output to the movements in monetary demand, there would be no reason why the trade cycle should be regarded as a primarily industrial phenomenon.   In fact, however, agricultural output is, on the whole, so unresponsive to money incentives that the trade cycle is often regarded as confined (so far as production is concerned) to industry, and in particular to that branch of industry which is not supplied with its raw materials by agriculture —namely, the production of durable and investment goods.   It is not, however, altogether impossible that industrial fluctuations may influence agricultural output in the long run, though only after a period so long that the words " response " or " elasticity of supply " cease to have much meaning.   The " responses " in such case will have the same effect as spontaneous variations in output.   On the other hand, industrial fluctuations will affect both the demand for agricultural products and—to a lesser degree —their cost of production.

Effect on demand.
Many writers, including L. H. BEAN,[1] J. M. CLARK,[2] A. HANSEN[3] and J. H. KIRK,[4] recognise the important influence exercised on agricultural incomes by fluctuations in industrial activity accompanied by similar fluctuations in money demand in general.   There is a

---

[1] *E.g.*, "Post-War Interrelations between Agriculture and Business in the United States," *U.S. Department of Agriculture, Bureau of Agricultural Economics* I.9.Ec.752.Pa.

[2] *Strategic Factors in the Business Cycle.*

[3] "The Business Cycle in its Relation to Agriculture" in *Journal of Farm Economics*, 14 : 59-68, 1932.

[4] *Agriculture and the Trade Cycle*, Part I.

relationship of reciprocal causation (as will be shown in Part II of this work) between increasing supplies of effective money and increasing industrial activity; and the same holds true of the downswing. In view of the importance to consumers of products manufactured with agricultural raw materials, it is not surprising that part of the general rise and fall in *money* demand should be passed on to agriculture. But the process is tempered by two factors :

(1) The demand for consumers' goods as a whole is more stable than the demand for all goods;

(2) The demand for consumers' goods of agricultural origin is more stable than that for consumers' goods as a whole.

On the other hand, the inelasticity in the supply of agricultural output tends to make the fluctuations in demand greater, at least in the first instance, than they might otherwise be.

The close correlation between agricultural prices and industrial activity, due to the causal connection between industrial activity and the demand for agricultural produce, may be taken by the unwary as a proof that low agricultural prices and incomes, due presumably to agricultural over-production, are responsible for low industrial activity.

Effect on costs. The cost items of agriculture are largely of agricultural origin; and to some extent they will vary with the demand for agricultural produce—the variation being only another aspect of the inelasticity of the supply.

To some extent, however, industry competes with agriculture for factors of production; and this competition may be so strong as to force a reduction of agricultural output when demand is high, and *vice versa*.

(1) With respect to the supply of implements and the investment funds for buying them, it seems probable that the farmers' increased desire to acquire instruments in good times will outweigh the competitive demand of industry for both of these things. The farmer can finance increased purchase in part from his own increased earnings.

(2) On the other hand, there is an important tendency in many countries for labour to be drained off from agriculture to industry during boom periods and to flow back during slumps.[1]

Concluding remarks. The above review of the possible interactions of agriculture and industry on one another cannot be said to yield a clear picture. Industrial crises may arise for monetary or other causes, and then work out their effects on agricultural incomes and—to a lesser extent, and by obscure channels—on agricultural output.

Spontaneous agricultural fluctuations may have a positive or a negative effect on the general business cycle and on monetary demand and may react back on agriculture through this channel. Lastly, variations, however caused, in the demand for and cost of agricultural produce may, after a time, give rise to variations in agricultural output which will act on industry like spontaneous disturbances, and set up a vicious circle of expansion or contraction.

---

[1] See, especially, Gustav Cassel : *The Theory of Social Economy*, Vol. II, Book IV, Chapter XV, § 65.

CHAPTER 8

SOME RECENT DISCUSSIONS
RELATING TO THE THEORY OF THE TRADE CYCLE

_____

§ 1.   INTRODUCTION

The greater part of the literature to be discussed
General nature in this chapter emanates from, and centres around,
of the Mr. KEYNES' *General Theory of Employment, Interest*
literature *and Money.* It is not all business-cycle theory in
reviewed. a strict sense, but rather general economic theory
dealing with analytical tools which may be used
for trade-cycle analysis as well as for other purposes. To a
large extent, the theories to be discussed are not even of a dynamic
nature, but are static-equilibrium theories. (This point will come
up for detailed discussion in § 6 of this chapter.)

For a number of reasons, it is very difficult to review these
theories. First, they are comparatively young and have not yet
found anything like a definitive formulation. They are still in the
process of development and clarification; there exist, and continue
to appear, versions [1] which are by no means identical in all respects.
The points at issue are frequently very subtle, and the argument
necessarily becomes complicated and involved.

_____

[1] *Cf.* mainly contributions by various writers to recent issues of the
*Economic Journal, Econometrica, Economica, Zeitschrift für National-
ökonomie, Quarterly Journal of Economics,* etc.

Differences in terminology versus differences in substance.

Secondly, these theories suffer from the fact that their authors have not been able to make clear in all cases whether apparent differences between their views and those of other writers rest on different empirical assumptions or only on a different usage of terms; in other words, whether differences are of a material kind or of a purely terminological nature. There can be no doubt that, in recent years, the discussions on saving and investment and the possibility of their being unequal, on hoarding, liquidity-preference and the rate of interest, and similar topics, have made it increasingly evident that purely verbal misunderstandings and slight differences in the definition of terms have played a very great rôle.[1] The exaggerated impression of importance which prevailed with respect to the real (as against purely terminological) differences between different schools of thought, especially between what some writers[2] like to call the " classical " and the " modern " view, has already been modified. But it is safe to assume that this process of terminological clarification is not yet completed, and it is hoped that the present chapter will do a little to hasten it.

Even in those instances where the new theories amount to nothing more than a terminological innovation and cannot be said to be in material contradiction to the traditional views, they have sometimes served a useful purpose, by bringing to light hidden implications in the older theoretical schemes and forcing the propounders of " rival " theories to make all their assumptions clear and explicit.

All this will be illustrated in the following sections.

---

[1] Professor Robertson has recently made an attempt at separating terminological from substantial differences. *Cf.* " A Survey of Modern Monetary Controversy " in *The Manchester School*, Vol. 9, No. 1, April 1938.

[2] *Cf.*, for example, A. P. Lerner : " Alternative Formulations of the Theory of Interest " in the *Economic Journal*, Vol. 48, June 1938, *passim.*

§ 2. SAVING AND INVESTMENT[1]

Everyday meaning of S and I ambiguous. In preceding chapters, we have repeatedly had occasion to speak of saving and investment, and differences between them, without giving a precise definition of these terms. The reason is that the writers whose theories have been reviewed have refrained from giving careful definitions of the terms, consistent with the use to which those terms are put. They evidently thought they could safely rely on the everyday meaning of these terms.

The discussions in recent years have clearly shown that this is not the case. Not only is the everyday meaning of these terms not unambiguous—different writers interpret it in different ways—but also it has been demonstrated that one particular definition, which it is fair to call a good *prima-facie* formulation of the everyday meaning of those terms, makes it impossible to speak of differences between saving and investment, because, on that definition, S and I are not only equal by definition, but are in reality the same thing.

Neo-Wicksellian usage of S and I. In the Neo-Wicksellian literature and related writings reviewed above (Chapter 3) under the title of " The Over-investment Theories ", it is usual to speak of differences between S and I. Phrases such as the following occur again and again : " Investment may be financed, not only out of (voluntary) saving, but by inflation ", " out of newly created money ", " out of hoards ". Conversely : " Not all the current savings need be invested ", " a part of them may go into hoards ", " may disappear in the banking system ", " may be used for repaying bank loans " and thus " run to waste ".

---

[1] In the following pages, we shall frequently use the following symbols :
S = Saving, I = Investment, Y = Income, C = Consumption.

Equality of S and I has been used as a criterion of equilibrium.[1] Any divergence between S and I means a disruption of equilibrium. If I exceeds S, we get inflation; an excess of S over I means deflation. Prosperity periods are caused, or at least characterised, by an excess of I over S; depression periods, by an excess of S over I. This language is irresistibly convenient and seems to express very realistically what actually happens during the upswing and the downswing of the cycle respectively.

Mr. Keynes'   It has, however, been questioned by Mr. KEYNES
equality of   and his followers.[2] Why is it considered fallacious ?
S and I.   That is very simple to explain. We have only to reflect for a moment on what we really mean by S and I. Mr. KEYNES' definitions are these : For the economy as a whole—just as for any individual—saving is that part of total income which is not spent on consumption : $S = Y - C$. Investment is that part of total output (in value terms) which is not consumed : $I = $ Output $ - C$. On the other hand, income of society as a whole is defined as the value of output. Therefore $I = Y - C$. Hence, $S = I$.[3]

If we accept these definitions, which appear *prima facie* to correspond quite well to the everyday meaning of the terms, S and I are necessarily equal over any period of time, because they are identically defined : both of them as $Y - C$. It then becomes nonsensical to speak of, or to imply, differences between them.

---

[1] The use of the equality of saving and investment as an equilibrium condition has been ably criticised by W. Fellner in his article " Saving, Investment and the Problem of Neutral Money " in *Review of Economic Statistics*, Vol. XIII, November 1938.

[2] See especially : Keynes, *General Theory, passim* ; A. P. Lerner, " Saving equals Investment " in *Quarterly Journal of Economics*, Vol. 52, February 1938, and " Mr. Keynes' General Theory of Employment " in *International Labour Review*, October 1936 ; Mrs. J. Robinson, *Introduction to the Theory of Employment* (London, 1937), especially pages 14 to 16, " The Hoarding Fallacy " ; R. F. Kahn's review of the first edition of the present book in the *Economic Journal*, Vol. 47, 1937, page 671 ; and R. F. Harrod, *The Trade Cycle*, London, 1936, pages 65 *et seq.*

[3] *General Theory*, page 63.

Now a number of questions arise which will be
Controversial taken up one after the other. *First*, some readers,
issues. who are accustomed to speak of differences between
I and S, would probably like to see how, in typical
cases, the equality of I and S works out in detail. Such an analysis
will reveal that the definitions given above are, after all, not always
in harmony with the everyday usage of the terms.

Secondly, the question arises as to how S and I can be re-defined
so as to make sense of the whole body of doctrine which speaks of
differences between them. We shall see that this can be and has
been done in several ways, and that it would be superficial to
dismiss as meaningless all theories which imply a difference between
S and I, even if some of the theorists in question may have care-
lessly defined them in such a way that they are necessarily equal.

Thirdly, it might be asked whether, if we adopt Mr. KEYNES'
definitions, S and I are not, in reality, identical rather than necessarily equal. Do S and I not really denote, are they not only
different symbols for, the same thing—unconsumed output ? If
that is so, why retain two terms ? Why not drop the one or use
them interchangeably ?

Let us first do some exercises in the application
How S and I of our definitions by discussing a few typical cases.
are equated Assume that new investments are made either by
in the case the Government or by private producers and that
of inflation. they are financed by the creation of new money;
for example, a factory or a railroad is being constructed. Suppose that there are unemployed workers and idle
resources, so that total production can easily be expanded. The
money is created by the banks and handed over to the entrepreneur
(or the Government) either as a short-term loan or by purchasing
long-dated securities, new ones or old ones which have so far been
in the possession of the constructor of the railroad.

There is then a certain amount of (new) investment, but, if
we adopt Mr. KEYNES' definitions of I and S, we are precluded
from saying that these new investments have been financed by
" inflation ", instead of by " voluntary " saving.[1] According to

---

[1] I put " inflation " in quotation marks, because some writers would
like to reserve the word " inflation " to such an increase in the quantity

Mr. KEYNES' and his followers' account of the matter, there must be somewhere savings corresponding to the amount of new investment. Where are they ? The answer has been given most clearly by Mr. HARROD. " For a few days, the whole of the new net investment may be financed by those who receive the money; before they begin to spend that money, they save what they receive. "[1] That is to say, the workers who are engaged in constructing the railroad are said to save the money which they receive, say, on Saturday until they spend it during the following week. If they keep all the money over night, they are said to have saved it. When they then gradually spend it on consumers' goods and consume these latter, they are said to dissave. The expressions " receiving " and " spending " are replaced by " saving " and " dissaving ". But when people thus dissave, " the stocks of consumption goods will be depleted; this involves disinvestment. "[2] So the new investment is first matched by saving and then cancelled by disinvestment; S is always equal to I. If, on the other hand, the production of consumption goods increases *pari passu* with the rising demand (by chance, or because producers have correctly foreseen the coming rise in demand), there is no disinvestment to cancel the original new investment; but, since the new money must always be somewhere, those people who hold it and have not yet passed it on are said to perform the necessary saving.

This account of the matter may seem strange; it is not usual to say that the savings which finance the construction of new capital are provided by the workers who are engaged in that construction job and not by those who provide the money which

---

of money as leads to a rise, or to an " excessive " rise, in prices ; they resent the use of the word for cases where the increased amount of money (or of monetary demand) is matched by an increase in the flow of goods and hence does not bring about a rise in prices. (*Cf.*, for example, Mr. Kahn's review of the first edition of this book in the *Economic Journal*, Vol. 47, 1937, page 675, and my answer, *ibid*, Vol. 48, 1938, pages 326 and 327.)

[1] *The Trade Cycle*, page 72.

[2] *Ibid.*, page 72. If prices of consumers' goods rise, the income and savings of the retailers go up.

is used to hire those workers. It is furthermore not in accord with the everyday usage of the terms to say that a man saves if he keeps his income in the form of money for a short time, owing to the simple fact that income is paid out discontinuously and spent more continuously. Only if it is kept unspent for longer than the usual income period, would one ordinarily say that it has been saved.

It must, however, be admitted that this unusual way of putting the matter follows from the literal application of the definition : $S = Y - C$. On Saturday evening, the income of the worker has increased; his consumption has not yet gone up; hence he has saved.[1] We have here an example where this *prima facie* plausible definition of S diverges clearly from the everyday meaning of the term.[2]

---

[1] Mr. Lerner admits that " if we take artificial periods—say of ten minutes each—our definitions acquire an artificial flavour too. We would then have to say that in the ten-minute period in which a man receives his weekly wage, he saves (nearly) all of it, and that in all the other ten-minute periods in which he makes any expenditure, he dissaves " (*Quarterly Journal of Economics*, Vol. 52, 1938, page 304.) Mr. Lerner is, however, not right when he says that this artificiality disappears " if we take reasonable periods ". Owing to the overlapping of periods, it never disappears completely. Moreover, the order of magnitude of the phenomenon in question is not correctly indicated by speaking of ten-minute periods.

[2] Sometimes another account of how S and I are equated has been given by followers of Mr. Keynes. For instance, Mrs. J. Robinson, in her *Introduction to the Theory of Employment*, puts the matter in the following way. Assume £1 per week is invested in housebuilding. Then make certain assumptions about the saving by the successive recipients of the money. " At each round ", a certain proportion is saved by workers, profit earners, etc. On this assumption, the author constructs a series of acts of saving which add up exactly to the figure of investment outlay (pages 20 and 21). If by " round ", turnover (change of hand) of money is meant, and if money does not circulate with infinite rapidity, this account of the matter proves the contrary to what it is intended to prove. For it takes time (strictly speaking, an infinite period of time under Mrs. Robinson's assumption) before the savings made at successive rounds add up to the total which is equal to the investment. What can be said is that there is a tendency for S to approach I, but owing (a) to the infinite length of these series and (b) to the overlapping of series set up by successive acts of investment, there can never, or only under very special assumptions, be an absolute equality of S and I.

Let us now consider the converse case, where
How S and I money is withdrawn from circulation. Let us
are equated assume that some people do not spend the whole of
in the case their income, or more generally of their money
of deflation. receipts,[1] and accumulate cash or idle deposits.

This has been conveniently expressed by saying
that saving exceeds investment, because part of the savings are
hoarded[2] instead of being invested.

According to Mr. Keynes' definition of saving and investment,
this way of describing the matter is no longer permissible. There
can be no divergence between S and I. How are they then equated
in this case ? The answer is very simple. If some people save
part of their income and keep it in liquid form, one of two things,
or a combination of them, must happen : either goods which
otherwise would have been sold accumulate and that constitutes
investment which corresponds to the saving, or else sales are
maintained at the former level by cutting prices, and the retailers
suffer losses; these losses reduce their income—and hence their
saving—by an amount equal to the original decrease in spending.[3]
Hence, the original saving is cancelled by an equal decrease in
saving (which, if we start from a position of zero saving, becomes
negative—dissaving) by somebody else.

---

[1] Not all money received by an individual or a firm is (net) income.
Part of the receipts of a producer is to be set aside for the replacement of
capital, either of working capital or of fixed capital. In the first case, it
is sometimes said that the money constitutes " working capital " ; in
the second case, we speak of " depreciation allowances " or " amortisation quotas ". Naturally, the more durable a capital instrument is,
the greater is the freedom and arbitrariness in distributing over the
period of its life-time the corresponding amortisation allowances. Therefore many writers (for example, Mr. Hawtrey) define gross income
inclusive of depreciation allowances. It should, however, not be forgotten·
that the transition from fixed to working capital is gradual and that, in
principle, the same problems are involved in the replacement of either.

[2] It should be noted how easy it is to describe the phenomenon without
using the words " saving " and " investment " in terms of receiving and
spending of money.

[3] It could be objected that a retailer may cut his consumption and
maintain his saving. This is quite true, but this further decrease in
consumers' outlay (act of saving) can be treated exactly as the original
one : it must again reduce somebody else's income and cannot give rise
to a divergence between S and I.

It seems to be pretty clear that there is no real problem at issue between those who speak of a difference between S and I and those who maintain that S and I must be equal. Both schools speak about the same phenomenon in different terminologies. No statements about facts are disputed, for what may happen if some people reduce their rate of spending is *assumed* and can be described in a neutral terminology which avoids the word "saving" and uses instead the terms "receipt" and "expenditure" of money.

Alternative definitions. There remains, however, the question of how saving and investment should be defined to enable us to be consistent in speaking about differences between them.

Three sets of definitions under which S need not be equal to I will be discussed : first, Mr. KEYNES' definitions of S and I as given in his *Treatise on Money*; secondly, Professor ROBERTSON's "period analysis"; and, thirdly, the Swedish distinction between *ex ante* and *ex post* saving and investment, which is also made by Mr. HAWTREY.

The terminology of Mr. Keynes' Treatise on Money. It was Mr. KEYNES' *Treatise on Money* which made the catchwords "excess of saving over investment" and "excess of investment over saving" popular in English literature.[1] Since, however, this piece of verbal machinery of the *Treatise* has been abandoned by its author, we may be very brief. Mr. KEYNES defined income as exclusive of losses and profits. I was defined as the value of unconsumed output; and S as income minus consumption.[2] Hence, an excess of saving over investment

---

[1] Mr. Harrod, for example, speaks of "the new-fangled view, sponsored by Mr. Keynes in his *Treatise*, that the volume of saving may be unequal to the volume of investment" ("Mr. Keynes and Traditional Theory", in *Econometrica*, Vol. 5, 1937, page 75). On the Continent, the view that S and I need not be equal has been held at least since Wicksell, and, as Mr. Hawtrey has pointed out, in the classical English writings the equality of S and I has always been regarded as an equilibrium condition rather than an identity (although not all the implications of this view have been recognised or explored).

[2] The reader's attention might be called to the possibility of interpreting what Mr. Keynes was aiming at in terms of the Swedish *ex ante* and *ex post* analysis, which will be reviewed below (page 180). Y is clearly

was so defined as to mean losses; and an excess of investment over saving, so as to mean profits. In turn, profits and losses were defined as that amount by which actual entrepreneurial income exceeds, or falls short of, that level which would leave the entrepreneur under no inducement to change the rate of output and employment.[1] In consequence, entrepreneurs, *by definition*, had an incentive to expand output whenever investment exceeded savings, so that an excess of investment over savings was robbed of all the causal significance which was imputed to it.

We now come to Professor ROBERTSON's definition of saving, which seems to give the best and most precise expression to what is in the mind of those who spoke and speak unsophisticatedly of differences between S and I.[2]

Professor Robertson's definition of saving. Professor ROBERTSON explicitly introduces from the beginning the discontinuity of the income streams by adopting a " period analysis ". He assumes that money income[3] received in the current period—" to-day "—becomes available for expenditure only during the next period—" to-morrow ". Such a " day " may be longer than a day : it may be as long as, say, a week. The exact length depends on the habits and techniques of payments. For any day, Professor ROBERTSON distinguishes, accordingly, between disposable income and earned income. The disposable income of to-day is the earned income yesterday, and the earned income of to-day becomes disposable income to-morrow.

Saving for any day is defined as *disposable* income of the same day (= earned income of the day before) *minus* consumption expenditure of the same day. Investment, on the other hand, is

---

defined as an *ex ante* concept, while profits and losses are *ex post* magnitudes. Likewise, S is defined in *ex ante* terms and I in *ex post* terms. (This was pointed out to me by Dr. Redvers Opie, Oxford.)

[1] This has been pointed out by Professor Hayek, Professor Hansen, Mr. Tout and Mr. Hawtrey in their respective analyses of the *Treatise*. *Cf.*, especially, Hawtrey : *The Art of Central Banking*, pages 334 *et seq.*

[2] *Vide* his article " Saving and Hoarding, " *Economic Journal*, Vol. 43, September 1933, page 399, and the subsequent discussion between Professor Robertson, Mr. Keynes and Mr. Hawtrey, *ibid.*, page 699.

[3] The analysis must, of course, be extended to payments other than income payments.

defined as actual expenditure on new investment goods during the day. Hence, investment can be greater than saving, because money may be spent out of other sources than from (disposable) income. Expenditure may be made from newly created bank money or from hoards. This money becomes, of course, earned income on the same day and disposable income on the following day. Thus an excess of I over S implies an increase of to-day's (earned) income over yesterday's (earned) income. Similarly, an excess of S over I implies a decrease of to-day's income as compared with yesterday's income. This evidently expresses precisely what is meant, when, in an unsophisticated way, it is said that, if I runs ahead of S, inflation ensues, and that an excess of S over I implies deflation.

It should now be pretty clear how statements in the language of those who (explicitly, like Professor ROBERTSON, or implicitly, like many others) distinguish between disposable and earned income can be translated into statements in the language of Mr. KEYNES, which does not make this distinction. This has been clearly realised by Mr. KEYNES himself[1] and by Professor HANSEN.[2]

Money income versus money value of output. There is another point of ambiguity which may give rise to misunderstanding. Professor ROBERTSON and others use " income " in the sense of actual money income involving monetary transactions (a transfer of money). This need not be quite the same thing as income in the sense of the money value of the output as a whole.[3] A corresponding distinction should be made about saving, whilst investment is almost invariably used in the sense of money value of unconsumed output. Mr. KEYNES uses the terms " income " and " saving " in the value sense, and Professor OHLIN says explicitly that

---

[1] *General Theory*, page 78.

[2] *Cf.* his review of the *General Theory* in the *Journal of Political Economy*, Vol. 44, 1936, page 674, now reprinted in *Full Recovery or Stagnation*, New York, 1938, page 22.

[3] " Undeflated ", that is, at current prices, or " deflated " by any sort of price index.

income, in his sense, " has nothing to do with the actual receipt of cash ".[1]

The two magnitudes need not coincide, because income in the sense of money value of output comprises items which do not give rise to monetary transactions—*e.g.*, " imputed " income (example : the services of a house to its owner), or " bartered " income, or the accumulation of stocks. But even if all transactions of goods took the shape of purchases for, and sales against, money, there would be certain discrepancies between the two types of income, because money income is received at discreet intervals, while real income flows more continuously. Furthermore, if new money is created and handed to somebody not in exchange for a service performed by the recipient (*e.g.*, an unemployed), this might be called that person's money income to which, before the money is spent, there corresponds no increase in the value of output.

In the case of non-wage and non-salary income, the concept of actual money income is beset with further difficulties, which make it impossible to define it by looking at the monetary transactions alone without any reference to the sphere of real goods. Not all money receipts and expenditures of a firm are income receipts and expenditures. Which part of the total flow of money has to be regarded as income and which as " intermediate transaction " can be defined only with reference to the " real " sphere. But even if this has been accomplished satisfactorily, it is in many cases not possible, without more or less arbitrary conventions, to identify individual transactions (either the " real " or the corresponding " monetary " transactions) as income or non-income transactions. It is, for example, not admissible to regard all purchases of consumers' goods by the final consumer as income transactions; for consumption can exceed income, the difference being dissaving. Nor is it always possible to identify an individual purchase of a capital good as constituting new investment or replacement—that is, as belonging to the income sphere or not. Income and new investment can be determined only in the

---

[1] " Some Notes on the Stockholm Theory of Savings and Investment ", *Economic Journal*, Vol. 47, 1937, page 65. Mr. Lerner, on the other hand, always speaks of *acts of expenditure*, which are classified either as consumption or investment, while both together constitute income.

aggregate, as residuals. By deducting from total output what is considered necessary for maintaining the capital stock intact, we determine income; and by deducting consumption from income, we obtain the volume of new investment.

The Swedish ex ante and ex post analysis. We now come to another set of definitions which gives meaning to the concept of a difference between S and I. This scheme has been worked out by a group of Swedish writers such as Mr. Erik LUNDBERG,[1] Professor Erik LINDAHL,[2] Professor Gunnar MYRDAL[3] and Professor Bertil OHLIN.[4] A very similar scheme has been proposed by Mr. HAWTREY.[5]

The Swedish writers distinguish for all the magnitudes concerned —income, saving, investment and others—between an *ex ante* and an *ex post* sense.[6] Looking back at any period of time that has elapsed, one can measure—at least in principle—what Y, C, S, I, etc., actually were. This is the *ex post*, or registration or accounting, sense of these magnitudes. Like Mr. KEYNES, Professor MYRDAL and Professor OHLIN[7] define S and I *ex post* in such a way that they are always equal—*i.e.*, both as $Y - C$.

From the *ex post* sense of these concepts, the *ex ante* sense must be carefully distinguished, and what is true of the *ex post* phenomena of a certain kind need not be true of the corresponding

---

[1] *Studies in the Theory of Economic Expansion*, London, 1937.

[2] *Studies in the Theory of Money and Capital*, London, 1939.

[3] " Der Gleichgewichtsbegriff als Instrument der geldtheoretischen Analyse " in *Beiträge zur Geldtheorie*, ed. by Hayek 1933 (an English version of which will soon be published by William Hodge, London).

[4] " Some Notes on the Stockholm Theory of Savings and Investment ", *Economic Journal*, Vol. 47, 1937, pages 53 *et seq.* and 221 *et seq*, and " Alternative Theories of the Rate of Interest ", *ibid.*, pages 423 *et seq.*

[5] See especially his *Capital and Employment, passim.*

[6] Professor Myrdal was the first to introduce this distinction. Professor Ohlin's exposition is, however, more accessible and more developed. Therefore, reference will be made chiefly to him.

[7] Other members of the group seem to lean rather to Professor Robertson's definition. See Ohlin (*loc. cit.*, page 57) : " . . . my terminology has been viewed with great scepticism by some of the younger Stockholm economists, chiefly because of my way of defining income so as to make savings and investment always equal *ex definitione* ". We shall, however, see that the two analytical schemes, if fully thought out, are by no means exclusive of each other.

ex ante phenomena.   The *ex ante* manifestations of income, saving, investment, etc., are the expectations entertained by all the individuals and firms in respect of those magnitudes at any point of time for some period ahead of that point.   Any member of an economic society at any moment of time expects a certain income, and plans or intends to spend a certain part of it on consumption and to save another part.   The "plan to save" must be associated with the "plan to increase the quantity of cash" or with the "plan to lend ". (These are the only two alternatives " if the use of one's own savings for new investment is treated as giving credit to oneself ".)[1]

The entrepreneurs expect certain prices to rule, a certain demand situation, certain interest rates and production costs to exist, etc., and, on the basis of these expectations, they plan a certain amount of investment.

Summing up the expected income, planned consumption, saving and investment of all individuals, we arrive at the *ex ante* magnitudes of these phenomena for the economy as a whole.

How equality of S and I is brought about ex post.
" There is no reason ", according to this school of thought, " for assuming that planned saving and planned investment should be equal.   But when the period is finished, [realised] investment is equal to [realised] saving.   How does this equality come about ?   The answer is that the inequality of *ex ante* saving and *ex ante* investment sets in motion a process which makes realised income differ from expected income, realised saving from planned saving and realised new investment differ from the corresponding plan.[2]   This difference we can call *unexpected income, unexpected new investment*, and *unintentional* savings.
. . .   The business-man who, after the closing of his accounts,

---

[1] Ohlin, *loc. cit.*, page 425.

[2] It will be noted that, in spite of the appearance to the contrary, no statements about facts are involved in the following analysis.   What actually happens, if planned saving and investment differ, is *assumed* by way of illustration, and can be described in terms of receiving and spending of money and of movement of goods between individuals and into and out of existence without using the terms " savings " and " investment ".   No particular process is required to make S and I equal *ex post*.   All sorts of reactions are possible, but, whatever actually happens, they must be equal, because the terms are chosen in such a way.

finds that he has had a larger net income than he expected and that, therefore, the surplus over and above his consumption is greater than his planned savings, has provided ' unintentional savings ' which is equal to this unexpected surplus. Un expected new investment, which, like unintentional saving, may, of course, be negative, can mean simply that stocks at the end of the period are different from what the entrepreneur expected. . . . "[1]

" Assume that people decide to reduce their savings and increase their consumption during the next period by 10 millions, as compared with realised savings and consumption during the period which has just finished. . . Assume further that the planned investment is equal to the realised investment during the last period." (Since realised savings and realised investment are equal, these assumptions imply that *ex ante* saving falls short by 10 millions of *ex ante* investment.) " What will be the result ? Retail sales of consumption goods will rise 10 millions and the stocks of retailers will, at the end of the period, be down—*e.g.*, 7 millions, the remaining 3 millions being extra income of the retailers. This latter sum is ' unintentional ' savings. Thus realised saving is down only 7 millions, or the same amount as realised investment."[2] Realised investment is down because the depletion of stocks by 7 millions is counted as unintentional disinvestment.[3]

---

[1] Ohlin, *loc. cit.*, pages 64 and 65.

[2] *Ibid.*, pages 65 and 66.

[3] This analysis can be readily translated into Robertsonian language. We would have to say that investment actually exceeds saving by 3 millions. The difference is " financed by other means than by saving from (disposable) income ". This way of expressing the matter has the advantage that it calls attention explicitly to the fact (which is, of course, implied also by Professor Ohlin's analysis) that bank credits must be expanded or that some people must dishoard—*i.e.*, " reduce their quantity of cash ". (Ohlin, *loc. cit.*, page 425.) The supply of loanable funds must be elastic; otherwise the planned investments could not go ahead undisturbed by the fact that people spend more on consumption than was foreseen. This assumption about the elasticity of the money supply may be correct in many cases, especially if the period in question is sufficiently short. It need, however, not always be correct, and if it is not, the rate of interest will rise so much (or credit will be rationed in such a way) that the investment plans will be sufficiently scaled down. This may very well lead to more or less serious disturbances in the

Similarly, other cases of differences between *ex ante* saving and *ex ante* investment can be analysed. " When the State finances public works with the printing of new notes, the increased investment is matched [*ex post*] by increased ' real ' savings ", although *ex ante* investments were in excess of savings, since it is assumed that no planned savings corresponded to the planned Government investment. " At the end of the period, some people hold more cash than at its beginning. This is evidence that they had an income which they have not consumed—*i.e.*, that they have saved. *Ex post*, there is *ex definitione* equality between savings and investment." [1]

The ex ante concepts as schedules. In a later article,[2] Professor OHLIN[3] has given important elucidations of his theories. He explains there that his *ex ante* concepts of savings, investment as well as the other closely related pair of concepts —viz., demand and supply of credit—are intended to mean the same thing as demand and supply *schedules*. " *Ex ante* saving " means the schedule showing how much people are willing to save at·different hypothetical rates of interest. And " *ex ante* investment " is the schedule showing how much people are planning to invest at different interest rates.

Demand and supply of credit determine the rate of interest. However, the rate of interest is not determined by the interaction of the curves relating to saving and investment; it cannot be explained by demand and supply of saving. " There is no such market for savings and no price of savings " (page 424). But there is a market for credit,[4] and " the price of credit [*i.e.*, the interest rate] is determined by the supply and demand curves for credit or, which amounts to the same, for ' claims ' " (pages 423 and 424).

---

capital-goods industries, as analysed by Professor Hayek. That shows again that Professor Hayek's theory can be well expressed with the help of the Swedish terminological apparatus.

[1] Ohlin, *loc. cit.*, page 69.

[2] " Alternative Theories of the Rate of Interest ", *Economic Journal,* Vol. 47, 1937, page 423 *et seq.*

[3] It is not quite clear whether his Swedish colleagues all agree on this.

[4] Strictly speaking, there are different markets for different kinds of credit—short-term, long-term, etc.

The two pairs of curves, relating to saving and investment on the one hand and to credit or claims on the other, are interrelated, but they are not identical. How are they interrelated? The supply of credit (= demand for claims—*e.g.*, for bonds) is not equal to planned savings (the supply of saving), because " it is possible to plan to save and to increase the quantity of cash instead of lending. Also, one can plan to extend new credits in excess of planned savings if one is willing to reduce one's own quantity of cash. "[1]

Similarly, the demand schedule for credit is not identical with the curve for planned investment, because there may be a " desire to vary the cash held, to cover expected losses or to finance consumption ".[2]

Obviously, a similar proviso as for " increases " or " decreases of cash " held (in other words, for hoarding and dishoarding) must be made for changes in the quantity of money made by the banking system or the Government. An increase in the quantity of money has the same effect as a reduction in cash holdings of some individuals : it increases the supply of credit beyond *ex ante* saving. The case of a decrease in the quantity of money is similar.

Diagrammatic exposition. Taking everything into account, it would seem that Professor OHLIN's theory can be precisely stated in the words of Mr. A. P. LERNER :

" The rate of interest is the price that equates the supply of ' credit ', or saving *plus* the net increase in the amount of money in a period, to the demand for ' credit ', or investment *plus* net ' hoarding ' in the period. . . . This is illustrated by [the following] Figure 7.

---

[1] *Loc. cit.*, page 425. There are some other possible differences between supply of credit and *ex ante* saving. " Besides, one can plan to extend credit instead of reinvesting ' capital made free '—*i.e.*, ' depreciation money ' " (page 425). A failure of reinvesting depreciation quotas can evidently be treated as negative investment, and could accordingly be deducted from the investment curve (demand curve for credit, of which the investment curve constitutes an element), instead of being added to the supply of credit.

[2] *Ibid.* The latter two items could be considered as negative saving and thus be deducted from the supply curve (curve of *ex ante* saving), instead of being added to the demand curve (curve of *ex ante* investment).

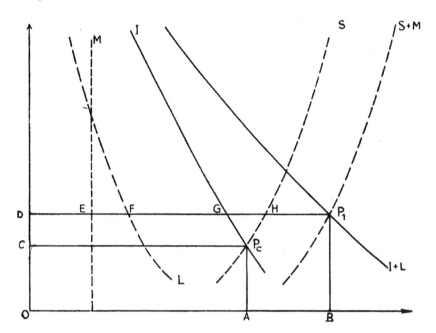

"*S* is the supply schedule of saving, showing how much would be saved (measured horizontally) at each rate of interest (measured vertically). *I* is the schedule of investment showing how much would be invested (measured horizontally) at each rate of interest. These two schedules intersect at P_c, the 'classical' point of equilibrium, which shows the rate of interest being determined at that level (AP_c) at which saving equals investment, both being equal to OA. *L* is the schedule showing the amount of net 'hoarding' that would take place at each rate of interest. In the figure, this is shown as a *positive* amount (*i.e.*, at all the rates of interest considered, there would be a net balance of 'hoarding' and not a net balance of 'dishoarding') which is greater for lower rates of interest. There is no reason for expecting 'hoarding' always to outbalance 'dishoarding' in the economy, and this is taken to be so in the figure merely for the purpose of simplifying the diagram. 'Hoarding' could be taken as a negative quantity at some or at all rates of interest (and shown by the L curve falling to the left of the vertical axis) without affecting the argument in any way.

" The M curve shows the increase in the amount of money in the period and is here shown as a positive amount and independent of the rate of interest. Both of these conditions are postulated merely for the purpose of simplifying the diagram. A *decrease* in the amount of money could be shown by drawing the M curve to the *left* of the vertical axis, signifying a negative increase in the amount of money. It might be the policy of the monetary authorities to take the rate of interest into account when deciding by how much to increase (or decrease) the amount of money. Thus if they increase the amount of money more (or diminish it by less), the higher is the rate of interest, then the M curve will slope *upward* to the right. But all such differences in assumptions would merely complicate the diagram without affecting our argument in any way.

" The M curve is now added horizontally to the S curve, giving the total net supply schedule of loans (or ' credit ') marked $S + M$. The L curve is added to the I curve, giving the total net demand schedule for loans (or ' credit ') marked $I + L$. The two new curves intersect at P_1, giving an equilibrium into which the complications due to ' hoarding ' and to changes in the amount of money appear to have been incorporated."[1]

---

[1] " Alternative Formulations of the Theory of Interest ", in *Economic Journal*, Vol. 48, 1938, pages 213 to 215. It is true, Mr. Lerner puts this account of the matter forward as an interpretation, not of Professor Ohlin's theory, but of " the position [of the theory of interest] as it appears after the first step [from the ' classical ' to the ' modern ' view] has been taken " (page 213). This first step consists of the recognition " that ' hoarding ', ' dishoarding ' and changes in the amount of money also have something to do with the supply of ' credit ' and the rate of interest—in the short period, at any rate " (page 211). This seems to me precisely the position taken by Professor Ohlin. Mr. Lerner merely does not take cognisance of the *ex ante* nature of supply and demand curves of saving in Professor Ohlin's theory. He interprets S and I throughout *ex post*. Hence, in a second graph (page 216), he draws just one curve, which is a saving and investment curve at the same time, whilst Professor Ohlin emphasises that S and I *ex ante* are not necessarily equal. Mr. Lerner probably has been misled by the fact that Professor Ohlin introduces the interpretation of the *ex ante* concepts of S and I in the schedule sense as an afterthought, as it were, in a reply to a criticism by Mr. Keynes ; in his original articles, he did not make it clear that he meant schedules when he spoke of *ex ante* saving and investment.

Let us draw a few corollaries from Professor OHLIN's interpretation of *ex ante* saving and investment as schedules and their relation to the demand and supply curves of credit which determine the rate of interest. Obviously, it is not strictly permissible to speak in the singular of *the* difference between *ex ante S* and *I*. There is a whole schedule of such differences, showing what that difference would be at different hypothetical interest rates. If Professor OHLIN speaks of the difference, he probably refers to the equilibrium[1] point, P_1, in our diagram.

This point P_1 in a sense denotes an *ex post* position; for it determines " the quantity of credit *actually* given ". At the rate of interest corresponding to that point, *ex ante* saving and *ex ante* investment need *not* be equal. In our figure, *ex ante S* exceeds *ex ante I* by *GH*. This difference is equal to the amount of money hoarded (*DF*) minus the increase in the amount of money (*DE*), *GH* being equal to *EF*.[2]

It should be observed that the diagram does not show savings and investment *ex post*; nor does it depict " the process ",[3] set in motion by the *ex ante* difference between saving and investment, which brings about the equality *ex post* between saving and investment.

---

[1] Equilibrium in the sense of immediate market equilibrium. There need be no equilibrium in any more ambitious sense.

[2] Mr. Lerner says that " this exactly portrays the disturbed state of mind of people who declare that saving can be greater than investment if the difference is hoarded " (page 215). Mr. Lerner is led to this statement by his erroneous and rather naive imputation to other writers of his own definition (*a*) of *S* and *I* and (*b*) of hoarding and dishoarding. He defines *S* and *I* throughout as identical and *ex post*, while in the above diagram it must be defined *ex ante* (or, as we shall see presently, *à la* Robertson). Mr. Lerner's definition of hoarding and dishoarding, which he shares with Messrs. Keynes, Harrod, Kahn and others, will come up for discussion in § 3 of this chapter.

[3] It may be noted once more that these words used by Professor Ohlin are rather misleading. Strictly speaking, no process is needed, because *S* and *I ex post* are equal at any moment of time. The word " process " suggests—erroneously—that there is only a tendency towards their becoming equal at the end of the process and that they are unequal at the beginning and during that process. In reality, according to the definition given, they are equal at any moment of time.

Let us investigate a little more the foundation
Relation of Professor OHLIN's theory and draw some further
between conclusions from it, not all of which have been
the ex ante stated by the author himself, probably for lack of
and the period space. We shall see that Dr. LUTZ's contention is
analysis. right,[1] that the Swedish *ex ante* analysis, if thought
through to its logical end, comes very near to
Professor ROBERTSON's period analysis. As Dr. LUTZ points out,
in order to make use of the apparatus of demand and supply curves
relating to credit, saving and investment, the period of time
taken into consideration must be very short, at least so short that
there do not occur any revisions of the various plans during the
period.[2] After the period has elapsed, people revise their plans
in the light of the experience gained during the period; in other
words, the curves relating to saving, investment, credit, etc.,
shift to new positions.

The choice of the length of the unit period which suits Professor
OHLIN's theory is not to be made on the basis of the same principles
as the choice of the length of Professor ROBERTSON's unit period.[3]
The latter, Professor ROBERTSON's " day ", is chosen so as to
make it impossible, in view of the existing habits of payment, that
money received during the day should be spent during the same
day; Professor OHLIN's unit period rests on the postulate that
plans should remain unchanged during the period.

Let us now concentrate on what happens during any unit
period. Professor OHLIN draws for the credit market an analogy
with a village market for eggs where people appear with " alternative purchases and sales plans " as represented in their demand
and supply curves.[4] It is not quite clear how far the author
wishes to carry this analogy, but if he carries it sufficiently far
by taking a very short period, his theory really coincides with that

---

[1] " The Outcome of the Saving-Investment Discussion ", *Quarterly Journal of Economics*, Vol. 52, August 1938, page 604.

[2] We abstract from a number of difficulties connected with the over-lapping of the plans, which is due to the fact that plans of different individuals are not always made at the same time and do not all extend over the same period.

[3] This problem has been well discussed by E. Lundberg, *loc. cit., passim.*

[4] *Loc. cit.*, page 423.

of Professor ROBERTSON, for *ex ante* saving then becomes saving out of the income received on the day before.   Perhaps he would not want to go so far, because *ex ante* saving would then no longer be savings out of a future, expected and uncertain income, but out of an income which has already been received.   On the other hand, the alternative construction presents very serious difficulties. Clearly, if planned savings were to mean savings out of a future income, which might not materialise at all, it would not be possible to say that " the price of 3 % bonds—and thus the long-term rate of interest—is fixed on the bond market by the demand and supply curves in the same way as the price of eggs or strawberries on a village market "[1] and to explain that planned savings constitue a part of the demand for bonds.[2]   How can future savings constitute supply of credit and affect the bond market before they are actually made ?[3]

We conclude that the most reasonable interpretation of Professor OHLIN'S concept of *ex ante* saving is " saving from disposable

---

[1] *Loc cit.*, page 424.

[2] This is said very clearly, although not with these words, *op. cit.*, page 425. " Will not the planned supply of credit [= demand for bonds] be equal to the planned savings ? . . . No, not quite." And then follow the qualifications about hoarding, dishoarding, etc., which have been mentioned above, page 184.

[3] An excess of *ex ante* saving over *ex ante* investment, we have seen, leads to a deficiency of demand for consumers' goods and causes losses to the retailers. This is one of the " processes " which bring about equality between *S* and *I ex post*. Clearly, if this construction is to make sense, *ex ante* saving cannot be interpreted as saving out of a future income. That could not affect retail sales now. To be sure, expectations about future income may affect present saving as a motive. But so will expectations about a hundred other things, and the manner in which, and extent to which, they affect the present situation is by no means uniquely determined.

These considerations illustrate a basic difficulty of the whole *ex ante* (expectation) analysis : How can mere plans about the future influence the present situation ? People are, on the whole, not so much influenced by other people's expectations or plans, as by their actions. Does not the whole expectation analysis stand in need of a behaviouristic re-interpretation ? As Professor Robertson puts it : " Changes in ' -nesses ' [he is speaking of thriftiness] and ' propensities ' do not in themselves exercise any effect on the external world. Nor does a decision to get up early necessarily indicate any reduction in the propensity to lie in bed—it may rather indicate an increased determination not to indulge in that propensity ! " (*Economic Journal*, September, 1938, page 555.)

income ". This conclusion is fortified by the fact (stressed by Dr. LUTZ) that an excess of investment over saving has the same consequences in Professor OHLIN's scheme as in Professor ROBERTSON's : in both cases, it has a stimulating effect and is a characteristic of an expansion of business (prosperity phase of the cycle).

If the foregoing interpretation of Professor OHLIN's theory is correct—that is to say, if it does not exceed what can be deduced from his theory, although it contains more than he explicitly says— there remain certain inconsistencies and difficulties which call for further modifications of the theory.[1]

How can alternative purchase and sale plans be disappointed? In so far and inasmuch as the actions of the individuals are determined by, and foreshadowed in, the various schedules, everything happens according to a plan—viz., to that one of the " alternative plans " of the various individuals which corresponds to the interest rate emerging as the actual market rate. Since Professor OHLIN identified the *ex ante* magnitudes with the alternative plans embodied in, or represented by, these schedules, it is difficult to see how he can speak of people's being disappointed by events going contrary to their plans. It is said, for instance, that retailers may find themselves with greater stocks than they expected (unintentional investment); or with lower receipts than they anticipated (unintentional dissaving). Are their actions leading to these results—viz., either leaving the sale price unchanged (which entails the accumulation of stocks) or reducing the price (which entails losses and a reduction in saving)— not predetermined in their supply schedule ? Everything happens according to the various schedules, and if all the possible plans of which Professor OHLIN speaks are embodied in these schedules, there can be no upsetting of the plans and no disappointment.

There are various ways out of this dilemma. The best, which rescues a maximum of Professor OHLIN's theoretical edifice

---

[1] These difficulties have been clearly noticed by W. Fellner, " Savings, Investment, and the Problem of Neutral Money ", in *Review of Economic Statistics*, Vol. 20, November 1938, page 188. *Cf.* also the criticism of the *ex ante* concept by Professor H. Neisser in *Studies in Income and Wealth*, vol. II, New York, 1938, page 172 *et seq.*

appears to be the abandonment of the identification of the *ex ante* concepts with the schedules mentioned. In other words, the plans which may be upset and the expectation which may be disappointed should be distinguished from what Professor OHLIN calls the " alternative purchase and sales plans " embodied in the various demand and supply schedules. The former stretch into the future, whilst the latter relate to a point or short period of time.

At any moment of time, a man may have (more or less consciously) alternative plans of action with respect to sales, purchases, savings, investment, borrowing, lending, etc., under different hypothetical prices, interest rates, etc., represented by various schedules. Nevertheless, he has probably been expecting for some time, more or less confidently, that one of these various possible situations would actually arise, or that the occurrence of some was more probable than of others. Moreover, he is likely to have acted in the past on the expectation that some things are more likely to happen than others : he has laid in stock or placed orders for the delivery of goods in the expectation that demand for, and the price of, his product will stand at a certain level; he has started certain constructions (investment) in the expectation that the situation in the loan market would enable him to borrow at a certain interest rate, etc. Hence the realisation of some of the situations foreshadowed in the instantaneous schedules of alternative actions will be in accordance with the long (or longer) range plans; the realisation of others will upset them. But events are still running according to schedule—that is, according to the instantaneous or short-run schedules. [1]

---

[1] There remain unanswered, of course, a number of questions—philosophical questions, we may perhaps say—about the precise nature of the instantaneous curves. Is it justifiable to characterise a demand curve, as Professor Ohlin does, as a series of alternative plans ? This language suggests that the various, strictly infinite, alternatives are thought out in advance in the mind of the individuals. A more behaviouristic interpretation may be better, because it allows one to dispense with this questionable assumption. We cannot here go into these problems and, fortunately, need not ; for, whatever we answer to these questions, it remains true that the plans which are upset must be kept apart from the " plans " or decisions represented in the instantaneous curves.

Mr. HAWTREY's distinction between " designed "
Mr. Hawtrey's or " active " and " undesigned " or " passive "
designed and investment is very similar to Professor OHLIN's
undesigned *ex ante* and *ex post* investment. Mr. HAWTREY
investment. refrains, however, from interpreting designed investment as schedules and thus avoids obscurities
from which Professor OHLIN's treatment suffers. The sum of
designed and undesigned investment is total investment, which
is defined as the " increment of unconsumed wealth " and is also
called " saving ". (There is no distinction between " active "
and " passive " saving in Mr. HAWTREY's scheme.) Designed
investment is defined as the voluntary acquisition of items of
unconsumed wealth in the expectation that they will be remunerative; this is what Professor OHLIN calls " *ex ante* investment ".
Undesigned investment is defined as an " increment of unconsumed
wealth, which is not acquired voluntarily in the expectation of its
being remunerative; this will be an involuntary accumulation
of unsold goods "—Professor OHLIN's unexpected investment.[1]
" Passive investment " may be a negative quantity; that is to say,
active investment may exceed saving, and the excess will be
represented by an undesigned disinvestment or decrement of
stocks of unsold goods. Thus active investment and saving
(= net total investment) may be unequal. If they are, the resulting
undesigned increment or decrement of unsold goods will be a
source of disequilibrium, leading to a decrease or an increase in
productive activity and possibly also in the price level.[2]

----

[1] It is not quite clear whether " undesigned investment " is identified
with " an involuntary accumulation of unsold goods " or whether the
latter is only a special case of the former. If the former interpretation
were correct, Mr. Hawtrey's undesigned investment would be a narrower
concept than Professor Ohlin's difference between *ex ante* and *ex post*
investment.

[2] *Capital and Employment*, London, 1937, pages 176 and 177. See
also *Economic Journal*, 1937, page 439, where Mr. Hawtrey discusses the
relation between his and Ohlin's concepts. The distinction between
ex ante and *ex post*, designed and undesigned, *S* and *I* has been clearly
anticipated in Professor Robertson's *Banking Policy and the Price Level*.
His " spontaneous lacking " corresponds clearly to *ex ante* or designed
investment and his " induced lacking " to undesigned investment, which
is the difference between *ex ante* and *ex post* investment. (This was
pointed out to me by Dr. J. G. Koopmans, The Hague.)

It remains to enquire why Mr. KEYNES finds it *Saving and* necessary to distinguish between saving and invest-*investment* ment. We have seen that the formal definitions *in* which he gives on page 63 of his *General Theory* are *Mr. Keynes'* such that, for society as a whole, S and I are not *system.* only equal, but identical; viz., the value of unconsumed output. If that definition were strictly adhered to, S and I would be synonymous symbols, they could be used interchangeably and there would be no necessity—in fact it would be rather misleading—to retain both expressions.

Now this is not Mr. KEYNES' practice. He uses both terms, deliberately and not for purely stylistic reasons. Moreover, he points out that the acts of saving and of investment are usually performed independently by different people.[1] He insists that a process is required to make S and I equal, and sees the " initial novelty " of his theory in his " maintaining that it is not the rate of interest, but the level of incomes, which ensures equality between saving and investment ".[2]

---

[1] *General Theory*, pages 20 and 21, 210.

[2] *Economic Journal*, Vol. 47, 1937, page 250. It is misleading to say that income must change, in order to ensure the equality of S and I. Whatever the level of income may be, S and I must be equal, because they are made so by definition. The change of level of income comes in as a condition only because Mr. Keynes takes the ' multiplier '— ' the marginal propensity to consume ' (compare § 4 below for a definition of these concepts)—as a constant quantity. He assumes that there is a certain relationship between a (small) increase in investment and in income. Suppose, for example, the multiplier is 3 (in other words, the marginal propensity to consume is 2/3)—that is, to any small increment in I, corresponds an increment in Y three times as great. If that assumption is to be borne out by the facts, we must find that, whenever a change in investment has occurred, income must have changed by three times as much. But the multiplier (alternatively expressed : the marginal propensity to consume) need not be a stable magnitude, independent of the nature of the change in I and the surrounding conditions. (This, Mr. Keynes himself has recognised.) Hence, if in a concrete case we find that income did not change as we expected on the basis of what we assumed about the multiplier, we shall not say ' this is impossible, because S is not equal to I ', or ' S can now not be equal to I ', but we shall say the multiplier (marginal propensity to consume) was different from what we expected.

The same in slightly different formulation : If we assume (expect) something about the magnitude of the multiplier, we implicitly assume

He expressly rejects Mr. HAWTREY's comment that S and I " are two different names for the same thing " and " that, in any sentence in which the word ' investment ' occurs, the word ' saving ' could be substituted for it without any change in the meaning ".[1]

The explanation given of the paradox that the two things, although identically defined, are not quite the same is this : S and I are different aspects of the same thing. They " are necessarily equal in the same way in which the aggregate purchases of anything on the market are equal to the aggregate sales. But this does not mean that ' buying ' and ' selling ' are identical terms, and that the laws of supply and demand are meaningless."[2]

The total purchases of a commodity must be identical with the total sales of that commodity, but an *individual's* purchases need not—and indeed are unlikely to—be equal to his sales of the same commodity. In the same way, total savings are identical with total investment, if we employ Mr. KEYNES' definitions; but an individual's savings need not be equal to his investment. It may be useful to retain the two separate terms " saving " and " investment ", since, even with Mr. KEYNES' definitions, they are not necessarily equal when reference is made to an individual.

There is a second reason for the retention of the two terms. Although the total purchases of a commodity are equal to the

---

(expect) something about the change in income subsequent to a change, say an increase, in investment. Income must change, not because it is necessary to ensure the equality between S and I, but because we have assumed it by assuming the multiplier.

We have here an example of a confusion between a terminological relationship between symbols (in other words : a relationship between concepts by definition) and an empirical relationship between conceptually independent magnitudes. In other words : the impression is created that a statement is made about an alleged regularity in the real world, whilst in reality a rule is given for the consistent application of the terms. On the relationship between ' multiplier ' and ' marginal propensity to consume' in Mr. Keynes' system, compare § 4 below and G. Haberler : ' Mr. Keynes' Theory of the Multiplier ', in *Zeitschrift für Nationalökonomie*, Vol. 7, 1936, pages 299 *et seq*. On the logical and methodological principles involved, see T. W. Hutchinson : *The Significance and Basic Postulates of Economic Theory*, London, 1938, *passim*."

[1] *Ibid.*, page 249.

[2] *Ibid. Cf.* also *General Theory*, Chapter 7.

total sales of that commodity, the motives of purchasers differ from those of sellers. In the same way, the motives for investment differ from those for saving; and the word " investment " may be used for the value of unconsumed income when the context refers to the motives of investors, while the word " savings " may be used for the same quantity when it is desired to emphasise the motives of savers.[1]

§ 3. HOARDING, LIQUIDITY PREFERENCE AND THE RATE
OF INTEREST

The theory of interest has for a long time been a weak spot in the science of economics, and the explanation and determination of the interest rate still gives rise to more disagreement among economists than any other branch of general economic theory.

The " pure " theory of interest. For a long time, the theory of interest has had two distinct branches or stages. There is (a) the " pure " theory of interest in essentially non-monetary terms explaining the rate of interest as the price of capital, determined by the marginal productivity of capital in a technological sense and by certain psychological factors (time-preference) influencing the relative urgency of present and future needs; Professor MARGET[2] calls these doctrines " real capital theories ". (That some writers, chiefly the followers of Böhm-Bawerk, go on to interpret marginal productivity of capital in terms of a lengthening or shortening of the period of production, whilst other writers object to that interpretation, has been mentioned on an earlier occasion.)[3]

---

[1] Further elaborations will be found in G. Haberler : " National Income, Savings and Investment ", in *Studies in Income and Wealth*, Vol. II, published by the National Bureau of Economic Research, New York, 1938.

[2] In a series of (unpublished) lectures delivered at the London School of Economics, 1933, and in an unpublished paper submitted to the American Economic Association at its meeting in Atlantic City, December 1937. The history of the two groups of theories and of the attempts at bridging the gap between them will be traced in Professor Marget's forthcoming Vol. II of his *Theory of Prices*.

[3] See footnote [1] on page 40 above.

We have (*b*) a monetary theory of the rate of
The "loanable- interest which runs in terms of demand for and
fund " theory supply loanable funds or credit or claims. Elabo-
of interest. rate attempts have been made at reconciling and
integrating these two branches. In the Wicksellian
and neo-Wicksellian literature—*e.g.*, as reviewed above in Chapter 3
—a detailed analysis is given of the mechanism by which, and the
routes through which, pecuniary surface forces realise or falsify
the fundamental relationship postulated by the " pure " theory of
interest. One may very well hold that this integration has not
been satisfactorily achieved, but one cannot say in justice that the
problem has not been recognised.

The monetary theory of interest in terms of supply of and demand
for loanable funds has to be regarded as a first approximation to a
more elaborate treatment of the matter. It has been presented in
the first edition of this book; it is the theory expounded by
Professor OHLIN, as reviewed above in § 2 of this chapter (page 183).
It is, as Professor ROBERTSON puts it, " a common-sense account
of events " which attempts to give " precision to the ordinary
view enshrined in such well-known studies of the capital and credit
market as those of LAVINGTON [1] and HAWTREY, as well as in a
thousand newspaper articles ".[2]

This " common-sense " explanation of the rate of interest,
and the more elaborate theory behind it, has been criticised by
Mr. KEYNES and other writers. He has replaced it by a purely
monetary theory, in which the rate of interest is completely
divorced from the demand and supply of saving and explained
instead by means of the " liquidity preference schedule " and the
quantity of money.[3]

---

[1] *The English Capital Market*, London, 1921 (3rd ed., 1934).

[2] *Economic Journal*, Vol. 47, page 428.

[3] Professor J. R. Hicks, too, in his book *Value and Capital* (which
appeared—Oxford, 1939—when this edition was already in print)
distinguishes between " real capital " theories of interest and " loanable
funds " theories (page 153). He calls this a " serious division of opinion "
which marks a " real dispute ". " But the real dispute has lately been
complicated by a sham dispute within the ranks of those who adhere to
the monetary approach." This refers to the dispute between Mr. Keynes
and his followers on the one hand, and the demand-for-and-supply-of-
loanable-funds theorists on the other hand.

Before we analyse more closely Mr. KEYNES'
Mr. Keynes' theory, we may clear the ground by reviewing the
criticism of the reasons, given by Mr. KEYNES and his followers, for
" *classical* " rejecting the traditional theory of the rate of
theory interest.
of interest. The greater part of Mr. KEYNES' criticism in
the chapter on " The Classical Theory of Interest "[1]
is directed against what we have termed above the " pure theory
of interest " and, more particularly, against that version which
explains the rate of interest by the interaction of demand and
supply of saving or capital. Mr. KEYNES points out that there is
no " material difference " between " the demand curve [for capital]
contemplated by some of the classical writers " and his " schedule
of the marginal efficiency of capital or investment demand-
schedule ".[2] Against this demand curve, some classical writers set a
supply curve of capital—that is, a curve showing how much saving
(or capital) would be supplied at different hypothetical interest
rates. The intersection of the two curves then determines simultaneously the rate of interest and the amount saved and invested.

Criticising this scheme, Mr. KEYNES rightly points out that the
amount saved depends, not only on the rate of interest, but also
on the level of income. In fact, most writers agree concerning
the manner in which the rate of saving depends on the level of
income : the higher the income level of an individual, the higher
tends to be the amount saved.[3] It is not so clear, on the other
hand, how a rise in interest rates will affect the rate of saving.[4]

---

[1] *Cf. General Theory*, Chapter 14, pages 175 to 193.

[2] *Loc cit.*, page 178.

[3] In some contexts, Mr. Keynes and many other writers make a
stronger assumption : they assume that when incomes rise, not only the
absolute amount of saving rises, but also the *proportion* of income saved
goes up. This is, for instance, implied by the widely accepted proposition that a more unequal distribution of the national income tends to
increase the amount saved by society as a whole.

[4] It has frequently been pointed out that some people may save less
at a higher than at a lower interest rate, although it has been widely
assumed that, for very low rates of interest, the saving incentive for
the community as a whole tends to vanish.

For short-run fluctuations, however, important *The propensity* qualifications must be made, even in respect of *to consume* the first-mentioned relationship—viz., that between *in the* the amount of saving and the level of income. If *short-run.* we say that there is widespread agreement among economists to the effect that the amount of saving is positively correlated to the level of income, that refers to individuals—not necessarily to society as a whole, because of possible changes in the distribution of income—and under settled conditions. Especially in the case of rapid changes, the rate of change of income and recent fluctuations of the income level undoubtedly play an important rôle. If, for example, the income of a person rises unexpectedly, at first consumption may not rise at all; later on, the level of consumption will be gradually raised. Furthermore, expectations entertained by the individual about the level of income in future periods play a leading rôle and these expectations will be profoundly influenced by the history of recent fluctuations. [1]

To return to the dependence of the rate of saving *Interdependence* upon the level of income : for each income level, *of demand for* a separate curve showing how much would be *and supply* saved at different interest rates ought to be drawn. [2][3] *of saving.* This being agreed upon, the next step in Mr. KEYNES' criticism follows conclusively : the demand and

---

[1] These remarks are by no means intended to be exhaustive. The problem could be settled only by extensive empirical studies. Some further observations will be found in Chapter 10, § 6, below. Here the aim is to caution the reader against accepting too easily the view now prevalent that the positive correlation between income and the amount of saving can be taken as a secure basis of further deductions for the purpose of explaining the business cycle as well as for long-run tendencies.

[2] It would be easy to construct a three-dimensional diagram exhibiting the dependence of the rate of saving on the two factors : level of income and rate of interest. A complete theory would have to take still other factors into consideration—*e.g.*, the rate of change of income.

[3] Mr. Keynes has not included in his theoretical scheme (although he has made some slight allusions to it) the obvious fact that investment (demand for capital), must be assumed to depend, not only on the rate of interest, but also on the level of income.

Mr. J. R. Hicks and Mr. O. Lange, in their respective diagrammatic expositions of the Keynesian theory (" Mr. Keynes and the ' Classics ' ;

supply curves of saving are not independent of one another. If, for instance, there appears a new stimulus to investment, if, that is to say, the investment demand curve shifts upward, income will, in general, rise and the supply curve of saving will shift too. Likewise, a shift in the latter will make the demand curve shift.

To sum up : the main defect of the " classical " theory of interest, according to Mr. KEYNES, is that it treats income as a given magnitude, as a determinant of the system and not as a variable.

If this criticism is valid as regards the static or equilibrium theory of interest,[1] it would not appear to apply to the short-run or monetary theory of the rate of interest as developed by the followers of WICKSELL. In this theory, the variability of income depending upon the shifts in the investment-demand and saving-supply curve is not neglected; for a continuous and sustained change in income is an essential feature of the Wicksellian cumulative process. A rise in income is characteristic of an expansion process; a fall of income, of a contraction process. Moreover, this theory allows for the purely monetary influences on the rate of interest; indeed, these influences operating on the actual market rate of interest are, as we have seen in Chapter 3, the very essence of the theory.[2]

What, then, are Mr. KEYNES' objections against the theory which conceives of the rate of interest as determined by demand for and supply of credit ?

A Suggested Interpretation "; in *Econometrica*, Vol. 5, 1937, and " The Rate of Interest and the Optimum Propensity to Consume ", in *Economica*, February 1938), have filled that gap. It would, however, seem to be more correct to say that the investment demand depends on the rate of change rather than on the level of income. That amounts to introducing into the system the acceleration principle which is a dynamic relationship (in a sense which will be discussed in § 6 of this chapter).

[1] Whether this theory, in spite of its admitted shortcomings, has not its merits, in relation to long-period equilibrium or as an ideal case realisable under certain special assumptions or as a purely theoretical standard of reference, we need not discuss in this connection, because we are here concerned more with the short-run (monetary) variety of interest theory which is used in business-cycle analysis.

[2] Mr. Keynes accuses the " orthodox " theory of having overlooked these monetary influences ; hence he must have the " pure " theory of interest in mind. *Cf.* his " The Theory of Interest " in *Lessons of Monetary Experience*, New York, 1937, page 147.

We are not here concerned with the concept of
Criticism of the " natural " or " equilibrium " rate of interest (as
the monetary discussed in Chapter 3), but with the underlying
theory explanation of the market rate by means of demand
of interest. and supply curves of credit, as developed in
Chapter 3, and more fully in § 2 of this chapter in
elaboration of Professor OHLIN's theory. We recall that demand
for and supply of credit is not the same thing as demand for and
supply of (*ex ante*) saving, but that the curves relating to the
latter form a part of the curves relating to credit.

Objections are raised against that theory on the ground of its
implying (*a*) that " saving is not necessarily equal to investment ",
(*b*) that " the amount of money hoarded is not necessarily equal to
the increase in the amount of money ".[1]

The first of these two difficulties has already been discussed in
§ 2 of this chapter; it would appear to arise from the various
possible meanings which may be attached to the terms " saving "
and " investment ". If these terms are defined in the manner
proposed by Professor ROBERTSON, the difficulty would seem to
disappear, and Profesor OHLIN's analysis, if carried to its logical
conclusion, gives the same result.

The second difficulty, concerning the term
The concept " hoarding ", requires careful consideration, because
of it has been an important source of confusion and
" *hoarding* ". misunderstanding in recent years.

The term " hoarding " is alien to Mr. KEYNES'
terminological system. It is used only when reference is made to
theories of other writers. In such cases, however, it would seem
that the term is used in two distinct senses, and the sense which,
in most cases, is applied and attributed to other writers would seem
to differ from the meaning attributed to it explicitly or implicitly
by those writers themselves.

According to this definition, " net new hoarding " (in the sense
of the amount hoarded; that is, of the result of this activity,
" hoarding ", during a certain period) is the same thing as the

---

[1] A. P. Lerner : " Alternative Formulations of the Theory of Interest ",
in the *Economic Journal*, Vol. 48, June 1938, page 215.

increase in the quantity of money during that period. For, if an individual's net hoarding in any period of time is defined as the addition which he makes to his holding of money during that period, the net hoarding of the whole community must be equal to the net increase in the amount of money in existence. "Dishoarding" (in the sense of the amount dishoarded) is the same thing as a decrease in the quantity of money. The total amount hoarded at any time "must be equal to the quantity of money ".[1] "Holding money" and "hoarding money" are thus synonymous terms, and since all the money in existence at any moment of time is held by somebody—if it were not "held" by somebody (if, for example, it had been lost), it would not be counted as being in existence—all the money is always hoarded.

In a few cases, however, another definition is given of hoarding—viz. : " the quantity of money *minus* what is required to satisfy the transaction-motive "[1]—in other words, idle or inactive money, including notes, coins and deposits or whatever is regarded as money. Net hoarding or dishoarding during a given period means, then, an increase or decrease of idle balances. This definition would seem to be roughly equivalent to the general meaning of the term.[2] On some occasions, however, the two concepts are used interchangeably although what holds true of one of these concepts need not and will not be true of the other. In particular, the theory[3] that any attempt of the public to hoard can only push up the interest rate, but cannot increase the aggregate amount hoarded unless the banking system increases the amount of money, is correct only if hoarding is defined in the wider (unusual) sense. If it is defined as an accumulation of *idle* balances, the public can hoard without any help from the banks. Even if the

---

[1] *General Theory*, page 174.

[2] As is usual with economic terms, there are points of detail where the general usage is not unambiguous. They will be discussed presently.

[3] This argument has been frequently expressed in recent years. See, for instance, J. M. Keynes, *General Theory*, page 174, and *Economic Journal*, 1937, pages 250-251 ; A. P. Lerner, " Mr. Keynes' General Theory of Employment, Interest and Money " (*International Labour Review*, Vol. 34, October 1936, page 435 ; R. F. Harrod, *Zeitschrift für Nationalökonomie* 1937, page 494. R. F. Kahn, *Economic Journal*, Vol. 47, 1937, page 671.

quantity of money is kept constant, the amount of *idle* balances can be increased by the public at the expense of *active* balances.

It is desirable, therefore, to define more precisely the meaning of the term and to state some of its implications and corollaries.

The concept of " idle balances ". The concept of " idle balances " presupposes the assumption of some sort of an average or normal rate of turnover or velocity of circulation. For, in order to make the concept precise, it must be specified how long a balance is to remain idle, so that it should be regarded as falling under the category of " idle balances ". Overnight, all balances are idle, and over a sufficiently long period, all may have been active, in the sense of having been turned over.

People sometimes separate the balances which they keep " idle " from those which they " use ", by putting the former on savings or time accounts while keeping the latter on checking accounts. But such is not always the case and, if it is not, one cannot ascertain whether an individual or society as a whole has hoarded or not by comparing the amount of money held (by the individual or by all individuals) at different points of time. We may express this by saying that hoarding has a time dimension.

Hoarding and the velocity of circulation of money. Hoarding and dishoarding thus means or implies a decrease or increase in the velocity of circulation of money V, or an increase or decrease in the reciprocal of V—that is to say, in the Marshallian[1] k. Should we then say that " hoarding " (" dishoarding ") and " decrease (increase) of V " are synonymous terms ? This is a terminological question which it is difficult to answer definitely on the basis of the general usage of the terms involved. Let us briefly and roughly consider the main forces responsible for changes in V (interpreting it, for the moment,

---

[1] It is hoped that further details lying behind the concept of " velocity " may remain undiscussed—viz.,the fact that we have, strictly speaking, to distinguish between a " transaction-velocity ", an "income-velocity " and some other varieties, and correspondingly between a " transaction-k ", an " income-k ", etc., the formal nature of the relation between V and k—viz., that of reciprocity—remaining in all cases the same. On this, compare the literature quoted above, Chapter 3, § 6, page 62.

as " transaction velocity "). V will change (*a*) if the habits of payment (*e.g.*, the income period) change, (*b*) if, with stable habits of payment, some money is " withheld from circulation ", or (*c*) if money flows into spheres (say agriculture) or regions[1] where its velocity of circulation is smaller than in those spheres or countries whence it came.

Some writers may prefer to reserve the term " hoarding " for such changes in V as are due to the factor (*b*), (or, perhaps, to (*a*) and (*b*)); they would then have to say that V is also subject to changes for reasons other than hoarding. To confine the term " hoarding " to phenomenon (*b*) would seem to correspond best to the definition of hoarding as the accumulation of idle deposits (unless the term " idle deposit " is given a rather wide meaning.) Suppose, for instance, that habits of payment so change that certain incomes which have been, so far, paid out in weekly instalments are, from now on, distributed in monthly payments. Assuming that before and after the change in the length of the income period has occurred, all money received is spent gradually during the respective income period, then the velocity of money is decreased, the money rests, on the average, longer in the pocket (or on the account) of the income receiver. Nevertheless, such deposits would presumably still be regarded as active, and not as idle, deposits.

The whole matter is, however, one of convenience and custom : one might just as well say that the deposits in question have become less active (that is, they are spent less frequently) and hence speak of an " act of hoarding ". But we need not here come to a definite decision or, rather, make a definite terminological proposal. Suffice it to call attention to the various possibilities.

From the point of view of the feasibility of statistical measurement, the definition of hoarding as equivalent to a change in V seems to be more convenient, because an actual separation of the influence on V of the three factors mentioned above will, in most cases, prove to be impossible.

---

[1] This has been frequently mentioned in connection with international flows of funds. *Cf.*, for example, J. Viner : *Studies in the Theory of International Trade*, Chapters VI and VII, *passim*.

One more word on the definition and measurement of hoarding by an individual (person, house-
hold, firm) may be in order. We shall say that an
individual has hoarded (dishoarded) if the fraction

$$\frac{\text{income (or transaction)}}{\text{average cash holding}}$$

decreases (increases). It
will be observed that this expression is the reciprocal of the
Marshallian k.[1] Hence, if an individual's volume of transactions
or income rises (falls) and his average cash holding rises (falls) in
proportion, the individual neither hoards nor dishoards. If, for
instance, somebody's monthly income used to be $200, was
received on the first of each month and spent evenly during the
month, and if the income now rises to $400, which is again received
on the first of each month and spent evenly during the month,
the average cash holding per day has become twice as high as
before; but no hoarding has occurred. The same is true if income
and average cash holding fall *pari passu*. It is, of course, possible
for a decrease in income to induce a person to dishoard—that is,
to reduce his expenditure by less than his income and to deplete
available cash resources. But looking at the average cash balance
alone, we cannot tell whether hoarding or dishoarding has
occurred or not. This point is frequently overlooked.[2]

*Definition of
hoarding by
an individual.*

---

[1] k usually refers to income ; it is then the reciprocal of *income* velocity.
But there is, as was pointed out above, a " transaction-k ". It will be
observed that it does not matter whether we express the magnitudes
involved (income, volume of transaction, average cash holding) in monetary or in " real " terms (*e.g.*, in wheat, as Professor Pigou, following
Marshall, does), because the denominator and numerator of the fraction
would have to be deflated by the same index number, if we changed from
one *numéraire* to another.

[2] If we adopt this definition in respect to individual hoarding, and if
we agree that any hoarding by society as a whole must be allocated to
certain individuals, we have implicitly answered the terminological
questions raised above as to the relation between the " hoarding " and
" velocity " concepts. Suppose there is no change in the habits of payment ; if, then, demand shifts in such a way that the income of people
who hold a small proportion of their income in the shape of money
(whose k is relatively small) decreases, while the income of people who
hold a large proportion of their income in money (whose k is great)
increases, velocity of circulation decreases for society, whilst nobody

Finally, it should be observed that the total amount which an individual or a firm is able to hoard during a given period is by no means always limited by the income received during this period or by net new saving. It would perhaps be better to refrain from saying that a part of income or of saving is hoarded and, instead, to speak only of the hoarding of money. But whether this terminological rule is observed or not, it should be clear that an individual (firm) may hoard, besides money income, all the money received from regular sales. We then speak of the hoarding of amortisation quotas and of working capital. In addition an indi.vidual may sell any asset in his possession and hoard the proceeds-Or he may borrow (sell claims) and hoard the proceeds of the loan.[1]

We can pass now to Mr. KEYNES' theory of the rate of interest and investigate whether or not it is compatible with the traditional views.

The definition of the rate of interest.   Mr. KEYNES holds that the rate of interest, contrary to the traditional view, according to which it is " the reward of not spending " (on consumption), is " the reward of not hoarding ",[2] " the reward for parting with liquidity for a specified period ".[3] It " is a measure of the unwillingness of those who possess money to part with their liquid control over it. The rate of interest is not the ' price ' which brings into equilibrium the demand for resources to invest with the readiness to abstain from present consumption. It is the ' price ' which equilibrates the desire to hold wealth in the form of cash with the available quantity of cash."[4]

---

need have hoarded, on our definition. This would, for example, be the case if demand for agricultural products increases (assuming that the farmer's k is greater than the industrialist's k).

[1] Mr. Keynes is, of course, quite right in saying that " the decision to hoard is not taken absolutely " (*General Theory*, page 174). It may depend on the price obtainable for certain assets. Given a certain situation, we may conceive of a demand curve for idle balances plotted against the rate of interest.

[2] *General Theory*, page 174.

[3] *Ibid.*, page 167. Precisely the same definition has been given by Professor Albert Hahn in his *Volkswirtschaftliche Theorie des Bankkredits*, Tübingen, 1920.

[4] *Ibid.*, page 167.

However, as Professor ROBERTSON[1] and others have pointed out, one alternative would not seem to exclude the other : the rate of interest may well be regarded as a reward both for not-consuming *and* for not-hoarding.   In order to earn interest, one must normally refrain not only from keeping money idle (from hoarding it), but also from spending it for consumption.   But the first (Mr. KEYNES') condition is, perhaps, less essential than the second. As everybody knows, banks sometimes pay interest on demand deposits.   If, then, hoarding takes the form of keeping idle deposits (rather than notes or coins), it does not preclude their earning interest on the amount hoarded, and the rate of interest cannot be said to be the reward for *not*-hoarding.   It is true that the rate of interest on demand deposits is usually lower than the rate on time deposits or the bond rate.   But this is not necessarily so; we can easily conceive of a situation where we have the same rate for all kinds of assets, and there have been instances when short-term rates of interest have been higher than long-term rates.   Hence, the deposit rate (reward for hoarding) may be higher than, for instance, the bond rate (reward for parting with liquidity).

About the definition of the rate of interest, there is no real difference of opinion.   Everybody means the same by " rate of interest " (at least, by the " explicit " rate of interest)—viz., " the price of debt "[2] or of a loan which is evidently the same as a debt.[3] Disagreement arises only when it comes to explaining the factors which determine the level of and fluctuations in the rate of interest.

---

[1] *Economic Journal*, 1937, page 431.   " The fact that the rate of interest measures the marginal convenience of holding idle money need not prevent it from measuring *also* the marginal inconvenience of abstaining from consumption.   Decumulation, as well as keeping-hoarded, is an alternative to keeping invested."

[2] Keynes : *General Theory*, page 173, bottom.

[3] Everybody means by " the rate of interest " the rate of interest on *money* loans—money loans of different duration, security, etc.   By a money loan, we mean a loan which is expressed in terms of money. Interest and principal could be expressed in terms of other things than money.   But even if they are expressed in money, the loan need not be paid out or repaid in money (cash).   It may be given and repaid in kind and still be a money loan.   Hence, what is needed is a *numéraire* and not actual money of exchange.

Liquidity preference demand for money. How does Mr. KEYNES' theory in this respect differ from the traditional views? According to Mr. KEYNES, the rate of interest is the resultant of two factors : liquidity preference and the quantity of money. " Quantity of money " we can translate by " supply of money ". The money is taken as fixed by the monetary authorities, or the banking system, according to some principles of monetary policy. It may conceivably be a function of the rate of interest—that is, the banks may, for example, pursue the policy of expanding the supply when the rate of interest rises. But, usually, this is not the case. It should be noted that by " supply of money ", Mr. KEYNES means the total supply for all purposes and not the supply of loanable funds alone. In this latter sense, the term " supply of money " is frequently used in the financial literature on the " money " market.

It is not so easy to interpret the term " liquidity preference ".[1] " The subject is substantially the same as that which has been sometimes discussed under the heading ' Demand for Money '."[2] Hence we may formulate : the rate of interest is determined by demand for, and supply of, money rather than by demand for, and supply of, saving or credit (loans).

At first sight, this theory seems indeed revolutionary and to run counter to many well-established doctrines. This impression is strengthened by Mr. KEYNES' apparent denials that an increase in the rate of saving, *ceteris paribus*, tends to lower the rate of interest; that a rise in the marginal efficiency of capital (demand for loanable funds) resulting, say, from a new invention or from a turn of the general sentiment towards optimism tends, *ceteris paribus*, to raise the rate of interest.[3] He seems to imply, furthermore, that any increase in the quantity of money, *ceteris paribus*, tends to depress the interest rate (at least in the first instance, notwithstanding indirect and psychological repercussions).

---

[1] On the various meanings with which it is used by Mr. Keynes in different places in his writings, compare, especially, Max Millikan : " Liquidity-Preference Theory of Interest ", in *American Economic Review*, Vol. 28, June 1938, pages 247 *et seq.*

[2] *General Theory*, page 194.

[3] *Ibid.*, pages 140, 165, 184 and 185.

A more careful analysis of what is meant by " liquidity prefer-ence " or " demand of money " will show, however, that the real difference between Mr. KEYNES' theory and the theory which explains the rate of interest and its daily fluctuations by the inter-action of demand for and supply of credit or loans (not saving) is not so great as may at first sight appear. A fundamental disagreement seems to arise, mainly because hidden assumptions are overlooked, especially those which are covered by the *ceteris-paribus* clause. The " other things " which are assumed to remain unchanged are not the same for all writers. Hence their disagree-ment is frequently due to their failure to realise the fact that they start from different assumptions, rather than to the fact that they arrive at different conclusions under the same set of assumptions.

Three motives for holding money. Mr. KEYNES distinguishes three motives for holding money : (*i*) the transactions-motive, (*ii*) the precautionary-motive and (*iii*) the speculative-motive. The transactions-motive is defined as " the need of cash for the current transactions of personal and business exchanges "[1] and is split up into the " income-motive and business-motive ".[2] " One reason for holding money is to bridge the interval between the receipt of income and its disbursement . . . and, similarly, the interval between the time of incurring business costs and that of the receipt of sales proceeds. "[2] In other words, a certain amount of money is required to " handle " a certain income and a certain volume of transactions. How much money is needed depends on the velocity of circulation of money and is determined by the habits of payment and other factors which have been touched upon in an earlier chapter, where references to the relevant literature are to be found.[3]

The precautionary-motive is described as the desire to hold cash " to provide for contingencies requiring sudden expenditures

---

[1] *General Theory*, page 170.
[2] *Ibid.*, page 195.
[3] Compare footnote [1] on page 59 (Chapter 3, § 6). The *locus classicus* of the discussion of these problems is Professor Marget's *Theory of Prices*, New York, 1938.

and for unforeseen opportunities of advantageous purchases ".[1] Mr. KEYNES assumes that the amount of money needed for this purpose, as well as the amount needed for transaction purposes, depends on, and varies with, changes in the actual level of activity (more precisely, volume of transactions).

By the speculative-motive, Mr. KEYNES means the inducement to hold money for the purpose " of securing profit from knowing better than the market what the future will bring forth ".[2] If, for instance, one expects the price of debt (*e.g.*, of bonds) to go down— that is, the rate of interest to rise—one will try to change from debt to money, to sell bonds and hold money. Mr. KEYNES believes that " general experience indicates that the aggregate demand for money to satisfy the speculative-motive usually shows a continuous response to gradual changes in the rate of interest—*i.e.*, there is a continuous curve relating to changes in the demand for money to satisfy the speculative-motive and changes in the rate of interest as given by changes in the price of bonds and debts of various maturities ".[3]

Hoarding and the rate of interest.   Mr. KEYNES believes, furthermore, that it is roughly true that the total amount of money, M, can be divided into two parts, M_1 and M_2, of which the first part, M_1, is held to satisfy the transactions- and precautionary-motives and the second part, M_2, to satisfy the speculative-motive.[4] M_1 may thus be called active or circulating money, whilst M_2 is hoarded or idle or inactive money. M_1 varies with the level of income or, rather, with the volume of transactions. M_2 depends on the interest rate in such wise that it rises when the interest rate falls and falls when the interest rate rises.

This would seem to be the most important new relationship introduced by Mr. KEYNES; new, not in the sense that it has never

---

[1] *General Theory*, page 196.

[2] *Ibid.*, page 170.

[3] *Ibid.*, page 197.

[4] *Ibid.*, page 199. Mr. Keynes realises that this is not quite correct, because " the amount of cash which an individual decides to hold to satisfy the transactions- . . . and precautionary-motive is not entirely independent of what he is holding to satisfy the speculative motive ".

been suggested in the literature, but in the sense that it has never been carried through consistently. We may formulate this theorem also by saying that hoarding tends to be stimulated by a fall, and checked by a rise, in interest rates. Hoarding becomes cheaper when interest rates fall, and costly when they rise. In still other words, we may say that the velocity of circulation of money[1] is positively correlated to the rate of interest.[2]

It will be convenient in the following analysis to distinguish sharply between liquidity preference in the wider sense and in the narrower sense. By the former, we mean the demand for money for all purposes, inclusive of the transaction purpose $(M_1 + M_2)$; by the latter, demand for idle balances, M_2, alone. The narrower definition corresponds better to the everyday meaning of the term " liquidity preference ". We shall therefore call it " liquidity preference proper ". If somebody sells an asset against money and keeps the proceeds idle or if he refrains from spending all his money receipts as usual, we may describe that as an increase in his liquidity preference. Suppose, on the other hand, that wages rise but interest rates remain constant because the banks increase the money supply; then the average cash holdings of the working population will rise, and we have to describe that in Mr. KEYNES' terminology as a rise in liquidity preference in the wider sense : more money is held for transaction purposes.[3]

---

[1] We think of the velocity of M, whilst Mr. Keynes (*General Theory*, page 201) speaks of the velocity of M_1 alone. Mr. Keynes speaks furthermore of *income* velocity rather than of transactions velocity.

[2] A very instructive mathematical and diagrammatic exposition of these relationships and of Mr. Keynes' *General Theory*, *in toto*, has been given by Dr. Hicks : " Mr. Keynes and the Classics ", *Econometrica*, April 1937, and by O. Lange : " The Rate of Interest and the Optimum Propensity to Consume ", in *Economica*, February 1938, pages 12 *et seq*. Of the latter, Mr. Keynes says that it " follows very closely and accurately [his] line of thought ". (*Economic Journal*, Vol. 48, June 1938, page 321.)

[3] Mr. Keynes himself states his theory sometimes in terms of liquidity preference in the wider sense and sometimes in terms of liquidity preference proper. An example of the latter will be found in *Economic Journal*, 1937, page 250. " If we mean by ' hoarding ' the holding of idle balances, then my theory of the rate of interest might be expressed by saying that the rate of interest serves to equate the demand and supply of hoards ".

This terminology does not appear to be in accord with everyday language.

Let us now consider how far Mr. KEYNES' liquidity-preference theory and the traditional demand-for-and-supply-of-loanable-funds theory of interest are really at variance.

How a rise in investment demand influences the interest rate. Take, first, an increase of the demand for capital—that is, in Mr. KEYNES' terminology, an upward shift of the schedule of the marginal efficiency of capital, which is characteristic of the prosperity phase of the business cycle. Suppose an increase in consumers' expenditure (however brought about) or improved expectations or inventions make entrepreneurs eager to invest. They demand investible funds, and, according to the traditional views, that will tend to drive up interest rates.

In spite of the impression to the contrary, this is not in contradiction with Mr. KEYNES' theory. We have only to translate what we have just said into his terminology. There are, in fact, two possibilities. First, if an entrepreneur borrows additional money from the market in anticipation of a future increase in his expenditure for investment purposes,[1] this represents an increase in his liquidity preference, for his demand for money has increased without either a fall in interest rate or, as yet, a rise in the volume of transactions. But, secondly, the entrepreneur may borrow additional funds no quicker than he spends additional funds on the increased investment. In this case, as indeed in the previous case also, there will be a rise in the volume of business transactions, and this will lead, sooner or later, to an increased demand for money to finance the larger turnover. This will involve a rise in interest rates, according to Mr. KEYNES, because less of the existing supply of money will remain available to satisfy the speculative motive for liquidity.

In either case, therefore, if the supply of money does not rise, the rate of interest must go up. This qualification about the supply of money cannot give rise to any disagreement, for it will

---

[1] This case is an example of the demand for " finance " for planned investment, which is discussed below, page 212.

be accepted by the adherents of the traditional views. All agree that, in spite of an increase in demand for loanable funds, the interest rate will not go up if (*a*) the banks supply the necessary funds or (*b*) the public supplies them by dishoarding at unchanged interest rates.

Case (*a*) has been recently described by Mr. KEYNES, alternatively, as an increase of the willingness of the banking system to become illiquid, which cancels the rise in the liquidity preference of the public. "One could regard the rate of interest as being determined by the interplay of the terms on which the public desires to become more or less liquid and those on which the banking system is ready to become more or less illiquid."[1] Apart from terminological differences, therefore, this theory and the loanable-fund (in this case bank-fund) theory would seem to be almost identical.

In Mr. KEYNES' terminology, case (*b*) would have to be construed as a decrease in the liquidity preference of those who are " willing to release cash "[2] which cancels the increase in the liquidity preference of the entrepreneurs and thus leaves the interest rate constant.

When the entrepreneurs then spend the money on wages, etc., they become less liquid (their liquidity preference decreases), but the successive recipients of the money become more liquid (their liquidity preference increases). This can also be expressed by saying that income (or transactions), which is one source of the demand for money, goes up. More money is needed to satisfy the transactions-motive, and this drives up (or keeps up) the interest rate, unless less money is needed for satisfying the specu- lative-motive—in other words, unless somebody "releases cash" (that is, dishoards).

Planned invest-   In a recent contribution, " The ' *Ex-Ante* ' Theory of the Rate of Interest ",[3] Mr. KEYNES has
ment and   modified, and elucidated, his theory in a way which
interest rates.   makes its similarity with the loanable fund theory
               still clearer. In his *General Theory*, he explained that the demand for money depended on the rate of interest

---

[1] *Economic Journal,* Vol. 47, 1937, page 666.
[2] *Ibid.,* page 667
[3] *Ibid.,* pages 663 *et seq.*

(determining the demand for idle balances) and on the actual level of activity (determining the demand for circulating balances). This, it is now admitted, was an incomplete statement. " The additional factor, previously overlooked, to which Professor OHLIN's emphasis on the *ex-ante* character of investment decisions has directed attention, is the following."[1] There is a third factor affecting the demand for money—viz., the necessity of providing what Mr. KEYNES proposes to call " finance " for planned investment. Before activity has actually gone up, funds for the intended outlay must be secured. " During the interregnum—and during that period only—between the date when the entrepreneur arranges his finance and the date when he actually makes his investment, there is an additional demand for liquidity without, as yet, any additional supply of it necessarily arising " (page 665). The adherents of the loanable-fund theory would merely substitute " credits " for the word " liquidity " in this sentence.

Mr. KEYNES rightly points out that this additional demand must meet with additional supply, if the rate of interest is not to rise. Somebody, the banks or the public, must " deplete their *existing* cash " (page 666), and he criticises Professor OHLIN for suggesting that *ex-ante* saving out of future income can satisfy the demand for finance. This is the same criticism as was made above when it was said that *ex ante* saving in the sense of saving out of a future income cannot affect the bond market *now*. This criticism loses its validity, however, if *ex-ante* saving is interpreted, as was suggested above, in the Robertsonian sense, as saving out of a previously received income. The demand for finance can be satisfied by increased saving in this sense or by dishoarding. Both sources can be described (in Mr. KEYNES' words) as a depletion of existing cash—cash from idle balances or, in the case of additional savings, cash released from transactions balances by the reduced expenditure on consumption goods.

One point regarding Mr. KEYNES' theory of " finance " has given rise to an interesting discussion which throws much light

---

[1] *Economic Journal, loc. cit.*, page 665.

on the whole issue.[1] It is Mr. KEYNES' insistence that " finance is essentially a revolving fund . . . . As soon as it is ' used ' in the sense of being expended, the lack of liquidity is automatically made good and the readiness to become temporarily unliquid is available to be used over again."[2]

Professor ROBERTSON objected that finance funds which have been spent can be made available for new financing only if they are saved (in Professor ROBERTSON's sense) by one of the successive recipients. Mr. KEYNES' reply clearly indicated that there is no disagreement except a terminological one, due to the different definition of the concept of saving. Mr. KEYNES explains : " The demand for cash falls away unless the completed activity (associated with the expenditure of the finance funds) is being succeeded by a new activity."[3] It would appear that this condition might well be accepted by Professor ROBERTSON : for the primary activity will be succeded by a new one, if the money is again spent on consumption; if it is saved, the " chain of activities " is interrupted, the demand for cash falls away unless the saving leads to a fall in interest rates which stimulates investment, or unless the marginal efficiency of capital rises—changes which are excluded by Mr. KEYNES' *ceteris-paribus* assumption.

The influence of saving on the rate of interest. On the question whether an increase in saving (a fall in the propensity to consume) affects the rate of interest or not, Mr. KEYNES' views still seem to be very different from the traditional views. He expresses the difference in principle between his and the traditional view as follows. Economists have " almost invariably . . . assumed . . . that, *ceteris paribus*, a decrease in spending will tend to lower the rate of interest and an increase in investment to raise it. But if what these two quantities determine is not the rate of interest, but the aggregate

---

[1] Compare Professor Robertson's article, " Mr. Keynes on Finance ", in *Economic Journal*, Vol. 48, June 1938, page 314 *et seq.*, and Mr. Keynes' reply, *ibid.*, page 318. See also E. S. Shaw, " False Issues in the Interest-Theory Controversy ", in *Journal of Political Economy*, Vol. 46, December 1938, page 838.

[2] *Economic Journal*, Vol. 47, 1937, page 666.

[3] *Economic Journal*, Vol. 48, 1938, page 319.

volume of employment, then our outlook on the mechanism of the economic system will be profoundly changed. A decreased readiness to spend will be looked on in a quite different light if, instead of being regarded as a factor which will, *ceteris paribus*, increase investment, it is seen as a factor which will, *ceteris paribus*, diminish employment." [1]

Some misunderstanding seems to have arisen in this connection from different interpretations of the *ceteris-paribus* clause. The classical writers, when they are not dealing with money and the business cycles, are in the habit of taking total monetary outlay as constant; it is included in the *cetera* that remain the same. Then a decrease in one division (consumption spending) implies an increase in the other (investment). Assuming the marginal efficiency of capital to be constant, this implies a fall in the interest rate. Mr. KEYNES, on the other hand, includes liquidity preference among the other things that remain unchanged; then, since M has remained unchanged, the rate of interest cannot fall. [2]

Now the loanable-fund theorists would not deny that this might happen, but they would describe it differently : people may hoard the money which they fail to spend. In Mr. KEYNES' theory, this has to be described as a rise in liquidity preference proper; [3] demand for money for " speculative purposes ", M_2, has risen. This implies a decrease in M_1, which is connected with the fall in activity. Thus total demand for money and the quantity of money remaining unchanged, the rate of interest remains unchanged too.

If, however, the producers of consumers' goods who experience a decrease in demand try to maintain activity by selling securities, the rate of interest will rise, and these sales will have to be construed as an increase in their liquidity preference.

There may be a difficulty in the timing of the processes; it is, however, clearly possible to conceive of a case where people spend

---

[1] *General Theory*, page 185. This passage conveys the incorrect impression that, in Mr. Keynes' opinion, an increase in investment does not tend to raise the interest rate.

[2] This point was also made by T. W. Hutchinson : *The Significance and Basic Postulates of Economic Theory*, London, 1938, pages 44 and 45.

[3] Compare the definition of this concept given above on page 210.

less on consumption (save), but direct the money *simultaneously* to the purchase of new securities.

It would appear from the foregoing discussion that Mr. KEYNES' views on the question of how the rate of interest is influenced by changes in the propensity to consume (save)[1] are not so radically different from the views of other authors as may at first sight appear. In a very recent exposition of his theory, Mr. KEYNES has himself suggested this.[2] " The analysis which I gave in my *General Theory of Employment* is the same as the ' general theory ' by Dr. LANGE on page 18 of his article."[3] On this page, Dr. LANGE states that " the traditional statement that the rate of interest . . . moves in the opposite direction to the propensity to save holds fully in our generalised theory ".[4]

Changes in M and the rate of interest. There remains one more case in respect of which the liquidity-preference theory seems to be at variance with the traditional views—viz., the effect of an increase in the quantity of money on the rate of interest. It would seem that, according to Mr. KEYNES, such an increase must always lead to a fall in the rate of interest. This is, however, not Mr. KEYNES' view, because in many cases, such an increase will, automatically and *uno actu*, raise the liquidity-preference schedule. " Suppose that M consists of gold coins and that changes in M can only result from increased returns to the activities of gold-miners. . . . In this case, changes in M are, in the first instance, directly associated with changes in Y, since the new gold accrues as someone's

---

[1] Since the propensity to save is equal to 1 minus the propensity to consume, any proposition regarding the propensity to save can be translated into a proposition regarding the propensity to consume and vice versa.

[2] See footnote 1, page 321, in *Economic Journal*, June 1938.

[3] *Economica*, February 1938.

[4] Hence we must conclude that Dr. Lange is not right when he attributes, rather unqualifiedly, to Mr. Keynes, not his *general* theory, but a *special* case of it—viz., that case where the " interest elasticity of the demand for liquidity is infinite " (page 19). It seems fair to say that Mr. Keynes holds that this situation obtains under special circumstances —viz., in deep depressions. It is " depression economics " (as Dr. Hicks, *loc. cit.*, says) and not the " general theory ". For further discussion of this special case, see the text below, page 218.

income. Exactly the same conditions hold if changes in M are due to the Government printing money wherewith to meet its current expenditure;—in this case also, the new money accrues as someone's income."[1] The increased level of income represents increased demand for money; hence the increased M does not lead at once to a rise in the rate of interest.

" The new level of income, however [Mr. KEYNES elaborates], will not continue sufficiently high for the requirements of M_1 to absorb the whole of the increase in M; and some portion of the money will seek an outlet in buying securities or other assets until the rate of interest has fallen so as to bring about an increase in the magnitude of M_2 and, at the same time, to stimulate a rise in Y to such an extent that the new money is absorbed either in M_2 or in the M_1 which corresponds to the rise in Y caused by the fall in the interest rate. Thus at one remove this case comes to the same thing as the alternative case where the new money can only be issued in the first instance by a relaxation of the conditions of credit by the banking system ", and thus automatically entails a fall in the interest rate.[2]

This passage calls for some comments. The statement that " money will seek an outlet in buying securities " must surely imply that the recipients of the money whose incomes have risen save a part of it, in Professor ROBERTSON's sense ? In this case, saving will reduce the rate of interest, although that entails part of the money going into hoards (increases the magnitude of M_2). If people did not save, but spent all the new money on consumption, M_1 would still absorb the whole increase in M.

The course of events might presumably differ from the one which Mr. KEYNES described : thus the increase in Y might stimulate investment, and this might more than compensate the tendency to a fall in the interest rate. Indeed, it is impossible to say what the outcome will be. But it is clear that Mr. KEYNES' theory does not imply that an increase in the quantity of money must in all circumstances entail a fall in the interest rate, and that

---

[1] *General Theory*, page 200.
[2] *Ibid.*

its stimulating effect is conditioned by its having previously depressed the interest rate.[1]

Apart from terminological innovations, the real contribution brought by Mr. KEYNES' *General Theory of Interest* would seem to consist, as we have seen, of the proposition that hoarding is a function of the rate of interest. This does not of course mean that factors other than the rate of interest may not also exert an influence as strong as that of the interest rate on the amount of inactive balances. In other words, even in the short run, shifts of the liquidity-preference schedule may be at least as important as movements along the curve.[2]

Infinite elasticity of demand for idle balances. Besides and in addition to the general empirical assumption about " demand for idle cash balances " (propensity to hoard), there is a more specific assumption about the shape of that demand curve (liquidity-preference schedule proper) which frequently plays an important rôle in Mr. KEYNES' theory. This more specific assumption constitutes Mr. KEYNES' " special theory ", as Dr. HICKS has aptly called it.

This assumption is to the effect that, for low interest rates, " say 2% " (page 202), the demand for idle balances (" demand for liquidity ") becomes more and more elastic and, at a rate well above zero, absolutely elastic—that is, insatiable. In technical parlance, the interest-elasticity of the demand for liquidity becomes

---

[1] Some economists, however, have interpreted Mr. Keynes' theory to mean that an increase in the quantity of money could operate on the economic system only via the rate of interest. For example, Mrs. J. Robinson, in a review of Professor Bresciani-Turroni's *Economics of Inflation*, remarks : " The author assumes that an increase in the quantity of money was the root cause of the inflation [in Germany, in 1919-1923]. But this view it is impossible to accept. An increase in the quantity of money no doubt has a tendency to raise prices, *for it leads* to a reduction in the interest rate, which stimulates investment and discourages saving, and so leads to an increase in activity. But there is no evidence whatever that events in Germany followed this sequence " (italics not in the original). *Economic Journal*, Vol. 48, 1938, page 509.

[2] The same difficulties have to be faced by any two-dimensional analytical apparatus when applied to such a complex phenomenon as the demand for idle balances and the rate of interest. Compare on this point M. Millikan, *loc. cit.*, pages 254 *et seq.*

infinite :[1] the schedule of liquidity preference proper becomes horizontal. It is very important to realise that this is equivalent to saying that, when this critical level of interest rates has been reached, any amount of money which might be created by the banks will be hoarded, in addition to any amount which people save in excess of the current demand for investment purposes (in Mr. KEYNES' terminology, we should rather say : any amount of money which is released from balances held for business or income purposes). Suppose, for instance, that, at the depth of a depression, investment demand for loanable funds is at a low ebb, and that the rate of interest has reached that critical level of (say) 2%; suppose, moreover, that there is a reasonable degree of competition, so that wages and prices continue to fall so long as there is unemployment : then money is constantly released from the transaction sphere. But instead of being directed to the acquisition of assets, thus driving up their prices (which is equivalent to reducing the interest rate) and stimulating investment and employment, all this money is being hoarded. Hoards grow without limit in terms of money and, because of the fall in prices, still faster in real terms.

A limit to the fall in interest rates.   If such a situation exists,—*i.e.*, if the demand for money-to-hoard (liquidity preference curve proper) is perfectly elastic—" a rise in the schedule of the marginal efficiency of capital only increases employment, and does not raise the interest rate at all ".[2] Likewise, a rise in the rate of saving (propensity to consume) decreases employment without decreasing the rate of interest. The idea that such a situation might arise is original and is of considerable theoretical interest.

Let us ask how, according to Mr. KEYNES, such a situation could come about, and whether, according to him, it has ever arisen.

The reason for the existence of a minimum, below which the rate of interest cannot possibly fall, we may paraphrase in the words of Dr. HICKS : " If the costs of holding money can be

---

[1] Lange, *op. cit.*, pages 18 and 19.
[2] Hicks, *op. cit.*, page 154.

neglected, it will always be profitable to hold money rather than lend it out, if the rate of interest is not greater than zero. Consequently, the rate of interest must always be positive. In an extreme case, the shortest short-term rate may perhaps be nearly zero. But if so, the long-term rate must lie above it, for the long rate has to allow for the risk that the short rate may rise during the currency of the loan, and it should be observed that the short rate can only rise, it cannot fall. This does not only mean that the long rate must be a sort of average of the probable short rates over its duration, and that this average must lie above the current short rate. There is also the more important risk to be considered —that the lender on long term [*e.g.*, bondholder] may desire to have cash before the agreed date of repayment, and then, if the short rate has risen meanwhile, he may be involved in a substantial capital loss."[1] Thus, in the words of Mr. KEYNES, " the rate of interest is a highly conventional phenomenon. For its actual value is largely governed by the prevailing view as to what its value is expected to be."[2] The argument is perhaps more intelligible when put in terms of asset prices (*e.g.*, bond prices) instead of interest rates. If asset prices are expected to fall (long-term rates to rise), asset prices cannot remain at a level much higher than the expected price, because people would prefer to keep their resources in cash, in spite of very low short rates.[3]

Weighty arguments against the assumption that the expected rate of long-term interest (asset prices) is likely to persist unchanged for any length of time, in spite of a fall in the current short-term rate, have been brought forward by Mr. HAWTREY.[4] We need

---

[1] *Loc. cit.*, pages 154 and 155. Compare also Professor Hicks' book, *Value and Capital*, Oxford, 1939, especially Chapter XI.

[2] *General Theory*, page 203.

[3] When put in terms of asset prices, it becomes clear that it is an optical illusion to say that the rate of interest cannot fall farther because it is " so near to zero ". Between, say, one *per cent* and zero *per cent*, there are still as many intermediate positions as there are between the price at $400 of a $100 4% bond (corresponding to a capitalisation at an interest rate of 1%) and the infinitely high price of the same bond corresponding to a capitalisation at a rate of zero *per cent*.

[4] *Capital and Employment*, 1937, Chapter VII. See also Mr. Kaldor's reply to Mr. Hawtrey's criticism of Mr. Keynes, " Mr. Hawtrey on Short and Long Term Investment ", in *Economica*, November 1938, pages 464 and 465.

however, not go into this matter more thoroughly, because Mr. KEYNES himself (quite rightly, it would seem) believes that this contingency of an " absolute liquidity-preference " is a theoretical possibility which has actually not yet arisen. " But whilst this limiting case ", in which " the monetary authority would have lost effective control over the rate of interest " (and in which, we may add, no fall in wages and prices could depress the rate of interest by releasing money from the transaction sphere), " might become practically important in future, I know of no example of it hitherto. Indeed, owing to the unwillingness of most monetary authorities to deal boldly in debts of long term, there has not been much opportunity for a test."[1]   Nor, we may add, has the alternative to a policy of increasing the quantity of money—viz., a sustained fall of *all* prices and wages—been put to a real test.[2]

Summary.   An almost perfectly elastic demand for idle balances up to a very considerable amount may occasionally occur, and has occurred temporarily (Mr. HAWTREY's temporary credit deadlock), but the hypothesis that it may exist indefinitely has not yet been put to the test of fact.[3]

---

[1] *General Theory*, page 207. It must, however, be admitted that there are many passages in Mr. Keynes' writings which are difficult to reconcile with this pronouncement and seem to assume the actual existence of cases of an insatiable desire for liquidity.

[2] It should be understood that, according to Mr. Keynes' theory, the two policies are alternative means only in one respect, which is, however (in the present context), the important one. Both policies serve to increase the quantity of money in terms of real purchasing power, " in terms of wage units ", as Mr. Keynes says. On page 234 of his *General Theory*, Mr. Keynes says, for example : " The only relief [for an excessive liquidity preference—that is, for an extreme desire to hoard]—apart from changes in the marginal efficiency of capital—can come . . . from an increase in the quantity of money, or—which is formally the same thing—a rise in the value of money." (Note that this passage contains an explicit statement to the effect that a fall in wages and prices will eventually bring relief. We wish, however, by no means to deny, nor does Mr. Keynes, that in many other respects the two policies are very different and cannot be regarded, from a practical point of view, as good substitutes. *Cf.* § 5 of this chapter below.)

[3] Chronic unemployment with stable money wages is no proof of an absolute liquidity preference.

§ 4. THE "MULTIPLIER" AND THE "MARGINAL PROPENSITY
TO CONSUME"

*The " psycho-
logical "
determinants of
 Mr. Keynes'
system.*
"Three fundamental psychological factors—
namely, the psychological propensity to consume,
the psychological attitude to liquidity and the
psychological expectation of future yield from
capital assets" (which govern, together with " the
given factors ", capital equipment, etc., the marginal
efficiency of capital or demand for capital)[1]—
constitute the skeleton of Mr. KEYNES' theoretical system which
" determines the national income and the quantity of employment ". Mr. KEYNES is careful to explain that these psychological
propensities (together with some non-psychological factors
such as the wage unit and the quantity of money) can
only " sometimes " be regarded as the " ultimate independent
variables " (page 246). He recognises that they are " themselves
complex and that each is capable of being affected by prospective
changes in the others "[2] and, presumably, *a fortiori*, by *actual*
changes in the others. (Thus we have seen that the liquidity
preference is influenced by actual and prospective changes in the
marginal efficiency of capital.)

As will be illustrated by various examples in the following
pages, we have here a source of frequent misunderstandings.
Those who have become accustomed to think in terms of

---

[1] *General Theory*, pages 246 and 247.
[2] *Ibid.*, page 184. In the course of the discussion, Mr. Keynes is
sometimes inclined to forget these limitations of his theory. This has
misled some economists to overlook them altogether. The usefulness of
the system clearly depends on the degree of independence of these
variables. If they were highly interdependent, they could not be regarded
as " ultimate independent variables ". This, is, of course, a difficulty
which any interdependence theory, especially one in macro-economic
terms, has to face. It is impossible to build up a theory which explains
national income and employment in terms of a few complex, strictly
independent factors without having regard to their internal structure.
Such a procedure can yield only rough approximations. Mr. Keynes is
well aware of these difficulties. See, for example, his remarks, *General
Theory*, page 297.

Mr. KEYNES' system take the determinant propensities, the wage unit,[1] etc., as given, and regard them as independent from one another, whilst other writers, brought up in traditional modes of thought, frequently make assumptions which imply a mutual influencing of Mr. KEYNES' determinants, or treat some of them as variables. These differences in the starting-point are concealed by differences in terminology.

Marginal efficiency of capital (demand for capital) and liquidity-preference having been discussed, we now turn to an examination of the concept " marginal propensity to consume " and the closely related " multiplier ".

The problem of the " multiplier ". Mr. KEYNES considers the theory of the so-called " multiplier " " an integral part of his theory of employment " (page 113). The multiplier—k— " establishes a precise relationship, given the propensity to consume, between aggregate employment and income and the rate of investment " (page 113). " It tells us that, when there is an increment of aggregate investment, income will increase by an amount which is k times the increment of investment " (page 115): $\Delta Y = k \ \Delta I$, and $\Delta Y = \Delta C + \Delta I$, if by ΔY, ΔI and ΔC we denote small increments of income, investment and consumption respectively. (We need not go into the question of the unit in which these magnitudes are expressed. Mr. KEYNES discusses this question carefully and elects to express all these magnitudes in " wage units ". We may, however, think of them just as well in " real " terms or in terms of money.) " The fundamental notion " underlying the theory is that, if " we conceive the monetary or other public authority to take steps to stimulate or to retard investment, the change in the amount of employment " will not be confined to the investment industries, but will extend to the consumption industries and " will be a function of the net change in the amount of investment "; and the theory aims " at laying down general principles by which to estimate the actual quantitative relationship between an increment

---

[1] In particular, the assumption regarding the stability of the wage unit, with its implication of rigid money wages, is apt to be lost sight of, but should be well kept in mind. (This will be discussed at greater length below, § 5 of this chapter.)

of net investment and the increment of aggregate employment which will be associated with it " (pages 113 and 114).

　　　　　　　　　　　The pure theory of the multiplier consists of the
The pure establishment of a precise relationship between the
theory of the multiplier and the marginal propensity to consume.
" *multiplier* ". The propensity to consume is defined as the func-
　　　　　　　　tional relationship between "a given level of income"
and " the expenditure on consumption out of that level of income "
(page 90). The *marginal* propensity to consume is then the relationship between an increment of income and the expenditure on
consumption out of this increment. It is measured by $\dfrac{\Delta C}{\Delta Y}$,
which is always smaller than unity, because " the normal psychological law " holds that, " when the real income of the community
increases or decreases, its consumption will increase or decrease,
but not so fast " (page 114).[1] The marginal propensity to consume
" tells us how the next increment of output will have to be divided
between consumption and investment " (page 115). A marginal
propensity to consume of, for example, $\dfrac{9}{10}$ means that $\dfrac{9}{10}$ of the
next increment of income will be consumed. If the marginal
propensity to consume is 1, the whole increment will be consumed; if it is zero, the whole will be saved. It follows that
the (marginal) propensity to save has to be defined as 1 minus
the (marginal) propensity to consume. If the latter is $\dfrac{9}{10}$, the
former is $\dfrac{1}{10}$, this being the proportion (of the next increment) of
income saved. If the marginal propensity to consume is 1, the

---

[1] It may be observed, *en passant*, that the marginal propensity
to consume of an individual may conceivably be greater than unity :
that is to say, an individual may be induced by an increase in his income
to spend more than that increment on consumption. This need not,
however, make his *average* propensity to consume greater than unity—in
other words, it need not mean dissaving. (An average propensity to
consume greater than unity means that $C > Y$—*i.e.*, that the individual
dissaves, " lives on his capital ".) Mr. Keynes does not consider this
case. (Compare, however, Mr. G. R. Holden's paper " Mr. Keynes'
Consumption Function, A Rejoinder ", *Quarterly Journal of Economics*,
August 1938, and Mr. Keynes' reply *Ibid.*, November 1938.)

marginal propensity to save is zero; if the former is zero, the latter is 1.

It should be kept in mind that the terms " propensity to consume (save) " and " marginal propensity to consume (save) " are usually used in the schedule sense—that is to say, they usually denote the whole schedule, showing what proportion of different hypothetical incomes or increments to income an individual or society as a whole would consume (save).   Sometimes, however, when speaking of the propensity to consume, reference is made to a particular point (mainly the point actually realised) on the schedule of alternatives.   Although it will usually be clear from the context in what sense the word is used, it would be better to speak, when not referring to the schedule as a whole, of " the rate of consumption (saving) "[1] or, better still, of " the proportion of income consumed (saved) ".

What is the relation between the marginal propensity to consume and the multiplier ?   The relationship is quite simple :

$$\Delta Y = k \Delta I$$

$$k = \frac{\Delta Y}{\Delta I}.$$

Since $\Delta Y = \Delta C + \Delta I$,

$$k = \frac{\Delta Y}{\Delta Y - \Delta C} = \frac{1}{1 - \frac{\Delta C}{\Delta Y}}$$

Thus, the multiplier k is, by definition, equal to 1 divided by 1 minus the marginal propensity to consume; and the marginal propensity to consume, $\frac{\Delta C}{\Delta Y}$, is equal to $1 - \frac{1}{k}$.   Since $1 - \frac{\Delta C}{\Delta Y}$ is the marginal propensity to save, we can also say that the multiplier is the repicrocal of the marginal propensity to save, and vice versa.   We

---

[1] It will be observed that what is meant is not the *time* rate of consumption (saving), the amount consumed (saved) per unit of time, but the *income* rate, amount consumed (saved) per unit of income.   This rate of consumption is measured by $\frac{C}{Y}$; the rate of saving by $\frac{S}{Y}$.   Since $S = Y - C$, the rate of saving is 1 minus the rate of consumption : $\frac{S}{Y} = 1 - \frac{C}{Y}$.

have thus three interchangeable expressions for the same thing. The expression " marginal propensity to consume " can always be replaced, without a change in meaning, by the expression " 1 minus the marginal propensity to save " or by " 1 minus the reciprocal of the multiplier ".

It follows that if, for instance, the marginal propensity to consume is $\frac{9}{10}$ (the marginal propensity to save being $\frac{1}{10}$), the multiplier is 10; " the total employment caused (for example) by public works will be ten times the primary employment provided by the public works themselves, assuming no reduction of investment in other directions " (pages 116 and 117). This result is clearly implied by the assumption made. If we assume that an increment in Y is divided in the proportion of 1 : 9 between I and C, then we assume that an increase in I by x units will mean an increase of $9x$ in C and an increase of $10x$ in Y. If we assume the marginal propensity to consume to be zero—in other words, that an increment in Y is wholly confined to I—then we assume that an increment in I increases Y by no more than its own amount. If the marginal propensity to consume is assumed to be 1—that is, if we assume that " the next increment of output will have to be divided between consumption and investment " in the proportion of 1 to 0—then, in order not to contradict that assumption, we must assume that any increase in I is accompanied by an infinite increase in C and Y : the multiplier is infinitely high. In plain English, there can be no increase in I.

It will be well to keep in mind the logical nature of the " pure theory of the multiplier "[1] which is clearly revealed by the foregoing discussion. The theory is not intended by Mr. KEYNES as a statement about a relationship in the real world between two distinguishable phenomena; there are not two facts, the marginal propensity to consume on the one hand, and the multiplier on the other, of which the former influences and governs the latter. The logical theory of the multiplier establishes a terminological rule

---

[1] Mr. Keynes calls it the " logical theory of the multiplier " (*General Theory*, page 122).

for the use of the two terms " marginal propensity to consume "
and " multiplier " and nothing more.

The practical problems behind the multiplier. The practical problem to the solution of which the theory of the multiplier and the attempts at a statistical measurement of its magnitude are directed is the determination, if possible in advance, of the indirect effects of Government expenditure on public works and the like.   The underlying idea is that, if the Government spends several hundred million dollars on public investment and thereby creates additional employment, the first recipients of the money will spend at least a part of their income on consumption; the consumption industries will be stimulated; the money will be spent again and again; and a whole series of successive income- and employment-creating expenditure will emanate from the first investment.   The question is, how big will be the secondary, tertiary, etc., effects flowing from the primary investment of a given magnitude ?[1]   For the reasons given below, the pure theory of the multiplier cannot provide a final answer to that question.

The problem of determining " net invest- ment ". (1) The multiplier refers to the effect of an increment of *net* investment.   Hence, as Mr. KEYNES states, " if we wish to apply [the theory of the multiplier] without qualification to the effect of (for example) increased public works, we have to assume that there is no off-set through decreased investment in other directions " (page 119).   In other words, a concrete amount of public works cannot, without examination, be accepted as *net* new investment; the public works policy may have unfavourable repercussions on private investment (*a*) by raising prices of material and labour; (*b*) by raising the interest rate, because of the method of financing employed; (*c*) owing to repercussions " through psychology ", if a Government deficit

---

[1] The idea that investment stimulates consumption is almost as old as business-cycle theory.   That it is inherent in the Wicksellian theory of the cumulative process of expansion has already been said (see Chapter 3, pages 33 *et seq.*, above).   Mr. Kahn, among others, has analysed the problem in his article " The Relation of Home Investment to Unemployment " (*Economic Journal*, June 1931), and has contributed the word " multiplier ".

shakes confidence; (*d*) through unfavourable influences on the international balance of trade and payments.

Some of these factors have been discussed by Mr. KEYNES (*General Theory*, pages 119 to 121), Mr. KAHN (*loc. cit.*), and by other writers in the considerable recent literature on expansionist policies in general and public works in particular.[1]

Secondary investment. (2) Mr. KEYNES speaks only of " *adverse* reactions on investment " of a public works policy, but it may have *favourable* reactions too. Indeed, it is generally considered as a condition of success of a " pump priming policy " that it should stimulate private investment. Public investment may stimulate private investment either directly or by first stimulating consumption.[2] All this is now well known and has been thoroughly discussed, but it all lies outside the pure theory of the multiplier.

The propensity to consume for society as a whole. (3) But the theory of the multiplier needs to be expanded and qualified in other ways. By expressing the multiplier in terms of the marginal propensity to consume, the impression is conveyed that it is possible to base the analysis on a fairly stable psychological magnitude. People's habits as to saving and spending are regarded as fairly constant, and this constancy and stability is transmitted by definition to the multiplier. A closer examination reveals, however, that this stability may be exaggerated. Mr. KEYNES speaks frequently of " the fundamental psychological law, upon which we are entitled to depend with great confidence both *a priori* from our knowledge of human nature and from the detailed facts of experience ";[3] this law is to the effect that " men are disposed . . . to increase their consumption as their income increases, but not by as much as the increase in their income ". He refers to the consumer, and sometimes to society as a whole. But the marginal propensity to consume of society as a whole (which corresponds to the multiplier)

---

[1] See, for example, A. D. Gayer, *Public Works in Prosperity and Depression* (New York, 1929), and J. M. Clark, *Economics of Planning Public Works* (Washington, 1935).

[2] This latter relationship is described by the acceleration principle.

[3] *General Theory*, pages 96 and 114.

cannot be identified with a psychological law about the behaviour of the individual consumer, for many other factors besides the consumers' behaviour determine the marginal propensity to consume of the society.

For a number of reasons, the stability of the multiplier must not be over-emphasised.

(*a*) As has been pointed out above (page 198), in the short run, the psychological traits of the individual in respect to saving and spending cannot safely be regarded as constant.[1]

Changes in income distribution. (*b*) As Dr. STAEHLE[2] has shown, changes in the distribution of income are very important for the propensity to consume of society as a whole, even from the short-run point of view. Since the propensities for different people or groups of people are different, a change in the distribution may give an unexpected turn to the marginal propensity to consume of society as a whole (contrary to the fundamental psychological law), even if the propensity of each individual is constant and conforms to " the fundamental psychological law ", to which Mr. KEYNES appeals. For this reason, in using the concept of the multiplier, allowance must be made for the changes in the distribution of income which are likely to be associated with a change in the level of incomes.

(*c*) Laws relating to consumers' behaviour cannot be directly applied to collective magnitudes, because what society as a whole invests and consumes is determined also by decisions of big corporations and of public bodies which cannot be so confidently assumed to be subject to the " fundamental psychological law " on which Mr. KEYNES depends for his empirical generalisations. In making use of the multiplier, allowance must be made for the proportion of any additional profit which companies are likely to save by adding to their reserves.

---

[1] Cf. Elizabeth W. Gilboy, " The Propensity to Consume " in *Quarterly Journal of Economics*, Vol. 53, November 1938, and Mr. Keynes' reply, *ibid.*, May 1939.

[2] " Short Period Variations in the Distribution of Incomes ", *Review of Economic Statistics*, Vol. 19, 1937 (pages 133 to 143) and the comments by F. C. Dirks, *Review of Economic Statistics*, Vol. 20, and rejoinder by Dr. Staehle, *ibid.*

Moreover, with respect to public expenditure,
Government the distinction between consumption and invest-
consumption ment is in many cases very arbitrary.   Expenditure
and connected with the construction of battleships,
investment. river-dams and the like will be classified as
investment.   Dole payments to unemployed and
expenditure for war veterans' bonus will be counted as consumption
expenditure and, if the Government borrows to meet this expenditure, as dissaving.   But how are we to classify money paid to
unemployed workers to perform "public works" of very doubtful
value ?   Suppose these works consist of digging holes in the
ground and filling them up again.   Or suppose a road is built
at a cost which far exceeds its value to the community. [1]   Evidently,
the classification, and still more the estimate of the value of
investment involved in such cases, is highly arbitrary and conventional.[2]   But the magnitude of the multiplier will be influenced
by such arbitrary decisions.   The fewer are the doubtful cases
regarded as investment and the lower is the investment value
assumed in each case, the greater will be the multiplier—that is, the
marginal propensity to consume of society as a whole.   Hence the
value of the latter will *pro tanto* depend upon these arbitrary
classifications and not on the psychological propensities of the
consumer.

Fortunately, in order to form an opinion on the probable
secondary effects of public expenditure, classification as consumption or investment is generally of minor importance.
What matters are the factors stressed by traditional theory : the
methods used by the Government in raising the money, the
rapidity with which the successive recipients spend it, the manner
of spending, etc.   In this latter respect, *individual* propensities
with regard to saving and consumption come into the picture, but

---

[1] Compare, for instance, this case with another one where the same
road is built with less labour and at a much lower cost, and the superfluous
workers receive a dole.   Part of the total money spent is investment
and the other part consumption, whilst, in the case mentioned in the
text, all is counted as investment.

[2] These problems are discussed at great length in various contributions
to *Studies in Income and Wealth*, Vol. I and II (ed. by National Bureau
of Economic Research, New York, 1937 and 1938).

together with many other determining factors, so that no simple and unique relationship between them and the multiplier (marginal propensity to consume of *society as a whole*) can be expected.

(*d*) Mr. KEYNES expresses the view that, in the short run, the marginal propensity to consume (multiplier) may deviate from its " normal " value, but he assumes that it will gradually return to it.[1]   Such a deviation will occur if producers of consumers' goods do not foresee the increase in demand resulting from an expansion in the capital-goods industries. Then, momentarily, prices of consumers' goods will rise or stocks be depleted. The same is true when full employment is reached or bottle-necks prevent consumers' goods industries from expanding. All these factors, which cannot be said to be governed by a psychological law, must be taken into account in order to determine the marginal propensity to consume of the community (multiplier).

(*e*) Certain difficulties arise when we consider
The multiplier the relation between the multiplier and the income
and income velocity of circulation of money. Suppose the
velocity of psychological marginal propensity to consume of
money. those who receive money from the Government
through public works is unity; that is, they save nothing, but spend the whole amount they receive on consumption. This is a conceivable situation, even if it is deemed unlikely. For reasons which will be discussed at some length in the second part of this book (Chapter 10, § 6), we should normally expect the secondary effects of a public works policy to be greater in that case than if the marginal propensity to consume was smaller than 1. But we should not expect to find an infinite rise in demand for consumption goods. This is, however, what follows from the assumption that Mr. KEYNES' marginal propensity to consume for society as a whole is unity; for this latter implies, as we have seen, that the multiplier is infinite. As Mr. KEYNES says, " the logical theory of the multiplier . . . holds good continuously, without time-lag, at all moments of time ".[2]   Hence, as there will,

---

[1] *General Theory*, page 123.
[2] *Ibid.*, page 122.

in fact, be some time-lag between the receipt of money and its expenditure, and since this time-lag will prevent an increase in investment from causing an immediate rise in consumption to infinity, we must say, in Mr. KEYNES' language, that there is a temporary distortion of the propensity to consume, and that consumption will only gradually tend to increase to infinity if the net increase in investment expenditure is permanently maintained. Hence, to determine the secondary effects, in time, of new public expenditure, we need, in addition to the information about the marginal propensity to consume of the various individuals, also information about the income velocity of money. This point has been well discussed by Professor J. M. CLARK (*op. cit.*).

Conclusions. We are now in a position to sum up the conclusions of our discussion. The pure theory of the multiplier shows the definitional relation between the " propensity to consume " and the multiplier. Many problems which are frequently discussed under the heading " multiplier " lie outside the pure theory of the multiplier. They can be divided into two groups, those relating to (*a*) the determination of the amount of *net* investment associated with a given amount of spending under varying circumstances and (*b*) the determination of the numerical value of the multiplier. The marginal propensity to consume of the individual to which Mr. KEYNES' fundamental psychological law refers, is only one of many factors which are causally important for the determination of the marginal propensity to consume (multiplier) of society as a whole. For this reason, care must be taken not to exaggerate the stability of the multiplier, which cannot be treated as a datum, but must be included among the variables (*quaesita*) of the theoretical system.[1]

---

[1] This is also the opinion of Mr. E. Lundberg (*cf. Studies in the Theory of Economic Expansion*, London, 1937, page 36), who believes that the multiplier will exhibit a cyclical movement over time.

§ 5.   THE THEORY OF UNDER-EMPLOYMENT

Application to the business cycle of Mr. Keynes' system.

Mr. KEYNES' theory does not furnish a ready-made answer to the riddle of the business cycle, but is intended to supply tools for the analysis of all sorts of problems concerning short-term fluctuations as well as long-run conditions. " The object of our analysis is . . . to provide ourselves with an organised and orderly method of thinking out particular problems; and, after we have reached a provisional conclusion by isolating the complicating factors one by one, we then have to go back on ourselves and allow, as well as we can, for the probable interaction of the factors amongst themselves. This is the nature of economic thinking."[1]

The analysis of the preceding pages should have made it abundantly clear that Mr. KEYNES' theoretical apparatus is not incompatible with any one of the theories of the cycle, or particular phases thereof, which have been reviewed earlier in this book. All these theories can be expressed in Keynesian language. Mr. KEYNES' own application of his theoretical apparatus to the typical business cycles, as contained in his " Notes on the Trade Cycle ",[2] have been briefly reviewed above in connection with the psychological theories (Chapter 6).

An over-saving theory of depression.

However, the theory, or theories, of economic depressions—cyclical and otherwise—which are generally associated with, or have emerged under, the influence of Mr. KEYNES' *General Theory of Employment* can be best described as a special sort of under-consumption or over-saving theory. All the determinants which play a rôle in Mr. KEYNES' system are always involved : the liquidity-preference, the supply of money, the marginal efficiency of capital and the propensity to consume. But it is the last one which is stressed most. This under-consumption theory is to be found in many passages of the *General Theory* and

---

[1] *General Theory*, page 297.
[2] *Ibid.*, pages 313 *et seq.*

in numerous writings of Mr. KEYNES' followers; it seems to refer primarily to depressions of longer duration; since, however, that is not always quite clear, we shall simply speak of periods of under-employment.

Let us first consider the description, in Mr. KEYNES' terms, of an equilibrium with less than full employment. Such situations are described in earlier parts of Mr. KEYNES' book, before all relationships (especially the liquidity-preference) have been introduced, and hence are there presented without all the necessary qualifications. This fact makes the theory appear more contradictory to traditional views than it really is. Suppose the liquidity-preference and the quantity of money are given. Hence the rate of interest is given. If the schedule of marginal efficiency of capital is given, the amount of investment is determined. And if the schedule of the marginal propensity to consume (multiplier) is known, the level of income and employment is also determined.

Let us now consider the interrelation of the last two schedules— the liquidity-preference schedule, the quantity of money and hence the interest rate being given and remaining unchanged. In wealthy communities, the propensity to save (consume) is great (small). Therefore much investment is needed to " fill the gap " between total output and that part of it which the " community chooses " to consume. There is no guarantee that at full employment there are enough opportunities to invest (at the given rate of interest) to maintain full employment.[1] If, as frequently happens, not enough investment is forthcoming, the level of employment and income must fall. This fall will induce people to save less of their income; some may even draw on accumulated resources and consume more than their income—*i.e.*, may dissave. Likewise, " the Government will be liable, willingly or unwillingly, to run into a budgetary deficit ", in order to provide for relief, etc., which is equivalent to a strengthening of the propensity to consume of society as a whole. Thus a new equilibrium will be reached when saving has fallen sufficiently for investment to fill the gap between ouput and consumption. It is not difficult to introduce here the liquidity-preference schedule : when income falls,

---

[1] Compare, for example, *General Theory*, pages 31, 98 and 105.

money is liberated from the transaction sphere, M_1 falls, M_2 rises, the interest rate falls, and equilibrium can be reached at a higher level than if interest rates had not fallen.

The three schedules, together with the quantity of money and some other data such as the available factors of production (labour, equipment, etc.) and the wage-unit,[1] determine the level of employment and unemployment. Hence it is impossible to blame any one of the three " psychological factors " (schedules) above for the absence of full employment. Or, if one chooses, one may attribute the existing unemployment to either one alternatively, if all the other data are given : other things being given, employment would be greater (smaller), if the propensity to consume was greater (smaller) than it actually is. Or : other things being given, employment would rise, if the liquidity-preference were to fall; or if the marginal efficiency of capital were greater, etc.

It is now easy to see that any one of the various *Other theories* hypotheses concerning the causes of the down-*in Mr. Keynes'* turn or the upturn of the business cycle which *terms.* we have reviewed in the earlier chapters is compatible with, and can be expressed in terms of, Mr. KEYNES' theoretical apparatus. Employment may start to fall, (*a*) because the propensity to save has become stronger without an offsetting weakening of the liquidity-preference; (*b*) because, for one reason or the other, the marginal efficiency of capital collapses (that is Mr. KEYNES' own tentative hypothesis for the crisis in the typical trade cycle); (*c*) because the liquidity-preference proper becomes stronger (*i.e.*, because M_2 increases—*i.e.*, people hoard) or the banks contract the quantity of money.[2]

Similarly, the various hypotheses concerning the forces which may bring about an upturn in employment can be classified according to the Keynesian categories. Employment and income may start to rise (*a*) because of a shift to the right of the schedule of

---

[1] See *General Theory,* pages 41 and 247. That the wage-unit—that is, "the money-wage of a labour unit "—must be given, is a highly important fact which is frequently overlooked and will come up for discussion below (page 238). It implies that an equilibrium with less than full employment can exist only if money wages are rigid.

[2] For further details and hypotheses, see Chapter 11, section B, below.

the marginal efficiency of capital : this may be due to inventions, to an increase of replacement requirements, or to an improvement in expectations of entrepreneurs, however brought about. In all these cases, traditional theory would add the condition that the supply of investible funds must not be wholly inelastic. If that were the case, the shift in the marginal efficiency of capital would raise the rate of interest, but not the volume of investment. In Mr. KEYNES' terms, we have to say that the liquidity-preference schedule proper must not be a vertical straight line. Mr. KEYNES always assumes this to be the case, and most writers now agree that this is true in times of depression. Employment will rise, (*b*) if the propensity to consume increases. Assuming other things to be equal and the liquidity-preference schedule elastic, this is clearly the case. Some writers, it is true, would object to the assertion that a decrease in saving will stimulate employment. The reason is, however, that they assume an inelastic liquidity-preference schedule. In that case, if some people save less and spend more on consumption, correspondingly less will be spent on investment, the rate of interest will rise and aggregate effective demand remain unchanged. But most writers will agree that this is an unrealistic assumption, at least in depressions.

Thanks largely to Mr. KEYNES, there is to-day almost general agreement that Government spending, barring psychological repercussions and assuming an elastic liquidity-preference schedule, will stimulate employment. This must be construed, in Mr. KEYNES' terminology, either as an increase in the propensity to consume or as a shift of the marginal efficiency of capital, depending upon the classification of Government expenditure as investment or consumption.

Similarly, dishoarding by private individuals has to be described as an increase of the propensity to consume (if the money is spent on consumption) or as a shift of the liquidity-preference schedule proper (if the money is lent out in the capital market). In both cases, it tends to stimulate employment.[1]

---

[1] For further details and other hypotheses, see Chapter 11, section A, below.

The cumulative nature of a process of expansion and contraction after it has once started cannot be deduced from Mr. KEYNES' theory. It requires additional assumptions of a dynamic character, as we find them in various business-cycles theories. These dynamic relationships can, however, be formulated in his terms. Assume, for instance, that the marginal efficiency of capital drops (rises) when income falls (rises) or that liquidity-preference proper (propensity to hoard) rises (falls) when activity contracts (expands).

Voluntary and involuntary unemployment. So far, we have detected a number of termino-logical differences between Mr. KEYNES' theory and the traditional views as represented by, say, Professor PIGOU's *Industrial Fluctuations*, Professor ROBERTSON's writings or the synthesis attempted in Part II of the first edition of this book, which is reproduced, with slight changes, in the present edition. In addition, we have suggested (*cf.* pages 209 and 218 above) that Mr. KEYNES has made an important contribution by his insistence on the relationship between " hoarding " and the rate of interest. Apart from this, we have not as yet discovered any essential differences between Mr. KEYNES' theory and that of the other recognised authorities. According to Mr. KEYNES, however, there is a fundamental discrepancy between the two, inasmuch as the " classical " theory cannot conceive at all of an equilibrium with less than full employment. " The classical theory is only applicable to the case of full employment."[1] More precisely, it is *involuntary* unemployment which is, according to Mr. KEYNES, incompatible with classical equilibrium; *voluntary* unemployment may, of course, exist in equilibrium; that is to say, if some people prefer not to work at the prevailing wage, they are not counted as unemployed; or " an eight-hour day does not constitute unemployment because it is not beyond human capacity to work ten hours " (page 15).

Involuntary unemployment, which classical theory is accused of having overlooked, or being unable to explain, is defined as follows : " *Men are involuntarily unemployed if, in the event of a small rise in the price of wage-goods relatively to the money-wage* [we could also say : in the event of a fall in real wages], *both the aggregate supply of labour*

---

[1] *General Theory*, page 16.

willing to work for the current money-wage and the aggregate demand for it at that wage would be greater than the existing volume of employment."[1]

Free competition in the labour market and unemployment. This is a new definition. The incompatibility of involuntary unemployment in this sense with classical equilibrium has therefore never been explicitly denied. Is such a definition implicit in the traditional position? The traditional view is generally taken to be that, under free competition in the labour market, unemployment is incompatible with equilibrium because, with free competition, money-wages will be flexible. Only if money-wages are rigid in the downward direction, if they are prevented from falling either by tradition, by trade-union pressure, or by Government action, can unemployment exist in equilibrium. This position does not, however, exclude the existence of involuntary unemployment in Mr. KEYNES' sense. Suppose there is unemployment and wages are rigid in the downward direction. Few classical writers will deny that employment may and will rise when aggregate demand and prices are raised by a revival of investment financed by new bank credit or by dishoarding. As there was then previously involuntary unemployment, its compatibility with equilibrium is not implicitly denied by the traditional view.

A difference of opinion can and does exist only in respect of the consequences and desirability of free competition in the labour market, which would ensure a complete flexibility of wages. However, the following two propositions would presumably be accepted both by Mr. KEYNES and by the classical school. First, if there is free competition in the labour market, money-wages will fall continuously, so long as there is unemployment. A situation in which wages fall continuously can hardly be called an equilibrium position.[2] Secondly, in point of fact wages are,

---

[1] *General Theory*, page 15. Italics in the original. An extensive discussion of this definition will be found in J. Robinson, *Essays in the Theory of Employment*, London, 1937, Part I. See also Viner's criticism, *Quarterly Journal of Economics*, Vol. 51, 1936, pages 147 *et seq.*

[2] Compare the following statement by Mr. J. E. Meade, " A Simplified Model of Mr. Keynes' System " (*Review of Economic Studies*, Vol. IV, page 99) : " If we suppose that the money-wage rate would fall so long

and probably have always been, rigid, because of trade-union resistance, unemployment relief, tradition, etc.

Money-wages and real wages. There seems to exist, however, a real difference of opinion between Mr. KEYNES and the classical school concerning the influence of a fall in money-wages on employment. Mr. KEYNES expresses the view that, " with a given organisation, equipment and technique ", an increase in output and employment necessitates a fall in *real* wages.[1] But whilst the "classical theory assumes that it is always open to labour to reduce its real wage by accepting a reduction in the money-wage ",[2] Mr. KEYNES' contention is that " there may exist no expedient by which labour as a whole can reduce its *real* wage to a given figure by making revised money bargains with the entrepreneur ";[3] the reason being that " prices change in almost the same proportion, leaving the real wage . . . practically the same as before ".[4] Mr. KEYNES is, however, careful to add that " this argument would . . . contain . . . a large element of truth, though the complete results of a change in money-wages are more complex ".[5] In Chapter 19, " Changes in Money-Wages ", he discusses the question in detail, and introduces many modifications into the original simple argument; but the argument is sometimes presented by economists

---

as any labour were unemployed, the system cannot be in equilibrium without full employment." Professor Alfred Amonn also points out that only with monopolistic wage rigidities can there be equilibrium with less than full employment. " Grundfragen der Konjunkturtheorie und Konjunkturpolitik " in *Festschrift für Oskar Engländer*, Brünn, 1937, *passim.*

[1] *General Theory*, page 17. Professor Viner considers this an unwarranted concession to the classical doctrine, as it is quite possible that real wages may rise with increasing employment. *Cf. Quarterly Journal of Economics*, Vol. 51, 1936, pages 149 and 150. This has been shown statistically by J. T. Dunlop : " The Movement of Real and Money Wage Rates ", *Economic Journal*, Vol. 48, 1938, pages 413 *et seq.* Mr. Dunlop's article has induced Mr. Keynes to modify his position somewhat. See his paper : " Relative Movements of Real Wages and Output ", *Economic Journal*, March 1939.

[2] *General Theory*, page 11.

[3] *Loc. cit.*, page 13. Mr. Keynes adds : " This will be our contention."

[4] *Loc. cit.*, page 12.

[5] *Loc. cit.*, same page, footnote [1]. See also page 269.

in its simple unmodified form.[1]   A closer analysis of this chapter seems to suggest that there is no fundamental difference between Mr. KEYNES' results and those reached by those more orthodox writers (such as Professor PIGOU in his *Industrial Fluctuations*) who pay attention to possible short-period repercussions of wage reductions.   Since there is substantial agreement, except in terminology, between Mr. KEYNES' analysis and the one given in Chapter 11, § 9, of the present book, only a few points will be raised in this connection.

Reduction in money-wages and aggregate demand.   According to Mr. KEYNES, the " accepted explanation " of the consequences of a reduction of money-wages starts from the assumption that aggregate effective demand remains unchanged; then, naturally, employment will rise.   Mr. KEYNES points out (as was observed in the first edition of this book[2]) that this assumption assumes away almost the whole problem.   It may be legitimate in a rigid equilibrium theory which deliberately argues under the simplifying assumption of constant aggregate demand; but it is certainly illegitimate in business-cycle theory, and it is usually not made there.

In his view, a " reduction in money-wages will have no lasting tendency to increase employment except by virtue of its repercussions either on the propensity to consume for the community as a whole, or on the schedule of marginal efficiencies of capital, or on the rate of interest ".[3]   This is true, because the three terms are so defined that any change in output and employment resulting from a fall in money-wages must be describable in terms of one or the other, or a combination of the three magnitudes mentioned.   If

---

[1] See, for example, Mr. A. P. Lerner : " Mr. Keynes' ' General Theory of Employment, Interest and Money ' ", *International Labour Review*, Vol. 34, 1936.   Mr. Lerner there " proves " that prices must fall " in just the same proportion as wages " (pages 441 and 442).   It is true that he qualifies that statement by admitting " that a reduction of money-wages may have all sorts of indirect influences ".   But this qualification is again qualified, and the short paragraph devoted to the matter gives a very cursory summary of Mr. Keynes' analysis.

[2] See Chapter 11, § 9, below.

[3] *General Theory*, page 262.

investment output rises, the rate of interest and consumption having remained unchanged, the marginal efficiency of capital schedule is said to have shifted; if consumption rises without an increase in investment and without a change in the interest rate, the propensity to consume of the community as a whole is said to have increased, etc.

Mr. KEYNES, however, characterises such influences of wage reductions on employment as " roundabout repercussions ",[1] and suggests that the classical theory erroneously supposes that there is a direct route by which wage reductions may affect output and employment without affecting the propensity to consume, the marginal efficiency of capital or the rate of interest. But, in fact, the repercussion may be quite direct, even though it can always be expressed in Mr. KEYNES' terminology if one desires to do so. Let us take the most straightforward case. Suppose wages in a pure consumption trade, say, of domestic servants, are reduced and the elasticity of demand for these services is unity. Then the consumption of these services and employment will rise. The effect of the wage reduction on employment is obviously direct; but in Mr. KEYNES' terms we must describe it as an influence via an increase in the propensity to consume.

Mr. KEYNES quite rightly stresses that, in order to evaluate the total effect of a wage reduction, it is not sufficient to consider it only in its cost aspects; effects through an increase or decrease of workers' purchasing power must be considered too. This matter will be taken up *in extenso* in Chapter 11 below. He then discusses various routes via which wage reductions may react, in an internationally closed system, or in an " open " one, through creating expectations on the part of entrepreneurs with respect to future changes of wages in an upward or downward direction or by producing " a more optimistic tone in the minds of entrepreneurs, which may break through a vicious circle of unduly pessimistic estimates of the marginal efficiency of capital and set things moving again on a more normal basis of expectation " (page 264).

---

[1] *General Theory*, page 257 and *passim*.

The most important influence which definitely

Wage operates in the direction of a rise in employment
reductions and output (whilst many of the others may cut
increase either way) goes via the liquidity-preference.
liquidity. " The reduction in the wages-bill, accompanied by
some reduction in prices and in money-incomes
generally, will diminish the need for cash for income and business
purposes; and it will therefore reduce, *pro tanto*, the schedule of
liquidity-preference for the community as a whole. *Ceteris
paribus*, this will reduce the rate of interest and thus prove favourable to investment " (page 263). A fall in wages and prices is
considered equivalent to an increase in the quantity of money.
" If, indeed, labour were always in a position to take action (and
were to do so), whenever there was less than full employment,
to reduce its money demands by concerted action to whatever
point was required to make money so abundant relatively to the
wage-unit that the rate of interest would fall to a level compatible
with full employment, we should, in effect, have monetary manage-
ment by the trade unions, aimed at full employment, instead of by
the banking system " (page 267).

In our terminology, that amounts to saying that unemployment with flexible wages leads—in the unfavourable case where
the wage-bill falls in response to a fall in wages—to an indefinite increase of idle funds (in liquidity) in terms of money
and still faster in real terms; and there must be somewhere
a limit at which people will stop hoarding and begin to
spend again, either on consumption or investment. (See below,
Chapter 11, § 8.)

We conclude once more that, according to Mr. KEYNES' theory,
his equilibrium with unemployment can exist only if money-wages
are rigid in the downward direction. This seems quite inescapable; and if Mr. KEYNES never quite admits it, at one point he
comes very near to doing so : if there were " competition between
unemployed workers ", " there *might* be no position of stable
equilibrium except in conditions consistent with full employment,
since the wage-unit *might* have to fall without limit until it reached
a point where the effect of the abundance of money in terms of the
wage-unit on the rate of interest was sufficient to restore a level of

full employment. At no other point could there be a resting-place."[1]

From this statement, with which all adherents of the classical school would agree, it does not, however, follow that very flexible wages (absolutely perfect competition in the labour market) are necessarily the best policy to get rid of unemployment. One may still hold with KEYNES that, under such conditions, prices may become very unstable, which may make business calculations difficult and affect unfavourably the marginal efficiency of capital.[2] The problem is a pressing one which has not yet been solved satisfactorily. Is absolute flexibility or is a certain degree of rigidity of prices and money-wages more conducive to stability of real income ? There is one section where competition has been strong and prices have been very flexible—viz., agriculture. During the last depression, for instance, prices of agricultural products fell drastically, but output and employment were maintained. In industry (especially in capital-goods and durable-goods industries), prices were better maintained, but output shrank. It goes without saying that, for the farming population, that is a very unfavourable situation. But many people would argue that, if industry behaved like agriculture, prices would fall all around, but production would be well maintained. This may be so, but it must be said that it has not yet been rigorously proven. It may well be, as KEYNES says, that violent fluctuations of prices, and in particular reductions of prices, would create great uncertainty and very unfavourably affect the demand for capital and the willingness to invest. Thus the result may be

Does flexibility of wages and prices promote stability ?

---

[1] *General Theory*, page 253 (italics not in the original). For this reason, it is clear that the alleged intractability of slump conditions (discussed in Chapter 17 of the *Theory*, especially on pages 229 to 235) can refer only to conditions in which money-wages are not allowed to fall indefinitely. It is therefore as true to attribute the persistence of unemployment to the rigidity of wages and prices as to attribute it to the peculiarity of money as compared with other assets. This does not, of course, exclude the view that unemployment may be relieved—perhaps more effectively—by measures other than a reduction in wages—*e.g.*, by an increase in the quantity of money combined with Government spending.

[2] *General Theory*, page 269.

that unemployment could be eliminated and the labour market cleared by a very drastic cut in wages, but at the price of a fall of *real* wages to a very low level. (Thus Mr. KEYNES' assertion that prices would fall *pari passu* with a fall in wages—which has been carried to extreme lengths by Mr. LERNER, *loc. cit.*—may be unduly optimistic.) In other words, if owing to rapid price changes entrepreneurs became very pessimistic, or at least very uncertain about the future, the demand for labour might become very inelastic.

Hence, although the classical theory is right in saying that an equilibrium with unemployment is incompatible with competition in the labour market, it does not necessarily follow that plasticity of wages would eliminate depressions. (Compare the cautious and well-balanced treatment of this problem in Professor PIGOU's *Industrial Fluctuations*, Chapter XX, " The Part played by Rigidity in Wage Rates ").[1]

Chronic depressions due to under-consumption. At the beginning of this section (see page 233 above), it was stated that the depression theory most frequently associated with Mr. KEYNES' theoretical system is an under-consumption or over-saving theory. This statement may not seem to have been borne out by the detailed analysis of Mr. KEYNES' *pure* theory in the preceding pages. It is nevertheless true in the sense that Mr. KEYNES, in many places, emphasises the low propensity to consume prevailing in rich countries as the main source of troubles. " But worse still. Not only is the marginal propensity to consume weaker in a wealthy country, but, owing to its accumulation of capital being already larger, the opportunities for further investment are less attractive " (page 31). Moreover, in various places, the spectre is raised of a lower limit to a fall in the rate of interest " which in present circumstances may perhaps be as high as 2% or 2½% on long term. If this should prove correct, the awkward possibility of an increasing stock of wealth,

---

[1] It is always possible to conserve the favourable effects of a policy of wage reductions in its cost aspect, and at the same time to eliminate the unfavourable ones, by combining the policy of wage reductions with a policy of public works (or similar measures), so as to make sure that total purchasing power does not fall.

in conditions where the rate of interest can fall no further under *laissez-faire*, may soon be realised in actual experience." [1] " The post-war experiences of Great Britain and the United States are, indeed, actual examples of how an accumulation of wealth, so large that its marginal efficiency has fallen more rapidly than the rate of interest can fall in the face of the prevailing institutional and psychological factors, can interfere, in conditions mainly of *laissez-faire*, with a reasonable level of employment and with the standard of life which the technical conditions of production are capable of furnishing " (page 219). " I should guess that a properly run community equipped with modern technical resources, of which the population is not increasing rapidly, ought to be able to bring down the marginal efficiency of capital in equilibrium approximately to zero within a single generation " (page 220). Mr. KEYNES believes " it to be comparatively easy to make capital goods so abundant that the marginal efficiency of capital is zero " (page 221).

Among writers who accept, as well as among those who reject these diagnoses and forecasts, the impression seems to prevail that they can be deduced from Mr. KEYNES' *General Theory*, but not from the traditional theoretical apparatus. This impression appears to be unfounded. In either case, additional empirical assumptions are required to establish the validity of those diagnoses, and, given these assumptions, they can be deduced from, or rather expressed in terms of, either one of the two theoretical systems.

The empirical foundation and justification of these visions need not be examined in this book, where we are interested more in the formal logical structure of the general theory. If they are not new, they have at least received a strong impetus from Mr. KEYNES' *General Theory*. The views expressed have been elaborated by various writers on the empirical side and much raiment has been put around Mr. KEYNES' bare contentions. We may mention a few broad facts which have been adduced to support his thesis.

---

[1] *General Theory*, page 219. See also, however, the passage on page 203 already quoted.

Investment opportunities are said to have become *The drying-up* scarcer, as compared with the nineteenth century, *of investment* because of the less rapid growth of population; *opportunities.* the cessation of migration on a large scale and of the opening of new territories and continents; the reduction of international lending for the reason just mentioned and others of an institutional and political character. More precarious assumptions are also made—for instance, that capital-consuming technical inventions are less likely to be made in the future than in the past.

On the other hand, reasons are given which make it unlikely that the volume of saving will decrease, and it is stressed that important changes in the structure of the supply of saving have occurred which impede their smooth absorption into the available investment channels : savings are increasingly made by institutions such as life insurance and social insurance companies, which are, in most countries, prevented from investing in equities. In other words, capital has become less venturesome, more timid than it used to be in the heydays of capitalism. This tendency creates a situation of scarcity amidst plenty in the capital market and eliminates a number of important outlets for investment.

These speculations about secular tendencies and developments are necessarily vague and are easily coloured by the subjective attitude of the particular writer and the surrounding conditions. Their persuasiveness often depends less on the logical force of the argument than on the way in which relevant facts are selected. Temporary hitches in the flow of investment, due to psychological shocks, rigidities, etc., are frequently interpreted as being due to a chronic lack of investment opportunities. The conditions necessary for chronic unemployment are overlooked or not clearly stated : for example, it is often not realised that either money-wages and prices must be rigid against downward pressures, or else, if they are allowed to fall gradually under the pressure of competition, it must be assumed that people are willing to hoard unlimited amounts of money.

However, the clear realisation of all the necessary qualifications of these theories cannot definitely disprove their validity, although it may reduce their persuasiveness. Only the careful scrutiny of a mass of experience and the study of historical processes can make the hypothesis more or less probable.[1]

§ 6.   STATIC VERSUS DYNAMIC THEORIES :
       SOME METHODOLOGICAL OBSERVATIONS

We may properly terminate the first part of this book by reflecting briefly on certain fundamental characteristics of the theories reviewed, thereby reverting to the logical problems touched upon in the first chapter.

General versus   On an earlier occasion, we characterised
partial Mr. KEYNES' *General Theory* as a general inter-
equilibrium. dependence (equilibrium) theory in macro-economic terms. The theory is a *general* interdependence theory in the sense that it explicitly embraces the economic system as a whole and represents it by means of a limited number of magnitudes interrelated by a few easily comprehensible relationships. This explicit generality distinguishes Mr. KEYNES' system favourably from many business-cycle theories which give only a *partial* picture, confining themselves, consciously or unconsciously, to exhibiting only some particular relationships, which are supposed to be the crucial ones, and leaving the rest hidden, so that it is left to the reader to supply from general economic theory the missing relationships which are necessary to make the system determinate.

---

[1] The most balanced and best considered statement is to be found in Professor Hansen's *Full Recovery or Stagnation*, New York, 1938, *passim*, and in his paper, " Economic Progress and Declining Population Growth ", *American Economic Review*, March 1939.   A very good but rather unqualified statement is to be found in *An Economic Program for American Democracy* by Paul M. Sweezy, R. V. Gilbert and others, New York, 1938.   Compare also Gerhard Colm and Fritz Lehman, *Economic Consequences of Recent American Tax Policy*, Supplement I to *Social Research*, New York, 1938 ; and G. Haberler, " Interest Rate and Capital Formation ", in *Capital Formation and its Elements*, ed. by the National Industrial Conference Board, New York, 1939.

Mr. KEYNES' system is conceived in terms of
Macroscopic macro-economic concepts, inasmuch as its fun-
versus damental data consist of complex magnitudes which
microscopic relate to society as a whole, such as national income,
analysis. savings, investment, volume of production of
producers' or consumers' goods, effective aggregate
demand, price levels, etc. Its macroscopic nature Mr. KEYNES'
theory has in common with most business-cycle theories. If a
theory which aims at representing the economic process as a whole
is to be manageable, it cannot avoid using broad averages and
aggregates of a collective nature. It is very well to preach a
microscopic approach and to urge the investigator to go back to
the individual units (households and firms). It is true, of course,
that direct and indirect observations of *individual* behaviour and
happenings are the only source of information about the magnitude
and behaviour of collective phenomena. But the final[1] statements
at which the theory aims (as distinguished from the methods by
which they are reached) must practically always run in terms of
aggregates and averages.[2]

The broader these aggregates, the smaller their number, the
more easily manageable (theoretically and statistically) the resulting
system. Unfortunately, however, it is usually not possible to find
between very broad aggregates significant relationships which can
be relied upon to be borne out by the facts. If so, the aggregates

---

[1] " Final " in a relative sense.

[2] Professor Frisch (" Propagation and Impulse Problems ", in *Economic Essays in Honour of Gustav Cassel*, London, 1933, page 172)
uses the term " macro-analysis " in the sense of " general " (embracing
the economic process as a whole) and " micro-analysis " in the sense of
" partial equilibrium analysis ". He points out that a *general* interdependence theory can be given in all detail (in our terminology : in microscopic terms) only " if we confine ourselves to a purely *formal* theory.
Indeed, it is always possible by a suitable system of subscripts and
superscripts, etc., to introduce practically all factors which we may
imagine (all individual commodities, all individual entrepreneurs, all
individual consumers, etc.), and to write out various kinds of relationship
between these magnitudes, taking care that the number of equations is
equal to the number of variables. Such a theory, however, would have
only a rather limited interest. In such a theory it would hardly be
possible to study such fundamental problems as the exact time, shape
of the solutions, etc." (page 172).

must be subdivided, the method must be made more miscroscopic. But so long as aggregates, even restricted in scope, are used, there is always the danger that the internal structure of these aggregates (in other words, the relationships between their subdivisions) may prove to be significant; this would force the economist to split up the aggregates so far undivided and to try to construct his system in terms of subdivisions of these aggregates. Thus the business-cycle theorist is always torn between the temptation, on the one hand, to go into minute details and to work out an endless number of individual cases where the course of events is decisively influenced by small details, and the passion, on the other hand, for constructing sweeping theories with a few bold strokes of the pen. The stony path of the economist working in this field leads constantly between the Scylla of a maze of individual cases of an unmanageable casuistry and the Charybdis of ingenious and clean-cut but lofty and half-true theories.

Static versus dynamic theories. Mr. KEYNES' theory has still another characteristic which distinguishes it from all business-cycle theories : it is essentially static. By a static theory, we mean a theory where all the variables (magnitudes to be explained) relating to a certain point or period of time are explained by data relating to the same point or period of time.[1] Such a theory can never explain a movement in time. It can only answer the question : Given certain data at a certain moment, what will be the result at that moment ? True, if the data change in time, then the results will also change. But a change in data cannot be explained. (If it could, then the data would cease to be data and become variables.) They must be given (or assumed) anew for each successive point in time. This method of dealing with economic change is frequently called " comparative statics ".[2]

---

[1] *Cf.*, for example, Frisch, *loc. cit.*, and J. Tinbergen, " Suggestions on Quantitative Business-cycle Theory ", *Econometrica*, Vol. 3, 1935, page 241.

[2] Usually, the assumption is made that, after a change in the data has occurred, a certain period of time must elapse before a new equilibrium emerges. Comparative statics in the strict sense confines itself to describing the two equilibria, the starting-point and the destination of the economic system. Any attempt, on the other hand, at analysing in

To explain the business cycle, or any change of the economic system over time, we need either a law about a (cyclical) change in certain data or a dynamic theory. In the first case, we speak of an " exogenous " theory of the cycle. (See Chapter 1.) The *paradigma* is the weather theory of the cycle. But explanations of this sort can be discarded at once as insufficient.

By a dynamic theory, we mean " a theory that explains how one situation grows out of the foregoing. In this type of analysis, we consider not only a set of magnitudes in a given point of time and study the interrelations between them, but we consider the magnitudes of certain variables in different points of time, and we introduce certain equations which embrace at the same time several of these magnitudes belonging to different instants."[1] We may also say that a theory is dynamic, if a magnitude is explained by another relating to an earlier (or, more generally, to another) point of time. In still other words : if there are lags in the causal nexus. If we say, for instance, that the volume of production (of a particular commodity or of commodities in general) is governed by the relation of cost and prices, we obviously must allow for a certain lag : cost and prices to-day govern production to-morrow. The acceleration principle is a dynamic relationship : investment is explained by a previous change in demand for the product. The " multiplier relationship " may be formulated dynamically, by allowing a time-lag between investment and the resulting increase in consumption demand. (In Mr. KEYNES' system, it will be recalled, it is a timeless terminological rule; only incidentally are some remarks made about the probable change of the value of

---

detail the process of transition from one equilibrium to the other (*e.g.*, in Marshallian manner, by distinguishing between short- and long-period effects) marks the first step towards a " dynamisation " of static theory. For it leads inevitably to the recognition of the fact that, as the result of certain reactions, the process of transition, and hence the final equilibrium, may be different. It also suggests that, after a given change in the data, a stable position will be reached only under special assumptions (stability conditions), which cannot be taken for granted without careful analysis.

[1] Frisch, *loc. cit.*, page 171. Tinbergen formulates : " A theory [is called] ' dynamic ' when variables relating to different moments appear in one equation " (*loc. cit.*, page 241).

the multiplier, or of the marginal propensity to consume, over time.[1]

Such a dynamic theory is *endogenous* in character. The determinants at any moment of time cease to be simply assumed. To-day's determinant data are yesterday's variables (and are thus explained), and to-day's variables become to-morrow's data. The successive situations (short-run equilibria) are interconnected like the links of a chain. Hence, in order to explain a movement (cyclical or otherwise), we need not assume a corresponding change in the data;[2] we need be given only the first position or an initial change in data, at the beginning of the process.

The skeleton of Mr. KEYNES' theory, as it is represented precisely in diagrammatic form by Professor LANGE,[3] is essentially static. There are no time-lags, and all the data and variables relate to the same point of time. There are, however, many allusions to dynamic relationships in incidental remarks and illustrative observations which are thrown out in great number all over the book. Moreover, dynamic theories can be grafted upon (or, as it is more correct to say, may be expressed in terms of) Mr. KEYNES' system. This has been done, for example, by Mr. HARROD,[4] who introduced the dynamic acceleration principle (and seems to interpret the multiplier dynamically). Another example is Mr. M. KALECKI's theory,[5] which introduces a lag between investment decisions as determined by the current situation and the actual volume of investment.[6]

---

[1] Professor Tinbergen, *loc. cit.*, has enumerated many different dynamic relationships which have been used at one time or another in business-cycle theory.

[2] This was the definition of an *endogenous* theory. *Cf.* Chapter 1, page 9.

[3] *Economica*, February 1938. Mr. Keynes has accepted this exposition as correct. See also J. E. Meade : " A Simplified Model of Mr. Keynes' System ", in the *Review of Economic Studies*, Vol. IV, 1936/37, page 98.

[4] *The Trade Cycle*, Oxford, 1936.

[5] " A Theory of the Business Cycle ", in *Review of Economic Studies*, Vol. IV, February 1937, pages 77 *et seq.*, reprinted in *Essays in the Theory of Economic Fluctuations*, London, 1939.

[6] These theories, although inspired by Mr. Keynes' *General Theory*, can be and have been expressed in a more classical terminology.

There is, however, one feature about Mr. KEYNES'
Are system which has given the impression to many
expectations readers that the *General Theory of Employment* is a
a dynamic dynamic theory—namely, the fact that, following
element ? the lead of Swedish writers such as MYRDAL
and LINDAHL, it runs in terms of expectations.
Almost every concept is defined in terms of expectations :
" aggregate demand function ", " supply function ", " effective
demand ", " marginal efficiency of capital ", etc., are defined
with the help of such concepts as " the *prospective* yield of
capital ", " proceeds which entrepreneurs expect to receive ",
etc.[1] Now, in a sense it is true that the explicit introduction
of expectations *tends* to make a theory truly dynamic. In the
sense, namely, that the introduction of expectations into the causal
nexus is essentially an incomplete idea which requires, in order to
become at all useful, a complement which makes the theory
dynamic : if we confine ourselves to saying that it is not actual
(current) prices, costs, profits, etc., but expected prices, costs,
profits which induce an entrepreneur to produce and to invest,
we do not say very much, unless we give some hint as to how
these expectations are determined.

A theory which takes the expectations as given at any point of
time, and does not say anything on how they grow out of past
experience, is of very little value; for such a theory would still be
static, and it is almost impossible to determine expectations as
such.[2] Only if it is possible to give some hypotheses about how
expectations are formed on the basis of past experience (prices,
state of demand, costs, profits, etc.) can a really useful and verifiable
theory be evolved. And such a theory is evidently dynamic in the
sense explained above, for it links the past with the present : past

---

[1] *General Theory*, pages 24, 25, 46 *et seq.*, 141, 147 *et seq.* Compare
also what has been said earlier in this book in Chapter 6, § 2, on the rôle
of expectations.

[2] Expectations may almost be called " non-operational concepts ".
The only way of finding out something about them would be to question
individual business-men—a very questionable procedure.

prices, costs and profits via the state of expectation with present production, consumption and investment.[1]

Mr. KEYNES has, of course, much to say on the formation of expectations and the difficulties and limitations confronting any theory on this subject. But all this is contained in the wealth of remarks, observations and *obiter dicta* which—elaborating, supporting, illustrating and, at times, contradicting and blurring— surround the main outline of his theory : the dynamic aspects do not penetrate the heart of his theory.

Professor ROBERTSON's " period analysis ", on the other hand. is a clear step in the right direction of a truly dynamic analysis, Similarly, a number of Swedish writers, especially Dr. Eric LUNDBERG in his *Studies in the Theory of Economic Expansion,*[2] have visualised the problem clearly. Dr. LUNDBERG characterises the method as " sequence analysis " and has constructed a number of macroscopic dynamic models—"model sequences" as he calls them.[3]

Dr. LUNDBERG's models are theoretical—that *Theoretical* is to say, the figures are assumed (not found statisti- *versus* cally); the relationships postulated, although assumed *statistical* and selected so as to be not impossible on *a priori* *models.* grounds, are too simple and too few in number to

---

[1] From a strictly logical point of view, the psychological link between the past and the present consisting of expectations may be dropped and the theory stated in terms of a direct relationship between observable pheno- mena at different points of time. Psychologically it may, however, be useful to retain the word " expectations ", or a similar concept, as a link, because it reminds us of the fact that those dynamic " laws " (relation- ships) are nothing but hypotheses ; that they can hardly ever be stated very precisely in great detail ; and that they may always be subject to rapid change " without notice ".

[2] London, 1937, especially Chapter IX.

[3] Compare the following remarks from his book : " The introduction of causal elements linking up economic factors in successive periods of time means a more radical departure from equilibrium-theories than the dynamisation claimed by Myrdal, and later by Keynes, when paying atten- tion to the independent rôle of expectations and anticipations. . . . The introduction of expectations can, in a way, be said to mark the stepping-stone to dynamic analysis, because they express the connection linking present plans and activities with future events. However, economists have indulged in too much purely formal exercise with this term. . . . It is sensible to link actions with expectations, only if the latter can be explained on the basis of past and present economic events.

give an adequate picture of the enormous complexity of real life.[1] Professor TINBERGEN, on the other hand, in a number of pioneering studies, has tried to evaluate statistically a great number of dynamic ·relations for particular countries and to construct concrete models which give at least a rough quantitative approximation of the principal economic magnitudes and of the dynamic laws by which they are interrelated.[2]

A dynamic theory of the business cycle, if fully elaborated in precise terms, so as to do some justice to the enormous complexity of the real world, requires a highly complicated mathematical technique and presents formidable problems from the purely formal logical point of view.[3]

Total lack of correlation here would mean. the complete liquidation of economics as a science. . . . In every process of economic reasoning, we. . . . have to make certain assumptions, often not specified, concerning the relation between expectations, on the one hand, and current or past prices, profits, etc., on the other " (*loc. cit.*, page 175).

[1] Dr. Lundberg is, of course, well aware of these limitations.

[2] See, for example, *An Economic Approach to Business-cycle Problems* and the companion volume, *Les Fondements Mathématiques de la Stabilisation du Mouvement des Affaires*, Paris, 1937 and 1938. For a detailed discussion of the statistical methods and measurements involved, compare Professor Tinbergen's memoranda published by the Economic Intelligence Service of the League of Nations, Geneva, 1939, in the series : *Statistical Testing of Business-Cycle Theories*.

[3] Hence this branch of economics has been cultivated by mathematical economists. See especially the work of Frisch and Tinbergen.

Part II

SYNTHETIC EXPOSITION
RELATING TO THE NATURE AND
CAUSES OF BUSINESS CYCLES

CHAPTER 9

DEFINITION AND MEASUREMENT
OF THE BUSINESS CYCLE

---

§ 1. INTRODUCTION

"*Crisis*"
and
"*Depression*".

There is complete unanimity among economists that the problem of the recurrence of periods of economic depression and the cognate problem of acute economic or financial crises cannot fruitfully be discussed in isolation from the major problem of which they form part—viz., the problem of the business or trade cycle ; by which is meant, a wavelike movement affecting the economic system as a whole. It is therefore with the major problem that this study is concerned.

To define " depression ", we must also define " prosperity " : for the two are correlated concepts, since each is the negative of the other.

Before we try, however, to define more precisely these two concepts, it may be well to say a word about the meaning of the two related terms " crisis " and " depression ". They are frequently used indiscriminately. Throughout this paper, they will be sharply distinguished.

" Depression " will be used to mean a process or a continuous state of affairs of more or less extensive duration, which will be described and defined in following sections of this chapter.

The term " crisis " has two meanings. In the technical sense of business cycle theory, it means the turning-point which marks the passage from prosperity to depression. In the ordinary sense of everyday language, in which it is used also by the financial Press and frequently in economic writings, it means a state of acute financial stringency, panic, runs on the banks, drain of gold, bankruptcies, etc. A "crisis" in the technical sense—*i.e.*, a turn from prosperity to depression—is usually (but not always) accompanied by an acute "crisis" in the ordinary sense. On the other hand, an acute financial crisis may, and occasionally does, occur at a time when there is no "crisis" in the technical sense; in other words, it does not always mark the turn from a period of prosperity to a period of depression, but occurs sometimes during a depression or even during a prosperity period without turning the latter into a depression.[1]

§ 2.   DEFINITION OF PROSPERITY AND DEPRESSION
IN THE GENERAL SENSE

A closed economy.   Depression and prosperity may exist in the case of a branch of industry, a region, a whole country or the whole world.

The international aspects and complications of the cyclical movement will be considered in Chapter 11 below. In the earlier chapters, the reference will always be to the case of a closed economy—by which is meant, not a completely isolated country, but a country in possession of all the attributes which we shall find necessary for the full development of the trade cycle. We may therefore have occasion to allow for outside influences on our "closed" country, even before we turn *in extenso* to all the complications and qualifications in the argument necessitated by the fact that in the real world we are concerned, not with a number of independent economic systems, but with a system of interdependent and interrelated countries.

---

[1] But, as has been touched upon in connection with the discussion of the "psychological" theories, the "detonation" of a financial crisis is likely to deteriorate the general situation, even if it does not bring about an actual turn from prosperity to depression.

Alternative criteria. Depression means a state of affairs in which real income consumed or volume of consumption per head, real income produced or volume of production per head[1] and the rate of employment are falling or are subnormal in the sense that there are idle resources and unused capacity, especially unused labour.

Prosperity, on the other hand, means a state of affairs in which the real income consumed, real income produced and level of employment are high or rising, and there are no idle resources or unemployed workers, or very few of either.

Depression and prosperity differ in degree rather than in kind. It is not so much a question of a sharp line of demarcation between the two, as of a scale of more or less depressed or more or less prosperous conditions, ranging from deep depression to high prosperity and from severe unemployment to full employment of all the factors of production.

Real income consumed, real income produced, rate of employment—the three are comparatively precise concepts and even to some extent measurable quantities. There is little to be gained by looking deeper, though it is always possible to regard each of the three as in one way or another an index or a measure of a more fundamental magnitude, *i.e.*, of economic welfare. But "economic welfare" is a vague expression which itself calls for definition in terms of more precise and measurable magnitudes—and, as such, real income consumed, real income produced and rate of employment are at once indicated. For all practical purposes, therefore,

---

[1] Professor Fisher, in his various writings, defines "national income" as volume of consumption (see his *Nature of Capital and Income*, New York, 1912, his *Theory of Interest*, New York, 1930, and his article "Der Einkommensbegriff im Lichte der Erfahrung" in *Die Wirtschaftstheorie der Gegenwart*, Vol. III, Vienna, 1928, page 28). It has, however, become more and more usual to define national income as consumption plus net investment—that is, for a closed economy, the same as what we have called above "national income produced" or "volume of production". Since investment can be negative (disinvestment, dissaving, capital consumption), the volume of consumption may exceed the national income. In Chapter 10, we shall have to come back to these questions of definition. (*Cf.*, *e.g.*, Eric Lindhal : "The Concept of Income" in *Economic Essays in Honour of Gustav Cassel*, London, 1933, pages 399 *et seq.*, and the statistical literature which has sprung up in recent years.)

prosperity and depression are sufficiently precisely defined in terms of one or the other or all three of these magnitudes.[1]

" Employ- In recent years, unemployment has frequently
ment " been taken as the sole criterion of the economic
criterion. situation of a country. It must not be forgotten in this connection that a certain amount of unemployment is always present (frictional unemployment), and that there is a seasonal fluctuation of employment in many trades and countries. Even if these two factors are disregarded, the fact remains that in some countries unemployment remains on a high level over long periods—*e.g.*, in England or Austria after the war. In such a case, we speak of a chronic depression : but this does not mean that cyclical fluctuations are absent. They are merely superimposed on the mass of "structural" unemployment.

Even with all these qualifications—which are equally applicable incidentally to the two other factors of real income consumed and real income produced—the employment index cannot be regarded as an unfailing criterion in all cases. In agricultural countries, for example, depressions, whether due to crop failures or to

---

[1] The precise definition of the three variables—real income consumed, real income produced and rate of employment—and the method of measuring them open up, of course, the possibility of infinite discussion and raise a host of intricate problems. The whole literature on the construction of index-numbers of the price-level and volume of production and the cognate problems which they raise, has its relevance in this connection. It need not, fortunately, detain us at this point, since (as we shall see) the fluctuations with which we are concerned are so marked as to be visible, whichever of the current definitions and methods of measurement of the fundamental magnitudes is adopted. Exceptional cases are conceivable where reference to other criteria is indicated—for example, where adverse influences on the real income consumed or the real income produced are offset by harder work. In such a case, though the real income consumed and real income produced are unchanged, we are compelled to record a deterioration of the position, because the economic welfare is reduced. The additional criterion which must be introduced in this case is the length of the working-day. An alternative would be to define real income in such a way as to cover the quantum of leisure achieved and to make allowance in some manner for the toil and trouble involved. The statistics, however, afford no ground for supposing that such exceptional cases are of any considerable practical importance. Hence we may refrain from going into the matter in greater detail.

low prices, are not commonly accompanied by unemployment. The farmers and agricultural workers indeed may even work harder, and more people may be called in to work—wives and children, for example—in bad times than in good. The same may be true, to a certain extent, in countries such as Japan or Yugoslavia where industrial labour is not completely divorced from the soil. Even in a purely industrial country, if wages were perfectly plastic, unemployment could possibly—although this is an open question—be reduced to a very low point. On the other hand, there are cases where unemployment is due to rapid technological progress : in such cases one can hardly speak of depression or deterioration of the situation in spite of the high or rising level of unemployment.[1]

In such cases, we fall back on the two other criteria above mentioned—namely, real income consumed and real income produced.[2] The difference between the two consists in the fact

---

[1] No reference is made in this connection to statistical difficulties in the measurement of unemployment—a frequent source of spurious changes in unemployment figures. The introduction of schemes of unemployment relief or insurance and alterations in existing relief schemes always involve changes in the number of registered unemployed, for the reason that numbers of persons previously not registered are included in the registration, while numbers of persons previously registered are excluded. Changes in the situation in regard to unemployment relief are also bound to influence the real volume of unemployment owing to changes in wage-rates and the willingness of the workers to accept work at the prevailing rates.

[2] It may be urged that, in manufacturing industries, which are not dependent upon the weather, a divergence between volume of production and rate of employment is impossible in the short run. But this is not the case—even apart from the destruction caused by earthquakes, fires, explosions and the like. Where there is no reduction in the labour strength, a fall in the volume of output is conceivable, if less capitalistic methods of production are employed. There are theorists who maintain that this actually happens during the depression. Quantitatively speaking, however, in the absence of unemployment, fluctuations in production would certainly be reduced to relatively small proportions.

Professor F. Machlup says : "If wages were perfectly flexible, there would perhaps be no sharp fluctuations in employment, but there would be fluctuations in wage-rates instead" ("Professor Knight and the Period of Production" in *Journal of Political Economy*, Vol. 43, October 1935, page 624). See also J. Robinson on "Disguised Unemployment" in *Economic Journal*, June 1936, reprinted in *Essays in the Theory of Employment*, London, 1937, pages 82 *et seq.*

that real income consumed is confined to consumers' goods and services—that is to say, is equivalent to "volume of consumption" or, if we disregard changes in stocks of consumers' goods, to "flow of goods and services ready for consumption",[1] while real income produced includes also additions to the stock of goods of a higher order (producers' goods, raw materials, etc.).

"Consumption" criterion. If wages or incomes in general are flexible, and unemployment is avoided more or less completely by a fall in wages rapid enough to offset the deterioration in the economic situation, the deterioration will take the form of a fall in the real income consumed by the community. In the case mentioned above of an agricultural country, the rate of employment and the volume of production may even rise in spite of the prevailing depression, if the foreign demand for the product of the country has fallen as a result, *e.g.*, of a depression in certain foreign countries or the expansion of a competitive source of supply.[2] The criterion of the deterioration is then a fall in the real income consumed represented by a reduction of the consumption of imported goods due to the fall in price of home-produced exports.

"Production" criterion. In a closed economy, the situation is usually less involved. But even here the movements of the volume of consumption and real income produced may diverge. It is conceivable that the volume of consumption should remain constant or even rise while the volume of production falls—*e.g.*, in the case of a community living on its capital. Obviously, in such a case, the volume of production and

---

[1] It is convenient to regard durable consumers' goods (such as motorcars or dwelling-houses) as goods of a higher order, and their services as the finished product. Professor Irving Fisher's *Nature of Capital and Income* (New York, 1912) would seem to contain the most satisfactory discussion of the various accounting problems which arise in this connection.

[2] It is worth pointing out that the term "volume of production" may be defined as meaning, not the volume of home production, but the final outcome or result of the national labour, including (that is) the volume of goods obtained for that part of the product which is exported to foreign countries. Volume of production = amount produced at home — exports + imports. If we adopt this definition, the discrepancy in this case between volume of production and real income consumed is avoided.

the rate of employment have to be taken as criteria rather than the volume of consumption.[1]

On the other hand, if a community adds to its capital equipment, the volume of production may rise or remain constant, while the volume of consumption falls or does not rise so rapidly. In this case, clearly the volume of production and the rate of employment should be regarded as the true criteria.

This situation frequently arises, to a greater or smaller extent, when business is recovering from a deep depression. The production of producers' goods rises and additions are made to the capital stock; but the flow of consumers' goods and services usually rises only to a lesser extent.

Conclusion. We may conclude that a combination of the three indices—(1) employment, (2) real income consumed and (3) real income produced—can be regarded as the criterion of the existence, and measure of the degree, of prosperity and depression and changes in the same. If all three indices point in the same direction, the situation is clear. If they diverge, it is as a rule possible to arrive at some indication on the basis of the considerations above set forth.

We shall see that the fluctuations are usually so marked that the doubtful cases are of no practical importance. But, before we proceed to statistical examples, we may discuss briefly two other criteria which are often used in the literature on the subject.

Other criteria. Fluctuations in profits (and losses) are frequently regarded as the essential characteristic of the business cycle : but it would not seem advisable to rank them with the three fundamental elements indicated above. The term " profit " is vague and misleading. What are recorded statistically as " profits " (*e.g.*, profits of corporations) do not consist purely of profits in the sense in which economic theory uses the term : they are, rather, a mixture of interest, rent, monopoly gains, etc. Profits in the sense in which economic theory uses the term are part of the national income

---

[1] Volume of consumption can be taken as the criterion, if the time element is introduced. A community living on its capital is prosperous for the time being; but the prosperity cannot last.

and, as such, are included in " real income ". The *absence* of profits—or losses—in this, the strict, sense of the word is the very essence of perfect equilibrium of the economic system; and a state of perfect economic equilibrium, with full employment of all available resources, is surely a state of high prosperity.

The term " loss " also lacks precision. An individual, commercial loss need not be a loss to the community. The invention of a new productive process, for example, may involve losses on the fixed plant used in the process supplanted : but such losses do not constitute a deterioration in the economic situation of the community. Profit-and-loss statistics are no doubt a valuable symptom of the business cycle in the technical sense : but they are not an unfailing criterion of the business cycle in the general sense (§ 3).

Our employment- and production-criterion seems to express precisely what is meant by " economic activity ", which is frequently used, more or less loosely, as criterion of prosperity and depression. Evidently, if it is to be at all useful as such a criterion, the concept must be capable of quantification, and if we ask ourselves how the degree or intensity of economic activity is to be measured, the answer will be in terms either of input or output, in terms, that is to say, of the effort applied or the result achieved. This is doubtless equivalent to measuring it in terms of employment (not necessarily of the available labour factor only) or of production.

§ 3.   THE BUSINESS CYCLE IN THE GENERAL SENSE AND IN THE TECHNICAL SENSE

The business cycle in the general sense may be defined as an alternation of periods of prosperity and depression, of good and bad trade. This definition is, however, provisional, for it is obviously too wide. It covers more than the business cycle in the technical sense of business-cycle theory. That the general economic situation is subject to fluctuations, that the volume of production, national income and level of employment should sometimes be above and sometimes below the average or trend is not indeed surprising. An alternation of periods of depression and prosperity is what we should normally expect. What calls for explanation is, in the first place, the duration and wide amplitude of the fluctuations—particularly those in the negative direction, since the upward movement, the approach to full employment, might be explained as a natural consequence of the inherent tendency of the economic system towards equilibrium. Why do we not find short irregular oscillations around a trend, but long swings in both directions ?

It is not merely, however, the magnitude of the fluctuations, but their peculiar nature, which constitutes the problem of the cycle. What that nature is can be indicated at this point only in negative terms. With the positive explanation of these fluctuations, the whole of the rest of this study is concerned. The mysterious thing about them is that they cannot be accounted for by such " external " causes as bad harvests due to weather conditions, diseases, general strikes, lock-outs, earthquakes, the sudden obstruction of international trade channels and the like. Severe decreases in the volume of production, real income or level of employment as a result of crop failures, wars, earthquakes and similar physical disturbances of the productive processes rarely affect the economic system as a whole, and certainly do not constitute depressions in the technical sense of business-cycle theory.[1] By depression in the technical sense we mean those prolonged and conspicuous falls in the volume of production, real income and employment which can only be explained by the operation of factors originating within the economic system itself, and in the first instance by an insufficiency of monetary demand and the absence of a sufficient margin between price and cost.

If external disturbances of the kind referred to have a causal relation to the occurrence of depressions in the technical sense— which is unquestionably the case—it is not so much the material obstruction of the production process that accounts for the fall

---

[1] This by no means excludes the possibility of such external disturbances having an indirect influence on the business cycle in the technical sense. On the contrary, we shall see that those disturbances play their rôle by starting or reversing, retarding or accelerating, internal processes of expansion and contraction of output and employment.

GENERAL INDICES OF CYCLICAL MOVEMENT IN VARIOUS COUNTRIES

For explanations, see Appendix I, page 453.
The principal crises are indicated by arrows.

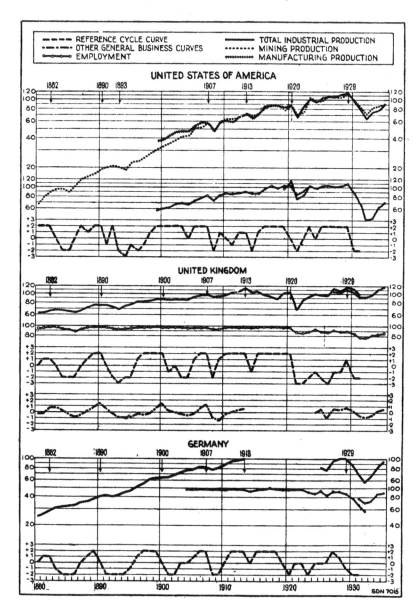

GENERAL INDICES OF CYCLICAL MOVEMENT IN VARIOUS COUNTRIES

For explanations, see Appendix I, page 453.
The principal crises are indicated by arrows.

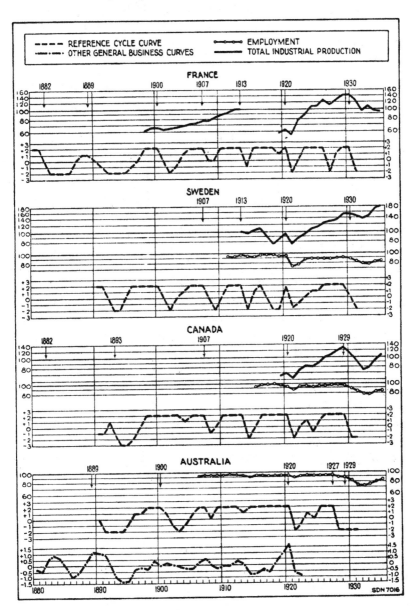

in the volume of production as the peculiar response of the economic system.[1]

The continuance of production is materially perfectly possible. The necessary capital equipment is there; so is the labour-power : so are the raw materials and semi-finished products.   Yet somehow a large part of the factors of production cannot be put to work; the economic machine does not function smoothly : the price system is out of equilibrium.

§ 4.   BASIC FACTS ABOUT THE BUSINESS CYCLE

Four phases of the cycle. In any attempt to apply our fundamental criteria of prosperity and depression in order to locate and measure in exact form, over any considerable length of time, the phenomenon which is the subject of our study, we are at once confronted with the difficulty that the statistical data, especially for the earlier periods, before the war and in the nineteenth century, are very inadequate.   Indices of national income and employment (or unemployment) are very unreliable, and in the case of a number of countries do not exist at all.   Indices of the volume of production are also far from being complete or sufficiently representative.

The fluctuations with which we are concerned are, however, so marked and extend over such a wide range of phenomena that it is possible to identify them with a high degree of accuracy on the basis of the existing material, even in periods for which the latter is not so complete.   We begin with the attempt to determine the length of the successive periods of prosperity and depression in the case of a number of countries by fixing as exactly as possible the turning-points from boom to slump and slump to boom.   The whole cycle is divided into four phases or parts :

(1) The upswing (prosperity phase, expansion);

---

[1] This is clearly revealed by the fact that external disturbances, such as a war or an earthquake, which directly obstruct the productive process and destroy wealth, nevertheless frequently tend to bring about an expansion rather than a contraction of employment and production.

(2) The downswing (depression phase, contraction);[1]

(3) The upper turning-point—that is, the turn from prosperity to depression (down-turn, crisis in the technical sense);[2]

(4) The lower turning-point—that is, the turn from depression to prosperity (up-turn, revival).

This distinction of four phases, or rather two phases and two turning-points, should not be taken to imply more than is actually said. It is not suggested that the duration of cycles should necessarily be counted either from trough to trough (from revival to revival) or from peak to peak (from crisis to crisis). It is not maintained that each cycle (whether counted this way or that way) is to be regarded as (so to say) an individual unit or an indivisible whole, so that it must be explained by a single principle, or, again, that one phase grows out of the previous one and must be explained with reference to it. Such statements may have a definite meaning and value at the end, or in a later stage, of a study such as the present one. At this early stage, we shall do no more than register certain basic facts.[3]

Various indices recording the cycle.   In the preceding graphs, the cyclical movement in a number of countries is represented by various indices, a description of which is given in Appendix I. An inspection of the diagrams shows an almost perfect concordance in the movements of different curves. There are sometimes slight deviations; but they seldom exceed one year. They can often be explained

---

[1] The terms "expansion" and "contraction" are sometimes used in the purely monetary sense of expansion and contraction of credit or money. We shall use them, where no other meaning is implied by the context, to denote the complex phenomenon—expansion and contraction of production and employment *plus* expansion and contraction of the circulating medium. For the purely monetary aspect, we shall usually employ the terms "inflation" and "deflation".

[2] See page 257.

[3] Various writers have elaborated different typical cycle patterns. The Harvard Economic Service, *e.g.*, distinguishes five phases : depression, recovery, business prosperity, financial strain, industrial crisis. Spiethoff has a still more complicated scheme. But these schemes are based from the outset on a particular view as to the causation of these fluctuations. They imply generalisations which do not fit all cases. Therefore they cannot serve as starting-points, but are the result of the analysis.

by inaccuracies in the figures or in the description in the annals. The conventions which have been adopted for the graphical representation of the "Annals" must be kept in mind, if a misleading impression is to be avoided. Only a few gradations of prosperity and depression are distinguished, so that neither the amplitude of fluctuations nor the speed of recovery and decline at various points can be adequately indicated. Both the high and the low conjunctures tend to be represented by horizontal straight lines masking the turning-points which come either in the latter part of the last year of the horizontal or in the first part of the following year.

It must also be remembered that, whereas the production indices show a pronounced trend movement, on which the cyclical fluctuations are superimposed, in the employment series—except in the case of the United States of America—and the Reference Cycle Curve, the trend is eliminated by the method of their construction.

These curves represent the business cycle in the general sense—that is to say, they record the changes in production and employment irrespective of the cause. But there is no doubt that, with a very few exceptions, the ups and downs of production in our curves are not the direct effect of material obstructions to the production process caused by strikes, earthquakes, etc. The direct influence of the weather on the volume of agricultural production plays no rôle, since our production and employment figures relate to industry alone.

Since reliable direct measurements of our fundamental criteria— employment and volume of production—are not always available, it is necessary to have recourse to other statistical series, which are either themselves constituent parts of the index of production, or are empirically so closely related that they can be taken as highly symptomatic for the direction of the movement or magnitude of fluctuations in the fundamental variable. Such "auxiliary" or "symptomatic" series, as they may be called, are bank clearings, bank deposits, other monetary series, price series, transportation figures, bankruptcies, etc.

§ 5. THE SECULAR TREND

Various components of time-series.
The economic cycle in which we are primarily interested is that alternation of relatively prosperous and depressed times, together with all the concomitant changes in all parts of the economic system, which extends over the period of three to twelve years. This movement we call the business cycle proper.

Besides (1) the business cycle proper, we find other movements reflected in the time-series of important economic magnitudes— namely, (2) a secular trend, (3) seasonal variations within the span of one year, (4) occasional disturbances attributable to erratic forces from outside the economic system in the strict sense, and (5) the so-called "long waves" covering periods of fifty years or more.

The meaning of the trend in different series.
The secular trend relates to the continuous rise in volume of production, real income, production of particular commodities, real wages, etc., which has taken place, with relatively short setbacks, during the nineteenth and twentieth centuries. Such a tendency of the fundamental magnitudes to grow is the criterion of a progressive economy. As we usually think of societies as progressive, we assume—and have hitherto been lucky enough to find—upward-sloping trend curves for production and consumption. But it is by no means necessary that the secular change should take place at a constant rate, or that it should always slope upward along a smooth curve which can confidently be extrapolated into the future. Nor is it excluded that the forces which create the trend may tend to operate spasmodically or cyclically.

Furthermore, it is evident that the secular trend may have quite a different significance according to the economic magnitude concerned. A gradual rise of the total volume of production and consumption is the natural consequence of growth of population. An upward-sloping trend of physical quantities of production and consumption per head of the population is the essence of material progress due to the accumulation of capital and the increasing stock of technical knowledge. Obviously, the situation is quite different in the case of money prices and money values. Rising prices and money values are not an essential characteristic of material progress. It is quite conceivable that, because of the peculiar working of the money-profit-price mechanism in an individualistic economy, a certain trend of prices is required to ensure the smooth, uninterrupted working of the productive apparatus, and to make possible the complete and rapid realisation of all the benefits of technological progress. But this is only a hypothesis, as to which there is unfortunately no agreement among economists. Some writers believe that prices should gradually fall when production expands : others predicate a stable price level : others, again, incline to think a slightly rising trend of prices is the most beneficial for the working of the economic machine. In any case, it seems to be clear that a price trend—if there is one—should be interpreted in quite a different way from a trend in the physical quantities of production.

At this stage, being primarily interested in cyclical movements of the order of magnitude of three to twelve years, we are concerned not so much with the " secular trend " as with the departures from it which our series exhibit. As for the other movements in the various economic magnitudes, the seasonal fluctuations —not shown in the annual data—do not constitute a serious theoretical problem, nor do the irregular changes or disturbances, such, for example, as the general strike in the United Kingdom in 1926.

§ 6. BUSINESS CYCLES AND LONG WAVES

A word of justification and explanation must, however, be said as to why we concentrate on the short cycle instead of on the long waves which according to many writers (KONDRATIEFF, WOYTINSKI and others) show themselves quite clearly in a number of long series such as those of production, wages and prices. These long waves or trend cycles extend over a period of fifty to sixty years; and the short cycles, for which we reserve the expression " business or trade cycle ", are superimposed on them (in much the same way as the seasonal fluctuations are superimposed on the business cycle).

Facts about the long waves. Avoiding figurative language and leaving aside all speculations and dubious hypotheses, the broad facts about these long waves seem to be as follows. It is possible to distinguish during the nineteenth and twentieth centuries alternating periods in which depression years and prosperity years respectively predominate. These periods extend from twenty to thirty years, and each of them comprises two to five complete business cycles of the short type. These periods are, according to Professor SPIETHOFF, for Western Europe (1) 1822-1842, (2) 1843-1873, (3) 1874-1894, (4) 1895-1913.[1] The *first* of these periods contains two business cycles in which the depression phase was much longer than the prosperity phase. In this whole period, Professor SPIETHOFF counts nine prosperous and twelve depressed years. In the *second* period (1843-1873) prosperous times prevail. In three and a-half business cycles there are twenty-one prosperous and ten depressed years, depressions being short and mild. The *third* period (1874-1894) begins with the prolonged and extremely severe depression of the seventies. It contains two and a-half cycles, and Professor SPIETHOFF counts six prosperous and fifteen depressed years. This gloomy period is followed by a *fourth* period (1895-1913) which is overwhelmingly prosperous. It contains two and a-half cycles, the last one being interrupted by the world war. Only four depression years stand against fifteen years of prosperity, depressions being short and mild.

Necessity for previous analysis of short waves. We do not deny that there is an interesting phenomenon in the " long waves " which calls for explanation. Some *prima facie* plausible hypotheses have been put forward to this end. There are stimulating and depressing forces, which do not exhaust themselves within the span of one short cycle but persist through a number of them, such as the up-and-down trends of gold production, the exploitation of technical

---

[1] According to other investigators, the dates are approximately the same.

innovations (equipment of a country with railroads) or newly discovered countries.[1] These forces may conceivably produce a long wave in production and prices. But is not that a purely fortuitous phenomenon ? Is each of these long cycles the result of the same type of force ? Is there the slightest probability that a cycle of fifty years or so will always be produced ? Are we at all justified in extrapolating these waves ? Is there any sense in such statements as that the depression of the nineteen-thirties was so severe because we were not only in the downgrade of a short, but also of a long, wave ? Why is it that periods which are under the spell of one of these long-range forces are themselves divided into shorter periods of prosperity and depression ? It would seem that all these and other sceptical questions about the nature of the long waves can be answered only after a fairly full insight into the mechanism of the short cycles has been attained. For the forces which are said to produce the long waves do not work independently of, and alternatively to, those that produce the short cycle. They work through the latter—*e.g.*, by tending to increase continuously the supply of money (gold production), or by continual creation of new investment opportunities (*e.g.*, railway development of a country or rapid growth of its population). Until the working of the mechanism of the short cycle has been explored, the nature of the long waves cannot be understood. We are therefore compelled to attack first of all the problem of the business cycle.

§ 7. IS A GENERAL THEORY OF THE CYCLE POSSIBLE ?

Each cycle an historical individual. Until now we have discussed the essential characteristics of the business cycle—that is, those qualities in the absence of which the phenomenon " business cycle " does not exist. Besides these, there is an endless variety of changes in all spheres of economic and social life which, without being essential features of the cycle, are more or less regular concomitants of its progress. These concomitant changes furnish the material which we have to seek

---

[1] This is Professor Schumpeter's hypothesis about the long waves.

out and analyse in order to find such clues to the causation of the cycle as will enable us to verify or reject the explanatory hypotheses (theories of the cycle) which we find in the literature.

Most of these changes do not appear regularly in all cycles. Close inspection of the facts reveals very many irregularities and far-reaching differences between the characteristics of the various cycles—over and above the differences in the length and amplitude of the cycles (as defined in terms of our fundamental criteria): Each cycle, each period of prosperity or depression, has its special features which are not present in any, or not in many, others. In a sense, each cycle is an historical individual : each is embedded in a social-economic structure of its own. Technological knowledge, methods of production, degree of capital-intensity, number, quality and age-distribution of the population, habits and preferences of consumers, social institutions in the widest sense including the legal framework of society, practice in the matter of interventions of the State and other public bodies in the economic sphere, habits of payment, banking practices and so forth—all these factors change continuously, and are not exactly the same in any two cases. It is therefore not at all surprising to find great dissimilarities between cycles in different countries and different periods. On the whole, it may be said that the differences and dissimilarities between different cycles are much greater than many cycle theorists seem to assume.

A general theory possible. This point with regard to the dissimilarities between different cycles raises the question whether it is possible to make any general statements at all as to the causes and conditions of cycles—in other words, whether the same theory holds for the cycles in the first half of the nineteenth century and for those in the second quarter of the twentieth century, for the cycles in the industrial countries of Western Europe and the United States and for those in the agricultural countries of Eastern Europe and overseas. ("Cycle" is here used in the technical sense as defined previously, disregarding those changes in volume of production, employment, etc., which can be attributed to the *direct* influence of the interruption or obstruction of the productive process by external disturbances.)

The question cannot be answered *a priori*. Logically, it is quite conceivable that, under different social and economic conditions, periods of prosperity and depression should be produced by entirely different sets of causes, so that for different groups of cycles separate theories would have to be devised.

We believe, however, that this is not the case. We believe, on the contrary, that a very general theory of the most important aspects of the cycle can be evolved, which will not on the one hand be so formal as to be useless for practical purposes, while, on the other hand, it will have a very wide field of application. The precise conditions of its applicability will be discussed in the following pages. They relate to monetary and banking arrangements, the wage-price system and some elementary technological facts—all deeply rooted in our present individualistic money-price economy.

It should be noted that the mere fact that each cycle is an historical individual is not a sufficient argument against a general theory. Are there two men who are in all respects alike? Does this dissimilarity in many respects destroy the possibility and practical usefulness of anatomy, physiology, etc. ? That each cycle is unique in many respects does not prevent all cycles from being similar in other respects, over and above those similarities which constitute the fundamental elements of the cycle. These latter do not constitute causes of the cycle any more than *pauvreté* is the cause of poverty. In other words, that each upswing shows a rise in production and employment and each downswing exhibits a fall of the same is not surprising, since that is how we have defined the cycle. But, if there are other similarities, they may, as symptoms, throw light on the causes.

Order of the argument. It will be shown that any economy organised on such lines is liable to cumulative, self-reinforcing processes of expansion and contraction. The first thing to prove is that these processes are self-reinforcing—that is to say that, once expansion or contraction has started (for whatever reason), forces are released which make for further expansion or contraction. In other words, certain deviations from the equilibrium are not corrected automatically, but lead the system farther away from equilibrium. (This is, of course, figurative language. Its purpose is not to prove a proposition, but to convey a general meaning. It will presently be replaced by precise analysis.)

The next step will then be to discuss why these processes of expansion and contraction always come to an end. Must they come to an end ? Cannot they go on indefinitely ? Why does expansion not lead to stable equilibrium ? Are periods of expansion interrupted and reversed by accidental disturbances, or do they necessarily give rise to maladjustments ?

We shall see that in these respects various possibilities are open, which do not exclude one another, and that there is no reason to postulate a single solution which must apply to all cases.

The guiding principle of our approach is to proceed cautiously step by step. We do not assume from the outset that there is a cycle in the sense that prosperity must necessarily be followed by depression and *vice versa*. That may be the final conclusion of such a study as the present; but it cannot be assumed from the beginning. Therefore we start with the most general aspects of the problem, which do not yet imply the existence of a cycle in the strict sense just indicated, and then proceed to less and less general features, where the conclusions depend to an increasing extent on the particular social-economic environment. This procedure has the advantage that it does not close the door to more ambitious theoretical constructions. But it would seem that such constructions cannot be safely undertaken except on the basis of such preparatory analyses.

§ 8. TWO REGULAR FEATURES OF THE CYCLE

Parallelism of production and monetary demand.
There are two features which we can observe in every cycle, probably without exception, although they are not implied by our definition of the cycle. They are therefore of the utmost suggestive value and must be kept in mind from the beginning.

The one is the fact that the cyclical ups and downs of production and employment are accompanied by a parallel movement of the money value of production and transactions; the second is the fact that the cyclical fluctuations are more marked in connection with the production of producers' goods than in connection with the production of consumers' goods.

The first of these facts is so indubitable that it hardly calls for special statistical verification. at this point.   It is only necessary to recall that production rises in the upswing, falls in the downswing, while prices in general (including factor prices, especially money wages and prices of real estate and property rights) rise or remain constant[1] in the upswing and fall in the downswing.   It follows that the money value of production and of transactions rises and falls.   In other words, the volume of work which the medium of exchange has to perform expands and contracts with the rise and fall of the business cycle. MV, the quantity of money × velocity of circulation—*i.e.*, the flow of money against goods or the aggregate demand for goods in terms of money per unit of time—grows during prosperity and shrinks during depression.   This proposition is certainly true of the money value of production and the money value of transactions relating to goods—of the " industrial circulation ", to use an expression of Mr. KEYNES.   It may not always be true—or at any rate irregular fluctuations may occur—if stock-exchange transactions (that is, the " financial circulation " in Mr. KEYNES' terminology) are included.

It should be noted that these propositions do not follow from the definition of prosperity and depression, and are by no means self-evident.[2]   It is not a logical necessity that fluctuations in thy material volume of production should always be accompanied be parallel changes in its money value.   Fluctuation in real income need not show itself by fluctuation in money income.   Prices might conceivably fall during the upswing and rise during the downswing.[3]   That the contrary is true, that a higher national

---

[1] The best-known case of constant or even falling prices is that of the 1926-1929 boom in America.   Even in this case it was only true of commodity prices : factor prices and stock-exchange prices rose.

[2] This has, *e.g.*, clearly been overlooked by Mr. R. F. Kahn, in his Rejoinder to my Comments on his review of the first edition of this book. (*Economic Journal*, Vol. 48, June 1938, page 335, last sentence of second paragraph.)

[3] Where the fall in the volume of production is due to a physical obstruction of the process of production, unaccompanied by changes on the money side, that is what one would expect.

income in terms of goods always appears as higher money income, is a highly significant additional fact which calls for explanation; and its explanation is almost bound to afford clues to the understanding of the business cycle.[1]

It would be rash to conclude from the fact that the monetary circulation (in the sense of MV) rises and falls with the general movement of the cycle that money—or rather monetary forces in the sense of monetary policy (*i.e.*, action on the part of the monetary authorities)—is the impelling cause of the cyclical expansion and contraction of production and employment. We shall come back to this point later. At this stage, we cannot answer the question definitely; we must confine ourselves to pointing out that money may conceivably play a rôle of minor importance. It is possible that in some, or even in all, circumstances it adjusts itself to changes in production without exerting an active influence.

Specially wide fluctuations in producers' goods. We pass to the second regular feature of the cycle, a less self-evident feature—namely, the fact that the production of producers' goods fluctuates much more violently than the production of consumers' goods. As may be seen from the following graphs, this is true in a relative, and in many cases also in an absolute, sense. If we measure the amplitude of the cycle either by changes in the total volume of production or by changes in the total number of unemployed or employed workers, we often find that the changes in the volume of production of producers' goods (goods of higher order) and changes in the number of unemployed in these industries contribute more to the change of the total than do changes in the volume of production of consumers' goods and in the number of workers employed thereon. Historically speaking, with the accumulation of capital, the producers' goods industries have grown relatively to the consumers' goods industries, till to-day they are in many countries approaching or outstripping the latter in importance, as measured, *e.g.*, by the number of workers employed in both branches. It may happen, however, in countries

---

[1] Mr. R. F. Harrod, in his book, *The Trade Cycle* (London, 1936), has also found it worth while to lay special stress on this fact.

PRODUCTION AND EMPLOYMENT BY GROUPS OF INDUSTRIES.

For explanations, see Appendix II, page 456.
The principal crises are indicated by arrows.

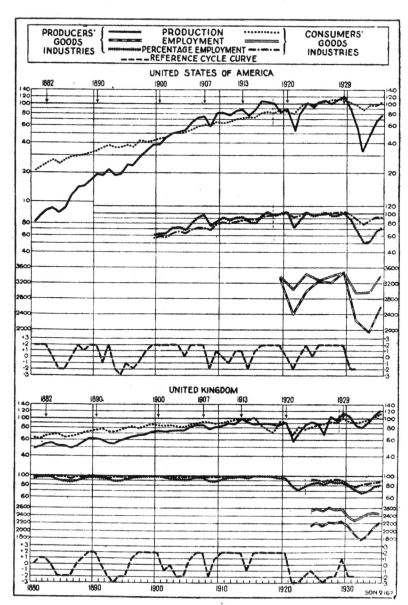

PRODUCTION AND EMPLOYMENT BY GROUPS OF INDUSTRIES.

For explanations, see Appendix II, page 456.
The principal crises are indicated by arrows.

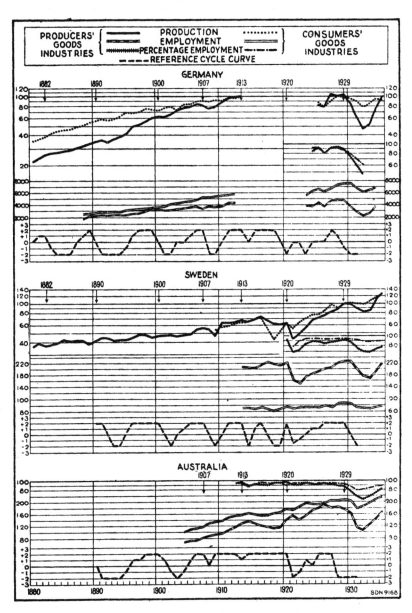

or semi-closed economies where the producers' goods industries are relatively undeveloped, that the absolute magnitude of these fluctuations in production is greater in the consumers' goods industries. But in almost all cases it will be found that the amplitude of the fluctuations measured with reference to "normal" production (*i.e.*, the relative fluctuations) is greater in the producers' goods industries. Moreover, not only is their amplitude greater, but the fluctuations in these industries are much more regular, and conform much more closely with the business cycle in general, than the fluctuations in the consumers' goods industries.

When we speak of consumers' goods, we mean perishable consumers' goods (such as food) and semi-durable goods (such as clothing, shoes and furniture). Durable consumers' goods (such as apartment houses) show very wide fluctuations, and belong rather to the category of capital goods, for reasons which have already been discussed and will be touched upon again.

CHAPTER 10

THE PROCESS OF EXPANSION AND CONTRACTION

---

§ 1. INTRODUCTION

The problem stated. In this chapter, the mechanism of the expansion and contraction processes will be analysed. We assume that the process of expansion (or contraction) has been started in one manner or another and we investigate what is meant by saying that the process is cumulative and self-reinforcing, and on what factors this cumulative quality depends. How such a process can be started, how in fact it is normally started, whether it can or cannot go on indefinitely, how it can be, and how it is in fact, interrupted, whether it is automatically brought to an end—all these questions will be taken up *in extenso* in the next chapter, although it will be impossible to avoid all reference to them in the present chapter, if only by way of implication or illustration.

On the whole, it may be said that the problems considered in this chapter are less controversial than those which form the subject of Chapter 11. If there is anything like common ground in modern business cycle theory, we are likely to find it here.

A.   The Expansion Process

§ 2.   GENERAL DESCRIPTION OF THE MECHANISM UNDER THE ASSUMPTION THAT THERE ARE UNEMPLOYED PRODUCTIVE RESOURCES

Elasticity of supply. We begin our analysis of the process of expansion at its starting-point—viz., at the bottom of the depression. This means in effect that we start with a situation where there are unemployed productive resources. The analysis of an expansion which has started with, or has advanced to the attainment of, a state of full employment is more difficult : it will be attempted in § 3.[1]

If there is much unemployment, the supply of labour is completely or almost completely elastic in the upward direction—that is to say, an increasing demand can be satisfied at the same or only a slightly higher wage. The supply of other means of production is also elastic, since there are stocks of raw materials, under-employed capital equipment, etc. In such a situation, there are no technical reasons why production should not be increased at short notice all along the line in almost all stages and branches of industry.

Suppose, now, expansion has been started for any reason whatsoever—*e.g.*, because new investment opportunities have been opened up and large sums are being invested over a considerable period of time at some point in the economic system (to build, say, a new railway line).

---

[1] It has often been argued—*e.g.*, by Professor Hayek—that an analysis of the cycle must start from an equilibrium with full employment. One cannot assume unemployment from the beginning, it is said, because it is the thing which has to be explained. But surely it must be possible and legitimate to investigate what happens when business has begun to expand after a depression which has created much unemployment and over-capacity, without first explaining how the depression has been brought about. This latter question we shall take up later. The order in which the various problems connected with the cycle are considered is a matter of exposition rather than of logical necessity. Furthermore, the question whether an expansion can start from a situation of full employment, and what it looks like and how it develops when it does, is not neglected, but only postponed.

It should be noted that the equilibrium concept of theoretical economics by no means implies full employment of all the factors of production. There are, *first*, apparent exceptions which really turn on the proper definition of unemployment. (*Cf.* A. C. Pigou, *The Theory of Unemployment*, London, 1933. Part I, Chapter 1.) In any economy, there are means of production which could be used but are not used because it does not pay—submarginal land, unemployable workers, etc. *Secondly*, voluntary unemployment does not count. If, at the prevailing wage-rate, certain people do not care to work, they are not to be counted as unemployed. *Thirdly*, if the prices of some factors of production (*e.g.*, wages) are kept too high by a trade union, by State intervention, by tradition or for any other reason, there may be some unemployment (unused factors) consistently with perfect equilibrium. In a sense, this kind of unemployment, too, may be called " voluntary ". (On this concept of " involuntary unemployment " compare Chapter 8, § 5.)

Reciprocal stimulation of investment and consumption. Assume that the necessary sums are raised in such a way as to bring about an increase in the effective circulation of money. The funds for the investment are not withdrawn from other uses, but consist of money newly created by the banking system, or come out of hoards of unused purchasing power. The monetary details will be discussed in § 4. Here it is enough to assume that, in one way or another, the aggregate demand for goods in terms of money increases. Workers are hired; raw materials, semi-finished goods and implements, etc., are bought or ordered. Note that there is no sort of guarantee that all the money thus injected will remain in circulation. On the contrary, there will be numerous leakages (which need not be discussed here in detail)[1] through which a smaller or larger proportion of the new purchasing power will be withdrawn from the active circulation and so sterilised. Assume, however, that a part of the new money goes on circulating—that is to say, is spent by the successive recipients. It is easy to see how it will stimulate other branches of industry and spread the expansion to all parts of the economic system.

The producers of materials and implements will increase their production.[2] They may draw on idle funds at their disposal, or borrow from the banks, or float a new issue in the market, in order to hire workers and buy the material or equipment they need. The additional earnings of the workers will be at least in part spent immediately. The demand for consumers' goods will go up and production of consumers' goods will be stimulated. This reacts favourably on the higher stages of production. Idle monetary funds are set in motion; and the demand for all kinds

---

[1] The point has been discussed at length by Mr. Kahn, Professors Arthur D. Gayer, J. M. Clark, etc., in connection with the probable effects of public works.

[2] Additional supplies may be available, even of those raw materials which are of agricultural origin, if quantities have been held in store during the depression. Whether the production of fixed capital rises at once or with a lag will depend on the existence of excess capacity at the moment when revival starts, on the "accumulation of investment opportunities" during the preceding depression, and a number of other factors which will be discussed at various points in the following pages.

of goods is further increased, which generates income. The process is likely to proceed slowly at the beginning and then to gather momentum. At first, it may easily be interrupted by adverse influences. Later on, when demand for many goods has grown for some time and the expansionary movement has spread to many parts of the system, the increase in the total demand for goods in terms of money per unit of time becomes greater. Adverse influences which tend to decrease the flow of money against goods will now only be able to decrease the rate of increase in the flow of money and to slow down the general expansion, whereas in the early stage of the upswing they would have nipped the expansion in the bud. This is what is meant by saying that " the process has gathered momentum "; it has become strong enough to overcome obstacles of lesser magnitude.

Rise in prices, costs and profits. There are other factors which are likely to come into play after a while and to reinforce expansion. A sustained and rapid increase in output due to, or accompanied by, an increase in the flow of money will certainly lead to a rise in production costs and commodity prices at various points, even if the labour supply is, for the time being, perfectly elastic. (See Chapter 4, § 2, above for a detailed description.) Profits will also rise all along the line, owing to the fact that rigid overhead costs can be spread over a larger output and wages lag behind prices.

Investment in fixed capital stimulated. A continued rise in demand, coupled with rising prices and profits, is bound to create in the business world a more optimistic outlook in general and in particular an expectation—no matter whether justified or not—of a further rise of prices. This will induce entrepreneurs to embark on more ambitious schemes of investment in fixed capital and either borrow more freely from the money or capital market or use idle funds at their disposal for the purpose. There will always be technological improvements waiting to be made, especially at the end of a depression during which investment has been at a standstill—improvements which necessitate the installation of additional machinery (fixed capital) and are profitable only at a certain ratio between price and cost. Given the profitability at the existing price-cost ratio, the investment will be undertaken only if the profitable price-cost ratio is expected to last long enough to permit the amortisation of the invested capital, and there are no other disturbing factors such as State interventions, revolutions, currency inflation, etc., to prevent the reaping of the expected profit. Naturally, the more durable the investment projected the more important the expectation factor.

Thus the expansion proceeds in a progressive and cumulative fashion. As it advances, restraining forces come more and more into play. These will be analysed in the section on the upper turning-point.

The above analysis of the expansion process can be put in more technical language. If we describe the initial expansion as being due to a divergence between the natural or equilibrium rate of interest, on the one hand, and the money or market rate of interest, on the other, the cumulative continuation of the expansion has to be ascribed to the fact that the price rise (and profit rise) induced by the initial divergence forces the equilibrium rate up, with the result that the gap between the two rates is widened—which in turn intensifies the rise in prices and profits, etc.

There are other terminological alternatives,[1] and terminological as well as analytical niceties, which need not detain us here : the non-technical description of the expansion process as given above is for the time being clear and precise enough. We shall come back to the monetary details in § 4.

§ 3. THE MECHANISM OF EXPANSION UNDER THE ASSUMPTION
OF FULL OR ALMOST FULL EMPLOYMENT

Can full employment be attained?   In what sense can the expansion continue beyond the point of full employment ? How can it start from a situation of full employment of all factors of production ? These questions are not intended to suggest that the upswing is always, or generally, carried to the point of full employment. On the contrary, it

---

[1] The reader will observe that the reactions so far analysed have to be described in Mr. Keynes' terminology as a shift to the right of the schedule of marginal efficiency of capital coupled with an elastic liquidity-preference schedule.

will be shown that the economic system becomes increasingly vulnerable when it approaches full employment, and that there is a consequent possibility that the full employment level will not be fully attained or, if attained, will not long persist. But for completeness' sake the question must be considered.

Obviously, after full employment has been reached, output can no longer expand at the same pace as before, since there are no idle factors which can be drawn into employment. But it can still expand in so far as improved methods of production are introduced, the working population grows, and additions are made to the capital stock.

Monetary expansion can of course go on, just as before; but the consequences will not be the same.

From rise in output to rise in prices. As more and more unemployed factors of production are drawn into employment, the supply of factors of production and of goods in general becomes more and more inelastic, and a constant expansion in terms of money will lead to a smaller and smaller increase in output and to a larger and larger rise in factor and commodity prices. In other words, at the beginning of the expansion, a large part of the increase in monetary circulation will have been absorbed by a rise in the output and turnover of goods, and a smaller part by increasing prices. When full employment is being gradually approached, this necessarily changes.

So long as the supply of factors of production is plentiful and elastic, output can be increased all along the line at the same time. For reasons which will be discussed in § 5, the output of producers' goods and durable goods rises much faster than the output of consumers' goods. When one category of factors after the other is becoming scarce—the transition to full employment is of course gradual and not sudden—it becomes more and more difficult to expand at various points at the same time. If one industry increases its demand for means of production and succeeds in attracting labourers by offering higher wages, it lures them away from other industries. The same holds true of raw materials and semi-finished products. The expansion of the industry is possible only at the expense of a contraction somewhere else.

If the monetary expansion through the creation of new money by the banks for productive purposes goes on, there will be a tendency for producers' goods industries to expand at the expense of consumers' goods industries, the former drawing away factors of production from the latter. We shall see that this process is not very likely to continue for long—if it has a chance to start at all ! But for some time it may continue; and thus the expansion may go beyond, or start from, the level of full employment.

Having sketched the process of expansion in general, we may go on to consider various points in detail. This will be done in §§ 4-6.

§ 4. THE MONETARY ANALYSIS OF THE PROCESS OF EXPANSION

Importance of total demand. An expansion of the monetary circulation, in the sense that the money value of the volume of production and total demand for goods in terms of money per unit of time increases, is (as we have seen) a regular feature and, we may add, an indispensable condition for a rapid expansion of production after a slump. If the monetary circulation could not somehow be expanded, prices of goods and productive services, especially money wages, would have to fall *pari passu* with the rise of employment and production. We need not pause to explain why in that case re-employment and recovery would come very slowly, if they came at all. Certainly such a fall in prices is the contrary to what actually happens during a recovery after a slump.

The market for investible funds. We have seen (Chapters 2 and 3 above) that the expansion may be described in technical language as being due to a discrepancy between the money or market rate of interest, on the one hand, and the natural or equilibrium rate of interest, on the other. If the former is below the latter, a cumulative process of expansion (a " Wicksellian process " as it is called) sets in. Since it is difficult to define the natural or equilibrium rate,[1] it seems advisable

---

[1] Different interpretations have been given of the term "natural" rate. By some it has been defined as that rate (in terms of goods) which

to adopt a slightly different approach to the problem, more in accordance with the modern method of marginal analysis.

We may conceive a market for investible funds which is divided into a demand side and a supply side. This is not quite the same thing as those sections of the demand and supply which actually appear in the market for loans or credit, because abstraction is made of the contractual element in the debtor-creditor relationship. Entrepreneurs or corporations, for example, who invest their own money appear both on the demand and on the supply side of the market : they advance investible funds to themselves.[1]

---

would obtain in a barter economy where capital is lent out *in natura*. This definition raises a host of difficulties which need not be discussed here. By others the "natural" rate is defined as the equilibrium rate. But what are we to understand by "equilibrium" ? Four or five different possible interpretations at once suggest themselves. Which one is best calculated to preserve stability of output and employment ? The rate which, in given circumstances, tends to keep the price level—in one or the other sense of this ambiguous term—stable ? The rate which tends to stabilise aggregate income, income per head, the price level of the factors of production, MV, etc. ? Every one of these alternatives has been, at one time or another, proposed as the right criterion. Our discussion has, however, already made—and will make it abundantly clear that it is very doubtful whether—is possible at all, by mere manipulation of the interest rate, to iron out short-term fluctuations in any one of these magnitudes. In any case, it would require drastic and rapid changes of the rate which in themselves would probably become a de-stabilising factor.

These difficulties need not—fortunately—be discussed here. It will be sufficient to say that it is premature and inadvisable at the beginning of the analysis to come to a decision as to what interest rate is best calculated to preserve the economic equilibrium. It is not proposed, therefore, in the present study to make any use of the terms "natural" or "equilibrium" rate ; and it is hoped that the theoretical terminology which is developed in the text will make it possible to express clearly and correctly all that is indicated by these terms in trade-cycle literature.

[1] Since we assume as a first approximation a perfectly smoothly working market for investible funds with only a single rate of interest, the problem of self-financing does not present special difficulties. It is assumed that it makes no difference whether the money invested is borrowed or not. The opportunity cost is in all cases the market rate of interest. In other words, the entrepreneur who invests his own money must put on the debit side of his account the interest which he could earn if he lent out the money in the market for investible funds.

This assumption is of course regarded by many writers as incorrect. It is alleged that self-financing leads easily to "over-investment", because people are not so careful when investing their own money in

Investible funds are supplied, and demanded, at a price which we shall call the interest rate. For the moment, we may ignore differences in the type and quality of investible funds, and speak as if there was only one, instead of a whole range, of interest rates. We may suppose both the supply and the demand for investible funds to be expressed in the form of curves or schedules in the familiar Marshallian manner. Along the horizontal axis of a system of rectangular co-ordinates we measure amounts of investible funds, and along the vertical axis the price of investible funds—*i.e.*, the rate of interest. For each amount we suppose the demand price—that is, the rate of interest at which this amount would be taken up by entrepreneurs for investment purposes—to be determined. If we join these points together, we get the demand curve for investible funds. We shall have occasion to make various hypotheses about the elasticity of this curve. In general, we may assume that it slopes downward from the left to the right, to represent the fact that at lower interest rates larger quantities are demanded and invested for productive purposes. Similarly, for each amount the supply price is determined; and by joining these points together the supply curve of investible funds is obtained. It may be horizontal for a certain range—in which case the supply is said to be perfectly elastic over that range; that is frequently Mr. KEYNES' assumption. It may be vertical—in which case the supply is said to be perfectly inelastic. We may assume that, generally, it slopes upward from the left to the right—that is to say, that investors exact higher rates of interest when they are called upon to provide larger amounts of investible funds.

It should be remembered that a system of these curves refers always to a point of time or a short period of time. We shall

---

their own enterprise. In other cases there may be a separation of ownership and disposition. It is frequently the director of the corporation who decides how much of the corporate income is to be " ploughed back " into the business, and not the owner—viz., the shareholder. These complications have been discussed to some extent in Chapters 3 and 5 above in connection with the theories of F. Vito (page 44) and E. Preiser (page 141). It may be added that the rationale of such measures as an " undistributed-profit tax " is closely connected with the problem on hand.

soon have to speak of shifts of these curves in time—that is, between successive points or short periods of time.

Let us now enquire about the factors which determine the shape of these curves.

The demand *curve for* *investible* *funds.* The demand curve for investible funds bears a close relationship to the curve of the marginal profit rate. By profit rate we understand the rate of profit in terms of money which an entrepreneur expects to derive from a concrete piece of investment. We may conceive the various investment opportunities existing at a given moment of time as being arranged in order of decreasing profitability, and construct a schedule or curve sloping down from left to right. If, now, we suppose that all the risks of investment are borne by the suppliers of investible funds—and it is convenient to allocate all risks to one or the other side of the market—this schedule is identical with the demand schedule for investible funds and the lowest or marginal profit rate for a given amount of investment is identical with the demand-interest rate for that amount of investible funds.[1]

The reader will have noticed that this description of the capital market is substantially the same as Professor OHLIN's and Professor ROBERTSON's market for credit or loans which was discussed in Chapter 8, § 2, above (pages 177 *et seq.*). The only difference between Professor OHLIN's scheme (as represented by the graph on page 185) and ours is that we choose to take on the demand side only demand for purposes of real investment. Demand for credit (loans) for other purposes—*e.g.*, for the purpose of strengthening cash resources

---

[1] It will be seen that we do not speak of *the* profit rate obtaining in a country. Naturally, for different investment plans different profit rates are expected. We speak of the *marginal* profit rate and we do not say that there is a difference (or equality) between the interest rate and *the* profit rate, but we say that the interest rate is equal to the *marginal* profit rate.

An alternative way of dealing with the risk factor would be to define the profit rate so as to include the risk. There are further complications about the risk. The same risk may be counted twice over, by the borrower *and* lender, or it may not be counted at all. These complications we ignore for the time being. Compare, however, footnote [1] on page 328 below.

(for hoarding purposes)—we prefer to deduct from the supply curve instead of adding it to the demand curve.[1] But the reader can easily make the slight adjustment, if he prefers Professor OHLIN's scheme.

It may furthermore be observed that we need not exclude short time-lags between the floating of a loan in the market for investible funds and the actual expenditure for the purchase of material, equipment, labour, etc., of the money raised.[2]

"*Net*" *investment and* "*gross*" *investment.* There is another point to be cleared up. Do we count as investment only "net" (or "new") investment or "total" (or "gross") investment? The difference between the two is reinvestment or replacement requirement. Gross investment = net investment + reinvestment. Gross investment is roughly the same as production of producers' goods, the only difference being production of consumers' goods which are not consumed, but stored up in the shape of stocks, or of durable consumers' goods (motor-cars, houses) : but the latter are better regarded as producers' goods producing consumable services. If we define investment as net investment, we must consider the possibility of its becoming negative (although this contingency will not arise so long as we deal with the expansion process). If, namely, gross investment does not cover replacement requirements, the difference between the two is negative investment : disinvestment, capital consumption. Since we are concerned with what actually happens in the market and "negative demand" for investible funds is a difficult concept, we had better refrain at this point from using the concept "negative investment".

---

[1] Hence our demand for investible funds is more nearly equivalent to Mr. Keynes' schedule of marginal efficiency of capital than Professor Ohlin's demand for credit.

[2] That would seem to be the most "natural" use of the terms, that is, the one which follows most closely their everyday meaning. But there are alternative constructions (terminologies) available and it should be noted that the one proposed in the text implies that a current excess of satisfied demand for investible funds—in short, of investment—over saving (see below) will lead to an increasing income only with a short time-lag. Hence there is a slight deviation from Professor Robertson's definitions.

Hence, in some contexts, we may elect to interpret investment as gross investment.[1] There are other reasons which would justify this decision. First, the definition of the concept " net investment " presents great difficulties, because it implies definition of what is meant by " keeping the capital stock intact ".[2] Secondly, since we assume that people act rationally, it should really make no difference whether a certain sum which is spent by an entrepreneur for productive purposes represents new investment or reinvestment. In the latter case, too, the prospective yield of this investment should be compared with what can be obtained from the same sum if lent out in the market for investible funds or if kept in liquid form (hoarded).[3]

In thus defining investment on the demand side as including reinvestment, we must be careful to apply a correspondingly broad definition on the supply side, to the discussion of which we now turn.

Supply of investible funds. The supply of investible funds may be said to flow from three sources—from amortisation quotas, from new savings and from " inflation " in the broad sense (including, not only newly printed notes and newly created bank money, but also withdrawals from existing hoards of money). The first two items, which we may lump together as " gross saving ", leave the total demand for goods (MV) constant. Inflation implies an increase in total demand for goods, a rise in M and /or in V.

---

[1] We may put the matter also this way : Gross investment is what actually is invested. It is always a positive figure. Replacement requirement is a calculated magnitude—viz., that amount which will have to be invested if the existing capital stock is to be maintained.

[2] Compare on the subject of these difficult points : Hayek, " Maintenance of Capital ", in *Economica*, August 1935, pages 247 *et seq.* ; Pigou, *Economics of Welfare*, Part I, Chapter V ("What is meant by maintaining Capital intact "), and *Economic Journal*, June 1935, page 225 ; Keynes, *The General Theory of Employment, Interest and Money*, pages 38 *et seq.*

[3] There may be psychological, and (in the case of corporations) institutional, differences between new investment and reinvestment, similar to those mentioned above in connection with self-financing. But we shall ignore them for the moment.

This statement requires elucidation in various respects.[1]   First, a word of justification must be said about the inclusion of amortisation quotas.   This corresponds to the inclusion of replacement under investment on the demand side.   For the individual firm, the setting-aside of amortisation quotas out of total receipts and their expenditure for replacement of outworn equipment do not always coincide in time.   Amortisation will usually—though not necessarily—be a continuous process, whereas the replacement of durable means of production is usually discontinuous.   For the economy as a whole, both processes are more continuous and run parallel.   During any period of time, a number of firms use their amortisation quotas to accumulate balances or to repay loans, thus adding to the supply of investible funds in the market, while others draw on their balances or borrow from the market in order to replace their equipment.   The reason why it seems advisable to include replacement on the demand side and amortisation quotas on the supply side has been given above.   Since, however, during the process of expansion with which we are now concerned net additions to the capital stock are supposed to be made (whatever the exact definition of this magnitude may be), we may deduct

---

[1] Compare also Chapter 8, § 2. V must not be interpreted for our purposes as " transaction velocity ".   I have not outrightly defined it as income velocity, because of the difficulties connected with the definition (not to speak of those connected with the measurement) of *net* income.   As Mr. Hawtrey points out (see his review of the first edition of this book, *Economica*, Vol. V (New Series), February 1938, page 94), the use of the concept of " trade velocity " also presents certain difficulties for our purposes, because " MV so defined includes all purchases of goods by one trader from another.   But such purchases, whether for the purpose of use as materials in manufacture or for simple resale, do not take the goods off the market.   The goods continue to be offered for sale ".   Mr. Hawtrey would prefer a " final-purchases velocity ", and would include the purchase of new investment goods (*e.g.*, of a machine) in the volume of final purchases.   But what is the relevant difference between the purchase of raw material (say coal) for manufacture which will eventually be sold in the shape of output as, say, pig-iron and the purchase of a not very durable machine which will also be sold in the shape of its services which enter the output ?   Mr. Hawtrey seems to have overlooked that a qualification has been made about the degree of " integration " of industry (Chapter 3, § 6), which seems to exclude from MV precisely those changes in the volume of purchases which Mr. Hawtrey wishes to exclude.

amortisation from the one side and replacement from the other without running the risk of obtaining a negative figure for investment and consequently for demand for investible funds. Therefore, so long as we are dealing with the expansion, investment may be interpreted as net investment.[1] If we adopt this procedure in order to simplify the further discussion, we have to distinguish only two sources of supply—viz., saving and inflation.

Savings and inflation. The statement that the supply of investible funds which would be forthcoming at a given point of time or during a short period of time at various hypothetical rates of interest may be made up partly by current saving and partly by inflation implies that actual investment need not be equal to saving. During an expansion process, the volume of investment is normally larger than the volume of savings, the excess being financed by inflation. In other words, demand for investible funds is so large that it cannot be satisfied by current saving, so that inflationary sources of supply are tapped.

As we have seen in Chapter 8, § 2, this convenient language, which has been used by many writers, has given rise to intricate terminological difficulties. We need not again go over the controversies discussed there. Suffice it to say that the definition of saving to be given presently is identical with that of Professor ROBERTSON.[2] The reader who has read Chapter 8 will have no difficulties in translating, if he so desires, what will be said in the following pages into other terminologies—*e.g.*, the Keynesian, which avoids speaking of differences between saving and investment.

Supply of saving. By saving we understand—as everybody does—income minus expenditure for consumption. But it is necessary to introduce the time factor. We must distinguish between currently earned income, which is simply the money value of the net output of the economic

---

[1] This we may do, even if we refrain from giving a perfectly exact definition of net investment.

[2] See, however, the slight qualification alluded to in footnote 1 on page 293 above.

community, and income currently available for consumption. This distinction rests upon the fact that, in the real world, income earned is distributed, not continuously, but periodically. Wages are paid weekly, salaries monthly, dividends quarterly, half-yearly or yearly : rents are paid at similar intervals; while farmers' incomes also come in to a considerable extent annually. There are, of course, exceptions to this rule, particularly in small-scale trade and handicraft where entrepreneurial withdrawals may take place practically continuously ; but the exceptions are of so little practical significance that they may be neglected in consideration of the immense analytical advantage of such a simplification.

The fact that incomes are earned continuously, expended continuously, and distributed periodically has the consequence of creating a time-lag between the moment when a given sum is earned and the moment when it becomes available for expenditure on consumption. On the average, wages are available for expenditure half a week after the moment of earning, salaries half a month later, dividends (assuming six-monthly payments) a few weeks to almost a year later, and so on. Of all the income earned at a given moment, part will become available for expenditure almost immediately, and other parts at various intervals up to (say) a year.

This distinction between earned income and available income is of considerable importance in the description of the process of change in investment and in total demand, through time.

Supply from inflationary sources. If in any short period chosen as a unit of time the income currently earned (that is, the sum of consumption expenditure and investment) exceeds the income available for expenditure, the excess must be financed out of inflationary sources. That is to say, the hoards of individuals and the reserve proportions of banks must—in the absence of State inflation—be diminished in comparison with the previous period.

Thus the money invested to-day is financed partly by savings out of income earned yesterday and becoming available to-day, and partly by inflation. But all that is invested to-day, inclusive of the part financed by inflation, becomes to-day's earned income [1] and to-morrow's available income. If, then, a part of the latter is saved to-morrow, it constitutes again current saving, although it is historically of inflationary origin. (The influence which changes in the rate of saving are likely to have on the development of the expansion process will be discussed below in § 6.)

Having discussed savings and inflation as two separate sources of the supply of investible funds and the implied inequality of saving and investment, we have now a few observations to make in regard to the shape of the supply curve at a given point or during a short period of time.

The shape of the supply curve. We shall have to make further assumptions as follows. The supply of investible funds is sometimes very elastic, so that a higher demand can be satisfied at slightly higher interest rates. At other times it is inelastic, so that a rise in demand is calculated to lead to a rise in interest rates rather than to evoke a greater supply. Any hypothesis of this sort about the behaviour of supply as a whole must be supported by an analysis of the behaviour of the constituent parts of the total supply.

Let us first take that part which is furnished by saving from current income. It is very probable that, *ceteris paribus*, the amount of saving becoming available for investment does not react strongly to changes in the interest rate. If there is a reaction at all, its direction is not clear. When the rate of interest rises, people may just as well save more and spend less on consumption or save less and spend more of their income.

On the other hand, the elasticity of saving in respect to magnitudes and factors other than the rate of interest is probably great. It is, *e.g.*, generally assumed that the rate of saving rises with rising

---

[1] A reservation must be made as to that part of the invested money which does not at once become income, but becomes amortisation quota. If we work with gross investment on the one hand and gross saving on the other (as, strictly speaking, we should), this qualification becomes superfluous. In this case, income which is a "net quantity" is replaced by the corresponding " gross quantity "—viz., net income plus amortisation for fixed and working capital.

income. It is not unlikely that it varies, not only with the level of income, but also with the rate of change of income. There are yet other factors which make it probable that the rate of saving exhibits a systematic movement during the course of the cycle. We shall come back to this point later.[1] Here, where we are concerned with the shape of the supply curve at a given point or during a short period of time, we may in all probability regard the supply of savings as a constant magnitude, insensitive to changes in the interest rate. In technical parlance, the supply of saving is, at least in the short run, inelastic in respect to changes in the interest rate. Hence the asserted elasticity in the total supply must depend on the elasticity of that part of the total which is furnished by " inflation ".

We shall have to discuss the factors which determine the degree of elasticity of supply of investible funds from inflationary sources at various points in our analysis. Here a few introductory remarks will suffice. There are various inflationary sources of supply— the central bank, the commercial banks and, last but not least, liquid reserves of purchasing power (hoards) in the hands of business firms and individuals.

The concept of elasticity of supply from the first two sources does not present analytical difficulties, and we know approximately what the factors are on which it depends, how far the banks are willing at any given moment to vary the supply of investible funds in the face of variations in demand and in the rate of interest which they can obtain.

In the case of the third source—hoards of firms and individuals —the situation is more involved. All the considerations which have been put forward in recent times under the head of " liquidity preferences ", " liquidity motives " and " propensity to hoard or dishoard " and the like are relevant here. In a general way, we may assume that, *ceteris paribus*, the higher the rate of interest the greater the temptation to dishoard—that is, the larger the supply of investible funds coming on the market from this source.

---

[1] Compare Chapter 8, § 3, and this chapter, § 6, below.

The clause *ceteris paribus* calls to mind the limi-
Movements tations of our elasticity concept. If we say that
along, and the supply has a certain elasticity, this refers to a
movements of, point or short period of time. But what we want
the curves. is an analysis in time; we have to compare what
happens in successive periods of time. This we
can accomplish with our apparatus of demand and supply curves
by introducing movements of these curves in time. We substitute, so to say, a ciné-camera for a simple snapshot camera : that
is, we take pictures of our demand and supply schedule at successive points of time and watch the movements of the curves. This
will become clearer when we proceed to put our simple analytical
instrument to work. It is hoped that it will enable us to describe
more precisely and simply the processes and relationships which
have been analysed in the literature in terms of differences between
the money or market rate of interest on the one hand and the natural
or equilibrium rate on the other. It is hoped, furthermore, that
it will be possible with the help of our method to clear up a number
of difficulties and paradoxes which have not been adequately
explained so far.

It should, however, be kept in mind that there
Subdivisions are other difficulties which are not removed by our
of the capital treatment of the matter. We speak of *the* rate of
market. interest for investible funds, whereas there are in
reality a multitude of rates with complicated interrelations—short-term and long-term rates with intermediate rates
and a great variety of gradation according to the standing of the
borrower, the nature of his business, the possibilities of furnishing
security, the risk involved, etc. The assumption of a homogeneous capital market is a drastic simplification. For the time
being, we try to overcome this difficulty by interpreting the market
rate of which we speak as somehow a properly weighted average
or composite of the existing rates. If we say the rate has risen
or fallen, we mean the complex of the rates which we find in the
market.[1]

---

[1] Compare especially R. M. Bissel : "The Interest Rate " in *American
Economic Review*, Supplement to Vol. XXVIII, 1938, pages 23 *et seq.*

Let us now put our apparatus to work and try to analyse the monetary side of the expansion process which was indicated in outline in §§ 2 and 3.

Cumulative expansion process.   It has been assumed that, in one way or another, the expansion has been started. The various initiating forces or " starters " will be discussed in detail in the section on the revival. Here we assume by way of illustration that new investment opportunities have appeared and that a certain number of people are prepared accordingly to borrow new money, or to utilise their own reserves hitherto lying idle, on a larger scale. This can be expressed by saying that the demand curve for money has shifted to the right to such a degree that more than the current flow of savings is taken up and inflationary sources are being tapped. The total demand for goods in terms of money increases, and the cumulative continuation of the process may be described, in terms of our analytical scheme, by the statement that this increase of the demand for goods causes the demand curve for investible funds to shift further to the right. If the flow of current savings does not suddenly rise to an extent sufficient to satisfy the growing demand—which would seem very unlikely—and if the supply of investible funds from inflationary sources is not inelastic, the result will be a further inflow of new money, which in turn will tend to force the demand curve further to the right, and so on.

Repercussions on supply of funds.   The force of the expansion is usually further intensified by a change on the supply side which is, in itself, a consequence of the expansion. The supply is likely to become more plentiful—that is to say, the supply curve is likely to shift to the right —because of a tendency to dishoard on the part of the public and the banks. When production increases and prices rise, not only the entrepreneurs—*i.e.*, the borrowers—but also the lenders, banks and investing public are likely to take a more optimistic view. During the contraction, a series of bankruptcies and failures will have made them more and more reluctant to lend. Now, with the progress of expansion, many bad debtors unexpectedly begin to pay interest on their debts or even to repay them. Frozen credits begin to thaw, and fear of compulsory conversions and currency instability recedes. All this tends to make lenders willing to lend at lower interest rates funds which they had kept in cash or other liquid forms.

Time sequence. It is impossible to generalise as to the time sequence of these various changes. The change on the supply side may precede the revival in demand and, once the process has started, one factor tends to stimulate the others. If, with a rising demand, people are induced to disgorge the content of their hoards on the capital markets, it may very well happen that for a considerable time the rising demand for credit and rising prices and production go parallel with falling interest rates—a development which, superficially regarded, might seem to contradict all accepted principles of economic theory.[1] The situation in the gold- and sterling-*bloc* countries in 1933 to 1936 seems to offer a good illustration. In the sterling *bloc*, continued recovery, rising transactions and demand have been coupled with comparatively low or even falling interest rates. In the gold countries, contraction and liquidation have been accompanied by comparatively high interest rates and a tight capital market.[2]

Volatility of demand for funds. It is extremely important to realise from the beginning that both the demand curve and the supply curve for investible funds are subject to frequent and rapid shifts. They are influenced, not only by technological factors—*e.g.*, by a new invention or the destruction of instruments by wear and tear or fire tending to move the demand curve to the right, which is tantamount (loosely speaking) to increasing the demand for funds—but also by " psychological " factors (optimism and pessimism), changes in demand for particular goods, etc. Much

---

[1] This can be expressed in Keynesian terms by saying that the liquidity-preference schedule shifts, or that the liquidity preference of the community as a whole becomes weaker. The transaction motive to hold money has become stronger ; but this is over-compensated by an opposite change in the speculative motive ; M_1 increases ; M_2 decreases. For details see Chapter 4, § 3.

[2] This explains also the fact that sometimes increased borrowing by the State for unproductive purposes (*e.g.*, armaments) makes the money and capital market more rather than less liquid.

theorising in this field has been vitiated by the tacit assumption that the demand curve for funds is more or less fixed by technological circumstances (viz., the superior productivity of longer roundabout ways of production). If the demand curve is considered as relatively fixed, changes in the flow of investible funds must be explained by shifts in the supply (in the other terminology, by changes in the money rate of interest rather than the equilibrium rate). This assumption cannot be reconciled with the facts, and hence the conclusion is unavoidable that the demand for funds is highly variable and sensitive to all kinds of influence.

An important corollary of this proposition is that MV, the flow of money or total demand for goods in terms of money, is also highly changeable. Static economic theory for the most part assumes a constant MV. It is very important to recognise in principle that this need not be, and rarely is, the case. In the investigation of concrete cases such as the probable influence of some measure of economic policy (*e.g.*, imposition of a tariff, devaluation of a currency, public works, etc.), or of spontaneous changes such as changes in the demand for particular commodities, many perplexing consequences which are quite inexplicable on a rigid static analysis, which assumes MV constant, can be cleared up by taking into consideration changes in MV produced or induced by the measure or event studied. We shall have many occasions to recognise the fruitfulness of this principle.[1]

Forms of monetary expansion. An expansion in the monetary circulation, in the broad sense in which the term is here employed, may originate in different ways. It remains to investigate the ways in which it can, and the ways in which it will usually or normally, be brought about.[2]

As a first step, we may say that a change in the money stream may be due either to a change in M or in V, in the quantity of money outstanding or in its velocity of circulation. This does

---

[1] There is, of course, no intention to assert that this has been completely overlooked. It is only suggested that the variability of MV has not been sufficiently stressed and that one of the disparities between business-cycle theory and general equilibrium theory seems to have its root here.

[2] Statistical explorations in this field have recently been made by Professor J. W. Angell. See his book, *The Behavior of Money*, New York, 1936.

not, however, help very much, since neither M nor V is statistically ascertainable (except by way of complicated indirect estimates which are not very reliable). We shall do better to start with those magnitudes which are statistically measurable, viz. :

(*a*) Legal tender money, notes, coins;
(*b*) Bank deposits subject to cheque;
(*c*) Velocity of circulation of (*b*).

These three items constitute, of course, only a fraction of the total in which we are interested. We cannot readily measure the velocity of (*a*). Furthermore, credit instruments (bills) frequently function like money, and a number of transactions are settled by direct offsetting without the use of money. (It is immaterial whether one construes such cases as implying changes in the velocity of circulation of money proper or in the quantity of money. In any case—and this is the important thing—an increase or decrease in the total demand for goods in terms of money can be effected by such practices.)

§ 5. WHY DOES THE PRODUCTION OF PRODUCERS' GOODS AND DURABLE GOODS RISE FASTER THAN THE PRODUCTION OF PERISHABLE CONSUMERS' GOODS ?

The essence of the " acceleration principle ". Many writers have pointed out that, for technical reasons, changes in the demand for, and production of, finished goods give rise to much more violent changes in the demand for, and production of, producers' goods. This is one of the most important applications of the so-called principle of the acceleration and magnification of derived demand which we have stated and discussed, with all necessary qualifications, in an earlier part of this study (see Part I, pages 85 *et seq.*). It remains to determine its place and function within the mechanism of expansion.

The essence of the acceleration principle can, as we have seen, be summed up in the statement that, to enable the output to be expanded, it may be necessary to make heavy immediate investments which will continue to bear fruit for some time into the future. The fact that capitalistic production utilises durable instruments means that services or goods of a given sort currently produced are in joint supply with services or goods of the same sort at various future dates. Thus, if demand is expected to rise over a certain future period, the supply will be provided in a lump at the beginning and (as it were) stored up in the shape of stocks and durable instruments.

Repercussions on demand for finished goods. Since consumers' demand can be profoundly affected by changes in capital construction, it is illegitimate to presuppose a cyclical fluctuation of consumers' demand, and then to use the acceleration principle to explain the larger fluctuations in the production of capital goods.

The principle therefore—quite apart from the necessary qualifications previously discussed—must be given its proper place within the framework of a more elaborate theory of investment, in connection with which it expresses the one-way causal relationship from the demand for consumers' goods to the production of producers' goods. The volume of production of producers' goods (which, in order to avoid double reckoning, should be measured as the sum of the value added to the product in successive stages) is equal to the sum of new investment and replacement or reinvestment. As has already been pointed out, it may be convenient to speak of "total" or "gross" investment in distinction to "new" or "net" investment (which may also be negative). Gross investment is then another way of saying production of producers' goods plus changes in the stock of consumables.

As we have seen, it is very difficult to give an exact definition of new investment for the economy as a whole, since it involves defining what is meant by maintaining the capital stock of society intact. It is still more difficult to measure it statistically—that is, to distinguish during a given period between replacement of worn-out capital and additions to the capital stock. Fortunately we do not need for many purposes to make the distinction. It suffices to speak of production of producers' goods. But, roughly speaking, the fact that production of producers' goods fluctuates more violently than the production of consumers' goods—which is taken as an index for consumption[1]—indicates that there is net investment during the upswing and a drastic reduction of net investment, or probably even net disinvestment, during the downswing of the cycle.

Rôle of expectations. The acceleration principle deals with one of the factors which determine the volume of investment—namely, changes in demand for the finished product. Obviously, demand must not be defined in too narrow a fashion as actual demand. What matters is, strictly speaking, anticipated demand. The investor expects that demand for his product will be forthcoming. But actual demand is certainly one of the most powerful factors in shaping the expectations of business-men as to future demand. If actual demand rises, and if the new level has been sustained for some time, or if the rise has continued for a certain period of time, there is a good chance that a continuation of the higher level or a further rise will be anticipated. There is, however, no absolute certainty that this will in every case be so ; many special reasons are conceivable which might prevent these optimistic expectations from being induced in the mind of the producers.[2]

Ratio of capital to labour. Supposing, however, that a producer of a certain commodity has formed his conclusions as to the probable volume of the future demand and is resolved to act on his anticipation, and increase production accordingly, then the acceleration principle postulates a rigid relationship between the volume of production of the finished product per unit of time and the volume of investment. The relationship is determined by the durability of the equipment and machines which are required for the production of the commodity in question and by the

---

[1] A reservation must be made regarding the fluctuations in stocks of consumers' goods. There is no consumption corresponding to that part of the production of consumers' goods which goes to stocks.

[2] Strictly speaking, a whole scale of more or less optimistic anticipations should be distinguished, ranging from the expectation that the increase in demand is only temporary, via the expectation that it will be maintained to the expectation that it will go on rising at a constant or increasing rate. In other words, there are various ways in which an actual increase can be extrapolated into the future.

importance of the machine services relative to other input items (working capital and labour) in the production process—which is as much as to say, roughly speaking, by the degree of mechanisation.

Here an important qualification is called for. This relationship is not rigid for various reasons. In the first place, surplus capacity may—and at the beginning of the expansion after a more or less severe depression usually does—exist. If there is unused or under-employed machinery or equipment, production can be increased by simply applying more labour and raw material to the existing equipment. The acceleration principle will then come into play only after production has been increased by so much that new machinery is thought to be desirable. But the point where it becomes desirable is not determined exactly by purely technological considerations. Usually the existing plant can be worked more or less intensively, although at rising cost. The decision to increase the plant is influenced—apart from the anticipations about future demand—by the rate of interest and certain other factors which will be discussed presently.

Importance of rate of interest. Supposing, now, it has been decided in principle to extend the fixed equipment, it is then necessary to determine how it should be done. As a rule there is a choice between different methods of production. More or less durable equipment can be installed, the more durable varieties involving as a rule higher cost. In other words, methods of varying degrees of " roundaboutness ", involving investments of different magnitude, are usually available. The magnification of derived demand—that is, the increase in investment induced by a given increase in the demand for, and production of, a finished product—depends accordingly on the choice between these available methods, on the durability of the instruments (or, in other words, the " roundaboutness " of the process chosen). And this choice, in turn, depends : (*a*) on the rate of interest, that is the terms on which the necessary funds can be raised, (*b*) on the estimation of the risk[1] involved and on the general outlook. The

---

[1] *Cf.* M. Kalecki : " The Principle of Increasing Risk ", in *Economica*, 1937, page 440, reprinted in *Essays in the Theory of Economic Fluctuations*, London, 1939.

lower the rate of interest, the more durable the instrument, the longer the roundabout way of production, the heavier the investment and the larger the magnification of derived demand. Furthermore, in an atmosphere of optimism and confidence in an undisturbed development of economic life, people will be more inclined to undertake heavy investment by which they are committed for a long period than in a state of uncertainty and apprehension.

Contribution of the acceleration principle. We are now in a position to formulate the contribution of the acceleration principle to the explanation of the mechanism of expansion, and especially of its cumulative nature. The technical fact that, in order to produce certain finished goods or services, one must construct durable instruments, because the finished goods cannot be produced otherwise or only at much higher cost or in inferior quality, operates as a powerful intensifier of the cumulative force of the expansion. If demand for such goods and services rises, investment becomes profitable. The profit rate rises or, to formulate it correctly in terms of our demand and supply schema, the demand curve for investible funds is pushed to the right. If the supply of funds is elastic, more money is drawn into circulation, with the result that demand for the finished product is further augmented and the expansion proceeds with accumulated force.

Application to durable consumers' goods. It should be noted that our argument applies also to durable consumers' goods. In their case, the finished product consists of the services which flow from the durable goods. If the demand for apartments rises (or is expected to rise), the demand for investible funds for the purpose of constructing houses will rise. The construction of the houses is usually undertaken by entrepreneurs, not by the prospective dwellers. Thus an increase in the annual demand for apartments may give rise to investment many times the amount of the annual rent. The service is being provided, so to speak, *en bloc* for many years to come.

In the case of semi-durable consumers' goods such as motor-cars, furniture, radio sets and the like, there is the institutional difference that these goods are usually bought by the consumer out of his own resources. But an instalment selling scheme may enable consumers to extend their current purchases beyond their current income. Thus slight increases in current income may bring about a much larger increase in demand in general.

Inelastic supply. We have here a factor which accelerates the expansion of the total demand for goods in terms of money, and (if supply is still elastic in all branches and stages of industry) of production and employment as well. The restraining forces which gradually make their appearance when full employment is being approached will be discussed in the section on the upper turning-point. It suffices here to point out that the acceleration principle cannot work unobstructed when supply becomes less elastic. Production cannot then be expanded all along the line. It remains true, however, that an increase in the demand for a commodity, the production of which necessitates the installation of durable instruments, may still, by increasing the price of these instruments, increase the amount of money required to purchase them. The physical quantity of investment may remain unchanged, but its money value increases, and the demand for funds rises likewise.[1]

Methods of financing. The question now arises how the increased production of producers' goods is financed. The workers who are engaged in producing these durable and non-durable means of production, and the owners of other factors of production which contribute thereto, must be paid. The answer has in fact already been given. The necessary funds come partly from inflationary sources, partly out of current savings.

---

[1] Consequently, if the supply of investible funds is perfectly elastic— *i.e.*, if the rate of interest does not change—the increase in demand for consumers' goods, and the resulting price rise, will spread throughout the whole structure of production, replacement demand in terms of money rising parallel with or even faster than the demand for the product. If consumers' demand starts to rise from a given level, this will speedily induce a proportionate or more than proportionate rise in the total demand for goods in terms of money (including demand for intermediate goods and replacement demand). Since consumers' demand is only a fraction of total demand, a given increase in consumers' demand gives rise to a greater increase in total demand. In this sense, the acceleration principle can still be said to be in operation.

We have seen that the cumulative nature of expansion hinges on the growth in the total monetary demand—*i.e.*, on the increase in the flow of money. Therefore, the larger the proportion of new investment financed by way of inflation (newly created bank money or more intensive utilisation of existing funds) in preference to voluntary saving, the more rapid the expansion—viz., the expansion primarily of the circulating medium and in addition (so long as the supply of factors of production of various kinds is elastic) of employment and production.[1]

---

[1] A word must be said on the concept of "forced saving", which has been much misunderstood. If investments are financed by inflationary means—if, that is to say, the flow of money against goods increases— those who spend the new money attract for their purposes goods which would otherwise have accrued to somebody else. These other people, whose purchasing power in real terms (real income) is now reduced, because of the new entrants to the reservoir of goods, are said to be forced to save. Forced saving is inflicted upon them. If total demand for goods in terms of money had not gone up, prices would not have risen, or they would have fallen ; and those members of society whose money income has not been changed by the inflation could have consumed more—*i.e.*, their real income would have been greater.

This sounds quite unambiguous if we assume that (*a*) the magnitude of the total flow of goods (output) is not changed by the inflation and that (*b*) there are no secondary influences (apart from the addition in question) on the flow of money. If the latter condition does not hold, and there are secondary increases or decreases in the flow of money induced by the primary injection, the problem becomes more complicated ; but it is still possible to apply to these secondary additions or reductions the same reasoning as to the first.

If, however, the magnitude of the total flow of goods is changed, the situation becomes more involved. Suppose, *e.g.*, that the increase in the flow of money calls for an equal increase in the flow of goods—in other words, that supply is perfectly elastic and, when the demand for goods rises, production and supply rise equally, so that prices remain on the average unchanged. In this case, it is difficult to speak of forced saving or a forced levy on particular persons. In practice, however, perfect elasticity of supply is almost unthinkable, even at the bottom of the depression. In other words, the flow of goods will increase in a smaller proportion than the flow of money : some prices will be higher than they would have been without the inflationary increase in demand— that is to say, some prices will rise or be prevented from falling ; and therefore forced saving will be inflicted upon some persons to some extent, although not necessarily to the extent indicated by the increase in the money stream.

But this raises the very important question of the rôle of saving in, and the influence of changes in the rate of saving on, the mechanism of expansion. This question, which has received much attention in the recent literature on the trade cycle, we must now discuss systematically.

§ 6. SAVING AND THE EXPANSION PROCESS

Importance of savings. Allusion has been made more than once in the course of the preceding argument to the actions of income-receivers with respect to spending and saving. On page 285, it was noted as an essential link in the expansion process that the increased earnings of the workers due to increased investment would in part be spent immediately. Later (page 296) saving was mentioned as one of the two sources of the supply of investible funds, the other being inflation in the wider sense of the term. It is therefore of importance to enquire, in the first place, what are the probable consequences on the expansion of a change in the proportion of income saved by the public as a whole and, secondly, what are the factors which, at the stage of the business cycle with which we are now concerned, determine whether the proportion saved will be great or small, whether it will rise or decline ?

Income not at once disposable. By the proportion of income saved is meant the average proportion of income not spent on consumers' goods in the income period in which it becomes available. The distinction between the period in which income is earned and that in which it is available to be spent or saved must be kept in mind. Even if no saving whatever takes place, this does not mean that the incomes are spent as soon as they are earned. Allowance must be made for the fact previously mentioned that incomes are paid out periodically and spent in the course of the ensuing period. Thus, even apart from saving in the sense here employed, income earned at a given moment of time will be spent about a week later, if it takes the form of wages, a month later in the case of salaries, and a few weeks to a year later in the case of dividends.

Expansion with zero saving. Suppose, now, that an impulse ("starter") is given to the recovery by some act of credit-expansion on the part of the banks, or dishoarding on the part of individuals or the State, whereby goods and services are bought and additional money income created. How should we expect the expansion to proceed in the absence of saving? After a distributed time-lag, determined (as explained above) by habits of payment and expenditure, the *entire* additional income is spent on consumption goods.[1] This increase in demand for consumption goods does not evoke an *immediate* and equivalent increase in their production. Time has to be given for the merchants to order new stocks and for the manufacturers to produce the goods. In the meantime, the merchants' stocks are reduced and the extra money receipts are kept in easily available form. They may be added to the merchants' bank balances, or used to repay a part of their debts to banks or to their own suppliers. It is here assumed that any effect this may have in increasing the supply of investment funds, and so affecting investment, is negligible. Ultimately, if we assume that merchants and manufacturers in the consumption-goods section of industry desire at least to maintain their stocks and working capital, the increased expenditure on consumption goods evokes an equivalent rise in income, which, after a further lapse of time, is again spent, and so on indefinitely. Thus, in the supposed circumstances of zero-saving, extra income, once created, will never disappear.

---

[1] It will be remembered that this assumption is *not* equivalent to a marginal propensity to save of zero in Mr. Keynes' terminology, because Mr. Keynes does not allow for time-lags. (See Chapter 9, § 4, above.) One may, of course, use Mr. Keynes' concept just as well, but one should not forget that these little time-lags for "technical" reasons are absolutely essential for a money economy, and that, in everyday language, when one speaks of zero-saving one automatically takes these time-lags for granted. The assumption that there are no such lags—the assumption, in other words, that the money was spent and respent instantaneously—would imply an infinite velocity of circulation of money, which would be tantamount to assuming away the use of money altogether and assuming instead a barter economy with a *numéraire* but without a medium of exchange (money).

Income velocity of money. While these time-lags between the earning and receiving of incomes, and again between the receiving and spending of them, are highly relevant to the determination of the proportion of money which the economic community will hold relative to its money income, it is not possible to deduce the " average lag " between the primary and the secondary increases of income directly from the magnitude of the average "income-" or " circuit-velocity " of the total stock of money, or *vice versa*. In part, this is because a certain portion of the community's cash holding is primarily a reserve store of value in no close connection with the routine receipts and disbursements of firms and of individuals. Only a part rises and falls regularly as receipts exceed and fall short of disbursements as determined by the lags which have been mentioned. But even if we proceed to exclude from consideration that money which is locked up in hoards, a distinction must be drawn between what may be called *average* and *marginal* time-lags between receipts and disbursements. Our assumption that no part of the income is saved excluded the possibility of a divergence between average and marginal time-lags in the case of income-receivers. But it is quite likely in the case of business firms that *extra* receipts will take a longer or shorter time to be disbursed than the average lag between all receipts and all disbursements.[1] In a very interesting passage in his *Economics of Planning Public Works*,[2] Professor J. M. CLARK estimates that the *marginal* period of flow of purchasing power from ultimate income recipient to ultimate income recipient (the length of the " cycle of secondary effects ") in the United States of America is very much shorter than the *average* period expressed in the " income-velocity of money ".

After some time, the " braking " influence of some of these time-lags will tend to disappear. Capitalists, at any rate, will probably begin to anticipate the payment of their increased

---

[1] This may, of course, also be expressed by saying that the *average* time-lag or *average* income velocity is likely to be changed by new additions to the income stream. It is not safe, therefore, to regard it as a comparatively stable magnitude.

[2] Washington, 1935, pages 87 and 88.

incomes. Merchants and producers of consumption goods will anticipate the rise in demand, and will create new incomes in advance of demand. Even apart from further investment than is involved in an increase in working capital corresponding to the increase in output, the rise in incomes will soon gather a terrific momentum. Moreover, investment in fixed capital will not in fact stand still : on the contrary, it will expand in the manner analysed above to a much greater extent even than the production of consumers' goods. The movement will gather momentum continuously until checked by the appearance of a shortage of factors of production and/or of investible funds from inflationary sources.

Immediate   What difference now will saving make to this
effect of   process ? An act of saving is necessarily two-sided.
saving.   It means a fall in demand for consumers' goods in terms of money and a rise in the supply of investible funds. If we look at saving only in its aspect of a reduction of expenditure—for example, if we suppose that money saved is simply destroyed or hoarded—it is obvious that, even in the absence of money-scarcity, credit restrictions and a rise in the rate of interest, a habit on the part of the public of saving a certain proportion of its income will tend to damp down, and finally extinguish, this increase in money income. At each revolution of the money stream, each time income is spent, it will undergo a reduction. Obviously, continual additions by way of investment will have to be made to the income stream in order to counteract the deflationary pressure of saving. The question then arises whether an act of saving in itself tends to produce an act of investment. Answers to this question are usually of an extreme nature. Some economists, of whom Mr J. M. Keynes is not the least eminent, reply that saving has no immediate effect on investment and that its ultimate effect, owing to the deflation which it induces, is to diminish the incentive to invest.[1] Others[2] assume that in normal conditions saving will give rise to an equivalent amount of investment.

---

[1] See, however, Chapter 8, § 3, pages 217 *et seq*, above.

[2] *E.g.*, Professor Pigou, in his review of Mr. Keynes' *General Theory of Employment, Interest and Money* in *Economica*, May 1936, page 125.

The truth probably lies somewhere between these extremes. The supply of investible funds from dishoarding, credit expansion, etc., even where it is not completely elastic, is probably always to some degree sensitive to the price of borrowing (*i.e.*, the interest rate).

Saving and hoarding. This is true at any rate for the stage of the trade cycle which we are now considering, though it may cease to be true at a later point in the boom. The lower the interest rates, the more money will be withdrawn from entrepreneurs and hoarded in some form. Anything which lowers or even prevents a rise in the interest rate will increase the quantity of money withheld from entrepreneurs and hoarded, or reduce the quantity of money which would otherwise have been dishoarded and offered to entrepreneurs. It is probable that the effect of savings will be to bring about a reduction or prevent a rise in the interest rate. If this does not happen, there can only be two possible explanations. Either the savings have been completely hoarded in the first instance, or the entrepreneurial demand for investible funds is perfectly elastic over a range equal to the amount of savings which is offered for investment. As for the first alternative, if even a part of the savings is hoarded, it is obvious that they cannot give rise to an increase in demand for producers' goods equivalent to the reduction of demand for consumers' goods which they occasion. In order to produce this compensating increase in investment, *all* the savings must be invested. But, even if the savers should in the first instance seek to invest all their savings, this will not increase actual investment to an equivalent extent unless the demand for investible funds is such that entrepreneurs can absorb the supply as increased by the full amount of the savings, at the same rate of interest as that at which they might have absorbed the same supply *minus* the savings. If they are unable to do this, the saving will be in part sterilised by hoarding, or a reduction in dishoarding, due to reduction of the rate of interest, or to its failure to rise; and the net effect will be deflationary.

We may suppose that, in the case of an increment of saving which is not expected and which entrepreneurs have made no plans to meet,[1] the demand for investment funds will show very little elasticity and investment will scarcely increase at all. On the other hand, where investment projects, which (consciously or otherwise) rely on such an increase in saving, have been conceived in advance, the fall in the interest rate will be much slighter and the relative deflation less severe. But always and in all circumstances—short of a complete insensitiveness of banks and capitalists to the rate of interest in their decisions to hoard and dishoard—saving must tend to reduce the total demand for goods in terms of money. The comparison, it must be noted, lies not between the state of affairs *after* the saving and *before* it, but between the state of affairs at a given time with the saving, and what it would have been had there been no saving. It may well be that the extra saving is fully counteracted by an increase in investment ; but, unless this investment would not have taken place in the absence of such saving, it remains true to say that the saving has a relatively deflationary effect.

Consequences of continued saving. An increase of saving, we have found, normally exercises a deflationary effect at the moment of its appearance. The amount of dishoarding is diminished, and the community's currently- earned income rises less fast than it otherwise would have done. If we pursue the consequences of this saving in subsequent periods, we find the deflationary effect is, as it were, cumulated. A relative fall in demand now leads to a relative fall in investment later, this to a further fall in demand and so on.

If the increase in saving is repeated in subsequent periods, it may not merely slow down the expansion but even prevent it from reaching the height it would otherwise attain, and finally turn it into a decline. This can be easily demonstrated on somewhat abstract assumptions. The higher the proportion of income saved, the less will the income level require to rise in order that a given rate of saving may be attained. On the other hand, according to the acceleration principle, the rate of investment will

---

[1] *Cf.* C. Bresciani-Turroni, " The Theory of Saving " in *Economica*, Vol. III (New Series), 1936.

be greater or less according as incomes are rising more or less fast, and, since the greater the proportion of income saved the slower will be the expansion of incomes, it follows that the higher the proportion of income saved the less will be the rate of investment at any given income level. But the expansion will cease when saving catches up with investment, and the higher the proportion of income saved the lower will be the income level at which the expansion will cease.[1]

The general conclusion of the foregoing argument is that saving which is in progress during an expansion process tends to slow down the expansion. *Ceteris paribus*, the more people save the slower the expansion, and the less they save the more rapid the expansion.

Quali-fications. It must, however, be kept in mind, if serious misunderstanding is to be avoided, that our analysis is limited at this point to the peculiar economic circumstances which are supposed to prevail during a typical upswing. We assume that a credit expansion is under way and that the supply of investible funds from inflationary sources is to some degree elastic. If that is so, then an increase in the rate of saving leads to a slowing-down of the inflow of new money (inflation), and a decrease in the rate of saving to an acceleration of the inflow of new money. If the money supply is completely inelastic, the situation is different; for in that case we cannot assume that a deficiency in the supply of investible funds caused by a decrease in the rate of saving will be automatically made up, wholly or partly, by inflation. This is, however, not the typical situation during the upswing, which is, on the contrary, characterised by an elastic money supply from inflationary sources. But, since (as will be shown in detail at a later point) this elasticity in the money supply is likely to diminish with the progress of the boom, the deflationary effect of saving is likely to become less and less pronounced.

---

[1] Compare Mr. Harrod's treatment of the interactions of the acceleration principle (which he calls " the relation ") and the propensity to save (or " the multiplier ") in *The Trade Cycle*, London, 1936, Chapter 2.

Furthermore, exceptions to our rule are conceiv-
Institutional able in special institutional circumstances. Take,
complications. for instance, the following situation. Hitherto
we have assumed a homogenous capital market
with a homogeneous object of transactions—viz., investible
funds. In reality, however, there are subdivisions in this market,
and the different types of investible funds which are marketed in
these subdivisions are not perfect substitutes. We are thinking
here primarily of the distinction between long- and short-term
credit—that is, between the capital and money market. Now, it
may be that the inflationary sources of supply (*e.g.*, bank credit)
serve mainly the money market, while the capital market is fed
chiefly by saying. It is true that in the real world this separation
is not complete. The sources from which the demand for long-
term credit is satisfied include inflationary sources. Banks, for
example, invest, not only in commercial paper, but also in securities;
money hoards of individuals and corporations go into long-term
investment and play a large rôle during the first phase of the
upswing. On the other hand, to a certain extent, short- and
long-term credit are also substitutable on the demand side. Investment in fixed capital may be financed by means of short-term credits
which are continuously renewed.[1] But the substitutability is
certainly not perfect either on the demand or on the supply side.
If that is the case to a considerable extent, if (that is to say) the money
market and the capital market are separated in the sense indicated
above and short- and long-term credit are not substitutable for
the entrepreneur, then the progress of the expansion may be
seriously hampered, and not accelerated, by a low rate or a fall
in the rate of saving. The capital market may become tight ; the
rate of interest there may be driven up and the volume of investment, so far as it requires long-term financing, will be reduced.
To the extent that different kinds of investment are complementary
so that long- and short-term funds are in joint demand, the inflow
of new money through inflationary faucets into the money market

---

[1] On this, compare M. Breit : "Ein Beitrag zur Theorie des Geld- und
Kapitalmarktes" in *Zeitschrift für Nationalökonomie*, Band VI, Heft 5,
1935, pages 632 *et seq.*

will be impeded. In order to appraise this possibility correctly, it should be remembered that money flowing from an inflationary source, after it has become income and is saved, has to be counted as saving. It has been assumed by many writers—*e.g.*, by Mr. HAWTREY—that profits which have been brought about by an inflationary rise in demand are the most important source of supply of investible funds during the upswing of the cycle.

But, even if such exceptions are deemed unimportant and our rule that savings during the expansion slow down the latter remains substantially unimpaired, it does not by any means follow that, for the purpose of obtaining the maximum *long-run* productivity, a low rate of saving during the upswing of the cycle is desirable. We are not yet in a position to give a definite answer to this question. There can, however, be no doubt that good reasons can be adduced for the proposition that an expansion which develops slowly will last longer and give rise to less serious maladjustment than one which progresses very rapidly.

Saving during the early expansion.   We turn now to the second problem presented at the beginning of this section. What proportions of available incomes are likely to be saved as the expansion develops? Are there any reasons for believing that the proportion of income saved by the economic community varies at different points in the cycle?

Unfortunately, for lack of statistical data, there is no possibility of measuring directly how savings behave during different phases of the cycle.[1] We have to rely on very general considerations which cannot provide a precise answer to the above questions.

So far as the wage-earning section of the community is concerned, there are various considerations which do not all point in the same direction. The real incomes of those who were employed during the slump probably fall during at least the first part of the upswing. The proportion of income saved by such people will probably tend to diminish, particularly as the danger of unemployment recedes. On the other hand, as the unemployed of the slump are re-employed, they obtain a saveable surplus, and in some

---

[1] *Cf. America's Capacity to Consume, passim.*

cases may have a strong incentive to save for the purpose of repaying debts to tradesmen which they have contracted. Since the real income of the working-class as a whole probably rises during an upswing—especially in post-war cycles—it is possible that the tendencies to increased saving prevail, but it seems unlikely that the increase in saving from this source can be of much importance.

Among the propertied classes, the fluctuations in the proportion of income saved are probably much more important, because their incomes fluctuate more widely. They skim the cream off the boom and bear the brunt of the depression. Considering that their standard of living is much less flexible than their incomes, it appears plausible that they should even dissave during the slump and save considerably during the upswing and boom. This is likely to be accentuated by the fact that they are, to some extent at least, cycle-conscious. During good times, they save not only for old age, children's education and inheritance, calamity, etc., but also to some extent against the eventuality of a slump. Business corporations pursue a policy of " dividend-stabilisation " by accumulating reserves out of net revenue in good times to disburse them in bad.

It is true that the bond-holding section of the propertied class is to some extent in a position analogous to that of wage-earners who find their real incomes diminishing during the upswing. This, however, is not likely to be important in the earlier stages of an expansion; and if we take capitalist-entrepreneurs, holders of equity shares and holders of industrial bonds in the mass, there can be no doubt that their real incomes greatly increase during the expansion. Where there is a big national debt, the situation is a little different. Here it is conceivable that the transference of real income from taxpayers (poor and rich) to rentiers (mainly rich) will be considerably diminished during the upswing, and this will counteract the redistribution of income in favour of the rich which will otherwise take place at that time, and to some extent limit saving.

Consideration of public finance in a wide sense (including social insurance institutions), however, brings in a further element which decisively tips the balance in favour of increased saving. During the slump—largely as a consequence of the increased real weight of social services, maintenance of unemployed and national debt— Governments are normally forced into budget deficits which we may regard as dissaving. During the upswing, these deficits disappear and may even be succeeded by budget surpluses.

Saving during the later expansion. The considerations set forth above are applicable to the expansion in its beginnings and in its heyday : but, as the boom reaches its height, they may lose some of their force. There are reasons for the view that, in the later stages of an expansion, people begin to spend once again a larger proportion of their available incomes.

Workers, farmers, and business-men alike will probably have accumulated a certain amount of debt during the depression, which represents a psychological burden and a threat to their security out of proportion to the actual money burden of interest. Any additional income coming their way during the expansion will be used to a considerable extent to repay these debts. Once this is accomplished, however, it is very unlikely that the same rate of saving will be maintained merely with the object of adding to capital. A larger proportion of incomes received will tend to be spent; and the consumers' goods trades will receive a fillip thereby, which will transmit itself, if there is still a sufficiency of unemployed funds and physical resources, to the investment-goods trades. The new *élan* which will thus be given to the expansion will provoke a further fall in the proportion of income saved, because the business world will be aware that bigger profits are being made and bigger dividends will in due course be distributed, so that a spirit of confidence will spread, which is very favourable to spending.

Another influence may make its appearance which will have more or less effect according to the social and economic structure of the country concerned. Rising business profits, and the anticipation of a continuance of rising profits, will bring about a recovery of equity values on the stock exchange. As time goes on, this boom may interest a larger and larger number of people in a speculative capacity. They may be disposed to utilise gains on the stock exchange as additional income, or they may feel that, since the value of their shares is so high, the future is well provided for and they can afford to do less saving out of current available income.

Saving at the peak. When the boom arrives at the stage where shortage of materials and men develops and prices rise rather than production, it is probable that the tendency to greater spending is increased. Wages in the latter stages of a boom no longer show the same " stickiness ", workers' organisations become more and more active, and wages rise as fast as profits. Further, it is probable that the farmers and other producers of raw materials succeed in getting a bigger share than before in the total income : and, since they are on the average much poorer than the industrial population, they will probably spend a larger proportion of their incomes.

In this way, the position envisaged by the monetary over-investment theorists at the end of the boom may possibly arise. The proportion of spending to saving tends to increase. The consumption-goods trades may draw labour away from the investment-goods trades and so create difficulties for them. Suppose now that, before the shortage of material means of production becomes a factor of much importance, the liquidity of the monetary system declines to such an extent that banks are unwilling to expand credit or individuals to dishoard to any considerable degree, even though interest rates rise very high. In such circumstances, increased saving will only be slightly deflationary, and a fall in saving only slightly inflationary. If, as has been asserted, the proportion of expenditure to income tends to increase at the later stages of the boom, the stimulating effect will be reduced to a minimum by the inelasticity of the supply of credit. The money added to the demand for consumers' goods will in large part be abstracted from the demand for producers' goods and the dislocation caused thereby may precipitate a deflation.

B. *The Contraction Process*

§ 7. GENERAL DESCRIPTION OF THE MECHANISM

Rôle of deflation. The process of contraction, like the process of expansion, is cumulative and self-reinforcing. Once started, no matter how, there is a tendency for it to go on, even if the force by which it was provoked has in the meantime ceased to operate.

The contraction may start from a state of full employment or partial employment; and the mechanism is, in principle, the same in both cases.

Deflation in the sense of a gradual decrease in the total demand for goods in terms of money plays an essential rôle in the contraction process. Deflation must not, however, be interpreted in the narrow sense of a deliberate act or policy on the part of the monetary authorities or commercial banks. A deflation in this narrow sense may, of course, act as a starter to the process, and it usually comes in sooner or later as an intensifying element ; but, when the process has once got under way, a sort of automatic deflation or self-deflation of the economic system (in contradistinction to a deflation imposed on it by the monetary authorities) is just as much an effect as a cause.[1]

---

[1] Writers on the subject have frequently used the term "secondary" deflation. Their attention has been concentrated mainly on the maladjustment which, they maintain, is the cause of the crisis. They conceive of the depression, not as a cumulative self-reinforcing process, but as a period of adaptation during which the economic system reverts to equilibrium and eliminates the maladjustments which have developed during the preceding upswing and have been brought to light in the crisis. The deflation is regarded as an unfortunate accident.

More recent writers have, however, come to realise increasingly that the above view is a misconception, that what it treats as an accidental phenomenon is in fact the most important element in the depression, that the deflation may continue long after the maladjustment by which it was started has been removed, that it may be started by purely monetary forces without anything being wrong with the structure of production, and that it does not revert directly to equilibrium, but, on the contrary, carries the economic system a long way away from equilibrium.

In many respects, the contraction is the exact counterpart of the expansion, so that large parts of the analysis of the latter can be adapted to explain the former.

Spread of deflation. Suppose contraction has been started for any reason whatsoever (*e.g.*, because a large construction scheme which was under way has had to be interrupted owing to inability to raise the necessary funds for financing it). Demand for construction materials and implements falls off, and production in the industries which provide those things is curtailed. We might equally well take the case where an act of deliberate deflation by the monetary authorities (which again may be due to a great variety of reasons or motives) starts the ball rolling. In the section on the down-turn (crisis), the question of the possible or usual starters will be taken up. Here we simply assume that a *net* contraction has been produced, and that the total demand for goods in terms of money has shrunk by a considerable amount.

When demand flags at various points, merchants will give lower orders to producers, production will be curtailed and workers will be dismissed. This reduces income. When incomes fall, the demand for all kinds of goods is further reduced and depression spreads to other parts of the system.

Like the expansion process, the contraction process will probably proceed slowly at the beginning and then gather momentum.[1] At first, when demand has fallen off in the case of only a few commodities, the contraction may easily be stopped or reversed by favourable influences elsewhere. Later on, when the demand for a greater number of goods has fallen for some time and contraction has spread to many parts of the system, expansionary influences, which in the early stage of the process would have been strong enough to outweigh the forces of contraction, will no

---

[1] The spectacular events in the financial sphere which usually mark the turn from prosperity to depression should not be allowed to obscure the fact that the downward movement of production and trade usually takes time to get under way. This was, *e.g.*, the case after the crisis of 1929. *Cf.* Slichter in *Review of Economic Statistics*, February 1937, on the 1929 down-turn. In the autumn of 1937, the fall in production and employment was much more rapid than in 1929, although there were no spectacular breakdowns in the financial sphere.

longer be sufficient to reverse the downward movement, but will merely slow it down.   This is what is meant when we say that " the process has gathered momentum ".

Intensifying factors.   After the process has continued for a while, intensifying factors are likely to come into play. Prices will soon begin to fall, and losses will be made everywhere, because wages and other cost items cannot readily be reduced.   There will be a strong tendency to reduce stocks and to curtail orders and purchases by more than the amount by which sales have gone down.   A sustained fall in demand and prices is bound to create in the business world a more pessimistic outlook in general and an expectation, whether justified or not, of a further fall in prices.   The profit rate will be reduced all along the line, and new investment or reinvestment of amortisation quotas will be curtailed.   Nobody dares to embark on ambitious schemes of investment; and this will intensify the tendency to reduce commodity stocks and to increase money stocks, that is to hoard—the counterpart of the tendency to dishoard during expansion.

It is important to note that such a contraction process can happen even in a pure cash economy with constant quantity of money (M).   In a modern banking and credit economy, powerful intensifying factors come in.   If a large part of the circulating medium consists of bank money (demand deposits subject to cheque) and if the banking system as a whole or a number of individual banks get into difficulties, the banks will restrict credit.   They will call in outstanding loans and be reluctant to grant new ones, and as a consequence M will shrink.   If a run on the banks occurs —if, that is to say, depositors want to change their deposits into notes—the deflation becomes still more serious.   The same may happen in the international sphere.   There may be a run on the central bank in order to exchange notes for coins and foreign money—that is to say, gold hoarding may develop or a flight of capital may intensify the deflation.

Owing to the rigidity of a number of cost items, each decrease in the total demand for goods in terms of money is followed by a certain shrinkage in production, and any reduction in the production of finished goods tends to be transmitted with increasing violence to the preceding stages of production, which again tends to reduce the demand for finished goods, and so on in a long and painful process.

This general description of the contraction process may probably be taken as a correct description of the common opinion on the matter. The most important thing to remember is that the depth to which the contraction develops depends on a number of circumstances, partly of an institutional nature, of which many are—or, at any rate, may be—quite independent of the factor which first initiated the contraction or even of the intensity of the preceding boom. The circumstances which are responsible for the cumulative nature of the contraction process we must now analyse in detail.

§ 8. MONETARY ANALYSIS OF THE CONTRACTION PROCESS

Fall in total demand. The monetary manifestation of the cumulative process of contraction is the prolonged fall in MV —*i.e.*, in the total demand[1] for goods in terms of money. If MV did not fall, there would be no such rapid deterioration of the economic situation, no such swift fall in production and employment, as is in fact exhibited in the course of cyclical depressions.[2] In this sense, one may call the contraction a monetary phenomenon. But the description is wrong, if it is taken (as it frequently is) to imply that the responsible factor for the shrinkage in MV is always a deflationary policy pursued by the banking system, or that the monetary authorities can always effectively prevent a fall in MV if they refrain from contracting credit, or if they expand credit, by the ordinary

---

[1] "Demand" in the sense of "actual demand" or "expenditure", not in the sense of "demand schedule".

[2] It should be noted that this is not a tautological statement following from the definition of depression. We have defined the latter, not in monetary terms, not in terms of MV, but in terms of volume of production and employment. Logically, a decrease in employment and production may be accompanied by a rise instead of a fall in MV. This will imply a rapid rise in wages and prices. Something like that seems to have happened during the last phase of the German post-war inflation. But this is surely not the typical picture of a cyclical depression.

measures of credit policy. Within the limits set by existing monetary organisation and banking practice, the monetary authorities can regulate the supply of money. But, in order to arrest a fall in MV during a contraction, it will frequently be necessary to regulate and stimulate demand as well as supply; and this may require very drastic interventions, which are hardly possible without far-reaching changes in the present institutional framework.

Cumulative fall in investment. We shall now analyse the contraction process broadly in terms of our demand-and-supply schedules of investible funds. It may be that not much is gained thereby; but, as the analysis recapitulates the essence of the theories which explain the slump by an excess of the market rate of interest over the equilibrium or profit rate, it may serve as an introduction to a more realistic treatment of the matter.

When the demand for goods in general falls and production shrinks, the demand for investible funds falls too—*i.e.*, the demand curve shifts to the left. Assuming that the supply curve is unchanged, and is fairly elastic over the given range, the new point of intersection will be to the left of the old one—*i.e.*, the amount of investment is reduced. But we cannot assume that the supply of savings is as elastic as the supply of investible funds. This means that part of the supply of investible funds which is not taken up by the demand will be diverted, not into expenditure on consumption goods, but into hoards—*i.e.*, it will be withdrawn from circulation. Hence the total demand for goods in terms of money falls further, prices fall still lower and production and employment are reduced. This provides a further discouragement to the demand for investible funds, and the demand curve is shifted further to the left.

Drying-up of supply of funds. On the other hand, the contraction process is bound to give rise to unfavourable reactions on the supply side. Losses are made everywhere : defaults and bankruptcies threaten or actually occur. The effect is to make the banks and the investing public cautious and pessimistic. The risk of lending rises and the supply of investible funds decreases. In technical parlance, the supply curve, too, shifts to the left. The interest rates are thereby pushed up, or are prevented from falling, in spite of the falling demand, which intensifies the deflation. As Mr. KEYNES and Mr. M. BREIT have both pointed out, the same risk factor may be counted twice over, on the demand and the supply side, by the lender and the borrower, thus widening the gap between demand and supply.[1]

For a more detailed study of the monetary aspects of the contraction process, especially a study which lends itself to statistical verification, it will be useful to start with the following considerations. MV, the total demand for goods in terms of money, shrinks:

---

[1] See Keynes : *The General Theory of Employment, Interest and Money*, pages 144 and 145. Mr. Breit (" Ein Beitrag zur Theorie des Geld- und Kapitalmarktes ", in *Zeitschrift für Nationalökonomie*, Band VI, Heft 5, page 654, footnote) describes five possible ways in which lender and borrower may anticipate the sharing between them of the risk involved in a given investment. Each may believe that he will have to bear the weight of the possible losses—in this case there is a double reckoning of risks. Both may regard the risk as falling on the creditor alone, or on the debtor alone. In either case there is a single reckoning of the risk. Each may regard the other as the risk-bearer, and in this case no allowance for risk is made by either party. Lastly, extremes may be avoided and a single reckoning achieved where both estimate that the risk will be shared in a given way between the two parties. Mr. Breit, however, believes that the first possibility, that of the double reckoning, is less unrealistic than the other possibilities. It might perhaps be added that the question of the sharing of risk between lender and borrower cannot be considered without reference to the wealth of the borrower, and also to the probable distribution of returns expected from the investment. If the risk consists in a considerable possibility of a small loss, there is more likelihood that the creditor will ignore the risk factor than if it consists in a slight possibility of a very large loss, which the borrower could not possibly make good. In the course of a deflation, the money value of the wealth of the debtor is likely to diminish, the entire probability curve of returns is reduced, and, in consequence, the range of possible losses which the debtor could not make good increases. The debtor finds that a greater part of risk consists, not in the danger of having to sell part of his property in order to pay his debt, but in having to go through bankruptcy courts. The creditor finds that he stands in greater danger of not being able to recover his money. In those circumstances there is a greater likelihood of a double-counting of the risk. A particular application of this principle occurs where the debt is secured on specific assets. The deflation reduces the amount of cover that borrowers can offer, and in consequence increases the risk premium they have to pay on their borrowings.

this may be due to a shrinkage in the quantity of money and/or to a decrease in its velocity of circulation. It must be possible to demonstrate that (1) a part of the monetary circulation is destroyed or leaves the country, and/or (2) money does not change hands so frequently against goods, because it is hoarded or used for other purposes. (3) In addition to the factors mentioned here as effecting a reduction in MV, or the flow of money against goods, it is conceivable that a deflationary influence may be exerted by another development which does not affect the flow of money, but adds to the work which money has to do—and that is an increase in the turnover of goods. Goods in general will in this case change hands for money more frequently in the course of their journey from the primary producer to the consumer. There is, however, no reason to believe that this disintegration of the structure of production is a characteristic or necessary feature of the downswing.[1] (4) Financial transactions may immobilise a larger part of the circulating medium, and demand for goods falls.

Forms of deflationary pressure. We have now to answer the questions : At what point does the money leak out of the circulation ? Where is it held up ? Who hoards it ? In what shape is the money hoarded ? How is it destroyed ?

It is possible to enumerate a number of forms in which the monetary contraction may appear, beginning with the more extreme and conspicuous cases and proceeding to the less conspicuous and more subtle ones. Not all of these forms of monetary contraction are regular or unavoidable features of every cyclical depression. The attempt is here made to arrange them approximately in decreasing order of regularity and conspicuousness.

Outright deflation by the central bank. Deflation by the central bank is a straightforward case which does not require much comment. A restriction by the central monetary authorities of the circulation of gold coins, notes and short-term liabilities (central-bank money) means a decrease in the flow of purchasing power—unless counteracted by other forces : *e.g.*, the substitution of bank credit for centralbank

---

[1] See Hayek : *Prices and Production*, 2nd ed., pages 118 *et seq.*

money or an increase in the velocity of circulation which will take place if the money flowing into the central bank comes out of hoards. This happens sometimes on a large scale after a period of panic which has led to a great drain of cash out of the banking system—*e.g.*, in the United States after the bank suspension in 1933.

Active deflation on the part of the central bank is nowadays almost always the consequence of a disequilibrium in the international balance of payments of a country, which may be due to the withdrawal of foreign credits, the cessation of the inflow of capital, a flight of domestic capital or a deficit in the balance of payments on current account because of a relatively high price and income structure (over-valuation of the currency).

An outright reduction of central-bank money is, however, not an invariable feature of every depression : at least, it is usually not pursued right through the whole course of the depression. It is a common experience at the beginning of the depression, or during the financial crisis which usually marks the turning-point, or in some later financial crisis in the course of the depression, to observe a sharp increase in the note circulation accompanied by a decrease in the total demand for goods. This is proof that, at some other point in the economic system, money is being hoarded, and that the central bank is providing the cash in order to avoid a collapse of private banks and firms and to mitigate the drain on the industrial circulation.

Hoarding of gold and bank notes by private individuals. This again is a clear case of deflation. In the first case, gold is sought from the banks by the public in exchange for notes so long as the latter are redeemable in gold. The circulation is thereby reduced and pressure is brought upon the bank of issue to contract further in order to improve the reserve ratio. In the second case, notes which otherwise would have been spent on goods are hoarded, or bank deposits are turned into notes ; and so pressure is brought to bear on the commercial banks to contract credit in order to preserve their cash reserves. It should be noted that the amount of money an individual can hoard is not limited to the magnitude of his current money income. He may sell other assets such as securities, real estate and commodities of all sorts against cash, and hoard the proceeds of the sales. This has a double effect. On the one hand, money is withdrawn from circulation (except in so far as the buyer of the assets manages to pay without decreasing his other expenditure—*e.g.*, if securities are taken up by banks which create deposits against them), and the demand for goods falls off at some point. On the other hand, the price of the assets in question is depressed, which may have serious repercussions. To this extremely important aspect we shall return later.

Clearly, hoarding of gold and bank notes by the public is not a feature of every cyclical depression. It happens only in exceptionally severe depressions and under special circumstances—*e.g.*, when the banking system is in bad shape, as in the United States of America in 1933, or when a flight into foreign currencies takes place, as in many European States during recent years. If money hoarding by the public develops, naturally it brings with it a severe intensification of the deflation.

Contraction of credit by the commercial banks. This probably has been, until now, an invariable feature of any contraction in an economy with a fairly developed banking system. It is one of the best known and most fully analysed aspects of the depression and need not long detain us.

Since bank deposits are, under modern banking organisation, a means of payment (bank money), a liquidation of bank loans and deposits is a clear case of deflation. This process may proceed in a slow and orderly fashion without spectacular bank failures, or rapidly to the accompaniment of bankruptcies. It may be hastened by pressure from above and below, from the central bank and from a public that demands cash for its deposits. Whether such complications arise or not and whether in consequence the contraction of credit goes a long way or not depends, not merely on the seriousness of the disturbance by which the contraction process was first set afoot, but also—and presumably in many cases to a larger extent—on institutional and psychological circumstances, on the policy pursued by the monetary authorities, on the international complications, on the methods of financing production (short-term or long-term credit, equities or fixed-interest-bearing bonds), etc. By way of example, the habit of indirect investment through the banks may be mentioned as a factor which tends to accentuate the deflationary possibilities of the economic system. The public, instead of holding securities directly, holds bank deposits (savings deposits or time-deposits) and the banks in turn hold securities, or loans backed by securities.[1] If and when—possibly as a result of a fall in security values which weakens the position of the banks—the public loses confidence in the bank deposits and desires to turn them into cash, the banks are forced to sell securities in order to find the money. This precipitates a further headlong fall in security values, which of course raises the real rate of interest at which business can raise long-term capital. It may be objected that, if the public which converts its deposits into cash does not use the money to buy up securities as fast as the banks unload them on the market, this shows that it prefers holding money to holding securities at the current price, the effect of which—even in the absence of indirect investment through banks—must be to force the price of securities down to the same extent. This objection probably assumes too much " rationality " on the part of investors. It is likely that people who have bought securities at a high price will hold on to them when the market is low, even where they would no longer be willing to buy the same securities at the same price. Moreover, the very fact that the banks hold securities may lead—as a result of the doubts which it engenders as to their ability to meet their obligations and the " runs " which it provokes—to a contraction of commercial credit which will be even more deflationary than the effect on security prices.

Even though an active policy of credit contraction on the part of the commercial banks is in practice—though not of logical necessity—an almost invariable feature in one phase or another of every depression, it does not follow that it always continues to the very end of the depression as the sole or principal deflationary

---

[1] For an indication of the importance of the movement towards indirect investment through the holding of bank deposits, especially in Central-European countries since the inflation and in the United States of America since the war, and for a discussion of the consequences involved, see *Commercial Banks 1925-1933*, League of Nations, Geneva, 1934. *Cf.* also Röpke : *Crises and Cycles*, pages 126 and 127.

factor. On the contrary, the contraction of credit may persist even after the banks have stopped pressing for the repayment of loans, the reason being that there are other, more subtle, forms of deflation than those so far discussed. To these we now turn.

Hoarding by industrial and commercial firms. Industrial and commercial enterprises tend, like the banks, during a general contraction to increase their liquidity : that is, they endeavour to strengthen their cash reserves and to reduce their debts with the banks. (The liquidation of other than bank debts, which is not so closely connected with the extinction of purchasing power as the liquidation of bank debts, will be discussed below in connection with certain aspects of the liquidation of debts in general.)

There is a twofold motive behind this attempt to increase liquidity. There is, *first*, the uncertainty as to the possibility of raising funds when they are needed to meet liabilities falling due. During a period of contraction, especially in its initial phase, it is difficult to get credit from the banks or from the suppliers of raw material and other means of production. There is the danger that such credits may be difficult to renew. In addition, one is not sure of being paid punctually by one's own debtors. All this makes increased liquidity seem advisable. *Secondly*, there is the fact that, when prices fall and losses are made and further losses are expected, the replacement of fixed and working capital (reinvestment), as well as new investment which may have been contemplated before the situation became too bad, is postponed or suspended for the time being. It does not pay to invest or reinvest; and, instead, idle balances are accumulated, or bank loans repaid even when the banks are no longer pressing for repayment. (In extreme cases, of course, the hoarding may be effected in the form of bank notes or gold rather than through the accumulation of idle bank balances and the repayment of bank loans.)

The immediate effect is in all cases the same, whatever may be the motives for, and the form of, the pursuit of liquidity. Demand for goods shrinks, prices fall, production is curtailed and the general situation is aggravated. So the initial achievement of greater liquidity creates a need for further steps to maintain liquidity, and makes things worse than they were. Gradually, however, with the fall in prices and wages and the curtailment of production, funds are liberated and—it may be, not till after a succession of setbacks and relapses—liquidity increases all round.

Needless to say, the policy of the central and commercial banks is a decisive factor. By supplying or withholding additional funds, they can intensify or mitigate the consequences of private hoarding. Both factors—viz., banking and monetary policy on the one hand and the liquidity policy of industrial and commercial firms on the other hand—interact in a complicated way. But it is nevertheless important to realise that the policy of the latter— *i.e.*, the hoarding by private business firms—is an independent factor which may make itself felt and provoke a general contraction, even in a pure cash economy with no bank money at all.

Liquidation of non-bank debts. Quite apart from bank debts, a strong deflationary effect is probably exercised, at least in the first stages of the cyclical contraction, by the liquidation of inter-personal and inter-business debts.

But the connection between the liquidation of debt in general and the decrease in the flow of money against goods is more complicated and indirect than in the case of bank debts.

The debts of a bank to its customers (that is, its deposits) are normally used as money. The owner treats them as cash : they constitute purchasing power and have a velocity of circulation. Hence the extinction of such debts through bank failures or through a contraction of bank credit diminishes purchasing power and demand for goods. Other debts may, of course, perform the same function. A bill may circulate as money ; and its settlement has then the same effect as the liquidation of a deposit. These cases, however, we may safely regard as quantitatively unimportant under our present monetary and banking arrangements (although economic history can show instances where they have been important). Usually it is in a less direct way that the liquidation of debts—or, if we prefer to take it from the opposite angle, credits —exerts its deflationary influence.

But, even if debts (credits) other than bank debts (credits) do not circulate as money, they may be highly liquid assets—the degree of liquidity depending on the standing of the debtor and the situation of the market. Therefore, such debts are used as liquidity reserves; and when during a process of general contraction they diminish in quantity or lose their saleability, they can no longer adequately fulfil this function and must be replaced by money, bank deposits or central bank money. The demand for money increases, its velocity of circulation tends to fall, and total demand shrinks according to the process previously described.

Forced sales of assets to repay debts. The liquidation of debts in general has, however, yet another aspect, which is of great significance. When a debtor is pressed to repay a loan, he is not always in a position to meet his obligation out of his current receipts. Ordinarily, he will be forced to sell assets in order to raise the fund for the discharge of his debt. He may sell securities, real estate, or commodities of different descriptions. These forced sales must have a depressing influence on the price of the assets, with deflationary consequences.

It is important to realise clearly why it is that such forced sales and the consequent price-falls produce or intensify deflation. It might be argued that these transactions themselves (*i.e.*, the sales and purchases of such assets) absorb money, temporarily at least, and withdraw it from other uses. Purchasing power which otherwise would have been spent for new investment or for consumption is now spent for old securities and other assets which are thrown on the market by harassed debtors. In the terminology of Mr. KEYNES' *Treatise on Money*, we may say that " the financial circulation is stealing money from the industrial circulation ". It would seem, however, that this temporary absorption of purchasing power in the actual transference of assets is a comparatively unimportant factor in the general scheme. A much more important factor is the indirect influence of the fall in the prices of the assets in question. If the price of securities falls, this is equivalent to a rise in the interest rate; and this must obstruct the financing of new investment through the issue of securities (bonds or shares). Bank loans are frequently granted on securities; and, if the latter fall in price, this will certainly not promote the willingness and ability of the banks to lend. If the price of real goods —*e.g.*, houses—falls, the production of these goods loses its profitability and will be curtailed.

We must not, however, forget the other side of the medal. What does the creditor do with the money ? If he buys the assets which the debtor sells, it is difficult to see why their prices should fall at all. Since, however, we are dealing with what happens during a general contraction, we may assume that the creditor will not promptly invest the money, but will keep it, at least temporarily, in liquid form. If that happens, then of course the whole procedure is highly deflationary. But the villains of the piece are in such case the hoarders who try to accumulate cash by calling in loans, and not the debtors who are forced to sell assets. Given the decision of the creditor to hoard (in other words, to increase his liquidity by turning debts into cash), the effect is deflationary, even if the debtor is able to refrain from selling assets and to meet his obligations by cutting down his expenditure on consumption or, if he is a producer, on producers' goods (investment and reinvestment).

Before leaving the question of debts, we may pause to point out that the indirectly deflationary effects of default on debts are probably much more serious than the directly deflationary effects which may follow from their payment, since defaults are bound to spread apprehension and to stimulate the liquidation of debts and the hoarding of cash.

Sales of securities, etc., to cover losses. A special variety of this case has been discussed by Mr. KEYNES and Mr. DURBIN.[1] They assume that somebody saves, that the demand for consumers' goods decreases, and that the producers of these consumers' goods make losses and cover them by selling " old " securities in their possession (as distinguished from new issues) in exchange for the savings which

---

[1] J. M. Keynes : *A Treatise on Money*, Vol. I, pages 173 and 174 ; Durbin : *The Problem of Credit Policy*, pages 95 *et seq.*

have brought about the losses.   We need not pause to discuss the likelihood of this rather artificial case.   We may consider instead the more general case where losses, however brought about, are covered by the sales of assets.

This case is very similar to the previous one but rather more general.   The idea is that a producer who is making losses does not cut down his expenditure (whether the expenditure for his personal consumption or his disbursements for labour, raw materials, semi-finished products, etc.) to a corresponding extent, but keeps them up by selling assets to somebody else.   His sales in such case will certainly have an indirect deflationary influence (as was pointed out in connection with the previous case) by depressing the price of the assets in question.   But it is difficult to see how any more direct deflationary effect is produced.[1] Money is transferred from a saver to the entrepreneur who *ex hypothesi* spends it in various ways.   Hence the demand for goods does not fall (except in so far as these transactions themselves absorb money temporarily).   We may describe the process by saying that the savings of a part of the public are compensated by dissaving on the part of entrepreneurs.   Savings are wasted to cover losses.   The situation is one which cannot of course continue for long ; but at any rate the procedure is not directly deflationary.[2]

---

[1] This was pointed out by Professor F. A. Hayek : " Reflections on the Pure Theory of Money of Mr. J. M. Keynes ".   Part II in *Economica*, February 1932, page 29.

[2] There may be in this respect a slight difference between the case envisaged by Mr. Keynes and Mr. Durbin (where an increase in the rate of saving is the cause of the losses) and the other case (where the losses have other causes).   In the former case, it might be argued that the path which the money has to travel from the moment when it becomes income in the hands of the saver until it constitutes demand for goods is lengthened, inasmuch as, before people decide to save, the money is spent by them directly for consumers' goods.   After they have decided to save, it goes first through the capital market buying old securities before it reaches the hands of the producers of consumption goods.   Its arrival at the final stage may be delayed en route—which is equivalent to a hold-up in the flow of money against goods.   In the other case, where the losses are independent from the fact that somebody saves who has not saved before, no turnover of money is interpolated, since the sums saved have in any case to pass through the capital market before

It is even conceivable that the direct effect is rather inflationary than deflationary. If the assets sold to cover losses are taken up by the banks and new deposits are created against them, or if somebody else is tempted to dishoard in order to buy them, the flow of money may be increased rather than decreased.

We are left with the conclusion that we have here no new form of deflation. It is the losses which tend to bring about deflation and not the fact that losses are covered by the sale of assets. On the contrary, the effect may even be to mitigate the force of the deflation. The alternative method of coping with losses—viz., retrenchment of expenditure—is certainly in its immediate effect in a higher degree deflationary.

Sales of securities, etc., for fear of a fall in their price. If the sales of securities and other assets are induced, not by the necessity for repaying debts or covering losses, but by the speculative motive—that is, by the expectation that prices will fall, or in other words that the value of money will rise—we have a deflationary move pure and simple. It is, however, important to note that what makes for deflation is not the demand for money for the purpose of these transactions, but the tendency to hoard—*i.e.*, to change less liquid assets into more liquid assets and to keep the latter unspent. It does not matter much whether the seller performs the act of hoarding after having disposed of the assets at a low price or whether the price of the assets falls without any transaction's having taken place. When everybody is equally pessimistic about the future trend of security prices, prices will quickly fall all round without any securities changing hand at all. On the stock exchange, this is a well-known phenomenon. Prices are " talked down " on a bear market, if there is a consensus of opinion. If there are actual transactions, that is because the consensus of opinion is not complete, those who buy being less pessimistic

---

being spent on real goods. Whether they buy old securities and cover losses or new securities and finance new investment, they reach the commodity market at the same time.

It is unlikely, however, that this difference is of much practical importance.

than those who sell. To be sure, the degree of pessimism will never be uniform; but the deflationary effect in no way depends on there being differences of opinion and therefore actual transactions. (If the pessimistic expectations of one part of the public are offset by the optimistic expectations of another part, the situation is of course different. Our present case is, however, only one of differences in the degree of pessimism.)

Scales of liquidity. Some writers have tried to devise a general formula for the motives which lie behind the various forms of hoarding that take place during a cyclical depression. They say that "liquidity preferences" in general rise.[1] Banks, business enterprises and private individuals tend to increase their liquidity—that is, they wish to hold a larger part of their wealth in cash or in more liquid forms than before. The attempt has sometimes been made to set up typical " scales of liquidity "—*i.e.*, to arrange the various types of assets in the order of their liquidity. If we start from the most liquid assets and proceed to less and less liquid ones, we arrive approximately at the following scheme : gold, bank-notes, bank deposits, short-term credits, long-term credits, bonds, shares, real goods.[2] It is, however, impossible to regard such a scheme as invariable. The order will differ in different circumstances, and all kinds of anomalies may arise. In a state of high inflation, for instance, shares will rank above bonds, real property above bank deposits, and so on.[3]

It does not seem that such generalisations can add much to what is revealed by a detailed analysis such as has been attempted in the previous pages.

---

[1] *Cf.* J. M. Keynes : *The General Theory of Employment, Interest and Money* and the various comments which this book has evoked, especially from Professor J. Viner, " Mr. Keynes on the Causes of Unemployment. A Review ", in *Quarterly Journal of Economics*, Vol. 51, October 1936, pages 147-168 *passim*.

[2] *Cf.*, *e.g.*, Professor J. R. Hicks : " Gleichgewicht und Konjunktur ", in *Zeitschrift für Nationalökonomie*, Vol. IV, 1933, page 441.

[3] *Cf.* E. F. M. Durbin : *The Problem of Credit Policy* (1935), page 106.

The operation of the acceleration principle in the contraction. Assuming the ratio of durable means of production (machines) to labour and raw material (working capital) required for the production of a unit of output to be rigidly fixed (within a certain range of output) by technological considerations—an assumption which would seem to be a good approximation in the short run—the acceleration principle[1] readily explains why demand for, and consequently production of, durable producers' goods and the various materials required for their production falls more rapidly than the demand for, and production of, the finished product.

When in the upward phase of the cycle all branches of the economic system are expanding and production and employment are increasing in all industries, the producers' goods industries and especially the durable-goods industries experience a particularly rapid growth. When the system stops expanding or even curtails output, people naturally stop adding to their fixed equipment. It is not at all paradoxical that no new investments should be made when the existing equipment is insufficiently employed owing to the fall in the demand for the product. The production of durable means of production is reduced to the replacement required for the maintenance of capacity and, in many lines of industry, virtually no replacement may be needed for some time in view of the fact that, during the preceding boom, the equipment has to a large extent been renewed, presumably on the most up-to-date lines. If the depression is particularly severe and long-drawn-out, it is possible that even replacement will be neglected and capacity allowed to shrink.

We may put the matter in a different way. Suppose consumers' demand falls to a certain level and production is curtailed so as to bring the output down to the level strictly required by the new

---

[1] Compare § 5 of this chapter and §§ 17-24 of Chapter 3.

(lower) level of " consumer-taking " (to use an expression coined by Professor FRISCH). Then the production of those goods and services of which there are excessive stocks (excessive in view of the new level of output) will be discontinued altogether until these stocks have been reduced to the level required by the new level of output. Now, as has been pointed out, durable goods—consumers' goods as well as producers' goods[1]—can be conceived of as a stock or bundle of services available at successive points of time. Such " stocks " are usually more considerable than the actual stocks of perishable goods.[2]

The possibility of postponing the acquisition of durable goods. For these reasons, we should expect a sharper decline in the production of producers' and durable goods than of consumers' and perishable goods— and that, even where the decline in consumers' expenditure is quite evenly distributed over all types of finished goods and services. But this need not and probably will not be the case. Consumers will cut down expenditure for different goods to a varying degree, and changes in income distribution will lead to different reductions in demand for different types of finished output. It is difficult, however, to generalise about the

---

[1] Assuming some arbitrary line of separation so that, *e.g.*, an apartment-house or an automobile is held to be a consumers' good and an electrical power plant a producers' good.

[2] There is furthermore this difference. If there are large stocks of transient goods—say sugar or coal—they can be " forced " upon the consumers and into consumption and thus eliminated from the market by price-cutting. Nothing of this sort can be done with durable goods. A machine or a house cannot be made to give up all its services in a short time, even if its price (or the price of its services) is reduced to zero. Sales of machines or houses can, of course, be hastened by lowering their price. But that does not eliminate them ; they are still there, and their very existence restricts the demand for similar goods. It is only by selling them and using them up for scrap that they can be eliminated outright. But this could only happen when their price had fallen so low that reproduction, not to speak of adding to capacity, was out of the question. It is, of course, another question whether a *general* reduction in prices could not revive production and investment all around. We are, however, here concerned with another problem : Why is it that, *given* a decline in production and activity in general, the production of durable goods and producers' goods declines more than the production of transient and consumers' goods ?

nature of the " marginal " expenditure, whether of the individual or the community.   One may characterise those goods which are the first to be sacrificed when income shrinks as " luxuries".   But it is not clear why durable means of production should enter into the production of luxuries to a particularly large extent.   This has, however, frequently been implied by those who say that the production of durable goods falls more rapidly, because it is easier to " do without them ", to postpone their purchase (or the purchase of their services), than it is in the case of perishable goods.   It is easier to go without a new motor-car or any car at all than to go without food.   To a certain extent, it may be true that durable goods and their services are at the margin of consumers' expenditure and will therefore be especially severely hit by any fall in consumers' outlay : but this reason for the comparatively rapid fall in the production of durable goods would seem to be less important and less inherent in the nature of the case than the reason given previously.[1]

The rôle of expectations.   This description of the place and operation of the acceleration principle in the mechanism of contraction must be supplemented and modified much as was the description of the operation of the principle in the expansion process.[2]   Strictly speaking, it is not actual but expected future demand for the product which gives rise to the demand for equipment.   The present level or recent movement (that is, in our present case, the recently

---

[1] If applied to producers' goods, the argument is more plausible and does not really differ from what has been already said.   It is frequently possible within a certain range to vary the methods of production.   In particular, more or less durable, and more or less up-to-date, machinery can be used.   But as soon as it is durable, expectations as to the future development of, demand for, and prices of, the product become relevant ; and, if these expectations are pessimistic, machinery will not be installed or replaced, even though it may be profitable on the basis of the present cost and output situation—that is, assuming that the present level of output and prices will persist.   Producers will " do without "—that is to say, they will work existing equipment beyond the " optimum " point (optimum, of course, only from the longer-run point of view).   It is obviously in most cases impossible to vary in this way the requirements for working capital, nor is there the same motive for doing so.

[2] *Cf.* above, § 5 of this chapter.

experienced *fall*) of demand (and/or prices) may be extrapolated in different ways into the future. We may arrange a whole scale of possible expectations, ranging from the more "optimistic" down to more and more "pessimistic" varieties. It may be assumed that the recent fall in demand is only temporary and will be followed by a rise, or that the new low level will persist or that the downward movement will continue at the same, or at an accelerated, rate. If we say, for instance, that a gloomy outlook is bound to be created by a prolonged contraction, what we mean is that people become more and more inclined to expect that a fall in demand which they have experienced in the recent past will continue (at the same or at an accelerated rate).[1]

Thus, logically speaking, the door is open for all kinds of reactions; and it is only a question of fact which one is the most frequent and typical. The supposition which underlies the rigid application of the acceleration principle is that the present level of demand is assumed to rule in the future also. Now, it is very doubtful whether it is possible to generalise as to the exact behaviour of producers in this respect. Fortunately for the broad result, however, it is sufficient to indicate a certain range of expectations as probable and to eliminate others as highly unlikely. Obviously, the cumulative process of contraction will go on—not necessarily indefinitely, but for a while—if the low level of demand reached at any point of time during the downswing is expected to persist, or if more pessimistic expectations prevail, the more optimistic ones being regarded as on the whole unlikely.[2] This

---

[1] Professor J. R. Hicks has tried to systematise the various possible reactions. He introduced the concept "elasticity of expectations" which he defines "as the ratio of the proportional rise in expected future prices . . . to the proportional rise in (the) current price". Thus the elasticity of expectations is unity, if a change in current prices will change expected prices in the same direction and proportion. (*Cf. Value and Capital*, Oxford, 1939, page 205.) He also expresses the cumulative nature of processes of change in terms of elasticities of expectations. As was also shown at various points earlier in this chapter, changes give rise to cumulative processes, if expectations move in the same direction as the current price—that is to say, if the elasticity of expectation is at least unity. (*Cf.* Hicks, *loc. cit.*, pages 251-252).

[2] It is sufficient if this is the case in the majority of industries. Occasional exceptions would not alter the result.

would seem to be a fairly plausible assumption and perhaps it may even be somewhat relaxed without any fundamental change in the result.

The result is the cumulative process of contraction through the interaction of consumers' and producers' spending, through the operation of the acceleration principle and the dependence of consumers' purchasing power on gross investment (production of producers' goods).[1] Expenditure on consumers' goods falls off. This in turn reacts violently on the production of producers' goods (acceleration principle). Demand for investible funds shrinks. MV is reduced in one way or the other as described in § 8 above. Income and expenditure on consumption are further curtailed, and so on.[2]

---

[1] This description of the dependence of consumers' purchasing power, and through it of the activity in consumption industries, on investment is analytically somewhat different from the use of the "Multiplier" concept by Kahn, Keynes and Harrod. But, substantially, the same thing is referred to in both cases, and it can be said that the idea of the multiplier is more or less explicitly implied in any description of the "Wicksellian process".

[2] How long this process will last before it is finally brought to an end will be discussed below in Chapter 11, section B.

CHAPTER 11

THE TURNING-POINTS. CRISIS AND REVIVAL

---

§ 1. INTRODUCTION

In the preceding sections, we have discussed the *The problem.* reasons why our economic system is subject to cumulative processes of expansion and contraction. We have shown why, once started, such processes are cumulative and self-reinforcing. The question now arises how they can be started, how they actually or usually are started, and how they can be, and usually or actually are, brought to an end.

The problem falls into two parts.

A. How can an expansion be, and how is it in the normal course of events, brought to an end ? Why does it not go on indefinitely ? Why does it not lead up to a position of stable equilibrium instead of being always followed by a more or less severe contraction ? The problem is closely connected—it is indeed almost identical—with the problem of how a contraction process is started. We therefore call it the problem of the upper turning-point or crisis.[1]

B. How can a contraction be terminated, and how is it usually reversed ? The problem is identical with that of the initiating causes of the expansion. We call it therefore the problem of the lower turning-point or revival.

---

[1] See remarks on pages 257 and 258.

In both cases, we can distinguish between two *"Accidental"* types of disrupting or mitigating forces—viz., *and "organic"* those which arise quite independently of the process *restraining* of expansion or contraction which they interrupt *forces.* and those which are usually or necessarily brought about by the process of expansion or contraction itself. In other words, an expansion or contraction may be interrupted on the one hand by an accident such as changes in the harvest due to weather conditions, influences from abroad (other than such as are induced by the contraction or expansion itself), spontaneous shifts in demand, etc., or it may on the other hand itself give rise to maladjustments in the economic system (counter-forces) which tend to check and reverse the very process (*i.e.*, the expansion or contraction) by which they were brought about. These maladjustments or counter-forces may be very various : they may be of a monetary or non-monetary character : they may be treated as the inevitable consequence of any expansion or contraction, or as dependent on circumstances not necessarily to be found in every expansion and contraction.

Most cycle theorists have tried to prove that the second type of restraining forces is all-important. Indeed, they usually accept the existence of such forces as a dogma, at least so far as the expansion is concerned. If this can be definitely established, the cyclical movement is in a higher degree an essential attribute of our present economic system[1] than in the first case. We shall investigate both possibilities. For, even if the second hypothesis can be proved to be correct—if, that is to say, a process of expansion or contraction cannot go on for ever because it generates forces which will counteract and ultimately reverse it—it is none the less important to show that it may be brought to an end by certain accidental factors, before those forces come into operation. An analogy will make this clear. It is true that every man must die

---

[1] The term "cycle" carries with it the suggestion that it is a coherent whole in the sense that one phase necessarily grows out of the other. We have used the term in the less ambitious meaning of a mere alternation of prosperity and depression, leaving it open whether one phase is the inevitable outcome of the preceding one, or whether the connection between the successive phases has to be conceived as less rigid.

sooner or later of old age : but it is none the less true—and deserving of attention—that many die earlier because they catch an infection or are victims of an accident.

The importance of this consideration lies in the fact that (as has already been indicated and will be shown in detail) an expansion becomes more sensitive to accidental disturbances, after it has reached a certain stage, and similarly a contraction can be more easily stopped and reversed by some stimulating factor, after it has progressed for some time. Therefore, even if we were not in a position to prove rigorously that expansion generates contraction and contraction generates expansion, a fairly regular succession of periods of prosperity and depression, of expansion and contraction, might be explained by accidental shocks distributed in a random fashion over time.

A. The Down-turn : Crisis

§ 2. THE METHOD OF PROCEDURE

Three stages of the argument. It has already been pointed out, by way of illustration, that a deliberate policy of deflation, pursued for whatever reason by the monetary authorities, or the interruption of an ambitious construction scheme may start a process of contraction. We shall now consider how this works out in detail and what other events or factors must be held in mind. As a first step (§ 3), we shall suppose that such disturbances occur, and enquire how they exert their depressing influence and, in particular, how an expansion may be interrupted and a general contraction be started by a factor which directly affects only a more or less restricted part of the economic system. At first we assume such disturbances to occur independently of the cycle. That is to say, they may arise in any phase of the cycle, during the contraction phase just as well as during the expansion. If they occur when a general contraction is going on, the contraction will be intensified. If they occur during a general expansion, the expansion may be slowed down or, if the shock is violent enough, cut short.

As a second step (§ 4), we shall show why the system becomes more and more sensitive to disturbances after the expansion has progressed for a while, so that such disturbances are likely to have much more serious consequences if they arise in the later phase of the upswing than in its earlier part.

The third step (§ 5) consists in discussing those unfavourable influences or maladjustments which are likely to arise during the course of the upswing, or which are inevitably brought about by the expansion.[1]

§ 3. THE PROXIMATE CAUSES OF CONTRACTION

Contraction in aggregate demand versus sectional disturbances. An outright and deliberate contraction of the circulating medium may be the proximate cause of the down-turn.   Then we have at once a decrease in the total demand for goods; and it is comparatively easy, as has been shown in the preceding sections, to explain the further development of the contraction.

It is much more difficult, however, to explain how a disturbance which does not in itself consist of a decrease in aggregate demand and which affects directly only a part of the economic system—as, for example, a particular branch of industry—can lead to a decline in aggregate demand rather than to a mere shift in demand from one commodity or group of commodities to

---

[1] In the literature on the subject, the group of problems listed under the third head have attracted most attention, and the first two categories have been somewhat neglected.   The first step in our scheme is, however, an indispensable preliminary to the third.   Even if we are able to demonstrate that the expansion process creates maladjustments in the structure of production, it remains to show how difficulties which affect a part of the industrial system are generalised and spread over the whole economy so that a partial breakdown brings about a general contraction.   The problem is the same, whether the maladjustment has arisen independently or been brought about by the expansion itself.   (There may, however, be a quantitative difference to the extent that maladjustments due to the expansion may be assumed to be especially serious.)

Until all the three groups of problems and possibilities distinguished in the text are clearly recognised and analysed, we cannot hope to build up a theoretical structure which will do justice to the manifold complexities we meet with in real life.

another. If we have explained how it brings about a decrease in aggregate demand, then we may rely for the further explanation on the cumulative forces of contraction as analysed in the preceding section.

We start by discussing the simpler cases where we have from the very beginning a decrease in the aggregate demand for goods due to a decrease in the supply of investible funds.

Deflation by Governments or banks. If a Government decides to deflate (that is, to retain a part of its revenue from taxation or other sources), the situation is quite clear; but this occurs only in very exceptional circumstances. A case of greater practical importance is that of a restrictive credit policy undertaken by the central bank of a country. It is not difficult to find examples in financial history. The motive is usually to stop an internal drain on reserves or to restore external equilibrium. The latter may be threatened by a great variety of causes. Prices in general may be too high in respect to prices abroad, because of an expansion at home or a devaluation or deflation abroad. A flight of capital or a cessation in the inflow of capital may have occurred. The loss of foreign markets due to a rise in tariffs or to some other reason (*e.g.*, the rise of a foreign competitor) may have rendered the international balance of payments unfavourable. A bad harvest in an important crop may reduce exports or necessitate increased imports.

Without being forced either by the external situation or an internal drain on its cash resources, the central bank may contract credit because it fears the consequences of a prolonged expansion, no matter whether these apprehensions are justified or not.

The commercial banks may contract credit for similar reasons on their own initiative without being forced or warned by the central bank.

The catalogue of possible cases might be lengthened. Each of the cases mentioned might be analysed in greater detail and minor variations might be distinguished. But, at this stage, it may be sufficient to say what is true of all cases equally—namely, that a tightening of the supply of funds by the monetary authorities has a depressing influence and is capable, if strong enough, of interrupting an expansion and of ushering in a contraction.

This explanation will frequently be adequate to explain why a process of expansion has been slowed down or turned into a contraction in a particular country at a particular point of time. It is not, however, a sufficient answer in all cases—other interrupting forces will be discussed presently—and, even if in a particular case a restriction of the money supply can be shown to have brought an expansion to an end, it does not follow that the expansion could have continued very long had the restrictive measures not been taken. This point will be discussed in § 5.

All these cases turn on a tightening of the supply of funds. The proximate cause of the contraction is a decrease in the supply of funds, while, in the cases to be analysed next, the demand for investible funds falls and ushers in a cumulative process of contraction. (As soon as this process has once got under way, contraction of demand and of supply interact and reinforce one another in a cumulative fashion as already shown.)

Consequences of a partial breakdown. We have now to discuss whether a disturbance occurring in a particular branch of industry can give rise to a general contraction and, if so, how. Suppose that, in an individual industry (say motor-car production), a number of firms are forced to curtail output or to cease operating altogether.

The causes and attendant circumstances of such a partial breakdown of an industry may be very different in different cases, so that it is impossible, without a number of specific assumptions, to say anything definite as to its probable consequences. The causes of the breakdown may be such as to exercise stimulating influences in some other direction in addition to the immediate depressing influences to which they give rise, so that the two tendencies may conceivably cancel out. This would be the case, *e.g.*, if the breakdown was caused by an unexpected shift in demand. Then we might have an increase in demand for commodity A and a decrease in demand for B. That which depresses industry B stimulates industry A. Even in this case it does not necessarily follow that the two influences offset one another in so far as the effect on total demand is concerned.[1] Moreover, in other cases

---

[1] See Chapter 3, § 24, above.

arising from different causes, there is no such instantaneous and automatic increase in demand at all, as we shall see presently.

We shall discuss first the probable influences on total demand of such a partial breakdown under different circumstances irrespective of automatic counter-influences set up by the cause which brought about the breakdown. Afterwards we shall enquire about the latter.

A reduction in the level of output of a particular industry will reduce the earnings of the factors employed : the wage-bill will diminish : and this will cause some decrease in the demand for wage goods. If sales go on for a while in the process of liquidating stocks, the proceeds may be used for repaying bank loans and other debts instead of being reinvested in the purchase of labour, materials, etc—and this will have a deflationary effect.

We have furthermore to consider the repercussions on the subsidiary industries. The magnitude of these repercussions will depend on a number of circumstances. It will be greater if the reduction in output occurs unexpectedly than if it has been foreseen. If the industry in question has been expanding for some time and a further expansion has been anticipated, a corresponding expansion in the subsidiary industry may come to a sudden end and the repercussions may be very serious. The conditions may vary in detail, international complications may come into the picture—*e.g.*, the industries furnishing raw materials and other means of production may be located in another country than the industries using them—and thus many cases with quantitatively different reactions and repercussions are conceivable. In any case, however, there is a clear tendency towards a reduction in the flow of money, a fall in total demand.

This tendency will be intensified if the firms involved happen to be heavily indebted to the banks. If a bank gets into difficulties and proceeds to contract credit, we have a clear deflationary move : we may refer to what has been said on earlier pages for an explanation of the consequences. But, even if no bank is so seriously involved that it is forced to liquidate credit, difficulties of an important industry or of particular big firms may be taken as a warning signal for caution and may make the banks more reluctant to grant or renew loans.

So much for the consequences of such a partial breakdown irrespective of the causes by which it was brought about. Now we turn to the latter and consider whether they are likely to set up stimulating counter-tendencies.

The curtailment in output of a particular industry may be due either to a decrease in demand or to an increase in cost. If a decrease in demand is the consequence of a deflationary move, we obviously cannot expect to find an offsetting increase in demand elsewhere. There is then no opposing force to the deflationary influences spreading from the breakdown in the industry concerned. But this case is ruled out in the present instance, because what we are seeking to explain is how a reduction in the total flow of purchasing power can be brought about by a disturbance which neither in itself involves nor results from such a reduction. If contraction is already under way, it is (as we have seen) comparatively easy to explain how it develops further.

If a decrease in demand for commodity A is due to a shift in demand to commodity B, then we have a decrease and an increase at the same time, and it depends on a number of circumstances which have been discussed in connection with the acceleration principle of derived demand[1] whether on balance it works out as an increase or decrease in total demand. In the absence of further indications, we may classify this case as neutral.

Suppose, however, that a fall in production has been brought about by the producers' being disappointed in their expectations about demand. Production has been begun or expanded in anticipation of a certain increase in demand. If this demand is not forthcoming, or if the expectations are revised in a downward direction, a resulting fall in production will not—except by chance—be offset in its influence on the flow of money by a simultaneous increase in demand somewhere else. This would seem to be a very important case : it will be specially apt to arise during the upswing of the cycle, when production is being carried in various directions into unknown territory.

---

[1] See Chapter 3, § 24, above.

It may be argued that a decrease of investment
Delayed   in a number of branches of industry will liberate
reaction of   investment funds, reduce the rate of interest, and
investment.   thus provide an incentive to invest the funds somewhere else. But this is unlikely to happen all at once.
Even in the most favourable case, where no business failures result
from the cessation of investment and no banks are affected so that
no special inducement to hoard is produced, there will usually be a
delay between the new funds' becoming available and their use for
new investment. Investment plans are not always prepared in
advance, so that they can be put into operation at short notice
when the situation changes. They must be planned; and, even
when they are planned, a certain amount of preparatory work is
usually required before orders are given and the money is actually
spent. Therefore, a temporary hold-up in the flow of money is
an eminently probable contingency.

The same is true where a shift in demand is such that the increase
is to the advantage of foreign goods, while the decrease is to the
disadvantage of home industries.

We turn now to the case where the curtailment
Rise in cost of output is due to an increase in cost items. If the
as cause   capital cost, that is the rate of interest, rises because
of a partial the banks are forced to restrict credit or because
breakdown.   capital goes abroad, the situation is clear. Here
the rise in cost is the *modus operandi* of a contraction
in the supply of funds and the reduction in output caused thereby
will intensify the contraction. There are, in this case, no automatic
and instantaneous offsets provided by the crircumstance (viz.,
the rise in cost) which is responsible for the reduction in output.

Nor, again, is there any direct offset in the important case where
the increase in cost is due to public intervention or to the monopolistic action of the owners or producers of one of the means of
production. Suppose that wages are being raised by trade-union
action or by Government decree and that this rise in cost leads
to a reduction in output. In this case, no offset is provided against
the deflationary influences set up by the reduction in output.

The same will usually be true where the price of a raw material or
semi-finished good is raised by the producers' monopolistic action.

A somewhat different situation arises where the rise in cost of industry A is due to increased competition for the means of production by other industries. Then a compensatory change is provided in the shape of the increased production of the other industries.

Conclusion. This discussion leaves us with the conclusion that a breakdown in an individual industry may very well cause at least a temporary fall in total demand below the level at which it would otherwise stand. Whether this will start a cumulative process of contraction or not depends, first, on the magnitude of the disturbance and secondly on the general situation. If a general expansion is going on which has not yet exhausted its force, such a disturbance may be overcome, provided it is not too strong. If, however, the expansion has already lost its *élan*, the economic system will be vulnerable and may easily be plunged into a process of general contraction. This point we propose to consider in the following section.

Static theory and the cumulative process. A word may be said as to the relation of this analysis of the probable consequences of partial disturbances to the familiar analysis of the same events on the basis of static equilibrium theory. According to the latter, a reduction of output and employment in a particular industry liberates forces which tend to restore equilibrium : wages should fall, and this should make for re-employment of the dismissed workers. Of course, wages may be kept up and the mobility of the workers may be defective—in which case unemployment may persist for a long time. But this need not cause a general contraction. On the other hand, if the process of investment in a particular industry is interrupted or scaled down, because expectations about the future demand have been revised in a downward direction (for any reason whatever), funds which otherwise would have been invested in the industry in question are set free : the rate of interest should fall, and this should induce investment somewhere else.

The tacit assumption underlying this reasoning, in so far as it applies to a monetary economy at all, is that the total flow of money, MV, is not reduced—so that on this assumption it is impossible to explain why such a partial disturbance should lead to a general contraction. Our analysis has shown that the static theory is inadequate. It describes (as it were) an ideal case which may occur, but only under particular favourable circumstances. In the probable event of a hold-up—even a temporary hold-up—in the total stream of purchasing power, the forces of contraction may drive the economy farther away from equilibrium; and the equilibrating tendencies may not have time to come into play or, if they do come into play, may not be strong enough to restore equilibrium, since the disturbance of the latter will have been still further increased in the meantime. What is treated in the static theory as an instantaneous adjustment may be a long-drawn-out and painful process of contraction. It may occupy the whole period of the downswing of a business cycle, during which the whole situation may undergo far-reaching changes, so that the equilibrium eventually attained will in all probability differ considerably from the equilibrium which in more favourable circumstances might have been reached, if not at once, at any rate soon after the occurrence of the disturbance.

§ 4. WHY THE ECONOMIC SYSTEM BECOMES LESS AND LESS CAPABLE OF WITHSTANDING DEFLATIONARY SHOCKS AFTER AN EXPANSION HAS PROGRESSED BEYOND A CERTAIN POINT

Why the expansion tails off. We have seen that an expansion is in its first phase of a somewhat precarious nature, so that it is liable to be reversed by an accidental disturbance. If it has a chance to develop undisturbed for a while, it is likely to gather momentum and then becomes, to a certain extent, immune against disturbances, such as those analysed in the preceding section, which tend to reduce total demand and bring about a general contraction. This immunity is the result of the fact that total demand is increasing so fast that an adverse influence, which in other circumstances would have initiated a contraction process, does not lead to an absolute fall of total demand, but only to a slowing-down of the upward movement. Expectations are not yet excessively optimistic and are again and again surpassed by results. We must now enquire why the movement should necessarily slow down after a while and eventually come to a standstill, so that there is a growing danger that a contraction process may be started by some chance disturbance, such as is at any time liable to occur.

Inelasticity of money supply. The two most essential conditions for the smooth progress of an expansion are, broadly speaking, an elastic supply of money and an elastic supply of means of production. Both conditions are essential. If either is lacking, the situation becomes precarious. Suppose that the money supply is inelastic in the upward direction (with or without full employment of the means of production—that is to say, with or without perfect inelasticity of the supply of means of production). By an inelastic money supply we mean in this connection that an increase in the demand for investible funds evokes no further increase—or only a small increase—in the total supply of money (*i.e.*, of MV, which is another expression for the aggregate demand for goods) and exhausts its effect instead in a rise in the rates of interest. It must not be assumed, however, that the supply of money is equally inelastic in a downward direction —that is, that a decrease in demand will produce at once a sharp fall in the rate of interest so as to stabilise MV. If, in such a situation, a partial disturbance arises of the sort analysed in the preceding section, tending to produce a hold-up in the stream of money, we get an absolute decrease in MV (not only a decrease in the rate of increase), which may easily engender a general contraction.

In a general way, it is evident—we shall come back to this point —that, under almost any monetary organisation with which we are acquainted, a continuous expansion will in practice lead sooner or later to a growing inelasticity in the money supply. The potentialities of monetary expansion which were stored up during the preceding depression are gradually exhausted—not to speak of restrictive counter-tendencies, to which we shall refer in the next section.

Inelasticity of supply of means of production. Let us turn now to the other requisite for a smooth development of the expansion—viz., a fairly elastic supply of means of production. Here, again, it is the elasticity in an upward direction— capacity for extension—which is in question. The supply of labour, at least, is presumed to remain extremely elastic in a downward direction : that is to say, a fall in demand does not lead to a heavy fall in wages in such a way as to stabilise employment. Elasticity of supply in the downward direction, coupled with inelasticity in the upward direction, is equivalent to a downward rigidity and an upward flexibility in wages. It is of the very essence of the expansion that it leads to fuller employment and that the supply of the means of production becomes less and less elastic in the upward direction. An increase in demand leads rather to a rise in wages than to an increase in supply and employment. Unfortunately, this lack of elasticity in the labour supply, which is a desirable thing in so far as it is due to increasing employment and to the exhaustion of the reserve of unemployed, has (as will be explained presently) the same effect as an inelastic money supply in that it makes the economic system less resistant to the impact of deflationary forces. The situation is the more serious in that—unlike an inelastic money supply—it cannot be remedied by purely institutional (*i.e.*, monetary) reforms.

Take first an extreme case. Suppose there is full employment of all factors of production. The money stream, MV, must then remain constant in face of the forces making for expansion—except to the extent to which the natural increase in the supply of factors (population growth) and in their efficiency (technological progress) permits of an increase in output—or else prices must rise and an outright inflation develop. If the latter happens, it is easy to see why the position is untenable, why the rise in prices will become progressive and will lead sooner or later to a breakdown.[1] If, on the other hand, MV is kept constant, in spite of the rise in the demand for funds, equilibrium may be preserved; but (as has been explained above) the system is then very sensitive to deflationary shocks and may easily be plunged by some accident into a spiral of contraction.

These considerations make it clear that, under full employment, a given deflationary shock is more likely to entail a general

---

[1] This statement might, perhaps, be somewhat modified : a slow rise in prices may perhaps be maintained for a long time without degenerating into a headlong inflation. This qualification does not, however, substantially affect the argument.

contraction than if the supply of labour and other factors of production is elastic. In addition, it can be demonstrated that certain events which necessitate a shift in production will cause more serious disturbances, and are therefore more likely to produce a deflationary shock, under conditions of full employment than when the aggregate supply of factors of production, and therefore the supply of finished goods in general, is capable of expansion.

Shift in demand with rigid factor supply. Suppose, for example, there is a shift in demand. The demand for commodity A increases and that for B decreases. An increase in the production of A must, under full employment, have an unfavourable effect on the cost of production in other industries. Since the factors are not perfectly mobile and interchangeable, we cannot assume (except in very special circumstances) that this pressure on other industries is at once relieved by the liberation of factors of production in industry B.

This case can be generalised. Anything that necessitates an increase of production in one industry will affect other industries adversely by raising their cost of production. Under full employment, one industry can expand production only at the expense of a contraction of output in other industries, whereas, under conditions of elastic supply of means of production in general, any one industry can to a certain extent expand production without raising costs to other industrie, simply by drawing on the existing reserves of unemployed labour and idle resources.

Sectional inelasticity of supply of labour. We have so far contrasted the two extremes— full employment on the one hand and perfectly elastic supply of all factors (and therefore with a certain time-lag of finished goods) on the other hand. What we find in reality is, of course, always an intermediate state. Even at the bottom of a severe depression, the supply of factors and of finished goods is not perfectly elastic, while at the height of the boom there is never absolutely full employment. Technologically speaking, there is almost always scope for increasing total production to a certain extent by drawing into employment hitherto unemployed factors, provided we assume sufficient mobility of the means of production.

But this does not by any means invalidate the argument, since it is sufficient to assume that, during the course of the upswing, the supply becomes less and less elastic, even if it does not start from the one extreme or ever fully attain the other.

This leads to a very important conclusion. The sensitiveness of the economic system to deflationary shocks will become great long before completely full employment has been reached. The reason is that the existence of a level of unemployment which might at first sight appear relatively high can by no means be taken as a safe indication of great elasticity of the supply of factors of production or of output in general. In other words, the mere fact that there is still much unemployment does not justify the conclusion that an increase in the total demand for goods in terms of money will elicit an increase in output and employment almost proportional to the increase in demand coupled with a comparatively slight rise of prices in general.[1]

The appearance of " bottle- necks ". The unemployed workers of a country as registered by the statistics at any particular moment are not a homogeneous reserve army from which each industry can draw the men needed with the required qualities at the prevailing wage rates. The total of unemployed is made up of unemployables, men of inferior quality, unskilled and skilled workers. Many of them, especially of the last group, are specialised for a certain type of work; and all of them are attached to a certain locality and cannot be easily moved to another part of the country. The existence of a large total does not in the least preclude the possibility of a shortage of labour in many special fields. When employment expands, there is naturally a tendency to re-employ first the better men; and the farther the expansion progresses, the greater the obstacle to general advance represented by the scarcity in particular lines. The same holds true, *mutatis mutandis*, for other means of production. " Bottle-necks " develop in the structure of industry at various points, with the result that, if monetary

---

[1] On these and the following considerations, compare L. M. Lachmann, " Investment and Cost of Production " in *American Economic Review*, Vol. 48, September 1938, pages 469-481 *passim*.

expansion continues and total demand increases, it is to an increasing extent prices rather than output or employment which rise.

In such a situation, it is clearly misleading to speak of elasticity of supply or output as a whole, or of elasticity of labour or factors of production in general, and to measure it by the total figures of unemployment or by some average over the whole industry of the technically possible increase of output. The elasticity of supply is not uniform : it depends very much on the path which expansion tends to follow. In other words, it depends on the increase in total demand and the distribution of the given increase in demand among the various products. If, in the course of the expansion, demand increases for the product of those industries where a large part of unemployment and over-capacity is concentrated, the elasticity of supply and employment will be greater than in the case when demand tends to flow into channels where there are no unemployed factors. In the latter case, a given increase in demand will lead to a rise in cost and prices, and the favoured industries may draw away factors of production from those industries where demand has not risen.[1] It follows that it is quite

---

[1] A striking illustration is provided by the situation in Germany during the years 1933-1935, which is described in *Die Wirtschaftskurve*, herausgegeben unter Mitwirkung der Frankfurter Zeitung (Heft III 1933/36, February 1936, pages 237-239) in a passage which may be summarised as follows :

Credit expansion in the form of notes and deposits took place in Germany in the years 1933 and 1934, though it was in part offset by the continuance of hoarding and debt repayment. At the time, however, the economy was just recovering from a deep depression ; and raw materials, plant capacity and labour were available in abundance. Owing to the elasticity of supply in all branches of industrial production, the additional purchasing power was fully compensated by a rise in production with scarcely any rise in prices.

In 1935, on the other hand, owing to the rapid recovery—and, in part also, to the foreign trade difficulties—shortage of raw materials developed in certain directions : stocks diminished : and here and there plant capacity was exhausted, and even the labour supply ran short. The elasticity of supply having thus declined, expansion became possible only at increasing cost; and, the writer considers, the limits of compensatory credit expansion were reached.

It is true that the industries producing for consumption hung behind the investment-goods industries to a greater degree than in any previous upswings ; and it was only in the latter that there was any evidence of approaching exhaustion of the forces of expansion. Conceivably, the

wrong to think that there is no danger of a rapid rise in prices from an expansion so long as there is considerable unemployment.

Conclusion.   We may sum up the findings of this section as follows.   During the course of an expansion which has started from the depth of a depression, the economic system becomes the more vulnerable the nearer full employment is approached.   That is to say, on the one hand the system becomes more sensitive to deflationary shocks, and on the other hand the deflationary possibilities of certain changes become accentuated.

§ 5.   DISTURBANCES CREATED BY THE PROCESS
OF EXPANSION ITSELF

Organic   Having now shown that, with the progress of
maladjustment.   expansion, the economic system becomes more and
more sensitive to deflationary shocks, and that certain changes in demand and production which may occur at any time become more and more liable to produce on balance a deflationary rather than an inflationary effect, we proceed to enquire into the likelihood of the expansion itself (or certain more or less regular features of the expansion process) giving rise to serious maladjustments in the body economic which operate as starters and intensifying factors of a cumulative process of contraction.   The analysis of existing theories of the cycle has furnished a number of hypotheses.   Few of these seem to be definitely wrong or *a priori* impossible.   What is unsatisfactory, however, is the exclusiveness with which many writers proclaim one or other of these hypotheses as the only possible solution.   Our task therefore will consist in setting out in a

---

expansion might have been directed to the consumption industries but for the programme of rearmament, under which Government orders continued to be concentrated on investment-goods industries.   In spite of the possibilities of expansion in the direction of the consumption industries, a continuance of the policy of financing orders for the investment industries by credit expansion would have meant (the writer argues) a transition from compensatory to inflationary credit expansion ; and it was for this reason that increased resort was had to taxation and to the savings of the public for the purposes in question.

logical order the various possibilities and determining their mutual relationship.

We may distinguish two groups of disturbances *Monetary* which may possibly be created by the expansion *versus* itself or, to speak more precisely, may be expected *non-monetary* to arise in the economic system in the course of an *disturbances.* expansion. (1) There may be a mechanism which works in such a way that a monetary expansion is after a while turned into a contraction without the latter being induced by previous loss, or the expectation of loss, in any particular industry. In other words, there may be no difficulty in any particular industry : cost may everywhere be covered by actual and expected selling price ; but there comes a hitch in the flow of money, the total demand for goods falls off, and this gives rise to a cumulative process of contraction. (2) The other and (as we shall see) much more promising hypothesis is that, as a result of the maladjustments in the structure of production which are regarded as inevitable in any expansion, some particular industry or group of industries is forced to curtail output and employment, and thereby start a general contraction in the manner described in § 3 of this chapter.

The first hypothesis may be called a purely monetary explanation of the down-turn, while the second has a non-monetary character. But it is not intended to attach special importance to this terminology.

We begin by discussing the first hypothesis. *The purely* Under any monetary arrangement which implies a *monetary* limitation of the quantity of legal tender money, *explanation* such as the gold standard, there is an upper limit *of the* (gradually approached during the upswing) to the *down-turn.* expansion of MV. This, as we have seen, explains the fact that the economic system becomes more and more sensitive to deflationary shocks. It does not, however, explain why, in the absence of such shocks, an expansion of MV should immediately be followed by a contraction rather than by a period of stability in MV.

Mr. HAWTREY (as was shown in the first part of this book) has endeavoured to establish the existence of a monetary mechanism in which the mere cessation of credit expansion leads to a subsequent contraction. His theory is based on the lag of cash reserves in the banks behind the expansion of credit. The drain of cash continues after the expansion of credit has come to an end. The banks watch only the present position of their cash reserves and do not foresee that these will shrink for a while after credit has ceased to expand. So they are led to expand too long, and later they are forced to contract in order to maintain their reserve proportions.

The theory is not very convincing. It implies that all that is required to forestall the contraction is for the central bank to furnish the commercial banks with the necessary cash to relieve them of the necessity for contracting credit. The discussion of our second hypothesis and of the different cases which it covers will show that this implication is hardly acceptable. Moreover, it is difficult to believe that the banks would not learn from experience, and would repeatedly make the same mistake of underestimating the drain of cash consequent on a given expansion of credit. The following discussion, by showing that the situation at the end of the boom is much too involved to be put straight simply by preventing a contraction in the money supply, will afford an effective criticism of this particular explanation of the down-turn.

Besides the reason given by Mr. HAWTREY, is there any other reason why a hitch in the flow of money should regularly occur in the absence of difficulties in any particular line of production ? It is easy to conceive of all kinds of chance disturbances of a purely monetary or institutional character, arising at home or abroad, which might be capable of inducing hoarding on the part of somebody. But it is difficult to see why this should be a necessary or probable result of an expansion, provided that it is not the consequence of a disturbance in the productive process. The rise in interest rates which we almost invariably observe during the upswing as a result of a rise in the demand for investible funds provides an incentive against hoarding. (High interest rates as such may, of course, be the result of a tendency to hoard. But this is rarely the case in the earlier part of the upswing. The question is only whether such a tendency does not manifest itself in the last phase of the boom.)

Structural mal-adjustments likely.

We turn now to the second group of possible disturbances which the expansion may bring about : viz., maladjustments in the structure of production arising out of the fact that, in some industries, the selling-price of the product falls short of the cost of production or, in other words, that demand is insufficient to take up production at remunerative prices. There is no initial decrease in the total monetary demand for goods—*i.e.,* in the money stream; but the flow of goods does not correspond in all its ramifications to the flow of money and its divisions, and therefore in some lines of production demand does not cover cost. The expectations of some people have been disappointed, which need not be offset by favourable surprises of others.

Prima facie, it is not at all surprising that serious dislocations in the structure of production should make their appearance during the course of a general expansion, when far-reaching changes occur in many parts of the production process. What we find during an expansion are not slight adjustments on the margin of production in this or that industry—in which connection it is safe to disregard indirect repercussions and to assume, if not perfect, at any rate approximately correct, foresight on the part of the producers. On the contrary, we find that far-reaching changes are under way : long-term investment is taking place in many lines : new commodities are being introduced (though the line between the introduction of " new " goods and the improvement of the quality of old ones is very hazy) : goods, the consumption of which was so far confined to the upper classes, are being made accessible for the consumption of the masses : new processes of production are being put into operation : and all these changes must profoundly influence conditions of cost and of demand for any given industry. Consumers are induced to rearrange the system of their expenditure. Relative prices of the various finished products and of half-finished goods and factors of production change.

Is it so astonishing that, under these circumstances, serious maladjustments should develop in the industrial structure as the expansion goes on ? Without as yet being able to specify the exact nature of these maladjustments, it would seem highly improbable that, in a rapidly expanding system, the expansion should proceed smoothly and eventually tail off into an equilibrium state of full employment. [1]

Operation of the acceleration principle.   If we go on to enquire what kind of maladjustments are likely to develop during an expansion, we must remember that an expansion always starts from a position of partial employment of labour and other means of production. For some time, output can and does rise all around—*i.e.* both in consumers' and producers' goods industries—although the rate of increase is not everywhere the same. As has already been pointed out, an expansion could not go on very long if it started from a state of full employment or after it has reached such a state in the course of its progress. Prices would rise rapidly. No industry could expand output except at the cost of a contraction in other industries. That is certainly not the situation we actually find during an upswing. We must put this picture from our minds if we are to view what happens at the end of the boom in the right perspective.

We have seen that an expansion, however it may have been originally set afoot (whether by an initial increase in consumers' or producers' spending, in consumption or in investment), is characterised by a rapid increase in investment. During the preceding depression, repairs, replacement and improvements in all industries which require the investment of capital have been postponed and, so to speak, stored up. Gradually all this latent demand for investment becomes effective and feeds the boom. The expansion in investment generates income and demand for consumers' goods. Consumption industries expand, and this enhances the demand for investment goods. Since there is a reserve of idle factors of production, the process may continue for some time unobstructed.

This is a fact of considerable importance. If a general expansion can proceed a long way smoothly, the acceleration principle of derived demand has time to work itself out. That is to say, a

---

[1] This *prima facie* argument for the likelihood of a serious maladjustment's arising has been especially stressed by Professor Schumpeter.

number of industries will be developed to a level which they can maintain only if other industries (or the system as a whole) go on expanding at a given rate. Quite apart from any limits which may be set by insufficiency of demand or any other cause, this rate of expansion is feasible only so long as there is a fairly elastic supply of unemployed factors of production. This type of maladjustment is not so likely to arise, or at least to develop to the same extent, if an expansion starts from full employment. In that case, it will very soon encounter strong resistance in the shape of steeply rising costs, and it is not likely that any considerable number of industries will be able, by the installation of highly durable equipment, to adapt themselves to a rate of expansion in other industries which it is not possible to maintain. At any rate, the danger of the development of a serious maladjustment in the structure of production is much greater in the case where an unusually rapid expansion all along the line is made possible by the existence of unused resources which are gradually drawn into employment than in the other case where we start from fairly full employment. If a certain industry expands production and hence increases its demand for producers' goods (say, machines), the producers of these machines will hardly jump at once to the assumption that this increased demand will continue to be forthcoming for a very long time. Consequently, they will not at once adopt the most up-to-date capitalistic methods of production requiring the installation of highly durable plant which cannot be amortised except over a considerable period of activity on an enlarged scale. The longer, however, an expansion of production in various directions continues unobstructed, the more optimistic will become the expectations as to its future continuation at the same or an increasing rate. Producers in a number of industries get accustomed to a level of demand which cannot continue for ever : possibly they are led to expect a rising demand, or even rising prices—which are still less likely to be long maintained. It is very improbable, therefore, that the system will be in equilibrium when it approaches the upper limit of the expansion. The mere cessation, or even the slowing-down, of the expansion will produce a serious setback in a number of industries ; and this may very well lead to a general process of contraction in the manner described in § 3 of this chapter.

Effect of credit shortage on derived demand. If this analysis is correct, the following important conclusion seems to be justified. If a general expansion which has been in progress for some time comes to an end for purely monetary reasons, the economic system will very probably find itself in the presence of serious maladjustments in the structure of production, which make it very likely that the expansion will be immediately followed by a contraction rather than by a period of stability. Let us analyse this case more closely. An expansion is going on, so far undisturbed by any maladjustment in the structure of production. There is scope for a further expansion of production since there are still idle factors which can be drawn into employment, and no serious "bottle-necks" have so far developed. There is a sufficient demand for investible funds; the output of the capital-goods industries increases; and so, although at a lower rate, does output in the consumers' goods industries. Now, the monetary authorities put the brake on the expansion of credit because of the international situation of the country or for some other reason. The total demand for goods in terms of money ceases to increase and the expansion comes to an end. It is possible, and even probable, that this cessation in the inflow of new credit will at once produce difficulties in the capital-goods industries, because a number of investment schemes have been started which cannot be completed in the absence of investible funds. But, even if we assume that the difficulty in raising the necessary funds for their completion can somehow be overcome—*e.g.*, by inducing people to provide the necessary capital through increased savings—there remains the other more fundamental difficulty that the scale of output in the capital-goods industries is geared to an expanding production in the consumers' goods industries. If the latter stop expanding, the former lose a part of their market and are compelled to scale down the level of their activity—even where they might be able to raise the necessary sums to carry on at the old level. Clearly, the situation cannot at once be rectified by increased voluntary saving for the reason that the money saved will not, in the situation assumed, find an immediate outlet in new investment.

It should be noted that this disrupting effect of a cessation of monetary expansion is independent of : (*a*) any credit restriction which the banks may be forced to make for the reason given by Mr. HAWTREY; (*b*) the fact that, when *MV* is no longer rising, the economic system becomes sensitive to chance deflationary shocks (as explained in § 4 of this chapter); and (*c*) the fact of a substantial rise in prices having taken place. The setback may occur in a comparatively early phase of the upswing, when supply of factors is still fairly elastic and prices have not perceptibly risen. If prices have gone up for a while and producers in various industries have been led to expect a further rise, the disappointment caused by the cessation of expansion and of the rise in prices will be all the greater; but the rise in prices is not an essential condition.

In this case, the collapse of the boom and the onset of the contraction could be avoided, for the time being, by removing the hindrances to a further expansion of credit. (Whether this is feasible from political, social, or psychological points of view is another question, which we need not discuss here.) But it goes without saying that it does not follow that the boom could go on indefinitely, if only the supply of credit were kept elastic.

Effect of shortage of factors on derived demand. Let us now drop the assumption that the expansion comes to an end prematurely because of an insufficient money supply. Let us suppose that it has a chance to develop without hindrance from the monetary side. What are then the possible and probable outcomes ?

In the previous case, we have assumed that the general expansion of production comes to an end because the increase in the flow of money is more or less suddenly stopped. Suppose now that the check to expansion comes at an advanced stage of the upswing when almost all idle factors, especially labour, have been drawn into employment. On this assumption, the general increase in employment and output must now come to an end (or, more precisely, slow down to the rate which is made possible by population growth, inventions, etc.). If at this point the level of activity in a number of industries is still dependent on the growth of employment and production in other industries— *i.e.*, if replacement demand has not yet picked up by so much as to absorb the whole output of machines [1]—the volume of output will not simply stop expanding and go on at the level which it has reached. It will actually decline in the capital-goods industries, which are geared to the expanding consumers' goods industries. [2]

Evidently, the situation cannot be put straight simply by trying to continue monetary expansion. The total production cannot go on increasing at the rate so far maintained. Some capital-goods industries are adapted to an expansion of the lower stages. Hence there must be some change in the direction of production (or else the production in the capital-goods industries in excess of replacement requirements must be taken on stock—an impossible assumption which we may discard *a limine*). Only a degree of foresight on the part of producers in general which it is too much to expect in the real world could obviate the appearance of such a situation. If it has once arisen, serious repercussions on employment could be forestalled only by a degree of adjustability of producers and mobility of labour which does not exist in reality.

---

[1] This possibility of smooth termination of a growth process has been discussed in the first part of this book (see page 91).

[2] If I understand Mr. Harrod rightly, this is also his diagnosis of the breakdown. " In a revival, consumption grows at a rate that cannot possibly be maintained. At the outset, the slack of human capacity available for work is greater than that of capital equipment, since the former has been maintained and grown at its normal rate during the slump, while the latter has not. After the revival has proceeded a short distance, therefore, the demand for capital goods arising out of the (abnormally high) prospective increase of consumption stands at a level at which it cannot be maintained. The increase of consumption must slow down, once a considerable proportion of the unemployment is taken back into work. Consequently, a point is bound to come at which the volume of orders for additional capital goods which it appears profitable to give is reduced, and this . . . spells a major depression. (*The Trade Cycle*, Oxford, 1936, page 165). The only difference between Mr. Harrod's position in respect to the explanation of the crisis and the one taken in these pages seems to be that Mr. Harrod puts forward the above as the exclusive explanation, whilst here it is treated as one reason among many others—although one which it is especially difficult to avoid.

Shift in production inevitable. Let us now try to compare this situation with those which we have analysed in the first part of this report. Can we classify the situation with which we are now concerned as a case of under-saving or over-saving ? In the first part of this work, we defined a maladjustment due to under-saving (shortage of capital) as one which could be avoided if people would save and invest more and spend less on consumption, and a maladjustment due to over-saving (under-consumption) as one which could be avoided by the opposite procedure. In our present case, there must be some shift in production. If this cannot be achieved, neither more nor less saving on the side of the public can prevent trouble. If such a change in production is possible, the further outcome depends on the direction in which it can technically be achieved with least resistance. If in the capital-goods industries which lose part of their market because the lower stages no longer expand output capacity can be comparatively easily adapted to produce other capital goods, an increase in saving will be conducive to re-establishing equilibrium, because it will enable various industries to adopt more capitalistic methods of production—that is, to increase their demand for capital goods without complementary resources being available.[1] On the other hand, it may be that an adaptation to the production of some sort of consumers' goods could be more easily achieved. In that case, less saving will be better calculated quickly to restore full employment. In both cases, however, it is a question, not only of changing the ratio of spending and saving, but also of consuming the required goods and investing in the required direction.

Thus, as soon as one goes into details, the problem becomes extremely involved : a number of variants have to be distinguished : and it is almost impossible to tell which is the most likely outcome.

---

[1] In Mr. Hawtrey's convenient terminology, we may say that a " deepening " of the capital structure must take the place of the " widening " which has come to an end, when the co-operating unemployed labour resources are becoming exhausted. (*Capital and Employment*, London, 1937, Chapter III.) Whether this can be achieved rapidly is very doubtful. Probably a certain delay will be unavoidable which may easily be sufficient to cause a hold-up in the money stream, which in turn will start a general contraction (as explained in § 3 of this chapter).

It is, however, practically certain that important shifts in production are necessary and that there is no guarantee that they can be effected smoothly. Temporary unemployment is almost inevitable and a certain number of breakdowns and bankruptcies are very likely to occur. Hence the probability that a contraction process will be started would seem to be great.

Where will "bottle-necks" arise ?
We have assumed so far that the expansion proceeds smoothly up to the point where all unemployed factors have found employment and then comes to an end rather abruptly. This is, of course, an extreme case, which will probably not (and need not for our theory to hold) be realised in a pure form. If the expansion does not happen to be directed along " the path of least resistance " as determined by the distribution over various industries of the available resources and their mobility, the situation which we have discussed will arise before all unemployed factors have been absorbed. This will manifest itself in the emergence of " bottle-necks "—that is, in the increasing scarcity of some factors of production leading to a rise in prices of certain commodities and a slowing-down of the expansion in this or that industry.

These bottle-necks may make their first appearance in any part of the economic system. They may first appear in the consumers' goods industries or in the capital-goods industries, or may be distributed in a random fashion over the whole economic system. It is hardly possible to generalise about their probable localisation, which depends—given the distribution of the available resources at the beginning of the expansion—on the direction in which the latter develops. Let us briefly consider the main determining factors. The boom may be concentrated to a higher or smaller degree in the capital-goods industries. In other words, the roundabout ways of production which are undertaken during the upswing may be longer or shorter. Whether they are longer or shorter depends : first, on the rate of interest and the elasticity of supply of investible funds as determined (*a*) by monetary factors (banking policy, supply of investible funds from private hoards, etc.), (*b*) by the public's propensity to save part of their current income and (*c*) to an increasing extent by the budgetary policy of

Governments; secondly, on technological opportunities to invest, the nature of the " new combinations " which have become available, etc.; and, thirdly, on the amount and direction of consumers' demand. Compare, on the one hand, a boom fed and propelled by armament demands and public constructions such as is in progress at the present time in various countries, where the share of the capital-goods industries in the increase of production as a whole is exceptionally great, and, on the other hand, one which relies more on current consumption for private purposes.

Clearly all these circumstances may be such that the physical limits of expansion of production are first reached either in the capital-goods industries or in consumers' goods industries; or the bottle necks may be distributed in any other fashion.

Now, when a number of industries to which others are so geared that their sales vary with the rate of the expansion of the former reach the limit of expansion, a serious setback in the latter is the consequence.

Monopolistic restrictions on supply of factors. If we say that an industry has reached the limits of expansion, we must interpret this in a broad way. It does not mean that it is physically absolutely impossible to increase production; but it means that cost of production rises so much as to make a further increase of production unprofitable.

This rise in cost may be due to the exhaustion of the supply of particular means of production. Complaints about a scarcity of this or that type of skilled labour in this or that industry become frequent in the later phases of any boom. It is, however, clear that this scarcity and the brake which it puts on the expansion of output can be due to other factors than the exhaustion of the reserve of unemployed. Two of these factors may be mentioned (to which we have already had occasion to refer) : viz., a rise in wages due to increased monopolistic pressure by trade unions and an all-round decrease in efficiency.

There is no doubt that the attitude of labour organisations stiffens during the upswing of the cycle. To be sure, money wages will rise even under a regime of perfect competition in the labour market. But it is equally certain that the bargaining position of the trade unions becomes stronger, financially and morally, with rising employment, and that they use it to accelerate the rise in money wages. The power of the labour organisations is also used to reduce the mobility of labour by preventing the entry of newcomers into particular industries, when the reserves of unemployed labour attached to these industries have been absorbed.[1]

Decline in efficiency. Labour cost is further enhanced—in other words, efficiency wages raised—by the fall in efficiency of the workers, which occurs everywhere during the upswing. As was pointed out in Part I (pages 108 *et seq.*), two tendencies must be distinguished. The average output per worker falls, because inferior plant, less-qualified workers and so on are drawn into employment when output expands. This is a consequence of the gradual exhaustion of the supply of idle means of production. We are here, however, concerned with the other tendency : viz., the fall in efficiency of each worker below the previous level for the reasons indicated by Professor MITCHELL.

These tendencies to a rise in money cost may be, and in many cases actually are, compensated or over-compensated by monetary expansion and a rise in prices. But this will again tend to stimulate the demands of organised labour, so that the spiral of rising cost and rising prices will be accelerated.

It is very likely that the attitude of labour and the rise of wages during the upswing will put a brake on the further expansion of employment and output in a number of industries long before the physical limits have been reached. This is especially true when the money supply is beginning to give out for one reason or another—*e.g.*, because the pace of monetary expansion in the country is more rapid than in neighbouring countries. Increasing monopolistic pressure on wages and reduced mobility of labour create an artificial scarcity of labour, as it were, long before the physically available stock of unemployed has been exhausted.

---

[1] Compare, *e.g.*, J. Robinson, *Essays in the Theory of Employment*, London, 1937, Section I. As the author says, " it is idle to attempt to reduce such questions as trade union policy to a cut-and-dried scheme of formal analysis, but it is plausible to say, in a general way, that in any given conditions of the labour market there is a . . . level of employment at which money wages will rise " (page 7).

It goes without saying that the monopolistic restriction of the supply of factors of production other than labour, and the raising of prices other than wages, have the same effect of slowing-down general expansion.

Drop in investment because of insufficient demand.　So far we have discussed the case where the expansion is allowed to develop up to the limit set by the amount and distribution and willingness to work of the available means of production, or where the expansion comes to a halt because of an insufficiency of the money supply. We have seen that it is very likely that serious maladjustments will make their appearance when the general expansion comes to a standstill for the reasons indicated, or even when it slows down to a certain extent.

We have now to enquire whether there is not a strong probability that the expansion will be interrupted at an earlier stage for the reason that it generates a type of maladjustment other than that which we have discussed, before it reaches the limits in question. The type of maladjustment which we have in mind is an insufficient demand either for consumers' goods in general, or for certain types of them, or for certain types of capital goods. It is that type of maladjustment which Professor ROBERTSON ascribes to the temporary " gluttability of wants ", or which Professor PIGOU has in mind when he says that the optimistic forecasts which have been made during the boom, and have materialised in heavy investments in different lines of industry, are brought " to the test of facts "—and, by that test, are found wanting—after the close of the gestation period for a number of things the production of which was started during the upswing. A maladjustment of this sort is also what Professor SCHUMPETER has in mind in his explanation of the collapse of the boom.

The idea is that the investment activity which takes place during the upswing is to a large extent concentrated in particular lines of industry—railway construction, automobile production, electrical machinery, etc. Then comes a day when the investment opportunities in these fields are exhausted; the want—or, rather the demand—is satisfied. Investment in these lines must come to an end. There is no guarantee at all that replacement demand will meanwhile have risen to such an extent as to enable it to keep the whole productive apparatus busy.

Repercussions or   When this point of saturation has come, suddenly *not foreseen* the gradually, there are several possibilities as to *by producers.* the outcome. The industries directly concerned may have correctly foreseen that demand is no longer going to rise, and may even fall, and may have adjusted their output so that they are not involved in difficulties. Alternatively, they may be taken by surprise : the " competitive illusion ", undue optimism, or any other reason may have led to an over-expansion of the particular industries concerned.

In the second case the boom will explode with a more or less strong " detonation " of bankruptcy, to use an expression of Professor PIGOU; and (as has already been shown in previous sections) it is easy to explain when and why this will lead to a general depression. In the first case, no such detonation occurs in the industries directly concerned. They simply reduce output and employment. But it is very likely that some tributary industries which supply raw materials or equipment will be taken by surprise, since it is unreasonable to suppose that all producers—including those who are removed by one or two stages from the point where the initial setback occurs—will foresee correctly what is about to happen at this point and what its repercussions on other industries will be. Moreover, there are always the unfavourable repercussions on the consumption industries which are still less likely to be foreseen by the producers. If output and employment fall at any point, the demand for consumers' goods is bound to suffer; and this then reacts on the higher stages of production. If the primary satiation of demand in some lines and the consequent drop in output have occurred, these repercussions on the consumption trades are almost unavoidable. They could be avoided only under perfect mobility of factors and a smooth working of the capital market; and (as has been already explained in detail) neither of these two conditions is likely to be fulfilled. We cannot assume that the sums which are liberated by a decline or cessation of investment in certain.lines will automatically and instantaneously find an outlet in other lines of investment. It is more than probable that at least a certain lag will occur, which will be quite enough to allow the deflationary tendencies to come into operation through the agency of a fall in the demand for consumers' goods and other developments.

There is no need to repeat our explanation of how these deflationary effects arising at any particular points may be compensated by inflationary tendencies in other directions. Such a development is not unlikely in the first part of the upswing, when the momentum of the expansion has not yet been lost, because investment is still going on or is being started in a number of directions. But, as has been explained earlier, this partial immunity against deflationary shocks must sooner or later give way to a state of greater vulnerability. If at that stage such a maladjustment as is described above should occur, it may easily lead to a general contraction.

But, to return to the nature of the first impact *This type of* with which we are here concerned, is it possible *maladjustment* to say generally that such maladjustments are bound *inevitable?* to occur during any expansion, or are likely to occur, or the contrary? It would seem that theoretical reasoning, backed by a limited amount of actual experience of broad tendencies, is not sufficient to prove rigorously either that such maladjustments are the absolutely inevitable outcome of any expansion or the reverse. We can only say there is a *prima-facie* probability that they are. We can figure out the consequences approximately—always again in terms of possibilities and probabilities : but only extensive empirical studies can show whether the contention of so many well-known writers is correct, and it is actually a fact that processes of expansion regularly develop a certain type of maladjustment and in turn are brought to an end by them.

Recently, Mr. N. KALDOR, in an interesting article,[1] adopted a very similar position and tried to classify the probable reasons of

---

[1] " Stability and Full Employment ", in *Economic Journal*, Vol. XLVIII, December 1938, pages 642 *et seq.* The author starts from the assumption that while it is not so difficult to say how a depression can be ended and to engineer a boom, it is still an open question how a state of fairly full employment can be maintained. It is the latter problem which he deals with.

the breakdown of a boom along similar lines as in the preceding pages, with some variations in detail (mainly of a terminological nature). He attempts to put them in the order in which they are likely to appear successively in time, and likens the boom to a peculiar steeplechase where the horse has to overcome a series of hurdles and is almost certain to fall at one of the obstacles.

B. *The Up-turn : Revival*

§ 6. INTRODUCTION

We have now to answer the question what the limits of a cumulative contraction process may be, and how it can be brought to an end. How is the downswing usually stopped and reversed ? In many respects, we need only adapt the assumptions and arguments adduced when we discussed the opposite problem : viz., that of the down-turn. Without pressing this parallelism too far, we may proceed in the same order which we adopted there.

The order of the argument.

In § 7, as a first step, we shall discuss the inflationary counterparts of the deflationary shocks analysed in § 3 of this chapter. We assume the occurrence of certain changes—such, for example, as an inflationary move on the part of the monetary authorities or anybody else, or a favourable turn confined to a particular industry—and investigate how this may bring about a general expansion. We leave open for the moment the question whether such changes are more likely to occur in any one phase of the cycle—*e.g.*, the latter part of the depression, rather than in any other.

In § 8, as a second step, we shall show why, after a contraction has continued for a time, the economic system becomes more and more sensitive to stimulating influences, in the same way as with the progress of an expansion it becomes more and more exposed to deflationary shocks.

In § 9, as a third step, we shall discuss those favourable reactions and stimulating influences which are likely to be brought about in the economic system after a contraction has gone on for some time.

The logical relation between the second and third steps may also be stated as follows. A process of contraction is likely in the course of time to exhaust its strength and lose its momentum.

The downward movement may then be easily reversed by any such favourable stimulus affecting a particular industry as is bound to occur from time to time. The same stimuli will not so easily start an upward movement, if they occur at an earlier moment, when the contraction has not yet spent its force.

Besides thus paving the way for the expansionary influence of some chance event, the contraction is also likely itself to give rise to inflationary stimuli. We shall see that it is sometimes difficult to draw the line between the two types of stimulating shock : that is to say, it is not always easy to decide whether a certain event, which actually played the rôle of the starter for an expansion, would have arisen in the absence of the previous contraction. Neither the validity, however, nor the usefulness of our distinction is destroyed by the existence of doubtful cases.

§ 7. THE PROXIMATE CAUSES OF REVIVAL

Asymmetry between turning-points. An expansion can always be stopped and a contraction process started by a restriction of credit by the banks. A contraction, however, cannot always be ended promptly merely by making credit cheap and plentiful. There will always be a rate of interest high enough to discourage even the most eager borrower; but, when prices and demand are falling and are expected to fall further, the demand for investible funds may be at so low an ebb that there is no rate (short of a negative figure) which will lead to a revival of investment and entail an increase in the effective circulation of money—that is, in the total demand for goods in terms of money per unit of time. There is thus a certain asymmetry between the upper and the lower turning-points which necessitates some departures in the method of exposition from that adopted in the corresponding section on the down-turn.

Producers' spending. We shall now attempt to set out the various possibilities and factors involved in an orderly and systematic fashion on the basis of our demand-and-supply schema for investible funds.

An expansion can be brought about by an increase in the expenditures either of producers or of consumers. In the further course of the upswing, each type of expenditure stimulates the other : but here we are concerned with the initiating forces. First we propose to discuss the possibilities of an increase in producers' spending—that is, of a revival in investment as the starter of an expansion.

A stimulus to investment can come either from a change on the demand side or, if there is still a latent demand for investible funds—latent, *i.e.* not effective, because the ruling rate of interest is too high—from a change on the supply side. Anything that has the effect (other things, including the demand for consumption goods, being equal) of shifting the demand curve or the supply curve to the right tends to bring about an expansion.[1]

Let us now discuss in turn those factors which affect supply and those which affect demand.[2]

Factors increasing supply of investible funds.　If the demand for investible funds is really so inelastic over a certain range that a change in the interest rate has no influence at all on the amount of money invested (that is to say, if the demand curve is a vertical straight line), a change on the supply side will make no difference to investment or to the effective quantity of money. This is, however, not the rule, even at the bottom of a depression. It may be the case for certain types of credit—*e.g.*, short-term

---

[1] In the Wicksellian terminology, anything that tends to raise the equilibrium or natural rate and/or to depress the money or market rate of interest has an expansionary influence. In Mr. Keynes' terminology we have to express the expansionary factors as an increase of the propensity to consume ; or as a shift to the right of the schedule of marginal efficiency of capital, both associated with an elastic schedule of liquidity preference proper (elasticity greater than zero) ; or as a downward shift of the liquidity-preference schedule. (See Chapter 8, §§ 3, 4, 5, above.)

[2] The distinction between factors affecting the demand for, and factors affecting the supply of, investible funds, although useful, should not blind us to the fact that there are many measures and events which obviously affect *both* demand *and* supply—*e.g.*, the imposition of a tariff. (Compare, on this particular case, Chapter 12.) Certain forces and motives, which we describe as general optimism or pessimism, work on the mind of both the borrower and lender, and thus influence both supply and demand. If a firm has idle funds at its disposal—*e.g.*, in the shape of demand deposits—and the question is whether it should use them for expanding production or not, it is borrower and lender at the same time, so that demand and supply are in the same hands.

loans : but usually there will be some latent demand which could be satisfied if the terms of credit for the particular purpose were less onerous. This is especially true of long-term credit and the branches of production financed thereby, notably the constructional trades. The demand for private houses is especially sensitive to the rate of interest on long-term loans, and shows a tendency to rise in the depression, when interest rates are low, in spite of the shrinkage of incomes. It is sometimes found, however, that the public evinces a reluctance to lend for long periods at times when short-term money is cheap. The reason for this is lack of confidence in general—*i.e.*, the fear of risks of every sort.[1] Modern economists are accustomed to describe this state of affairs by saying that the liquidity premium is high or the liquidity preferences are strong. It requires a large differential between long-term and short-term rates to induce people to part with their liquidity by investing for a longer period rather than for a short one.

Given, then, the state of demand for loans of various types and maturities, we may say that anything which makes supply more plentiful tends to initiate an expansion. We cannot give here a complete catalogue of all factors which might conceivably have an influence in this direction. One of the most important influences is that of the central and commercial banks, whether exercised through discount policy with a view to increasing the liquidity of the short-term (money) market or through open-market operations which affect primarily the long-term market. There are, however,

---

[1] In Chapter 8, § 3, page 220, it has been said that, according to Mr. Keynes (whose views have been strongly endorsed by Mr. Kaldor—*Economica*, December 1938, page 464, footnote [1]), only the expectation (risk) that the long-term rate of interest may rise (*i.e.*, that bond prices may fall) can explain the short-term rate remaining for any length of time much lower than the long rate. It would seem, however, that other kinds of risks and apprehensions may very well produce the same result. If people anticipate war, inflation, social upheavals or something similar, in a somewhat distant future without entertaining any particular view about the current interest rate, then they will be reluctant to buy long-dated bonds except at a low price (high current yield), because they will feel uncertain about the solvency of the debtor or the possibility of collecting the debt and of disposing of the receipts, though they may still buy short-dated debts at low interest rates. It would seem that these kinds of risk usually constitute much more powerful motives than mere expectation or uncertainty about the future course of interest rates.

technical difficulties in extending such a policy, at least so far as the central banks are concerned, to other than Government securities. Apart from the initiative of the banks, anything that removes risks and strengthens general confidence will have an encouraging effect on the supply of capital.

A change in the international economic situation of a country will often be a prerequisite to any increase in the supply of capital or reduction in the rates of interest. The existence of price discrepancies between countries and the consequent pressure on the balance of payments in the high-cost country frequently block a fall in the interest rates of the latter. The history of the post-war period and of the recent past offers plenty of examples of the various devices which may be employed to eliminate such price differences (*e.g.*, devaluation of the currency), or to prevent them from having an influence on the balance of payments and the internal money market (*e.g.*, rigid exchange control), or to remove the causes for flight of capital from a country or to hinder it effectively. These various measures need not be discussed here in detail.

Increase in demand for investible funds.   We turn now to the discussion of factors exercising a favourable influence on the demand for capital. Whilst it seemed necessary to show by a detailed analysis why a partial disturbance, which primarily affects production only in a particular branch of industry, may under certain circumstances produce a temporary hold-up in the money stream and thus engender a general contraction, it would seem to be more obvious that an event which leads to an increase in production in a particular industry will in most cases also lift the total flow of money to a higher level than it would otherwise attain, if only the money supply is elastic. If in an individual firm or industry output is being expanded, workers must be hired, raw materials bought, machines and other equipment ordered. If for that purpose money is used which would not be used otherwise, the money stream swells and the demand for other goods rises. It is of course immaterial whether new money is created by the banks or idle funds are utilised; in other words, whether the increase in total demand is financed by an increase in M or an increase in V.

Are there no offsetting influences which tend to nullify the expansion in the flow of money, corresponding to those which we have discussed in connection with the problem of the down-turn? In some cases there are; but it would seem that in most there are not.

If an increase in production in industry A is due to a shift in demand, then there is of course a compensatory change in the shape of a decrease in demand and output in industry B. We have already discussed on what circumstances it depends whether a shift in demand will have on balance an inflationary or a deflationary effect.

In many other cases there are no offsetting influences except perhaps in very special circumstances. If a capital-goods industry increases production because equipment must be replaced somewhere, or if an invention is made which necessitates the installation of capital equipment, or if the scale of output is raised somewhere simply because an increase in demand is anticipated, or if cost of production is lowered in a particular industry—*e.g.*, by the reduction of wages or of the price of some means of production, so that the industry is induced to expand production and to disburse more money for labour and means of production—in all these cases there is an immediate increase in the flow of money from the rise in output without offsetting influences coming into play. At any rate, they will not come into play at once (it is always possible, of course, to conceive of complicated attendant circumstances under which compensatory forces might be brought into operation indirectly). Any such change may therefore act as a starter for an expansion.

A general reduction in wages over the whole industry, on the other hand, is a doubtful case which we shall discuss laters (§ 9 below).

The imposition of a tariff will usually stimulate capital investment in the protected trades and thus raise their demand for investible funds. Moreover, the supply of money will be favourably influenced by a reduction in imports, except where there are indirect counter-effects (*e.g.*, retaliation by foreign States).[1]

---

[1] It should be remembered that we are here concerned only with the short-run influences. Many considerations, therefore, which play a considerable part in the literature on international trade do not affect

Reserves of gold and foreign exchange in the banks will be increased as a result of the reduction in imports, and this will tend to ease credit conditions. It should be noted that the two effects which a tariff has on the demand and supply of money are independent of each other. If, for example, durable plant is installed in the protected industries, the influence on the demand for investible funds during the period of construction of the plant may be much greater than the influence on the supply side. Under other conditions, the " indirect " influence on investment through the supply of funds may be more important than the " direct " influence through demand.

Increased consumers' spending. So far, we have discussed factors arising in the sphere of production, prior to a rise in consumers' demand, although leading subsequently to increased consumers' spending. We come now to the other important group of phenomena referred to above which may act as powerful stimuli on investment and on the demand for investible funds : namely, inflationary increases in the demand for consumption purposes.[1] An increase of

---

the argument. In the long run, exports will fall if imports are reduced ; but, in so far as the reduction in exports is not due to retaliatory measures of foreign States, the process must operate through the money mechanism —that is, by contraction in the one, and expansion in the other, country. It is precisely this transitional aspect of the matter which we are analysing. It goes without saying that it is no part of our intention to give a general recommendation to Protection as a policy for overcoming depression. There can be no doubt that the fact that all countries have during the last depression tried to alleviate their own position by protective measures has operated as a most potent intensifying factor for the contraction— in spite of the fact that each country could, to a certain extent, have attained its purpose, if all the others had refrained from doing likewise.

[1] How that has to be expressed in Mr. Keynes' terminology has been discussed in Chapter 8, §§ 3, 4, 5. When people spend from hoards on consumption we have to say that the propensity to consume has become stronger. This implies an increase in aggregate demand (in our terminology, an " inflationary " increase in demand) provided it is assumed that the other determinants of Mr. Keynes' system (the quantity of money, the schedules of marginal efficiency of capital and of liquidity preference, etc.) remain unchanged and that the liquidity-preference schedule proper (demand for idle balances) is perfectly or highly elastic. It may seem simpler to state explicitly that an increase in aggregate demand is assumed.

foreign demand for home-produced goods will have similar effects.

We have seen that an increase in consumers' demand is an indispensable link in the cumulative process of expansion. It is difficult to see a reason why an increase in consumers' spending should not stand at the beginning of such a process. Notwithstanding Professor SPIETHOFF's opinion to the contrary, there can be no doubt that, *ceteris paribus*, a net increase in consumers' demand will not only lead to revival in consumers' goods industries, but will also stimulate investment—always on the assumption that there is an elastic money supply.

A net increase in consumers' spending might conceivably be brought about by acts of dishoarding by private individuals. Precipitate purchasing because of the fear of rising prices is a case in point. This case, however, does not seem to be typical of the process by which revival is set going after a depression. A much more important influence—not so much for the past as for the present and the future—is the increase in consumers' spending deliberately induced by Government action in the shape of public works programmes, increases in ordinary expenditure and relief measures, all financed in such a way as to create a net increase in the total demand. We cannot here go into the numerous and complicated problems of a fiscal, administrative and political nature connected with such schemes. Only this much may be said—that from the short run economic point of view the main task is to finance these works in such a way that they stimulate demand for goods without restricting it in other directions, which would probably be the case if the necessary funds were raised by taxes. In the Anglo-Saxon countries it should furthermore not be forgotten that only a few other countries can borrow huge sums from the market without either making funds scarce for private investors or provoking psychological repercussions which may easily check private investment. Such a situation may be created by an alarming rise in central-bank money, especially in countries such as Germany, where the memory of a hyper-inflation is still fresh. It may be added that the budget deficit created by reduction of Government revenue (*e.g.*, tax remissions) may be just as effective as one created by an increase in expenditure (*e.g.*, public works).

The tax remission method may recommend itself to many people, in as much as it does not involve the danger of a permanent extension of Government activities.[1]

Summary. The upshot of the discussion in this section is that there are many different types of expansionary shocks and influences, each of which can conceivably act as a starter for a general process of expansion. Whether they actually do so or not depends in any given case on the magnitude of the particular change and on the general situation. If a process of contraction is under way, a strong expansionary impetus is required to restrain and reverse it. If the contraction has spent its force, a slight stimulus may be sufficient to start the system on the up-grade.

§ 8. WHY THE ECONOMIC SYSTEM BECOMES MORE AND MORE RESPONSIVE TO EXPANSIONARY STIMULI AFTER THE CONTRACTION HAS PROGRESSED BEYOND A CERTAIN POINT

The contraction loses momentum. We have seen that a process of contraction, if it has had a chance to develop unobstructed for a time, gathers force and becomes too strong to be reversed by expansionary stimuli such as those analysed in the preceding section, except when these are very powerful. This paralysis is the result of the fact that the total demand is shrinking continuously and idle capacity is piling up everywhere, so that a stimulating event which under other circumstances would cause an increase in the total demand is now unable to do more than retard the downward movement : it cannot turn the tide. We shall now enquire why the contraction is likely after a while to lose its strength, with the result that the economic system regains its responsiveness to such expansionary forces as may make themselves felt from time to time.

---

[1] For an exhaustive discussion, see : J. M. Clark, *The Economics of planning Public Works*, Washington, 1935 ; A. D. Gayer, *Public Works in Prosperity and Depression*, National Bureau of Economic Research, New York, 1935 ; E. R. Walker, " Public Works as a Recovery Measure ", in *The Economic Record*, Vol. XI, December 1935.

It has been demonstrated that the economic system during an expansion tends to become increasingly vulnerable when it approaches full employment, first, because the supply of means of production in general and labour in particular becomes more and more inelastic in the upward direction and, secondly, because the expansion of total monetary demand, of MV, must sooner or later slow down or else prices must rise continuously—which again cannot go on for ever. We have now to apply this reasoning to the inverse situation as its develops during a contraction process.

Restored elasticity in supply of factors. There is obviously a tendency for the elasticity of supply of means of production of all kinds, of labour and producers' goods (produced means of production) to become greater the farther a contraction goes. The supply of labour recovers its elasticity in the upward direction : that is to say, an increased demand for labour can again be satisfied at constant, or only slightly rising, wages by abandoning short time or taking on new men. (As has been explained earlier, the supply is elastic in the *downward* direction—*i.e.*, wages are rigid in that direction—even at the height of the boom.) Similarly, monopolistic restriction by entrepreneurs—whether by means of amalgamations, cartellisation, or other methods of organised joint action by producers, or whether it is the result of the lethargy of individual competitors and their fear of " spoiling the market "—often succeeds in maintaining relatively stable prices for certain goods and services right through the contraction. In this way, elasticities are created in the supply of means of production and products at various stages of preparation. An effect similar to that of increasing elasticity of supply may be brought about in the course of the decline by an increase in the quantity of sub-marginal agents of production—land, or industrial plant—which acquire a value and a use as soon as demand revives. The consequence is, as we have already demonstrated elsewhere, that it becomes easier for any one industry to expand production in response to an actual or expected increase in demand for its product, without thereby increasing the cost of production of other industries. In other words, the depressing consequences of certain changes are thereby mitigated, while the expansionary consequences have free play.

Restored elasticity of credit supply. The second prerequisite for an easy start and smooth development of the expansion process—viz., an elastic money and credit supply—is eventually restored in the course of the contraction. As prices fall, the value of central-bank money which is at the base of the credit structure will rise. So long as the structure itself remains undamaged, each tier will be broader-based than before. The gold reserve will cover a larger proportion of the central-bank money; the cash reserve of the banks will rise relatively to their short-term liabilities ; circulating currency and deposits in the hands of the public will rise relatively to the money income which they receive and the capital which they possess. But this process need not be continuous: it may encounter a whole series of setbacks. The mounting debt burdens and the struggle to avoid bankruptcy themselves create a need for ready cash, while bankruptcies and the fear of good debts turning into bad ones give rise to a flight to liquidity which is not satisfied even by increased reserve proportions and rising hoards. If the credit structure gives way spasmodically, we may see an oscillatory movement in which liquidity diminishes and increases several times in the course of the depression. It is, however, only a matter of time till the course to bankruptcy is arrested, and the monetary munition accumulates for a new expansion.

Limits to the fall of MV. But, we must now ask, is there a bottom to the fall of MV, the monetary contraction ? In the corresponding problem of monetary expansion, we were able to show that there is a limit to the rise in MV, beyond which the continuation of the expansion becomes very precarious. The limit in that case was found to be inherent in the tendency of the expansion to produce increasingly a rise in prices, rather than a rise in employment and production, as the state of full employment is approached. Is there a corresponding limit to the fall in MV ? The deflation can, of course, be stopped by any one of the factors making for expansion analysed in the preceding section. (These factors may arise by chance; but, as will be shown in the following section, they may be expected to arise in any case with the lapse of time as a reaction against the contraction process.) Supposing, however, that no such change for the better, strong enough to turn the tide, oc .urs—is there a general reason why the contraction of MV should come to an end ?

Logically it is of course conceivable that, in the absence of an expansionary impulse, the contraction should go on and on indefinitely : but there is good reason, based on general experience of human behaviour, to suppose it will not do so.   In this connection, there is one important consideration which is sometimes overlooked.   A persistent shrinkage in MV—i.e., in the total monetary demand for goods—must be accompanied either by a continued destruction of money or by a continued accumulation of money hoards.   How far the process of destruction will go in a concrete case depends on the monetary organisation, institutional factors and international situation of the country concerned. Nowadays, it is mainly deposit money, rather than central-bank money, which is exposed to destruction.   To what extent the destruction of deposit money goes depends on the organisation of the banking system and to a great extent also on factors which may vary from one depression to the other, such as the methods adopted in handling a panic, the special connections between the banks and the particular industries especially hard hit by the depression, and so on.   The way in which the banking organisation influences the severity of the deflation through money destruction is well illustrated by a comparison between what happened in the United Kingdom with its unified banking system on the one hand and the United States with its thousands of small insolvent banks on the other hand during the depression of 1929 to 1933 as well as in previous cycles.   It is common knowledge what happened : the sole purpose of the preceding remarks is to give the question of the influence of the banking organisation its proper place in our system.

Accumulation of money hoards.   After the destruction of money has come to an end—as sooner or later under any monetary system it must do—continuance of the contraction must be accompanied by a growing accumulation of money hoards in various shapes; liquidity increases, M_2 goes up.   The magnitude of these hoards will increase, as measured in terms of the monetary unit, at the expense of money in circulation : it increases still faster, owing to the fall in prices, in terms of real purchasing power.

These hoards will grow in relation to real income as well as in relation to real wealth.   In other words, people will hold an increasing proportion of their real income and wealth in the liquid form of money.   It should be noted that, so long as people are adding to their hoards—in other words, so long as " the struggle for liquidity " goes on—the rate of interest (on investible funds) will be kept relatively high in spite of the fact that the demand of producers for money for investment purposes is at a low ebb.   Under unfavourable circumstances, such a situation may last a long time : but, as it implies that money hoards are growing all the time in magnitude, we are probably justified, in the light of our general knowledge of economic behaviour, in assuming that there will be a limit to such hoarding.   After liquid resources have reached a certain high proportion of wealth, the need for liquidity will eventually become satisfied and people will stop adding to their hoards.   If the rate of interest remains high, because there is still a demand for credit for purposes of real investment (as will be the case in poor countries rather than in rich communities), hoarders will be tempted to put their funds on the capital markets sooner than if the rate of interest has already fallen to a low level. But, even if the rate is very low, there will come a point when hoards reach such a high proportion of income and wealth that there is no point in increasing them.   One or both of two things will then happen.   Either more money will be lent out on the capital market, with the result that interest rates will be forced down (beginning probably with the short-term rates and ending later with the long-term rates) and investment will revive; or, if the demand of producers for credit is absolutely inelastic, people will become less disposed to save—in Mr. KEYNES' terminology, the propensity to consume will rise in addition to the decrease in the liquidity preference—and the demand for consumers' goods will cease to fall, or may even rise.   Instead of putting away their money receipts in their hoards, people will either spend them on consumption or lend them out through the capital market.[1]

---

[1] The whole analysis might be put into technical language ; but it may be doubted whether much would be gained by so doing.   In terms of our demand and supply schema, we can take the hoarding factor either

The upshot of this analysis is that on very general grounds there is a strong probability [1] that there is a limit to the fall in MV, even in the absence of any special stimulus for expansion. An assumption to the contrary would imply an increase *ad infinitum* of money hoards in relation to income and wealth. When MV has ceased to fall, when (that is) contraction has come to an end, the economic system becomes very responsive to expansionary impulses and comparatively immune from deflationary shocks. [2]

This analysis is not intended to suggest that contractions always or usually develop up to that very distant limit or that it is safe or good policy to allow them to pursue their course to this " natural " end. The object has been to present the problem in its most general form to serve as an introduction for the following

---

on the supply or on the demand side. We may either say that the amounts which are hoarded reduce the supply of investible funds, or we may say that hoarding is a special sort of demand which competes with the demand for industrial purposes. We have chosen to take it on the supply side because we have defined demand as demand for the purpose of actual investment.

[1] There is no question, of course, of an absolute certainty. There may be a rational incentive for indefinite continuation of hoarding— viz., the expectation of a continued fall in prices. But, in all circumstances, it remains true that the incentive to dishoard must grow continuously with the growth of hoards in terms of money and goods. Compare the interesting analysis by Professor J. Viner on the abhorrence of idle cash—like the *horror vacui* of nature—displayed by the economic system, and the various devices employed by the modern financial organisation to satisfy the need for liquidity without increasing liquidity in terms of cash. J. Viner, " Mr. Keynes on the Causes of Unemployment : A Review ", in *Quarterly Journal of Economics*, November 1936, Vol. 51, pages 147-148 *passim*.

[2] This analysis does not exclude the possibility of a more or less stationary state with unemployment and fairly stable prices as envisaged by Mr. Keynes and his followers. This has been discussed in Chapter 8, § 5, where it has been shown that a downward rigidity of money wages and prices is a necessary condition for that to happen (which is admitted at points but not sufficiently stressed by Mr. Keynes). Here we are concerned not with such an equilibrium state with unemployment, but with the contraction process. A contraction may tail off into a more or less stationary situation at a low level of employment (" depression equilibrium ", " bumping along the bottom of the depression "), but the point made in the text is that it is more likely that the system will automatically start on the up-grade again as soon as it has come to a stable point.

section. Closely connected with—and sometimes almost indistinguishable from—the factors which operate to limit the shrinkage in MV, there are other forces or reactions which make for an expansion of MV. These it is now proposed to discuss in conjunction with other expansionary impulses which are more or less likely to arise, sooner or later, in connection with the progress of a contraction.

§ 9. EXPANSIONARY TENDENCIES WHICH ARE LIKELY TO ARISE DURING THE CONTRACTION

The "natural" forces of readjustment. In § 7 of this chapter, we analysed a number of factors which are capable of generating an expansionary impulse and so starting a process of expansion. The expansionary impulse was there taken for granted as a *point de départ*, and the question whether such hypothetical impulses arise by act of God or Government, or whether they may be expected to arise automatically with the operation of the mechanism of the market, was left for subsequent consideration. In the present section, we shall enquire whether the economic system is capable of putting an end to a contraction process and turning it into an expansion, on the assumption that (*a*) the Government does not take active steps (such as a public works scheme) to start an expansion, and (*b*) that no chance event (such as a new invention or a series of good harvests or an impulse from abroad) comes to the rescue. It is here that we shall have to analyse the " natural " forces of readjustment, the tendencies towards equilibrium which are frequently too readily taken for granted as being inherent in the economic system, if only the price mechanism is allowed to function unobstructed. We shall see that there are expansionary impulses of this kind which can be relied upon with a fair degree of certainty to occur automatically sooner or later and to turn contraction into expansion. (But, in so saying, we are not by any means arguing that it is desirable to wait until these "natural forces" start the system on the up-grade, in preference to taking action to expedite the revival and, possibly, to directing the expansion into channels other than those which it would take if left alone.)

In § 7, it was shown that an expansion can be started by some event or factor which brings about in the first instance an increase of consumers' spending, or by one that stimulates producers' spending (investment). (After the expansion has once been started, both types of expenditures stimulate each other : investment generates income and demand for consumers' goods, and an increase in consumption induces further investment.) When we look for automatic expansionary impulses, we shall find them primarily in the shape of factors which directly stimulate producers' spending (investment). Here, again, it is convenient to distinguish between changes on the side of the supply of, and demand for, investible funds; but it must not be forgotten that there are factors which affect demand and supply at the same time.

Return of confidence. We begin with changes on the supply side. We assume that demand for investible funds has not completely vanished—that is to say, that there is a latent demand at a positive rate of interest which cannot be satisfied because the ruling rate of interest is too high owing to the supply situation (lack of confidence on the part of the banks and the investing public, high liquidity preference). This being so, the cessation of the hoarding process, as described in the preceding section, will not only bring the contraction in MV to a halt : it will also lead in course of time to an expansion. When the banks, industrial firms and private individuals have on the whole reached the conclusion that their cash reserves are large enough—in other words, when they have attained the degree of liquidity which they deem in the circumstances to be desirable or necessary [1]—the rate of interest will fall, because a certain amount of money will be put on the capital market instead of going into hoards. Investment will pick up a little; and this will stabilise MV and the aggregate demand for goods. It will also bring about a stabilisation of employment and production. If such a state of

---

[1] If the theory put forward in the text of the automatic cessation of hoarding and contraction is not accepted, it will be necessary to rely on those active stimulants which are likely to arise sooner or later (as explained in the following pages). The rest of the argument is not affected. In particular, the proposition that MV is likely to rise, as soon as it has stopped falling, holds good—whatever the factor may have been which brought the fall of MV to a halt.

comparative stability has lasted for a while without new business failures and other shocks to confidence, confidence will return and people will be tempted to reduce their hoards.   When prices have once ceased falling, or when they are expected to remain stable or to rise, there is a strong inducement to dishoard, since hoarding means the sacrifice of the profits of investment.[1]   On the other hand, during the contraction, the debt burden of industry will have been reduced in various ways and thus the basis for a revival of financing increased production by loans, etc., will have been restored.

This process of a gradual restoration of the basis for a new expansion of investment has been frequently described.   The analysis could be much more detailed.   Such expressions as " general state of confidence " or " pessimism " and "optimism ", even if restricted to the suppliers of investible funds, relate to very complex phenomena.   Different types of risks and fears may be distinguished, some of which refer only to long-term investments while others refer to long and short-term investments of various types.   A number of institutional complications might be introduced.   We confine ourselves to analysing the process in outline.   The basic fact which one has to keep in mind is that the return of confidence and the disappearance of pessimism lead to dishoarding, to an increase in the supply of investible funds and, if there is demand for such funds, to an increase of MV (demand for goods) and of employment and production.

We turn to the demand side.   When a contrac-
Revival of   tion has continued for a long time, when prices are
investment. sagging and demand is falling almost everywhere,
the demand for investible funds may have reached almost the vanishing-point, so that a fall in the supply price (that is, of the market rate of interest) even to a very low level may have very little influence.   Nobody dares to invest.   But the reason is not that the accumulation of real wealth has gone so far that physically there are no investment opportunities left—*i.e.*, that there is no possibility of increasing output by adopting

---

[1] We need not pause to translate that into Mr. Keynes' terms.   Compare Chapter 8, §§ 3, 4, 5.

time-consuming processes of production.   The reason is rather the
fear that prices will fall and a lack of confidence, a feeling of
uncertainty about the future in general.   It follows that, when
total demand and prices have once settled down at some level
or other, the demand for investible funds will rise automatically
with the mere lapse of time.   The fear that prices will fall further
will gradually disappear and certain investments, which would
have been possible and profitable but have not been undertaken
because of the fear that demand and prices would fall further, will
begin to be made.

It is very likely that during the contraction, when investment was
at a standstill, new inventions may have been made which, in
spite of the fact that (at the ruling prices) they would reduce the
cost of production,[1] have not been put into application because they
necessitate more or less heavy investments which the entrepreneur
is not willing to make when he expects a fall in demand and prices.
Thus a stock of investment opportunities is accumulated, which is
likely to induce investment expenditure as soon as the general
price fall has been stopped.   The way in which, after a long spell
of depression, the ice is broken by some enterprising spirits who
have the courage to try something new in some line of production,
and the way in which the example they set is followed by others in
the same or other branches of industry, are described in classical
language in the various writings of Professor SCHUMPETER.
" Whenever . . . new things have been successfully done by
some, others can, on the one hand, copy their behaviour in the
same line . . . and, on the other hand, get the courage to do
similar things in other lines, the spell being broken, and many
details of the behaviour of the first leaders being applicable outside
their own field of action." [2]

---

[1] See Mitchell, *Business Cycles*, Berkeley. 1913, page 567.

[2] Schumpeter, *Economica*, December 1927, page 298.   See also his
Theory of Economic Development (English translation, 1934) and Pigou,
Industrial Fluctuations, 2nd edition, 1929, pages 92 and 93.   It should,
however, be noted that Schumpeter uses this argument, not so much
to explain how the lower turning-point is brought about, but to show how
the system is carried, during the upswing, beyond the equilibrium point
(compare footnote on page 81 above).   However, there seems to be no
reason why this dynamic factor should not in some cases make its appearance at an earlier point in the course of the cycle.

Replacement demand.   Another factor closely connected with, or even indistinguishable from, the revival of new investment (probably in new and untried combinations) is the increase in replacement demand. During the contraction, not only new investment, but also reinvestment has been curtailed. On the other hand, the capital equipment of industry deteriorates by wear and tear and obsolescence. Therefore, even with the reduced volume of output, it is very probable that sooner or later the need for replacement will make itself felt in one industry or another, which leads to dishoarding or new borrowing and an increase in MV.

There is a further point. Producers know from experience that prices will not fall for ever. When prices have fallen for a time, they will probably become more and more inclined to anticipate a reverse in the price movement. Accordingly, they will not put off improvements and replacements for so long as is possible from the technological point of view without impairing the process of production : they will rather seize the opportunity of having the improvements and replacements made when prices are still low.[1]

Fall in wages.   We must now discuss one very important type of adjustment which under a competitive price system would appear to be the natural cure for unemployment—namely, the reduction of money wages and other cost items.[2]

We are not here concerned with the social and moral aspects of the problem. Nor do we focus attention on the problem of whether a reduction in wages is the best method of bringing a depression to an end (assuming that it is a possible method and that there are alternative methods). The problem with which we

---

[1] The problem of " replacement waves " has been discussed in the first part of the book (see page 84). Mr. Keynes, too, has availed himself of this standard tool of cycle analysis (*General Theory*, page 253).

[2] An analysis in many respects similar to the following one was given by Professor S. Slichter in his book *Towards Stability*, New York, 1935, and in his paper " The Adjustment to Instability " in the *American Economic Review*, Vol. 26, 1936 (Supplement), pages 196-213 *passim*.

As was pointed out in Chapter 8, § 5, above, the following analysis has also many points in common with Mr. Keynes' treatment.

are concerned is a more modest one, although it would seem that its solution is an indispensable preliminary to any answer on the questions of policy.

The problem is this. Is the fall in money wages which we observe during any major depression to be regarded as a factor which tends to put an end to the contraction ? Would depression be alleviated and revival hastened if money wages were more flexible and fell more rapidly so long as unemployment persists ?[1]

This is a very-much-disputed question. Many economists see in a reduction of wages the unavoidable and infallible remedy against unemployment. Others denounce it as useless or even detrimental.

Monetary A large part of what has been written on the *implications.* subject has been vitiated by the fact that the mone- tary implications of the various theories have not been made clear. Many argue on the tacit assump- tion that MV can be taken as constant, or at any rate as independent of changes in money wages. If this were true, if total monetary demand were not influenced by a reduction in money wages, then of course, with lower money wages, employment and production would be greater than with higher wages, because, with lower wages and prices, the same amount of money would buy more goods and provide more employment. Others have assumed tacitly or without adequate proof that MV will fall by the same amount as pay-rolls have been reduced (or even by more), so that the general

---

[1] An equivalent to a decrease in money wages is an increase in the efficiency of labour which does not augment other cost items (*e.g.*, capital cost) at the same time. If the worker works harder, or if the work is better organised so that a smaller labour force can do the same work without an increase in capital equipment, the position, so far as the employer is concerned, is equivalent to a reduction in money wages. From other (*e.g* , the social) points of view, there may be important differences between the two methods of reducing labour cost. For the purpose of our problem they are equivalent.

The statistical measurement of efficiency presents extraordinary difficulties, which cannot be discussed here. It may, however, be noted that the ordinary statistical measure of "efficiency-wages"—viz., labour cost per unit of output (pay-roll : volume of output)—cannot be taken as a precise measurement of the magnitude we have in mind.

situation remains unchanged (or even deteriorates). Each of these extreme assumptions—or, for that matter, an assumption intermediate between the two—may be true under certain circumstances and false under others.   Without specifying the attendant circumstances and distinguishing a number of different cases, nothing definite can be said.

We begin by assuming an isolated country, leaving complications arising from international trade for later treatment.   What holds true of an isolated country holds true substantially also of any big country which need not allow its internal policy to be influenced by considerations of international trade.

Effect of wage reductions in a particular industry.   If an individual firm manages to reduce wages, it will usually be able to expand production at the expense of other firms in the same industry, so that the others will be forced to follow suit.   Therefore, we had better start with the assumption that money wages are reduced throughout the entire branch of industry concerned.   What will be the possible or typical reaction of the wage-cut on this industry—leaving aside for the moment indirect influences on other industries and repercussions of these secondary effects on the industry where wages were reduced? We shall try to answer this question with special reference to the problem of how MV is likely to be affected.

A priori, there is a wide range of possibilities.   At the one extreme the industry may expect a great increase in demand from a fall in price made possible by the reduction of cost, and may accordingly increase production by so much that employment increases by more than the wage has fallen, so that the sum disbursed for wages directly and indirectly through the purchase of raw material and equipment is actually greater than it was before.   (We characterise this by saying that the elasticity of the industry's demand for labour, including indirect demand exercised through the purchase of means of production, is greater than unity—which involves an even greater elasticity of demand for the product of this industry.)[1]   In the other extreme, there is the possibility that

---

[1] Even if the output of the industry in question does not increase as a consequence of a wage reduction, the industry may be enabled by the reduction of its labour cost to give more employment, if it uses the money

output and employment are not increased at all (the elasticity of demand for labour being zero) so that the amount saved is withdrawn from circulation—*e.g.*, by repaying bank loans or by not contracting new ones. The position of the banks is thereby improved : but, since we are speaking of a period of contraction, we cannot assume that the whole of the sums repaid will be re-lent to other borrowers. We are certainly nearer to the truth if we assume that at least a part will be used to strengthen the reserves of the banks.

In order to avoid a *post hoc ergo propter hoc* argument, we must make the preceding statement more precise. We may say that employment will, or may, rise to such an extent that wage disbursements (directly in the industry concerned, and indirectly in the preceding stages through the purchase of raw materials and other means of production, etc.) are raised above the level which they would have attained had the reduction in the wage rate not occurred. This formula covers the case (which during a general contraction may easily occur) of a wage reduction inducing an industry to refrain from contracting its employment and pay-rolls by so much as it otherwise would have been forced to do, so that the wage reduction does not bring about an increase in employment and pay-rolls in comparison with the preceding period but prevents it from falling to a lower level. The other extreme is then the case where employment is not increased at all above the level which it would have attained if there had been no reduction in wages—a level, namely, which would probably be lower during a general contraction than in the preceding period—so that the amount of money withdrawn from circulation is greater than it would be if no wage reduction occurred.

In the first case, the wage reduction has an expansionary influence, so that the contraction is mitigated or even reversed. In the second case, the influence is deflationary, and the contraction is hastened and intensified.

---

saved to improve or replace its equipment—or, in other words, if it was consuming its capital and the wage reduction puts a stop to such consumption. This is not, however, a typical case in a depression, since even the existing equipment is not then fully utilised, though it is not denied that capital consumption may be going on.

We now ask, Is it possible to decide on general
Will pay-rolls grounds which of the two possible outcomes of a
rise or fall? wage reduction is likely to prevail during a contraction process ?   Can the fall in money wages be
regarded as something which, on balance, mitigates and shortens
the contraction, or is it an intensifying factor ?   We may certainly
assume that employment and output in the industry directly
concerned will be influenced favourably.[1]   It is hardly conceivable that an industry would react to a fall in money wages by
giving less employment than it would otherwise do.   But it does
not necessarily follow that employment and output must rise to
such an extent that wage disbursements increase.   For various
reasons, during a depression, especially its first phase, wage reductions are less likely to have a strong expansionary influence than
during the upswing of the cycle.   There is excess capacity (surplus
equipment) in many lines of industry; and there may be large
stocks from which raw materials and semi-finished products can

---

[1] It may be, and has been, argued that, even if in principle a reduction
in wages may be expected to exercise a favourable influence, the latter
will not materialise at once and the delay will be sufficient to stultify its
operation altogether.   If an entrepreneur is led by a reduction in wages
to increase his investment, he will need some time to put his plans into
effect.   First, he is likely to wait for a while and see how things develop.
Secondly, his plans must be worked out in detail before orders can be
given and the money actually be spent.   In the meantime, wages and
pay-rolls will have been reduced, and consequently the demand for goods
in general will have fallen.   This will cause the general situation to deteriorate, and may well induce the producer to drop his plan of increasing
his output.   If, therefore, his investments are not made at once, they are
likely not to be made at all.
There is certainly much force in this argument ; and we have already
had occasion in our analysis (page 353) to refer to this inevitable lag
between the conception of investment plans (or the occurrence of a
change which makes the investment in principle a profitable proposition)
and the actual expenditure involved.
But at this point of the argument the situation is somewhat different.
In the first place, we are concerned not so much with new investment in
fixed capital as with a possible increase of production within the framework of existing plant.   In the second place, it must be remembered
that a reduction in wages may not only stimulate an increase in output,
but may also induce the employer to refrain from a curtailment of production and employment.   In this latter case, the effect of the wage reduction
may well be quite instantaneous.

be obtained—*i.e.*, output can be increased without heavy new investment. If new investment in fixed capital were required, it would be difficult to raise the necessary sums. Pessimism prevails, and people are reluctant to take the risk of investment for longer periods. But, as we have seen, these conditions are likely to change gradually when the contraction has progressed far enough. On the other hand, a reduction in wages is bound to have a favourable psychological effect on business-men, and will make them more inclined to invest and the banks more inclined to lend; and this tends to mitigate deflation.

Influence of cost reduction on sales receipts under competition and monopoly. There is another very important point to be mentioned. The case where producers use part of what they save through the cut in wages to strengthen their liquidity or to repay bank loans implies that total receipts from sales do not fall by so much as pay-rolls. In other words, if prices fall so much that all that is gained by cutting wages is passed on to the consumer, the position of the producer is not improved and there is no scope for additional hoarding so far as he is concerned. This could only happen under conditions of perfect competition and even then not to a full extent. Even on the assumption of perfect competition in the strict sense of economic theory, when every producer regards the price at which he can sell as given independent of his own action and expands his production accordingly up to the point where his marginal cost equals the price—even on this assumption total receipts will not fall by as much as pay-rolls except in the improbable case of marginal prime cost being constant—*i.e.*, the marginal cost curve being horizontal. In all cases where marginal cost rises, only a part of the reduction in the total cost of production which has been achieved by the cut in wages will be passed on to the consumer.[1] In other words, gross profits will be

---

[1] It may be added that the view which one can frequently hear expressed that a wage-reduction can have a stimulating effect only if prices are correspondingly reduced, is not generally correct. Even if prices are not reduced at all, more employment may result from a reduction in money wages, if entrepreneurs are induced or enabled to resume the replacement of their equipment which they had neglected.

increased—though *net* profits will still be negative, since the gross profits do not cover amortisation of the fixed capital—and there is therefore scope for increased hoarding or repayment of bank loans. This is *a fortiori* the case where there is not free competition in the strict sense of economic theory, and prices under monopolistic or quasi-monopolistic conditions (or simply as a result of friction or fear of spoiling the market) are prevented from falling to the point of equality with marginal cost—in other words, where producers fail to expand production up to the point at which marginal cost equals price.

We conclude, therefore, that the freer the competition and the more flexible the price the greater the favourable effect of wage reductions and the smaller the danger of an intensification of deflation. That conclusion is no more nor less than was to be expected. It does not follow, however, that such an intensification of the hoarding process as a consequence of a wage reduction is impossible, even under competition in the strictest sense.

Repercussions on other industries. Suppose employment and output in a particular industry to have been somewhat increased in response to a fall in money wages, but not by so much as wages have been reduced, so that there results a decrease in the disbursements of wages by the industry in question. This increase in employment and output is certainly desirable : but we have also to take into consideration the effect on other industries. This depends on what happens to the increased (gross) profits. Suppose a part of them is hoarded. Then demand for other products will be reduced,[1] and the increase in employment in the industry directly concerned will be partly or wholly offset by a decrease somewhere else. This may even react back on the first industry and partly nullify there the original increase in employment.

---

[1] Of course, an increase in wage disbursements need not result in an instantaneous increase in demand for wage goods since the wage-earner may hoard part of it or use it for repaying debts. On the other hand, a decrease may be temporarily offset by drawing on hoards or incurring debts. We disregard these factors here as being quantitatively unimportant.

It may be useful to put the same thing in a slightly different way. It may happen that, if wages had not been reduced in the particular industry, employment and output would be smaller in this industry, but the industry would have disbursed more money for wages, etc., and would have financed this either by borrowing more from the banks or by refraining from repaying bank loans or from building up monetary reserves or by drawing on idle funds at its disposal (by reducing its liquidity).

Wage reductions in many industries. So far we have analysed the case from the standpoint of one particular industry, assuming other things being equal. But, if wage reductions occur in a number of industries at the same time, or one after the other at short intervals, it is still more difficult to tell what the aggregate result will be. If the primary influences on each industry are such that on balance no change in MV takes place, the hoardings induced in some industries being balanced by induced dishoardings[1] in other industries, the net result will be an increase in total employment. If the dishoarding in some industries is larger than the hoarding in others, the result will be a still greater increase in employment. But this need not necessarily happen. On balance, the tendency to hoard

---

[1] Some writers have displayed a certain aversion for the word " hoarding " (*e.g.*, Mr. Kahn in his review of the first edition of this book). Others have obscured the concept by distinguishing all kinds of new meanings which the word is alleged to have in the writings of different writers without saying who those authors are (see Joan Robinson : " The Concept of Hoarding ", *Economic Journal*, Vol. XLVIII, June 1938, pages 231 to 237). It is difficult to attach any meaning to the statement that " ' hoarding ', except in the sense which is covered by the conception of ' liquidity preference ', has no causal force " (*op. cit.*, page 236). The meaning of " hoarding " which is used here and which was defined precisely in Chapter 8, § 3, is not the one to which alone Mrs. Robinson attributes " causal force ". But it has certainly causal significance in that the decision of individuals to hoard or not to hoard in this sense is of great importance for future events. How it can be translated into Mr. Keynes' terms has been repeatedly indicated. In the present context it may help to translate " dishoarding " into " greater disbursements ", with the additional condition (carried by the expression " dishoarding ", but not by the word " disbursement ") that the increase in expenditure is an addition to aggregate expenditure of society as a whole.

may be stronger than the tendency to dishoard. To be sure, a certain amount of net hoarding, as evidenced by a decline in MV, is consistent with an increase in employment and output. But, if it goes beyond a certain point, the stimulating effect of a reduction in money wages may be frustrated, the fall in wages being accompanied by a fall in demand and in prices. Employment and output will be no higher; they may even be lower than they would have been without the fall in wages.

But, even in this unfavourable and perhaps
Wage improbable case, where a reduction of money wages
reductions has the immediate effect of intensifying contraction,
increase the policy of reducing wages and prices, if pursued
liquidity. long enough, will be sufficient to create a situation out of which a revival (a new expansion) is likely to emerge sooner or later without any special expansionary stimulus from without being required.[1]

This follows from what has been said earlier in this and the previous section. We there demonstrated that, with the continuance of contraction, banks and individual firms become more and more liquid. Money hoards grow, both in terms of money and—since prices fall—still more in purchasing power. Now, it is clear that this process will be accelerated if wages are reduced and prices fall more than they would without a fall in wages. In other words, the fall in money wages and prices reduces the volume of work which money has to perform in mediating the exchange of goods and services in the different stages of production. Money is set free in this line of its employment, and becomes available for hoarding.[2] *Pari passu* with the fall in prices, existing money hoards (M_2) rise in real value and, sooner or later, the point will be reached where even the most cautious individuals will find an irresistible temptation to stop hoarding and to dishoard.

We may put the matter in yet another way. Assume for the moment that, independently of the behaviour of money wages,

---

[1] Compare footnotes 1 on page 390 and 392.

[2] In Keynesian terminology, less money is needed to satisfy the transactions motive and more becomes available for " speculative holding " : M_1 decreases ; M_2 increases.

there is a definite level of liquidity which must be reached before the economic system can again start on the up-grade. It is clear in this case that the more rapidly wages and prices are allowed to fall the more quickly the desired level of liquidity will be reached. Flexibility of money wages, and competition in the labour market as a means to the attainment of flexibility may be regarded as a factor conducive to the restoration of full employment. But the problem is not quite so simple as that, because the level of liquidity which must be attained need not necessarily be independent of the movement in money wages. If wages are very flexible, and if this flexibility has an initial deflationary effect (as explained above), disturbances may result, confidence may be shaken and thus a higher degree of liquidity may be required than when wages were somewhat more rigid. But, the argument runs, even in this unfavourable case—which is by no means the only possible case, or even the most probable,—there is somewhere a higher level of liquidity which is sufficient in all circumstances.

Conclusions. The question with which the above discussion began, as to whether a continued fall in money wages under conditions of general unemployment is to be regarded as a factor which will bring a contraction to an end, must therefore, if we carry the argument to its logical conclusion, be answered in the affirmative. It must, however, be emphasised once more that this does not imply the necessity for a process of contraction's always, or even in the majority of cases, running its course through to its " natural " end. One or the other of the expansionary impulses which have been analysed in the present and the preceding section will usually intervene. Nor again, in answering the question in the affirmative, is there any intention of prejudging the issue of the advisability or otherwise, in the absence of a spontaneous expansionary impulse, of attempts to check the course of the contraction by State intervention in one form or another. In answering that question, many extraneous considerations arise, some of them of a non-economic nature, which cannot be discussed here. But so far as the problem in hand is concerned —namely, the problem of the influence of the behaviour of money wages—the following conclusions may be drawn.

Some problems of policy. An isolated policy of keeping money wages up is very dangerous, although it is impossible to deny that a policy of wage-cutting may on occasion, up to a certain point, intensify the contraction before its favourable influence on employment and output makes itself felt. It may be very difficult to decide beforehand whether such a temporary intensification is, or is not, to be expected from a given reduction in money wages in a number of industries. If there are reasons to believe that even without a wage reduction contraction of MV will go on—and, as we have seen in the chapter on the contraction process, a certain shrinkage in MV is the invariable concomitant of a cyclical depression—it will certainly increase unemployment and prolong contraction if wages are not allowed to fall. If a contraction in a country is dictated by its international situation, the situation is still clearer. Wages and prices must be allowed to fall if a rise in unemployment and a fall in output are to be prevented. (It is another question whether, and in what circumstances, it is possible and advisable to cut short this process of adjustment by currency devaluation.)

On the other hand, where a country need not consider its international economic situation and has a free hand as to its monetary policy, it is comparatively easy to make sure that the possible deflationary influences of wage reductions are eliminated while at the same time the expansionary influences are not hampered. All that is required is to combine a policy of wage reduction with expansionary measures such as public works financed by inflationary methods. The effect will be to forestall any decrease in total wage disbursements, and consequently in the demand for consumers' goods, which might otherwise result from the wage reduction.

What has been said of wages is equally true of other prices which are kept up by monopolistic manipulation or State intervention.

CHAPTER 12

INTERNATIONAL ASPECTS OF BUSINESS CYCLES

---

§ I. INTRODUCTION

Previous treatment of international aspects. In the preceding chapters, the analysis of economic fluctuations has been pursued without much attention to their international aspects. In all references to " countries ", we have had in mind, not indeed completely closed economies, but areas within whose borders all the characteristic features of the business cycle—the swings of rising and falling money demand, the reciprocal interactions of demand for consumers' goods and demand for producers' goods, the variation through time in the degree of employment and scarcity of productive factors—could come into play. Repercussions on, and disturbances from, economic relationships with the outside world have made their appearance in the argument at various points, but only incidentally : they have been treated as isolated facts and have not been further analysed. The attempt has now to be made to deal with these international aspects in systematic fashion. The argument has to be adapted, as and where necessary, to the fact that the real world is neither one big economic unit nor a congeries of closed systems, but a complex system of economic relationships of various kinds between individuals. The closest connections these individuals tend to have with their neighbours and their own countrymen; but they are linked up—sometimes directly, always indirectly—with the farthest corners of the earth.

This adaptation of the argument incidentally links up two branches of economic theory which too often are kept apart

—the theory of international trade and the theory of economic change.[1]

Methods of exposition. In setting out the international complications in orderly fashion, there are two alternative methods of exposition which we may adopt. The first method would be to start from the assumption of two or more completely independent and isolated economies, and proceed to introduce one by one the various types of economic connections which we find in the real world (exchange of goods and services, capital movements, the various types of monetary connections), and so investigate the influence of each of these connections on the course of the cycle in the various countries, and the extent to which a parallelism in the alternation of periods of prosperity and contraction in the different areas concerned is thereby produced.

The other method of approach, which is that adopted in the following pages, is to start with the hypothesis of a spaceless closed economy embracing the whole world and to introduce one by one the circumstances which divide and disintegrate that economy. The disintegrating factors are so arranged as to start with the most general, natural and inevitable physical facts, and from these to proceed to the more artificial human devices, in such a way as to exhibit the operation of the earlier factors without the later factors but not of the later factors without the earlier.

The first disintegrating factor to be introduced is transportation cost—in other words, imperfect mobility of goods and services.

---

[1] In addition to the book by H. Neisser, *Some International Aspects of the Business Cycle* (Philadelphia, 1936), two articles may be mentioned which deal expressly with the international aspects of the business cycles, viz. : O. Morgenstern, " International vergleichende Konjunkturforschung" in *Zeitschrift für die gesamte Staatswissenschaft*, 1927, Heft 2 ; and A. v. Mühlenfels, " Internationale Konjunkturzusammenhänge " in *Jahrbücher für Nationalökonomie und Statistik*, 130, Band III, Folge 75, 1929 I. Moreover, the literature on international trade has become more " cycle conscious" in recent times and contains frequent references to cycle problems. *Cf.* B. Ohlin, *Interregional and International Trade* (1933) ; R. Nurkse, *Internationale Kapitalbewegungen* (1935) ; R. F. Harrod, *International Economics* (1933) ; C. Iversen, *Aspects of the Theory of Capital Movements* (1935) ; J. Viner, *Studies in the Theory of International Trade*, New York, 1937, especially Chapter VII, Section V.

The second is the localisation of investment, credit and banking (imperfect mobility of capital). The third, perhaps the most important, is national currency autonomy. Thus we have a series of situations representing an increasingly close approach to reality. In the discussion at each stage of approach, it will be necessary to make further distinctions in relation to what we conceive to be the distribution of resources (in the widest sense of the word) among the various " countries ". It is the uneven geographical distribution of economic resources and activities that gives the disintegrating factors their importance. If each area or country possessed all types of resources in sufficient quantity, the existence of high transport costs between them would be irrelevant.

It goes without saying that some of these disintegrating factors —especially the first, but also the second to some extent—operate, not only between countries separated by political borders, but also within political areas between different regions. When, therefore, we speak simply of " countries ", the expression is to be understood with the obvious qualifications implied by the context.

§ 2.   INFLUENCE OF TRANSPORT COSTS : IMPERFECT MOBILITY
OF GOODS

Localisation of expansion and contraction. The most natural and inevitable of all disintegrating factors is the existence of costs of transport. Costs of transport should be interpreted in a broad sense as covering, not only the expenses involved in transferring goods between producers, or from producer to consumer, in different localities, but also the trouble and expense involved in moving the consumer to the goods and services. It is assumed that resources are to a considerable extent localised, whether by nature or, in the case of labour, by a multiplicity of causes. It should further be kept in mind that, at this stage of the argument, we still assume a unified money and credit system for the whole world.

Given a certain geographical distribution of resources, the effect of transport costs is to permit of cumulative upward and downward movements in money demand, not wholly confined to but centred in, particular areas.   In the absence of transport costs in the sense defined above, the specialisation of particular areas to particular lines of production arising out of the unequal distribution of resources between localities would have full play.   Suppose now a fortuitous expenditure on the part of a group of people.   There will be a consequent primary increase of income accruing to the workers and entrepreneurs producing the articles to which the additional demand is directed.   Probably this primary income increase will affect some districts more favourably than others. When the primary increase in income comes to be spent, however, there will be a secondary increase in incomes; and there is no reason to believe that this will accrue particularly to those districts which enjoyed the primary increase, nor yet to those whose fortuitous increase in expenditure set the whole process going.   There is no presumption that the cumulative expansion process will be localised in or centred around its first starting-point; but it will spread in a random fashion all over the economic surface.

When we introduce transport costs, however, specialisation and division of labour between areas tend to diminish; and we find that the primary employment and income increase tends to accrue in a greater degree to those living near to the group which increased their expenditure.   The secondary increase in incomes will likewise tend to accrue to those living and working near the beneficiaries of the primary increase in incomes, and so on.

Counter-influence of uneven distribution of resources. The cumulative expansion movement need not, of course, be confined to any particular locality. The influence of transport costs tends so to confine it; but, on the other hand, the influence of the uneven distribution of resources tends to maintain a geographical division of labour, to promote inter-regional exchange, and so to ensure that some portion of the increased income of individuals in a given locality is expended in the period immediately following on "imports" of one sort or another.   Thus, the more strictly the various areas are specialised in particular types of economic activity the less scope there will be for local or regional monetary expansions and contractions.

In seeking to picture an expansion from the point of view of any particular country or area, we must bear in mind the fact that each locality is differently placed in respect to the given distribution of economic resources over the earth's surface. Each locality has its own characteristic potentialities for the production of different goods and services, and its own characteristic constellation of transport costs affecting its exchanges with other centres of production. As a result, a fortuitous increase in the monetary demand for goods and services in one area may tend to confine itself to that area, whereas in another area an increased demand may rapidly overleap its own borders.[1]

In a country like the United Kingdom, for example, the primary increase in income will be spent very largely on products (food, textiles, and so on), the earlier stages of whose production are located abroad. Thus, a considerable portion of the expenditure of secondary and subsequent income increases will be drained off to agricultural countries; and the favourable repercussion on British exports may be small and long delayed. A similar argument will apply to a country like New Zealand, whose inhabitants will spend a considerable portion of any increase in income on the manufactured products of the United States and Europe. On the other hand, we may take the United States as an example of a country in which only a very small proportion of an increase in consumers' incomes will find its way abroad.

It is necessary, however, to keep in mind, not only the expenditure on consumption goods, but also the expenditure on investment goods which is to some extent dependent on the former. In an undeveloped country, without heavy industries, the process of monetary expansion by way of reciprocal stimulation of consumption and investment—the so-called Wicksellian process—will be of minor importance. If a revival of British industry takes place, it provides a stimulus for the building and extension of plant. The

---

[1] *Cf.* the interesting article by F. W. Paish, " Banking Policy and the Balance of International Payments ", in *Economica*, Vol. III (New Series), November 1936.

existence of a world capital market (which in this stage of the argument is still assumed to function smoothly) ensures an unlimited supply of investible funds, so that the investment can proceed unhampered by rising interest rates. The funds invested will be spent on the products of British heavy industries, and the flow of money incomes will be enhanced. On the other hand, if the original impetus to prosperity develops in some part of China, it may become profitable to extend, *e.g.*, the railway system —in which case a large proportion of the money invested will be drained off to Europe or America, who supply the required capital goods.

Tendency of local expansions to overflow. It must not be assumed that the proportion of expenditure in any country which finds its way abroad in payment of imports will remain the same in all phases of a cyclical movement. As a local expansion or contraction develops, there will be changes in the distribution of income and expenditure which may involve a greater or smaller proportion of purchases from abroad; but there is no reason to expect any systematic movement. More important is the point already touched on that, as the volume of the demand for investment goods changes in relation to the volume of the demand for consumers' goods, the foreign drain will become less or more considerable. In this event, some systematic movement in the direction of a greater or smaller foreign drain is to be expected in each individual case; but we cannot say in general which direction the movement will take.

We can say, however, that the further a local expansion goes the more it is likely to " spill over " into other regions—and that for a different, a third, reason. Imports will increase, not merely *pari passu* with incomes, but faster. As the expansion goes on, stocks are taken up, unemployed workers reabsorbed, and plant is used to fuller capacity. Hence wages and other prices will rise and, by the operation of the mechanism described in the classical expositions of international trade theory, both home and foreign demand will be switched away from local products to foreign substitutes. For a local boom even more than for a general boom, the stage of price-inflation is a dangerous one and marks the beginning of the end.   On the other hand, where prices are kept steady as a result, *e.g.*, of technological progress, the boom may obtain a longer lease of life.

Coexistence of prosperity and depression facilitated.

The effects of transport costs are not, however, confined to the imposition of a check on the spread of prosperity and depression from one area to another.   They also make it possible that, at one and the same time, a cumulative contraction process should be taking place in one region and a cumulative expansion process in another region.   The simplest, though not the most likely, cause of such a development would be a change of taste or income distribution in the world as a whole, leading to a transference of demand from the products of one region to those of another.   In a " spaceless " economy, such " horizontal " demand shifts, while significant for the industries directly concerned and for their subsidiary industries, would be relatively a matter of indifference for the rest of the economic system, unless the consequence of the shift was to set afoot a net expansion or contraction.   In the real world, the effect may be to promote an upswing in one quarter and a downswing in another.

A somewhat similar case is the effect of innovations in methods of production or transportation, the introduction of new types of finished goods, etc.   In most of these cases, the stimulus provided for the new industries will find its counterpart in a check to the old competing industries—*i.e.*, those industries which produce the equipment or material replaced or rendered superfluous by the new processes, and those which have lost their market because demand has been drawn away by the newly invented types of goods.   This setback in the old industries may not become serious until after the new methods have been put into operation; but, when it does, it is calculated—in a " spaceless " economy—to precipitate the down-turn.   If, however, the new industries are localised in areas other than those in which their unsuccessful rivals are to be found, the continuance of prosperity in the former region may be but little hampered by the misery of the latter. The danger of excessive anticipations in one country need not drag the whole world down.

Influence of existing tariffs. Much of what has been said about the influence of transport costs is equally applicable to tariff barriers and other hindrances to international trade. Customs duties in particular resemble transport costs in that they impose an obstacle to the movement of goods; but the obstacle can be overcome if the price disparities in the exporting and the importing country are sufficiently high. For this reason it is convenient to mention them at this point, though they may be regarded as more "artificial" than some of the other disintegrating factors treated below.

Whereas transport costs tend to increase the proportion of demand directed to goods and services produced in nearer or more accessible regions, Customs tariffs—being levied at political frontiers only—tend to confine demand to the products of the same State, or to other States whose imports are relatively little affected by the tariff barriers. Often, this means that tariffs act as an additional factor tending to localise monetary expansions and contractions. It need not be so, however, since their effect may be to divert demand from nearer to more distant sources of supply. This will be the case for populations living close to political frontiers and hence to Customs barriers. The effect of high tariff protection will be that localities within the same country—or, it may be, within the same empire—may tend to have their periods of prosperity and depression at the same time, whereas other countries will tend to show a lesser degree of synchronisation.

Influence of changes in tariffs. Changes in tariffs have exactly the same consequences as changes in transportation cost—in which connection we may refer to the short analysis of the possible expansionary influence of the imposition of a tariff in the protected country which was given on page 382 above. (This type of analysis can be easily adapted so as to apply to the effects of the removal of a tariff on both countries concerned.)

Tariffs differ, on the other hand, from transport costs in the fact that they can be altered by legislation, and therefore may be changed as a matter of policy systematically throughout the course of a cycle. A country may conceivably succeed, by raising its tariff wall, in diverting demand from foreign to domestic sources of supply (though, be it noted, a part of the demand thus diverted from the purchase of foreign goods may be sterilised in the form of hoards). It is conceivable, therefore, that a country might use its power to vary its tariffs as a means of mitigating the violence of its own industrial fluctuations, raising them when threatened by deflation in other countries or by the appearance of deflationary tendencies at home, and lowering them in the opposite case of danger of inflation whether originating at home or in other countries.

Although the trend of international commercial policy has been steeply in the direction of protection ever since the beginning of the last quarter of the nineteeth century, a certain cyclical movement is unmistakable. Every major depression brought a new outburst of protectionism, whilst prosperity periods have usually been marked by short steps back in the direction of freer trade.

But while it is conceivable that a single nation might succeed, by a policy of raising tariffs in bad times and lowering them in good times, in damping the impact on itself of the great international business cycles, the consequence of such a policy simultaneously pursued by all nations would be precisely the reverse. The raising of a tariff means a limitation of the investment opportunities of the potential importers. The money which is prevented from leaving the country is in part hoarded. The demand for foreign products will fall by more than the amount by which the demand for home products rises : and, if such a policy is pursued all round by every country, the depression will be rendered still more severe in the world as a whole and very probably in each individual country as well. For similar reasons, a policy of reducing tariffs in the upswing, simultaneously pursued by all nations, will not lead to stability in the total money demand, but will rather afford a further expansionary impetus to each country.

§ 3.   INFLUENCE OF THE LOCALISATION OF INVESTMENT, CREDIT AND BANKING : IMPERFECT MOBILITY OF CAPITAL

Equalisation of interest rates.   In the last section, we introduced into our picture of the cyclical movement the influence of an uneven distribution of (*a*) resources and (*b*) transportation cost of goods and services. We have continued, however, up till now to assume a common money circulation within the whole of the area under consideration. This assumption we shall still maintain in the present section. We have further assumed perfect mobility of capital. This assumption will now be dropped; and in its place we shall introduce the assumption of a more or less complete localisation of investment and banking activity—in other words, we shall assume imperfect mobility of capital.

Let us first enquire into the exact meaning of imperfect mobility of capital and of its opposite. By perfect mobility of capital we mean perfect mobility of loanable funds, that is to say, a state of affairs in which loanable funds will flow to those parts of the world where demand is highest or, rather, in which they will be distributed over the various countries in such a way that the rates of interest in general—or, more precisely, the rates of interest for different types of loans with equivalent maturities and risk—will everywhere be the same.

Mobility of capital versus mobility of goods.   It should be noted that perfect mobility of capital, that is complete inter-local equalisation of the rate of interest is not incompatible with high, or even prohibitive, transportation costs (including artificial costs such as tariffs) for goods in general and capital goods in particular. Suppose two countries, *A* and *B*, between which the transportation of capital goods of all kinds is completely impossible, the trade between the two consisting exclusively of consumption goods. If the currency of the two countries is firmly based on gold, and if the position in respect of debtors' *morale*, legal protection of investors and possibilities of supervision of investments is the same in both countries, there is no reason why the investors in the country where the interest tends to be lower should not turn to investments in the other country. There will be a complete equalisation of the rate of interest; and capital will eventually be transferred in the shape of consumers' goods and luxuries. Short of the quite extreme case where there is no exchange of goods or services whatsoever (a case which need not detain us here), imperfect mobility of goods does not directly reduce the mobility of capital. It cannot, however, be denied that, indirectly, increasing restrictions on the movement of goods and services tend to restrict the movement of capital, and render foreign investment more and more risky. If the volume of trade between two countries is large, and if there are many actual and potential export and import goods, the repercussions of the transfer of a given amount of investible funds (money capital) will be slight. A mild expansion in one country relatively to the other[1] will suffice to produce an export surplus from the capital-exporting country. If, on the other hand, the volume of trade is comparatively small, the movement of the same amount of money capital will produce a more violent expansion, and probably a sharp rise of prices, in the one country, and contraction and a sharp fall of prices in the other country. The same thing can be expressed by saying that, where the volume of trade is large and the economic connections are close between two countries, the money which flows out of one country to seek investment in the other will soon find its way back through increased exports or reduced imports. If the volume of trade is small, it will not return so quickly. The slump in the capital-exporting country may drive up the interest rate and thereby remove, at least for the moment, the incentive for the migration of capital. But it may also incite a flight of capital and precipitate the crisis.

In the extreme case where no movement of goods or services is possible, a transfer of money capital will be wholly inflationary

---

[1] There need not in all cases be an absolute contraction in the capital-exporting country. A slowing-down of the expansion may be sufficient. There are also cases conceivable where no contraction—not even a relative one—is required from the capital-exporting country—*e.g.*, if the proceeds of the loan are spent directly on goods of that country.

in the one country and deflationary in the other; [1] but even in this case the transfer is not impossible, although it is difficult to see how an equalisation in the rate of interest can be permanently achieved, unless one believes the interest rate can be permanently lowered by monetary inflation or permanently raised by deflation.

We may sum up as follows.   The smaller the volume of trade the more violent will be the inflation in the borrowing, and deflation in the lending, country consequent upon the movement of a certain sum of money capital, or, if exchanges are allowed to vary, the more violent will be the fluctuations in the exchange rate.   If this development does not directly check the tendency of capital to migrate, it will at least afford incentives to State interventions such as transfer moratoria and the like, and is for this reason indirectly fatal to foreign investment.

The reasons for differences in interest rates.   So much for this digression.   We return to the main theme.   As everybody knows, equalisation of interest between different countries is not the typical situation we find in the real world.   What we find is, on the contrary, a persistence of discrepancies, sometimes of a very high order of magnitude. The mobility of capital is usually far from being complete.   People tend to invest their money at home in local land, physical capital, property rights, debts and so on, even though the rate of interest which can be earned is much lower than that to be obtained by equivalent investments abroad.   The reasons for this are rather obvious.   Partly they are, so to speak, of a physical nature. Transport costs and costs of communication place obstacles in the way of that personal supervision which is usually necessary to obtain the highest income from investment in physical capital, while they enhance the difficulty of obtaining that first-hand knowledge of the business and political situation in other countries which is necessary to dissipate uncertainties in regard to business propositions and the value of equities.   But, on the whole, the barriers to international lending and investment are less physical than political, social and institutional.   Ignorance of foreign tongues, inadequacy of legal protection, risk of transfer restriction

---

[1] *Cf.* Iversen, *loc. cit.*, page 47.

or outright confiscation—and, to anticipate a little, fear of exchange instability—are nowadays certainly more important factors than actual distances.

Changes in mobility of capital. We are not concerned here with the effects in the long run of the immobility of capital on the economic structure of the world and the economic development of the capital importing and exporting countries. We do not try to answer questions as to what, for example, the world would look like to-day without the enormous capital movements which took place in the nineteenth and twentieth centuries. We are here concerned with (*a*) the proximate influences of the imposition, removal, strengthening or relaxation of the impediments to international capital movements, and (*b*) the modifications brought to the short-run cycle of expansion and contraction by the very *existence* of a certain degree of localisation of investment, credit and banking.

On the basis of the analysis in the previous pages of the nature and causes of cyclical expansions and contractions, it is comparatively easy to answer the first of these questions. Naturally, the answer cannot take the form of a brief and comprehensive formula : each case has to be taken individually. But we can indicate broadly what are the factors which must be taken into account.

Obviously, we must first distinguish between the effect on the capital-exporting and that on the capital-importing country, and must ascertain in each case in which phase of the cycle the change takes place. What will be the influence on the supply of investible funds and the rate of interest in both countries ? Clearly, the imposition (removal) of restrictions on capital movements will tend to reduce (raise) the rate of interest in the capital-exporting country, and to raise (reduce) it in the capital-importing country. How will the demand for investible funds react to the change in supply ? This will, in turn, depend on the phase of the cycle.

Thus the final outcome may differ according to circumstances. But we are in a position to indicate what in any particular case are the circumstances which determine that outcome.

We turn now to the second question—that is,
Tendency to to the effects of a certain degree of localisation of
damp down investment, credit, and banking. They can be
local booms most clearly brought out by supposing the tendency
and depressions. towards localisation to be so strong as absolutely
to prohibit lending and investment outside regional
or national boundaries. In such circumstances, the general world
market for capital (or investible funds) will be divided up geogra-
phically or nationally into watertight compartments. In each
country, a different interest rate—or scale of rates—will prevail,
determined by the local demand for funds and the local supply.
The local supply will depend, among other things, on the
supply of money in the country, on the basis of which we may
suppose a more or less developed credit structure to have been
erected. What will be the consequence of such an arrangement
on the length and amplitude of cycles in the different countries ? Here, again, the answer cannot be contained in a single
formula.

On the one hand, localisation of credit tends to damp down
local booms and depressions. Suppose a local boom flares up—
because, *e.g.*, the demand for the export goods of the area in question has risen or because of a purely internal stimulus to investment.
With an international capital market in operation, funds may in
such case be drawn from the whole world. The interest rate will
rise much less quickly than it would, were only local funds available. A local depression may also be alleviated or shortened by
imperfect mobility of capital. When the demand for investible
funds is at a low ebb, the fact that such funds cannot leave the
country will so reduce the rate of interest that the chances of revival
are improved.

On the other hand, there are a number of reser-
Reservations. vations to this principle. While a boom, like a
fire, is more easily extinguished where the supply
of inflammable material is restricted, it may be that the causes of
the fire provide at the same time the inflammable material. If
the boom is caused by a rise in foreign demand, the influx of
money will increase the supply of investible funds as well as the
demand, and may, under a regime of localised credit, depress the

rate of interest below the rate which would have prevailed had capital exports been possible. In the same way, a depression due to an adverse movement in international demand may be accentuated by a restriction of the supply of investible funds consequent upon a drain of money from the country.

But even if we restrict the generalisation about the moderating effect of credit localisation to booms and depressions where external causation is lacking or unimportant, it is applicable only to *relative* booms and depressions : that is to say, it is when a country is more prosperous than other countries that it suffers from the absence of capital movements. In the course of a general world boom, countries which, though enjoying a cyclical upswing, are less promising fields for investment than others may be drained of funds if capital movements are possible. It will be seen that anything which tends to hinder such movements may in the circumstances prolong the prosperity of some countries while limiting that of others. Similarly, localisation of credit may put a brake on depression in the most-depressed countries, while prolonging it in less-depressed countries.

A still further limitation must be placed on the general principle to allow for cases where capital exports and imports are not merely cyclical phenomena, but trend phenomena. Suppose that in some countries the supply of investible funds tends on the whole— counting in all phases of the cycle—to run ahead of the demand, and so to depress the rate of interest below that prevailing in other countries. If capital exports are possible, they will take place. If not, a part of the funds will be invested at home, bringing down the interest rate, while a part will be sterilised in hoards and cash reserves. Taking an average over good years and bad, the hoards will be larger if credit is localised than if it is not. But these hoards may be invested in boom periods at home. Their presence ensures that the supply of investment funds from domestic sources will be fairly elastic. It is even conceivable that the localisation of credit, by promoting the accumulation of hoards in advanced countries which would otherwise be capital-exporting, may make the supply of investible funds available to the entrepreneurs of those countries more elastic than it would be if international capital movements were possible.

Effects on "spreading" of cyclical movements.   Having attempted to sketch the effects of credit localisation on the cyclical movements of individual countries, let us now turn to the question of its effects on the spreading of such cyclical movements from country to country. Suppose that investment opportunities appear in country A, and a boom develops accompanied by rising interest rates. With a perfect world capital market, this would mean that funds would be drained from foreign countries, raising the rates of interest there. Foreign countries would thus experience at the same time a rise in their export trade to A, involving a rise in the demand for investible funds and a fall in the supply of those funds. It cannot in general be said whether the inflationary effect of the former would outweigh the deflationary effect of the latter. If, on the other hand, capital movements are impossible, the effect of A's boom is unambiguous. A's trade balance will become less favourable and money will tend to flow abroad, with the effect of increasing there the supply of, as well as the demand for, investible funds.

It might seem to follow from this argument that the localisation of credit is a factor tending to spread prosperity and depression from one country to another. But, even in the case considered above, this is not necessarily true. It was pointed out in the foregoing pages that in general—though there were exceptions—the effect of localisation of credit was to limit the extent of booms and depressions. In so far as it has this effect, it also limits the rise in A's imports, which will take place during an upswing in A and so limit the extent of the stimulus to business in the outside world. If funds could be transferred to A from the outside world, the increased investment there would have its repercussion on imports, thus giving rise to an increased demand for goods in the outside world. On the other hand, the transfer of the funds will reduce the supply of investible funds in the outside world : but it is conceivable that the latter effect will be less important than the former. This is likely to be the case when, during a depression, the supply of loanable funds is very elastic, the rate of interest having reached a minimum level (set by institutional circumstances) in the face of a very low demand. Thus, localisation of credit may easily have the effect of hindering the spread of a boom by hindering the boom itself. [1]

International transfers of demand. The disparate organisation of the world capital market opens up a new series of possible repercussions from changes which involve a transfer of demand from one country to another. The unequal development of credit in different parts of the world means that any movement of the balance of trade in favour of a country with a relatively highly developed credit structure will, *ceteris paribus*, have a net inflationary effect in the world as a whole. [2]

But, apart from this unevenness in the development of credit, a movement of funds from one national credit market to another brought about through changes in commercial currents will be likely to have a net effect. Whether this effect is expansionary or deflationary will depend on central-bank policy, confidence and liquidity of the banks, elasticity of the industrial demand for credit—all of which conditions are themselves largely dependent on the phase of the cycle in which the countries concerned find themselves when the change in demand occurs. In particular, any very violent diversion of demand between countries, such as may occur in the course of a world business cycle or as a result of war or large-scale harvest fluctuations, will probably be deflationary in its effect. The country losing money may be forced to contract, while the country gaining money will be unable at first to employ its new funds in investment. [3]

Sectional mobility of capital. For the purposes of our exposition, we have so far contrasted two extreme cases : viz., a state of affairs with no international lending and investment at all on the one hand, and a world economy in which there are no hindrances to the flow of investible funds from any one area to any other. In reality, of course,

---

[1] Here the Neo-Marxian Theory of Imperialism referred to on page 85 comes to the mind.

[2] *Cf.* especially Viner, *loc. cit.*

[3] This factor, which is probably of very great practical importance, has been analysed with great force by Dr. Thomas Balogh, " Some Theoretical Aspects of the Central European Credit and Transfer Crisis " in *International Affairs* (Journal of the Royal Institute of International Affairs), Vol. 11, May 1932.

while on the whole people do tend to lend and invest funds in their home country to an extent which prevents the complete equalisation of interest rates in different countries, there is normally a certain amount of international lending and investment.

In order to investigate such intermediate cases more closely, we must abandon the simplifying assumption that the market for investible funds is completely homogeneous. In reality, there are many sub-markets. One type of debt is not completely substitutable for another. It is therefore not surprising to find that the markets for certain types of debts are much more international than the markets for others.

Some Government obligations, for example, command a world market, whereas small business-men must borrow from those who know them and have some legal redress against them if the debts are not paid. For reasons of security, certain classes of debts are held exclusively by co-nationals of the debtors.

Another factor closely connected with security of repayment is liquidity, or quick saleability—a quality which makes debts to some extent a substitute for money. It is obviously more convenient to have one's current account with a local banker than with one whose offices are abroad. Also, the fact that people prefer to buy local securities is in itself a good reason for anyone's keeping that part of his wealth which he wants to be " liquid " in the form of local claims.

Mobility of short-term and long-term capital. It therefore remains true that, even at a time when considerable international capital movements may be taking place, a flow of money from country A to country B on current account—*i.e.*, as payment for goods and services exported by B in excess of imports—will bring about a diminution in the supply of investible funds available in A and an increase in the supply of investible funds available in B. If the capital market were international in all its branches, this would not take place. There would be an increase in the supply of investment funds in B; but it would be available to entrepreneurs in any country. In fact, however, the increased money in B will be deposited with the banks, and will lead to an expansion in the loans of the banks to industry and to the bill market, as also to an increase in the banks' holdings of securities. If the bill market in B is well known internationally, the cheapness of discounting there may lead to an afflux of exporters from A and elsewhere desirous of benefiting by the low discount rates. Similarly, the high prices of bonds in B, due to bank purchases, may make it easier for other countries to float new issues in B, and in addition may induce holders of B bonds to exchange them for bonds of other countries. The reverse process will take place in A. In this way, a part of the money which leaves A on *current* account will " leak " back on *capital* account, without, however, completely nullifying the favourable effect on the supply of credit available to borrowers in B or the unfavourable effect in A.

It may be a permissible simplification of the situation to suppose that there is a world-market for long-term bonds and shares, but that working capital has to be provided by each nation from national sources. We may suppose that, in the case of two countries A and B, opportunities for the absorption of long-term funds are opened up in A, whether such opportunities arise in connection with real investment or with the phenomena of a stock-exchange boom. The result in either case is a flow of loanable funds from B to A, which may exceed the adverse trading balance that A will probably develop as incomes in A rise. Now, if all sections of the capital market were international in scope, business-men in B would suffer from the rise in interest rates consequent on the rise in the demand by A for loanable funds, and would gain by the increased demand for B goods in A. In the circumstances of the supposed case, however, they will suffer an additional handicap in that the flow of money from B to A will induce the banks in B to restrict credit, and may render the supply of working capital in B scarcer than it is in A.

Cyclical changes in the mobility of capital. Even in the case of those sections of the capital market which are comparatively international in scope, the degree of internationalism depends upon factors—such as the policies of Governments and the state of confidence of individuals—which vary with the times. It may be possible to make the generalisation that during the downswing of the world business cycle, when the confidence of investors is at a low ebb, foreign lending is specially avoided as more dangerous than domestic lending, so that the brunt of the depression falls on the borrowing countries, while countries which normally are capital-exporting obtain some relief through the improvement of their balance of payments. The rôle of capital movements in the course of the world business cycle, however, is largely determined by events on the foreign exchanges, to which subject we now turn.

Summary.   The broad result of our analysis in this section is as follows. The influences of a localisation of investment and credit on the cyclical movement are manifold. Sometimes the tendency is to damp down local booms and depressions : sometimes the influence is the reverse. Everything depends on the details of the general economic constellation. While it may be said that the existence of transportation costs (that is, of a certain localisation of real goods) tends definitely to disturb the uniformity of the cyclical movement in the world and to make local booms and contractions possible, no such general statement can be made about the localisation of investment and credit in general. Given the existence of transportation cost and the geographical distribution of resources, it cannot be said that increased mobility of capital tends to synchronise the cyclical movement in all countries nor yet the reverse.

§ 4. DIFFERENT DEGREES OF NATIONAL CURRENCY AUTONOMY
AND THEIR INFLUENCE ON THE CYCLICAL MOVEMENT

Degrees of independence.   We have hitherto assumed a single basic money throughout the world, in terms of which all prices and debts are expressed, constituting together with bank notes and deposits, which represent essentially promises to pay the basic money, the sole medium of exchange. We shall now attempt to bring out the full significance of this assumption for the course of the cycle by confronting this unified, worldwide system with a number of less unified systems.

Recapitulating partly what has been said or implied in previous sections, we shall have to work through a whole series of cases, in which the monetary systems of the various countries become increasingly independent of one another. We shall eventually arrive at the very opposite extreme to complete world unification— namely, complete independence in the monetary systems of different countries : *i.e.*, completely free exchanges.[1]

A unified money system with mobility of capital. When we were arguing on the assumption of a closed, spaceless system, we postulated the existence of some basic money such as gold and a note circulation on that basis issued by a central bank. The central-bank money (which includes deposits with the central bank) forms in turn the basis for a credit structure built up by the commercial banks. Evidently, we must make some assumptions about the supply of the central-bank money : that is to say, we have to define the policy of the bank of issue in respect to the ratio between the note circulation and the gold reserve which it seeks to establish at any given moment of time.

Our previous postulate was maintained when we first introduced the space factor by assuming a certain geographical distribution of resources and transportation cost for goods and services. The same money circulated everywhere, and the conditions of the supply of investible funds as furnished by the central bank, commercial banks or other sources were everywhere the same. We saw that in this case, in spite of the fact that the supply of investible funds was uniform—consisting, as it did, of a single pool to which would-be borrowers from all parts of the system had equal access— local booms and depressions were not excluded because, owing to a certain localisation of real resources, the demand for investible funds might be concentrated in particular localities.

We may conceive of the central-bank money as supplied by a single institution with branch offices in various localities, all of which pursue the same policy. They issue notes by discounting bills at the same rate (and under the same conditions) or by buying and selling securities at the same prices. The cash (gold) reserve—if any—is pooled and not kept separately for each branch.

---

[1] Professor John H. Williams has attempted a similar analysis : " International Monetary Organisation and Policy ", in *Lessons of Monetary Experience*, New York, 1937. *Cf.* also Viner, *loc. cit.*

Decentralised banking with mobility of capital. So long as we adhere strictly to the assumption that perfect mobility of investible funds implies 100% equalisation of interest rates, we do not raise any basically new problem if we proceed to assume that the issue of money in each area is effected by independent institutions. Each area has its own central bank; but the money such banks issue is expressed in the same units and is accepted everywhere. All of these banks are forced to pursue the same policy. If one of them charges a lower rate for discounts than the others, it will be overwhelmed by an increase in demand diverted from all the others. Either its rate will have to be raised again, or else the other banks will have to follow suit by lowering theirs in order to retain their customers. Supply conditions for investible funds will still remain the same everywhere, and it will be impossible for one country separately to effect a local expansion or contraction by a manipulation of the supply of funds. Differences in prosperity between countries can only come from the demand side. (An artificial increase in demand can of course be brought about for any particular country by State intervention —*e.g.*, by State borrowing for public works. Whether and to what extent the ensuing boom will be localised will in such case depend on the localisation of resources, transport cost and the flow of purchasing power—that is, on the way in which the flow of new money is distributed by the successive recipients as between home goods and import goods.)

The problem remains of how the terms of lending, which must be the same for all the banks of issue, are determined.[1] Several systems are conceivable. The system which is the most important in practice is to make the determining factor some ratio—not necessarily constant—of the note circulation to a gold reserve. If the gold-reserve ratio of any one of these banks falls to a level which is considered as the lower limit, it will restrict lending. But, since we still assume perfect mobility of capital, the effect of this will be that borrowers are diverted to other banks, and that there is merely a redistribution of borrowers as between the different

---

[1] The same problem arises in a "spaceless" economy, if there are several banks of issue, or in a "cashless" economy (as imagined by some writers) where the circulating medium consists solely of bank deposits.

banks. No differential rate can be charged by any one bank because we have *ex hypothesi* a perfect market for loanable funds.

Central-bank policy with localised credit. This analysis may seem somewhat strange and unfamiliar. Our actual gold-standard experiences are certainly very different. The reason is that we are not really accustomed to assume perfect mobility of loanable funds, although we are not always aware of the fact. The assumption of perfect mobility of loanable funds does not indeed correspond to reality. Any abandonment or relaxation of the assumption at this stage will bring us much closer to the familiar realities of our gold-standard experience.

We shall continue to argue on the basis of a gold standard, under which the money is everywhere convertible into gold and a certain minimum ratio between the monetary circulation and the gold reserve is maintained. But we now propose to assume a more or less complete localisation of credit, and especially of central-bank credit. This will give the monetary authorities a somewhat wider scope in the pursuit of a policy of expansion or contraction by means of variations in the supply of investible funds, independently of what happens in other countries. The central bank of any particular country need not be afraid of being swamped by an immediate flood of demand for credit if it lowers its rate below the rate ruling in other countries. Needless to say, there are other limits to an independent policy in the fact that we still assume a common monetary standard : viz., gold. These limits depend on (*a*) the degree of localisation of credit and (*b*) the degree of closeness of trade connections as determined by the localisation of resources, transportation cost and the direction which is given to the flow of money by its successive recipients.[1] Up to a certain point, these limits can be widened by increasing tariffs and other impediments to the import of goods.

Within these limits, the central bank of a country may try to offset expansionary or depressing influences from other countries. If, for example, the balance of payments takes an unfavourable

---

[1] *Cf.* Paish, *loc. cit.*, who introduces the concept of " the Marginal Propensity to Import ".

turn and gold is withdrawn from the central bank for export, the central bank may maintain or even increase the amount of its liabilities by the purchase of some other form of asset such as Government securities. The length of time for which a country on the gold standard can persist in a policy of neutralising inflows and outflows of gold is, however, limited, in the case of an outflow, by the stock of gold in the possession of the central bank and, in the case of an inflow, by its stock of saleable assets other than gold. Even within these limits, the monetary authorities may be unable to " insulate " the country against fluctuations in the money flow due to international causes. Few would question their power to check a tendency to expand by means of a restrictive credit policy : but the deflationary effect of an unfavourable change in the balance of trade may be too strong to be counteracted by any purely banking policy. A mere maintenance of the outstanding volume of central-bank money (notes and deposits), while it obviates the necessity for the commercial banks to pursue an active policy of credit restriction, is probably insufficient to compensate the deflationary effects of an adverse balance of payments. It cannot completely compensate these effects unless the adverse balance is " caused " by an export of capital in the shape of purchases of foreign exchange and sales of Government and other national securities. If the cause of the adverse balance is a switch-over of demand from home-produced goods to foreign goods, we may presume that the higher price of Government securities and the continued willingness of the banking system to lend on short term will be unable to obviate—at any rate immediately—the deflationary consequences of a worsening of the anticipations of business-men.

The chief advantage of such a system as has been discussed is its ability to prevent the " secondary " unemployment which will otherwise follow a temporary dropping-off in foreign demand, and to counteract to a large extent the export of capital and the decline in capital imports. The chief disadvantage of the system is its tendency to give rise to doubts as to the maintenance of the gold parity, and encourage large-scale capital movements which in turn render much more difficult the task of maintaining the gold parity.

Different national money units. By mentioning the possibility of a variation in the exchange ratios between the various currencies, however, we introduce a new factor of considerable importance into our analysis. This we must now investigate more closely. So far we have assumed that there is the same money in all countries. We shall now suppose that each country has a money of its own—dollar, pound sterling, franc, etc.—which within its frontiers is everywhere acceptable as payment for goods and services, taxes, etc., but is not normally acceptable outside these frontiers.

So long as we assume these currencies to be closely linked by a common standard which involves a constant exchange ratio between these currencies, and so long as we assume that no question arises in any quarter as to the stability of these exchange rates, and that nobody anticipates the possibility of a variation in these rates, no new problems of any importance are raised by the introduction of a variety of national monetary units.

A new element of great importance, however, is introduced into the analysis when the possibility arises of variations in the exchange ratios between the different currencies.[1] It is not even necessary that such exchange variations should actually take place. The mere anticipation or apprehension of exchange variations will suffice to give rise to speculative movements of capital from one currency to another. People will naturally prefer to hold money (and claims expressed in money) which is expected to appreciate than to hold money (and claims expressed in money) which is expected to depreciate. The movement of capital will probably affect also the equities of the two countries, as well as the bonds, unless there is some reason to expect that a relative rise in dividends will take place in the country whose currency is expected to depreciate.

Speculation on the foreign exchanges. Speculation on foreign exchange, like all speculation, plays a double rôle. It may have a tendency either to offset or to accentuate disturbances arising from other sources. If it is believed that no change will take place in the exchange rates, short-term

---

[1] This new element clearly may arise without the previous introduction of a variety of national monetary units. But it would seem convenient to introduce it together with the latter.

capital movements of a stabilising character will appear whenever the other items in the balance of payments tend to disturb those rates.   In the case of a long-continued movement in one direction, such as might be caused by a transfer of demand for goods from country A to country B, speculative capital movements from B to A may offset the effect on the exchanges for some time; but later, either money (gold) must flow from A to B, or A's currency must depreciate with reference to B's.   If, however, the adverse development of A's balance on trading account is expected to be sufficiently considerable and sufficiently·lasting to cause a transfer of gold from A to B on such a scale as to lead to the abandonment of the gold standard by A, there will be a " flight " from A's currency to B's, which will accentuate the gold export and either advance the day when the gold standard must be abandoned or force A to a more severe deflation than would otherwise be necessary.   Anticipations regarding movements in the foreign exchanges tend to their own fulfilment. Similar pessimistic expectations, with similar unfortunate consequences, are likely to be aroused by any signs of unwillingness on A's part to exercise a deflationary pressure in response to an adverse trade balance, or by such devaluation on the part of B as makes a more adverse trade balance for A probable.

Under a gold-standard regime, the appearance of capital movements of the type described is an unhealthy symptom.   It means that the regime is thought to be in danger of breaking down. When, on the other hand, national policies cease to regard the maintenance of exchange stability as something which must take precedence over all other considerations, and when even a single important group of countries decides to envisage the use of exchange variation as an instrument of economic policy, speculation regarding the probable movement of the exchanges, and capital movements in connection with such speculation, are normal and inevitable features of economic life.

" *Exchange standards.*"   Before proceeding to enquire what happens to the business cycle in conditions where countries use exchange variation as an instrument of economic policy, we should perhaps pause to consider the cyclical implications of some of the other methods—*i.e.*, the methods other than the gold standard—of maintaining exchange stability. So far we have assumed that each country offers to exchange gold at a constant rate against its own currency, and keeps a reserve of gold which varies in some ratio with the volume of the monetary circulation. An alternative method of keeping the exchanges stable consists in buying and selling foreign exchange at a fixed rate and in treating foreign means of payment and claims thereto (balances abroad) as reserve instead of gold. These are the famous " exchange standards "—" gold exchange standard ", " sterling exchange standard ", " dollar exchange standard ", etc. For convenience, we shall refer to the countries whose central banks hold their reserves in the form of assets expressed in the monetary unit of some other country or countries as " exchange-standard countries ", and to the countries whose exchange provides the standard for the first group as " reserve countries ".[1] A group of countries in which some (the " exchange-standard countries ") keep their reserves in the shape of the assets of the others (the " reserve countries ") may be called a single " monetary group" of countries—*e.g.*, the " sterling *bloc*". To maintain the unity of the monetary group, there must either be only a single reserve country whose currency, itself independent, provides the standard for the group or the reserve countries must have a common standard—*e.g.*, gold.[2]

From the point of view of the individual exchange-standard country which thus " pegs " its exchanges to some other currency, the external money mechanism is exactly the same as under the gold standard; and the limits and possibilities of action to obviate expansionary or depressing influences from outside also remain in principle the same. If the policy is carried through by the central bank, with foreign exchange taking the place of gold as the reserve against liabilities which constitutes the country's basic

---

[1] The term " gold-exchange standard " is a little too narrow, because it suggests that the " reserve countries" keep their reserve in gold or exchange their currency on demand into gold. This need not be the case, as the example of the " sterling group " (" sterling *bloc*") shows.

[2] A two-sided or reciprocal exchange standard would be an arrangement whereby each member of the group undertakes to treat claims on all the others (foreign exchanges) as reserve. Under such a system, clearly the country which pursues the most inflationary policy would set the pace for all the others and would force them to inflate too.

money, there is no difference from an ordinary gold standard. If it is carried through by some other Government department which issues no money, such as an Exchange Equalisation Fund, the effect is still the same, though the details are slightly different.[1] If the central bank sells foreign exchange, it diminishes its liabilities to the public (including the commercial banks) and so stimulates credit restriction. If the Exchange Equalisation Fund sells foreign exchange and adds to its balance at the central bank, the public's balances must diminish *pro tanto* and credit restriction will follow as before.

From the point of view, however, of the world as a whole, the adoption of the exchange standard in preference to the gold standard may make a considerable difference to the money supply and may thereby affect the cyclical movement.

The transition from the gold standard, where every country holds a gold reserve in a certain proportion to its circulation, to a system where a number of countries hold no gold is bound to have an inflationary effect on the world as a whole. A change in the opposite direction tends to have a deflationary effect.

The very existence of such a system—and not *The exchange* merely its introduction or abandonment—is likely *standard* to exert some influence on the supply of money in *in operation.* all the countries concerned. Under the gold standard, any one country that expands faster than the others will lose gold and be forced to stop expanding. With some qualifications, which follow from what has been said in the previous

---

[1] A policy of " offsetting " influences operating through the balance of international payments on the internal situation which has been pronounced to be the main object of the various equalisation accounts (*cf.*, *e.g.*, N. F. Hall, *The Exchange Equalisation Account* (1935), *passim*) can be pursued and has frequently been pursued without a separate fund by the central bank. It must, however, be admitted that the psychological, legal and administrative reasons for and advantages of a separate account may be very important. On the policy of the British fund compare also F. W. Paish : " The British Exchange Equalisation Fund in 1935 ", *Economica*, 1936. *Idem*, 1935-1937, *Economica*, 1937. S. E. Harris, in his *Exchange Depreciation, 1936*, discusses also the American experience. On various technical points compare also Th. Balogh : " Some Theoretical Aspects of the Gold Problem ", *Economica*, 1937, and the *Memorandum on Money and Banking*, Vol. I, published annually by the Economic Intelligence Service of the League of Nations.

sections, we may say that, under the gold standard, the country with the least-rapid expansion sets the pace for the whole system. Under the new system, where a number of countries belong to a single monetary group in the sense defined above, this restraining force will cease to operate in one direction. The reserve country or countries, even if they themselves are " on gold ", need not be afraid of losing gold to the dependent exchange-standard countries. This restraining force is, however, still effective in the opposite direction. When the exchange-standard countries expand more rapidly than the reserve countries, the monetary reserves of the former—that is, their balances with the latter—tend to be depleted.

The mechanism of the exchange standard may however, provide automatically a certain substitute for the gold brake, although an unreliable and a weak one. Suppose an expansion takes place in the reserve countries, and their balance of payments *vis-à-vis* the exchange-standard countries becomes unfavourable in consequence. The latter will find their central-bank reserves increased accordingly. Much will then depend on the precise form in which these reserves are kept. If they are held as demand deposits in the reserve countries, the latter—while suffering no reduction in their own gold, or other, reserves—will nevertheless experience some deflation. Money will have been withdrawn from circulation, as it were, and sterilised in the form of demand deposits. This deflationary effect will be attenuated almost to vanishing-point, if the extra reserves of the exchange-standard countries are invested on the bill market or in securities. In any case, the expansion in the reserve countries will not experience to the full the usual " braking " effect of the rise of the adverse trade balance—namely, a fall in the gold reserve and a consequent credit restriction by the banking system.

On the other hand, under a gold standard, if one country expands and loses gold to others, it exerts an expansionary effect on the latter by strengthening their gold reserves. With the exchange standard in operation, this expansionary influence ceases to be effective in the direction from the exchange-standard countries to the reserve countries. If an exchange-standard country expands, the reserve countries do not experience an increase in their basic money supply. On the other hand, this expansionary influence still operates in the opposite direction. When the reserve countries expand, the exchange-standard countries will find themselves with an increased money supply and will be tempted to expand also.

From this argument, it would seem to follow that an upswing (or downswing) starting in a reserve country will be likely to spread more easily to other parts of the world, and go farther than it would under gold-standard conditions, because the exchange-standard countries will benefit (suffer) both in respect of their trade and in respect of their reserves while the reserve countries will not, as under the gold standard, lose (increase) their reserves. Similarly, an upswing (downswing) starting with the exchange-standard countries will be less likely to spread, and will go less far, than under a gold standard.

So much, however, cannot be said without qualification, at any rate when we are considering a gold-standard system where localisation of credit is not complete. Suppose, for example, an expansion in reserve country A. A's trade balance with exchange-standard country B deteriorates; but capital movements from B to A may be induced in such quantities that A's balance of payments with B actually improves. Under gold-standard conditions, A's gold reserve will rise in spite of the adverse trade balance; and this will help to increase liquidity and the supply of funds through the machinery of the banking system in A. The effect of the exchange standard may well be such as to counteract the influence of these capital movements. When capital moves from B to A—that is, when B's citizens are buying A's equities—the central bank in B will be forced to realise on its reserves. It may, *e.g.*, sell A's Government securities if its reserves are invested in such securities. The favourable effect on A of the capital movement from B will thus be largely offset.

Variations in exchange rates.   We may now return to the discussion of the point raised earlier in this section—viz., the influence on the cyclical movement of systems which either use variations in the exchange rate as instruments of policy or allow the exchanges to vary whenever the forces of the market tend to bring about a change in the rate.

We have seen that a most important—and, we may say, very disturbing—consequence of systems in which stability of the exchanges is no longer regarded as axiomatic is to be found in the extensive and irregular capital movements to which such systems give rise. By "irregular capital movements" we mean movements which are not induced by differences in the interest rate and do not therefore necessarily proceed from the rich countries to the poor countries, but on the contrary (so to say) "up-stream", and—what is perhaps the most disturbing feature of all—are subject to rapid fluctuations and abrupt changes of direction.

Naturally, there are different degrees of uncertainty as to the future of the exchanges. Different people will react to a prospective change in the exchange rate with different intensity. In the case of small countries where exchange transactions are familiar, or populations (*e.g.*, in Central Europe) where the memory of drastic depreciation of the currency is still fresh, a slight change or the danger of such a change will mean more, and will induce a more violent reaction, than in other countries. Furthermore, the effect of changes in the exchange rate on international capital movements frequently cannot be separated from other factors often alternative to changes in the exchange rate, such as transfer moratoria, partial defaults and the like. Therefore, so far as the details and the magnitude of the reaction are concerned, it is impossible to generalise : each case must be considered on its own merits. In a general way, we can only say that unstable exchanges unquestionably hamper normal international lending. They are one of the most powerful obstacles in the way of equalisation of interest rates between countries. The irregular capital movements to which they give rise introduce an erratic factor which may considerably disturb the cyclical movement, giving it sometimes a quite unexpected turn.

After these general considerations, we shall now discuss two problems : (1) the consequences on the business cycle of a definite act of devaluation—that is, of a deliberate and substantial change of the exchange rate, and (2) certain peculiarities (not to say paradoxes) arising under a system of "free exchanges"—that is, under a system where the exchanges are allowed to vary with the variations of supply and demand in the market and no attempt is made to keep them stable.

Currency devaluation. Recent years have provided many examples of deliberate and substantial changes in exchange rates. Since the gold value of a currency is still regarded as the norm, and since the initiative is almost invariably taken by the country whose currency is depreciated, these changes in the exchange rate are commonly referred to as a depreciation or devaluation of a currency in terms of the other currencies, although the depreciation of one currency necessarily implies the appreciation of the others. The consequences of these changes on the international and domestic trade of all the different countries involved have been extensively discussed in connection with recent experiences.[1] It is not proposed to reproduce all the arguments which may be, or have been, advanced for or against devaluation under the various possible circumstances. It is proposed, instead, to apply our analysis of the cyclical movement in order to trace the main channels through which alterations in exchange rates are likely to exert an expansionary or depressing influence on the national economies concerned, and to indicate the relevant circumstances on which the resulting effect will depend.

We assume that, before and after the devaluation, the countries concerned will pursue a policy of stabilising the existing rate, at any rate for the time being. If the exchanges are allowed to fluctuate freely with the changes of supply and demand, we have the system of "free exchanges" which will come up for discussion later. In order to make it easier for the reader to follow the analysis, we shall refer to the country or countries whose currency has been devalued as " D countries " or simply " D " and to the country or countries whose currency has appreciated as " A countries " or " A ".

Effects on exchange of goods. We have first the effect of an act of devaluation on the flow of goods—*i.e.*, on international trade. (We shall disregard for the moment effects due to the stimulation of capital movements.) In the case with which we are concerned, the influence is clearly expansionary for the D country. Exports are stimulated; imports are made more difficult. Export industries and industries

---

[1] Compare the exhaustive treatment by S. E. Harris, *Exchange Depreciation* (Cambridge, Mass.), 1936.

which compete with imports will benefit. Their demand for investible funds will rise, or cease to fall off, or cease to fall off so rapidly; and this will have favourable repercussions on other trades. The fact that imported raw material rise in price in terms of the domestic currency is unlikely to nullify altogether the benefits referred to. So far as these raw materials enter into export goods, their rise in price will offset only a part of the export premium afforded by the depreciation of the currency. So far as they are used for domestic purposes, the adverse influence may possibly be more potent.

Devaluation has a favourable effect, not only on the demand for, but also on the supply of, investible funds. The augmentation in the supply is due to the increased gold reserve resulting, not merely from the improvement in the balance of trade, but also from the marking-up of the value of the existing reserve in terms of the local currency. If there was a pressure on the gold reserve of the central bank, it will be lessened or removed; and so an obstacle to recovery may be eliminated.

For similar reasons, in so far as the influences on exports and imports of goods and services are concerned, the effect of a variation in the exchange rate on the A country or countries will tend to be depressing.

Influence on the world as a whole. What will be the influence on the world as a whole? Will the combined effect on both the D and the A countries be expansionary or deflationary? So far as the influence exerted through the supply of investible funds is concerned, it is possible to make some generalisations. If, as is likely, the devaluation takes place under the pressure of a declining gold supply, and if the A countries have an ample gold reserve, the combined effect will be expansionary. The result will be an alleviation in the D countries and no particular " tightness " in the A countries. If the rôles of the two groups are changed, the result will be the opposite.

We may also put it this way. The result will be expansionary if the devaluation constitutes a movement towards an " international equilibrium ", and deflationary if it leads away from equilibrium— the criterion for an international equilibrium being the absence of persistent gold movements and of abnormal capital movements motivated by an anticipation of a fall or rise in the exchange rate.

Again, it will be expansionary when it corrects an "over-valuation" of the depreciated, and an "under-valuation" of the appreciated, currency : it will be deflationary when such a disparity is accentuated.[1] The criterion of over- and under-valuation is the divergence from the equilibrium level as defined above.[2] Naturally, the devaluation may be so strong as to create a disparity in the opposite sense. It is common knowledge that this has in fact frequently occurred.

It is much more difficult to say anything definite on the world effect, so far as the influence on the demand for investible funds is concerned. In the D country, owing to the encouragement of exports and discouragement of imports, the demand for investment funds will be stimulated. In the A countries, the demand will be unfavourably influenced, even if (owing to the existence of ample reserves) the supply of investible funds is not affected at all. It is impossible to say whether the expansionary effect in D or the deflationary effect in A will be stronger. Much will depend on certain lags. If, for example, a cumulative expansion process in D has time to develop before a contraction in A has got under way, it will have favourable repercussions on A, so that A may be relieved from the initial pressure produced by the devaluation.

Effect on capital movements. It is, however, probable that the total result will be decisively influenced by other factors to which we must turn now. We are thinking of the influences which a variation in the exchange rate may exert through capital movements and possibly through "psychology". (In practice, there are, of course, still other factors to be considered—viz., the probability of retaliatory measures in the sphere of currency manipulation or of commercial policy. There is also the effect on the international economic policy of the D country itself to be considered. The devaluation may enable a country to relax impediments to international

---

[1] Compare P. B. Whale : "The Theory of International Trade in the Absence of an International Standard" in *Economica*, London, February 1936, pages 33 and 34, for a discussion of the terms "over-valuation" and "under-valuation", and Harris, *loc. cit.*, *passim*.

[2] Measurements of "purchasing-power-parity" based on comparisons of price levels or of changes in price levels in both countries afford only very rough and unreliable criteria of over- and under-valuation.

trade such as quotas, tariffs or exchange restrictions. These considerations may sometimes be of vital importance : but they fall outside the scope of the present study.)

A devaluation is bound to have a strong influence on the movement of capital; and the fundamental effect on the trade currents may be blurred as a result. Since it is not probable that a devaluation will come quite unexpected out of the blue, it may be assumed that it will be preceded by capital outflows from the D country. After the operation has been accomplished, it is likely that these capital flows will cease or even be reversed. It will be apparent, if this happens, that the operation of these developments does not run counter to the fundamental influence exerted on the D and A countries through the effect on the export and import of goods and services, but, on the contrary, accentuates and anticipates it. In this case, the devaluation will be regarded as successful from the point of view of the D country. This result depends, however, on certain expectations being created—in particular, the expectation that the devaluation will be definitive for a considerable time to come. It does not necessarily follow that this expectation will be created. The devaluation may be regarded as no more than a first step, to be followed by others in the same direction. In that case, capital movements away from the D countries may be induced, and the favourable effect on the supply of investible funds in the D economy will be postponed.

While ordinarily the effects of devaluation in a single country on the world situation—through changes in the trade balances and revaluation of the gold reserves of the countries affected—may be said to be on the whole inflationary, the capital movements which may be induced will probably have a deflationary effect on the world as a whole; and the deflationary effect may be stronger on balance than the inflationary effect.

Deflationary effects of capital flights. Ordinary capital movements—*i.e.*, movements induced by disparities in interest rates or profit rates in different countries—must be counted as expansionary, because money which may have been in part hoarded in the country of origin owing to its lower rates of interest will be invested to a greater extent in the capital-importing country because of its higher rates of interest.

This presumption does not hold good of capital movements motivated by the desire to profit by, or to avoid losses from, expected exchange movements. It is even likely to be reversed if the movement of funds assumes large proportions. The potential extent of such " abnormal " capital movements, when people are thoroughly scared, is much larger than any " normal " capital movement could be; and they may expose the capital-exporting country to a much more serious drain of gold than is likely to develop in a short period of time from an adverse movement in the trade balance. Consequently, the funds will in all probability tend to move from a country with a high rate of interest to one with a low rate.

This in itself would render probable the view that the capital movement is deflationary : but, in addition, there is the attitude of the receiving country to the extraordinary import of capital to be taken into account. It will be realised that funds of this nature are liable to be withdrawn as quickly as they appear. Banks with which foreign balances are deposited regard them as "bad" or "hot" money, and will not re-lend more than a relatively small proportion of them. If the banks are incautious, the central bank will probably realise that the increase in its gold reserve occasioned by the afflux of foreign funds is liable to disappear at short notice, and will refrain from expanding central-bank money accordingly. Thus, while the flow of funds will cause a considerable reduction in investment in the countries from which it comes, it will be largely sterilised in those to which it goes.

Free exchanges. We turn now to the discussion of an extreme case in our scale of possible relationships between the currencies of different countries—viz., the case where the different national currencies are completely independent of one another. This is the exact opposite of a completely unified world monetary system. This system of " free exchanges ", as we may call it, gives rise to a number of peculiar reactions, which stand in sharp contrast to our familiar gold-standard experience. It is not suggested that such a system has ever existed in a pure form. It is nevertheless instructive to enquire into its probable consequences : first, because there are monetary arrangements which come near (and tendencies which would bring us near) to such a system and, secondly, because certain implications of familiar views derived from gold-standard experience are brought out very clearly by contrast.[1]

Let us first give a precise definition of what we understand by " complete independence of two national currencies ". Independence implies, of course, the absence of an international standard. The exchanges are allowed to vary according to the situation of demand and supply in the market. No central bank or other institution interferes in order to stabilise the exchange at any particular level. While, under the gold standard, a disparity between demand and supply in the exchange market leads to a flow of gold from one country (or region) to the other, no such money flows are possible under the "free-exchange system". While, under the gold standard, equilibrium in the balance of payment is eventually restored by contraction in the amount and flow of money in one country and expansion in the other, with free exchanges this equilibrating function is assumed by variations in the exchange rates. The free-exchange system may also be described in the following manner. The money circulating in any given country is strictly confined to the territory of that country. There is no arrangement to enable money in one country to be transferred to another country and used there for paying debts and buying goods, whether directly or indirectly through the intermediary of a central bank or an Equalisation Fund with a stock of foreign money which it sells at a more or less fixed price against domestic money, thereby contracting the circulation of the one, and expanding the circulation of the other, currency.[2] Anyone who wishes to buy foreign means of payment for the purpose of buying foreign goods or making investment

---

[1] Compare the very illuminating article by P. B. Whale, *op. cit.*, pages 24 and 38.

[2] We shall see that it would be incorrect or, rather, that it would beg important issues and exclude important eventualities if we were to conclude from this that, in any given country, the total demand for goods in terms of money (MV) remains constant in face of changes in the international transactions (owing to fluctuations in commodity trade or capital movements).

abroad must secure them through the market from those who desire, for similar reasons, to sell foreign means of payment.

The "impact" rate of exchange. When considering a state of affairs where variations in the exchange rate are used to restore equilibrium in the foreign-exchange market, we are confronted at the outset with a difficulty.[1] At any given moment, there is a volume of international payments to be made under existing contracts. If there is a deficit in country A's balance at a certain point of time, it is by no means certain that it can be wiped out by any variation in the exchange rate. Whether this is possible or not depends on the currencies in which the debts falling due at a given moment are expressed. "If all payments contracted for between two countries are fixed in terms of the currency of one of them, it is clear that no variation in the exchange rate can alter the relation between the two sides of the account."[2] If all the credit items of country D are expressed in D's currency and all debit items in A's currency, a deficit in D's account will for the moment be aggravated by a depreciation in D's currency (although, if the depreciation had time to exert its influence on exports and imports, it might restore equilibrium). The deficit could immediately be wiped out by an appreciation in D's currency; but it is difficult to see how the market mechanism can produce such an appreciation under the assumed circumstances : for, if there is a deficit in D's balance, D's demand for A's money will rise and A's currency will appreciate—which, as we have seen, aggravates the situation. (This is what GRAHAM calls a "self-inflammatory" exchange variation.) It is only when D's debit items are fixed in D's currency and its credit items in A's currency that we can expect the exchange market to achieve a smooth adjustment automatically through a depreciation of D's currency.

---

[1] F. D. Graham has called attention to this difficulty in his article "Self-limiting and Self-inflammatory Movements in Exchange Rates" in *Quarterly Journal of Economics*, Vol. 43, February 1929, pages 221-249. See also by the same author : *Exchange, Prices and Production in Hyper-inflation : Germany 1920-1923* (1930), pages 136 *et seq.* Compare also P. B. Whale, *op. cit.*, pages 27 and 28.

[2] P. B. Whale, *op. cit.*, page 27.

Transfer of demand under " free exchanges ".　We may, however, get round this difficulty (which is probably of no practical importance) by relaxing our assumptions a little, so as to allow of some private or official transactions with the object of preventing these short-term fluctuations. Suppose, then, that there are no capital movements at all other than those involved by the ephemeral transactions just mentioned. In these circumstances, a switch-over of demand from country D to country A occurs[1] by reason (say) of a change in the taste of the consumers in A and / or D, or the introduction of a new tariff in A, or a rise in cost of production in an export industry of D, or a reduction in cost in a competing industry in A. In the assumed conditions, the value of D's currency must fall relatively to that of A's currency. The farther it falls the cheaper will D goods become in terms of A's currency and relatively to A goods. If the elasticity of demand for imports in terms of the local currency can be assumed to be greater than unity both in A and in D, D will spend less D money on imports from A and A will spend more A money on imports from D. The rate of exchange will be such as to equilibrate the value of D's import (A's exports) and A's imports (D's exports). Thus, the more elastic the reciprocal demand of A and D for each other's products, the less the need for D's currency to fall in value relatively to A's currency.[2]

What will be the consequence of this change on the internal situation in A and D ? Under the system of " free exchanges ", there is no flow of money between countries. D's banking system is not any less liquid, or A's any more liquid, in consequence of the change in demand than before. There is thus no reason for a change in the supply of investible funds in the two countries. Nor is it clear how the demand for investible funds will be affected. The initial transfer of demand meant greater profitability in the

---

[1] We call the two countries A and D in order to keep in mind that **A** is the country the currency of which will appreciate, and D the country the currency of which will depreciate.

[2] If we suppose the two countries to have close trading connections, with competing industries and potential export and import capacity, we may safely assume an elasticity greater than unity. This is still truer of one country *vis-à-vis* the rest of the world.

A industries and less profitability in the *D* industries directly affected; but the modification in the exchange rate provided an exactly equivalent stimulus to the *D* industries and a setback to the *A* industries. The conclusion must be that, if the transfer of demand from *D* to *A* has any effect whatever of a stimulating or depressing nature on either *D* or *A*, it must be because of some peculiarities in the industries involved. In both countries, there is a horizontal shift in demand; and the outcome will depend on a number of factors which have been analysed in an earlier chapter. The only *a priori* justification we might have for expecting an upswing in *A* and a downswing in *D* is that the initial switch-over in demand may be anticipated by the industries concerned to a greater extent than the counter-effects on export industries as a whole due to exchange variations.

Comparison with gold standard. It will be noted that this is very different from what we are accustomed to expect under a gold-standard regime. We have, *e.g.*, argued that, under the gold standard, the imposition of a tariff has an expansionary effect on the country which imposes the tariff and a deflationary effect on the country whose goods are shut out from the market of the former. This rule does not hold good under a system of free exchanges. The difference between the two systems may become clearer, if we put it in yet another way. Assuming no capital movements, an increase in exports from country *A* to country *D* under a free-exchange system will produce an immediate equal increase in imports. Under the gold standard, some time will elapse before the effect is apparent. In the meantime, money will flow from *D* to *A*—or rather, under a one-sided or two-sided exchange standard, money will not flow physically, but the central bank in *A* will expand on the basis of increased balances in *D*. This intermediate step is cut out under a system of free exchanges; and thus the necessity for expanding in the one, and contracting in the other, country is eliminated.[1]

---

[1] It is interesting to note that, frequently, free traders use arguments which are appropriate (as a short-run proposition) only to a free-exchange system and not to a gold standard—*e.g.*, when they point out that a decrease in imports must be followed by a decrease in exports and *vice versa*.

By reasoning not essentially different from the
Localisation above, it can be shown that, under free exchanges
of prosperity without capital movements, there will be no
and tendency for prosperity or depression to commu-
depression nicate itself from country to country. On the
complete. other hand, they will tend to spread more thoroughly throughout all the industries within the
country than they do under gold-standard conditions.
Suppose an expansion process is started in country D. Prices
and incomes rise. Imports will go up, and D's currency will fall
relatively to A's currency. But, *pari passu* with the rise in imports,
exports will grow, so that the boom in D will develop unweakened
by a drain of money abroad. Country A, on the other hand, will
experience an increase in exports no less than in imports. Whether
on balance these two changes will be expansionary or deflationary
will depend on the same set of circumstances as the expansionary
or deflationary character of a horizontal shift in demand. Under
a system of free exchanges, the powerful factor which under a
gold standard dips the balance on the side of expansion—viz., the
inflow of money—is lacking. By analogous reasoning, it can be
shown that contractions also lose much of their contagious
character. The free-exchange system eliminates from the economic
interchange of different countries the most important carrier of
the boom and depression bacillus—namely, the flow of money
across frontiers.

Let us now consider the effect of capital movements
Capital under a system of free exchanges. Suppose people
movements in D seek to invest money in A for any reason, or
under free people in A seek to borrow money from D. No
exchanges. money can move; but the demand for A money rises,
and D's currency falls in value accordingly. D's
exports rise, and/or imports fall, by the amount which is being
invested abroad. The capital movement at once brings about
an export surplus in D's balance of trade, which is an import
surplus from A's point of view.

The effect of this movement on D, the capital-exporting country,
is very likely to be expansionary. Demand for goods as a whole
has certainly not fallen : but it may well have risen if even a small

part of the money which seeks investment abroad comes out of hoards, or would have been hoarded if the transfer abroad had not been possible.

In the capital-importing country A, the effects are the contrary— viz., deflationary. The money which people in D want to invest in A can be made available only by an import surplus in A—that is, it is withdrawn from the sales of A products. More goods are offered for sale in A : but total demand has not risen. It will be seen that this deflationary effect obtains even on the most favourable assumption : viz., the assumption that the money made available in A for investors in D is spent on goods—*i.e.*, is really invested. If—as may be the case with speculative movements of capital—a part of the money is kept in liquid form, the deflationary effect is accentuated.

Contrast with gold standard.   From the point of view of our gold-standard experience, it appears highly paradoxical that the capital-exporting country should be stimulated and the capital-importing country depressed as a result of capital movements !

The difference between the *modus operandi* of the two systems may again be put this way. Under a gold standard, capital export will usually not produce an immediate corresponding movement of goods.[1] It will first lead to a money flow, which will then induce a flow of goods. This intermediate phase is cut out under the operation of a system of free exchanges.

In the light of this analysis of the effects of capital movements under free exchanges, we may reconsider the case of a switch-over of demand from D goods to A goods. D's currency will depreciate. This may induce speculative capital movements. Suppose the movement of the exchange is believed to be temporary and likely to

---

[1] Under exceptional circumstances, it may happen that the money which D lends to A is spent in A entirely on D's or A's export goods, so that the change in the balance of trade is brought about without friction —that is, without a relative or absolute contraction in the lending, and a relative or absolute expansion in the borrowing, country. (Compare R. Nurkse, *Internationale Kapitalbewegungen*, Vienna, 1935, pages 121, 122 and 144.) Owing, however, to transport cost and the resulting localisation of demand for goods, this will rarely happen to the extent of 100% of the sum transferred.

be reversed—as it will be, *e.g.*, in the case of seasonal movements. In that case there will be a movement out of A values (money, debts and bonds) into D values. This flow of funds will run counter to the initial transfer of demand and will to some extent obviate a fall in D's money. It will also produce an import surplus in D. The result—in accordance with familiar gold-standard experience—will therefore be that the transference of demand stimulates business in the country to which the demand is transferred, and depresses it in the country from which the demand is transferred. The rôle of gold movements is thus taken over by speculative capital movements.

It is, however, clear that things may take an entirely different turn, and that the gold-standard reactions may be, not reproduced, but reversed under free exchanges. People in D may become fearful of their currency's falling still lower. In that case, capital movements from D to A will set in, and D's currency will be depressed still more. The result, as explained above, will be that D, the country which lost the trade in the first instance, will be stimulated by the export of capital, while depression will spread in the country which originally gained the trade.

Capital movements induced by the cycle. In the foregoing pages, we have assumed a capital movement to take place however occasioned, and have investigated its influence on the general economic situation and the cyclical fluctuations in the two countries concerned. But the cyclical variations themselves are likely to give rise to capital movements which in turn will react on the cycle in those countries. An analysis of these reciprocal influences leads us to reconsider a case discussed a few pages earlier.[1] Arguing under the assumption that *no* capital movements were taking place, we there reached the conclusion that, under the system of free exchange, the most important channels through which prosperity and depression spread from country to country are blocked. This result must now be modified through the application of our analysis of the consequences of capital movements.

Suppose that a boom flares up in country D because new investment opportunities have appeared. If this attracts foreign

---

[1] See above, page 446.

capital, the expansionary stimulus is at once transmitted to the other (capital-exporting) countries, while the expansion is hampered in the country D, where the stimulation first arose.[1] If, on the other hand, the expansion in D is brought about or fostered by a cheap-money policy and if thereby capital is driven out of the country D (to take advantage of the higher interest rates abroad), the expansion in D is still further intensified by the outward capital movement. The outside world, instead of basking in the rays of prosperity cast by D, feels a chilling wind from that quarter and may even be thrown into a vicious spiral of deflation.[2]

It would not be difficult to construct other cases and to analyse them along the lines indicated. But the general conclusion already stands out clearly : our previous result that under free exchanges the cyclical movement in different countries is independent needs modification if capital moves freely. It is, however, not quite correct to say without qualification (as has sometimes[3] been said) that capital movements tend to reproduce gold-standard conditions. On the contrary, they may produce exactly the opposite result from what we would expect under an international gold

---

[1] It is impossible in this case to decide on general grounds whether D's currency will appreciate or depreciate, because there are two conflicting forces at work. The inflow of capital tends to push up the value of D's money, the rise in prices and incomes tends to depress it. We may perhaps suppose that the first factor is likely to exert its influence first, so that the currency will appreciate. The result is, however, in principle independent from the direction in which the exchange rate moves. Compare next footnote.

[2] It should be noted that this is not because D's currency has fallen in value, but because of the export of capital from D. The same result that prosperity in one country spreads depression to others could obtain with the D currency appreciating. Suppose the present case is complicated by a fortuitous shift in demand from A- to D-goods, strong enough to over-compensate the influence on the exchanges exerted by the capital outflow from D, so that D's currency actually appreciates. It follows from our preceding analysis that, abstracting from fortuitous circumstances which may work out either way, this shift in demand is neutral ; it does not tend to stimulate the country to which demand has shifted and to depress the other from which it was drawn away. It goes without saying, however, that exchange fluctuations may become relevant by inducing speculative capital movements. Unfortunately, there is no possibility of telling in general which way these speculative capital movements will go.

[3] Cf., e.g., Whale, loc. cit.

standard. Under free exchanges with free flow of capital, the cyclical movements in different countries are not independent of each other; in that respect, the system of free exchanges with free mobility of capital resembles gold-standard conditions. While, however, under a gold standard an expansion (contraction) in one country tends to produce expansion (contraction) in the other, under free exchanges with capital movements expansion (contraction) in one country may just as well induce a contraction (expansion) abroad as an expansion (contraction).

Limitation of foregoing analysis. The short-run nature of the preceding analysis should be kept in mind. We have been concerned with the effects of temporary *fluctuations* in capital movements, not with the ultimate effects on the economic development of a country of a long-continued flow of capital imports or exports. Moreover, even the short-run effect of individual items in a continuous flow to which the countries concerned have already adapted themselves is a quite different matter from the effects of extraordinary fluctuations.

The classical contention that capital exports from the industrial countries of Western Europe and the United States to the other parts of the world were indispensable for the rapid development of the latter and beneficial to the whole world, including the capital-exporting countries themselves, is not in the least invalidated or made conditional upon the existence of an international gold standard[1] by our somewhat paradoxical result to the effect that, under free exchanges, capital *imports* and, under an international standard, capital *exports* are likely to have a deflationary influence. It should be remembered furthermore that this deflationary influence is relative to the situation which would otherwise prevail. If a rapid monetary expansion is in progress, the deflationary check which an inflow of capital provides may be very wholesome. This will be the case especially if the supply of unemployed factors of production is small and inelastic, as it is likely to be in poor and industrially undeveloped countries. Once again

---

[1] It is, of course, another question whether the absence of an international standard would not increase the risk of foreign lending so much as to restrict it considerably.

the reader must be requested not to ascribe indiscriminately a positive value to expansionary and a negative value to deflationary effects.

Possible extension of preceding analysis.
The reader would do well to regard this chapter as containing an exposition of a method of analysis rather than a presentation of definite results which can be applied without further investigations to concrete cases. With this caution, it is possible to apply the analysis of the effects of capital movements, *mutatis mutandis*, to other types of unilateral payments such as interest and dividend payments, reparations payments, war debts and the like. But this extension of the argument must be made with great care, keeping in mind all the assumptions, especially those as to the elasticity of supply of investible funds from inflationary sources, on which the results of our analysis were based.[1]

---

[1] It is quite likely that, say, reparation payments from one country to another will affect the " propensity to consume " or the " propensity to save " (to borrow these expressions from Mr. Keynes) in a different way from ordinary commercial capital movements. In the receiving country, *e.g.*, the propensity to consume might be stimulated. If that is the case, we must expect results different from those resulting from capital movements.

Part III

MONETARY AND REAL FACTORS AFFECTING ECONOMIC STABILITY

A Critique of Certain Tendencies in Modern Economic Theory

CHAPTER 13

CRITIQUE: TENDENCIES IN MODERN ECONOMIC THEORY

§ 1. INTRODUCTION

It is the conclusion of the present paper that a large part of contemporary economic theory has laid undue stress on "real" factors and that "monetary" factors and the closely related phenomena of institutional price and wage rigidities have been neglected or their importance grossly underestimated. Instability in general economic activity as well as in the external balances of payments are explained in terms of physical rigidities, fixed coefficients of production, stubborn inelasticities of demand and supply, instead of being attributed to faulty monetary arrangements and policies, to price and wage rigidities and similar factors.

§ 2. THE MEANING OF INSTABILITY

Let me explain first what I mean by instability. I define it as fluctuations in aggregate output and employment. However, even with stable aggregate output and employment, price instability is possible in the sense of changes in relative prices as well as of the price level (in any one of the possible meanings of this ambiguous term). Price instability introduces instability in the income distribution which may well present very serious social and economic problems. Sharp

---

This chapter is an abridged and slightly altered version of a paper read at the *First Congress of the International Economic Association* held in Rome 1956. The full text appears in the proceedings of the Congress (London, Macmillan and Co.)

changes in the terms of foreign trade, which are an especially
serious matter for highly specialized primary producing countries, are an example on the international level. But there can
be no doubt that in most cases violent changes in the terms
of trade between large segments of the economy on the national
or international level are the consequences or concomitants of
fluctuations in aggregate output and employment in the industrial countries.

For this reason I shall concentrate in this paper on the short run
fluctuations—the business cycle in the industrially developed
countries.

In the " underdeveloped " countries economic instability is to
a very large extent either the reflection of the business cycle in
the industrial world or the consequence of autonomous inflationary
policies. Much has been made of changes in demand, technology
and import policies of the industrial countries which may de-
stabilize the external balances of highly specialized primary
producing countries. Without wishing entirely to discount the
importance of these factors, I venture to say, however, that from
a global standpoint such sources of instability are of minor importance compared with the business cycle and inflation.

Inflation, to which I shall return briefly later in my paper, is by
no means an unimportant matter. On the contrary, I am convinced that long run (continuous or intermittent) inflation not
only introduces price instability but is also a factor seriously
retarding economic growth. But intellectually the problem of
rapid secular inflation[1] is much less challenging than the
problem of the business cycle to which I turn my attention
now.

Business cycles I take in the sense in which the term is used by
the National Bureau of Economic Research—that is ups and downs
in aggregate activity, more precisely in aggregate output and

---

[1] The slow, "creeping" kind of inflation which is now going on in many
developed countries is again a more insidious process, much harder to diagnose
and to evaluate than the rapid, open inflation which many underdeveloped
countries suffer.

employment, changes in output due to changes in employment.[1]
(Output can, of course, change without changes in employment—
harvest changes being the most important example. But the short
run changes in aggregate output that constitute the business cycle
are clearly not of that nature—which does not, however, exclude
that crop changes as well as other exogenous disturbances may
have great causal significance for the cycle).

I follow Mitchell and Burns in defining the cycle as the shortest
observable fluctuations in activity. In their words, " business
cycles vary from more than one year to ten or twelve years and
are not divisible into shorter cycles of similar character with
amplitudes approximating their own ".[2] Furthermore, I make
no attempt at finding a regular sequence or pattern of
" minor " and " major " cycles (as Hansen thinks there exists).
Cycles do, of course, differ greatly in duration and enormously in
amplitude; some depressions are mild, others severe; some
upswings strong, others weak and abortive.[3] But the most
careful investigations in *Measuring Business Cycles* have convinced
me that no regular and persistent pattern exists or at any rate has
yet been discovered; that it is not possible to interpret the succession of cycles of different length and amplitude as resulting from
the superimposition of independent or interdependent cycles of
different length (Schumpeter's three cycle schema); that it is even
less defensible to assign different quasi-independent cyclical
mechanisms to the different superimposed cycles. Each cycle or
depression is, in a sense, an historically unique case; that is to say
it is the joint product of endogenous and exogenous forces. The
result of the interaction between the cyclical mechanism and the

---

[1] In identifying fluctuations in activity with fluctuations in aggregate
output and employment, I deviate somewhat from the great masters of the
National Bureau. The deviation is, however, slight because their cyclical
chronology for "activity" is almost perfectly matched by the cyclical chronology in aggregate output and employment series.

[2] See BURNS AND MITCHELL, *Measuring Business Cycles*, p.3. Seasonal
fluctuations are not of "similar character ".

[3] This makes me doubt the usefulness of the averaging procedure adopted
by N.B.E.R. even with all the caution and reservations expressed by the
illustrious authors of *Measuring Business Cycles*.

historical environment and external disturbances is a complicated chemical compound and not a mechanical mixture whose constituent parts are separable by more or less mechanical statistical devices. The statistical decomposition of time series in cycles and trend is an insoluble problem.[1] But this does by no means exclude that it is often possible to explain particular cycles or phases (depressions or expansions) in terms of exogenous forces or endogenous processes or to point to strongly intensifying or mitigating factors which explain the mildness or severity of a particular depression, or weakness or strength of a particular upswing. Let me mention only one or two examples—more will follow later. The intensification of the boom following the outbreak of the war in Korea does not require any further explanation than reference to the wave of Governmental and private spending engendered by the war.[2] The great depression of the 1930's in the U.S., whatever its deeper causes, was undoubtedly tremendously intensified by the collapse of the banking system.

It is disturbing that economists do not see eye to eye on all these matters. But we can take consolation in the fact that despite great divergences in the interpretation and explanation, different

---

[1] It is perhaps more correct to say that the problem is meaningless, at least in the sense in which it is—or rather *was*, for it is no longer a very live issue—usually formulated. The question is usually framed as a causal one: How to separate the effects of the causes responsible for the cycle from the effects of the causes responsible for the trend. The further assumption is made that the two sets of effects are additive. This assumption is surely unwarranted. The causes making for cyclical fluctuations, when impinging on a growing system, will produce very different results than they would produce in a stationary system. And similarly the growth factors would produce different results in an economic system that, unlike the one we live in, is not subject to cyclical fluctuations. As a consequence, if we could make the experiment of abstracting from the actual system which is subject to the joint operation of both sets of causes, first those that make for cycles, and second those that make for trend, the sum of the two effects would not be equal to, but would probably greatly exceed the total observed change.

[2] It should be observed, however, that in the U.S. the lower turning point following the mild recession of 1948-49 had occurred already in the middle of 1949. The war in Korea was therefore not necessary to pull the American economy out of a depression, but was superimposed on an upswing that had started independently.

writers agree about the dates of cyclical turning points and about certain basic characteristics of the short cycle. For example. cyclical chronologies established independently by the most careful investigations of the N.B.E.R., by Edwin Frickey's painstaking researches,[1] and by Schumpeter's more impressionistic methods agree almost entirely. (Divergences in the dates for turning points of a few months are hardly surprising and serious in view of the complexity of the underlying data).

While the contours of the short run business cycle are, thus, fairly clear and generally accepted—further characteristics which throw light on the role of money in its causation will be discussed presently—the long "waves" which go under the name of Kondratief cycles, secondary or trend cycles, are a much more hazy thing. They find their expression mainly in wholesale prices and interest rates. But the chronology varies considerably from writer to writer and from country to country; and it is not quite clear whether the ups and downs in prices are always associated—as they invariably are in the short cycle—with ups and downs in output and employment.

It is better not to identify the problem of long run stability with a hypothetical long cycle—a phrase which suggests an endogenous mechanism and a degree of regularity that simply do not exist. We should rather think of the occurrence or recurrence at irregular intervals of rising or falling price trends stretching over several short cycles which may or may not be associated with similar trends in real output.

§ 3.   A STRIKING CHARACTERISTIC OF THE SHORT CYCLE

One of the most striking and revealing characteristics of the short cycle is that the ups and downs in output and employment are closely correlated with ups and downs in price levels. *A fortiori* fluctuations in *real* magnitudes (output, employ-

---

[1] EDWIN FRICKEY, *Economic Fluctuations in the United States*, Cambridge, Mass., 1942.

ment, real income) are paralleled by fluctuations in *money* flows (money income, money value of output). It should be noted that this does not follow from our definition of the cycle which runs in *real* terms. Conceivably, prices as well as money values could be uncorrelated or negatively correlated with fluctuations in real output.

It seems to me that this actual, almost[1] perfect parallelism cannot be a chance phenomenon. In fact, an increasing number of business cycle analysts explicitly or implicitly agree that the *proximate* cause of fluctuations in output and employment is fluctuations in aggregate expenditure or effective demand. To be sure there is plenty of disagreement on the deeper forces and processes that are responsible for the cyclical fluctuations in aggregate expenditure. It is nevertheless highly significant that very diverse theories agree on the role of expenditure fluctuations. To this group belongs not only the various types of monetary theories of the cycle, but also all the modern " capital stock adjustment theories " which rely on some sort of interaction of multiplier and acceleration principle to construct an endogenous oscillating mechanism and even Schumpeter's theory, whose logical structure is entirely different, belongs to this group. All these theories explain in different ways why expenditures fluctuate in cycles; it is then easy to see how this produces cycles in output and employment—so easy indeed that the necessary assumption of some sort of price and wage rigidity is rarely made clear. Let me add that a very large part of currently employed methods of forecasting the future course of business consists of attempts to form a judgment on the probable course of various segments of the expenditure stream—business spending on investment (plant

---

[1] I say "almost perfect" because there are sometimes shortlived deviations at the turning points between the movement of prices on the one hand and that of real activity on the other. But note that even if the timing between prices and real volume is not perfect, it is still possible (and probably the case) that money flows (price times quantities) are perfectly correlated with volumes.

For the hypothetical long cycle the parallelism is certainly much less close. This surely is a reflection of the fact that in the long run price and wage flexibility is much greater than in the short run.

and equipment, inventories), consumer spending, Government spending, foreign demand, etc.

The proposition that fluctuations in aggregate effective demand or expenditure are the proximate cause of the business cycle does by no means imply that it is always monetary factors in the sense of active measures of monetary policy on the part of the monetary authorities or of the banks that bring about the fluctuations in expenditures. The line of causation does not necessarily always run from the monetary to the real factors, although it can hardly be doubted, in my opinion, that monetary factors do often greatly contribute to cyclical instability and that, on the other hand, skilful monetary policy can help to counteract instability caused by " real " factors.[1] Suppose our economic system were not subject to cyclical fluctuations; it would then be an easy task to produce by monetary measures a business cycle with all the familiar features of alternating periods of expansion and contraction in output and employment associated with ups and downs in prices and aggregate demand. All that is required to bring about such a result would be to expand and contract credit or to produce sufficiently large surpluses and deficits in the Government budget.

§ 4.   REAL AND MONETARY FACTORS BEHIND THE FLUCTUATIONS
IN AGGREGATE EXPENDITURE

In order to gain perspective let me briefly enumerate and survey various possibilities of explaining cyclical fluctuations in aggregate spending by " monetary " and " real " factors and

---

[1] Hardly anybody doubts this any more. In that respect the situation is different from what it was at the time of the outbreak of the Great Depression. But let me add that this remark does not imply the endorsement of a naive version of "functional finance". However the criticism of the latter (see especially the forceful and convincing strictures by Milton Friedman) is based on the realization of the difficulties in diagnosis and timing of policies owing to lags and uncertainties and not on a denial of the basic proposition that correctly timed and properly dosed injections of money can counteract (although not always completely compensate) fluctuations in aggregate real activity.

their interaction—starting from cases of " purely monetary " causation and proceeding to cases of increasing preponderance of " real " factors.

At the one extreme we have the purely monetary explanations of the cycle which assume that the real economic system is inherently stable and that instability is introduced by misbehaviour or mismanagement of money. (It should be remembered that what may be purely monetary is the causal mechanism; the thing to be explained, the cycle, we have defined in real terms).

Of modern writers who have proposed purely monetary explanations, Irving Fisher and R. G. Hawtrey come at once to mind. Fisher flatly denied that there was such a thing as a cycle except to the extent that quasicyclical instability was introduced by monetary instability which he conceived in terms of changes in the purchasing power of money. Professor Hawtrey's endogenous theory, consisting of a dynamic mechanism of lagged interactions of monetary circulation, cash drains, and credit policy of the banks, changes in short term interest rates inducing changes in inventory investment is well known.[1]

Another school that explains the cycle by monetary factors starts from Wicksell's distinction between the market or money rate of interest, on the one hand, and the natural or equilibrium rate on the other. Wicksell himself did not hold a purely monetary theory of the cycle, but Mises and Hayek, to mention only two, did. They believe that the initiating cause of the cycle can always be found on the monetary side, on the supply side of money. Excessive supply of credit (that is to say, credit creation in excess of " voluntary savings "—the precise criterion of excessiveness not being always the same) depresses the market or money rate of interest below its equilibrium level; this starts a Wicksellian cumulative process which necessarily ends in crisis and depression.

In these monetary theories, which stress changes in the supply side of money, it is assumed explicitly or tacitly that the demand for money and credit, or to put it differently, the natural or

---

[1] It seems safe to say that his theory would have made a greater impression if it had been worked out in mathematical form.

equilibrium rate of interest is determined by the (physical) marginal productivity of capital which is fairly stable over time, although perhaps subject to a gradual downward shift as the capital stock increases.

Non-monetary factors make their appearance as soon as it is realized that the demand for money and credit (or the equilibrium rate of interest) is neither stable nor determined solely by the physical productivity of capital.

The main factors making for instability of investment demand, or in the terminology of the Wicksellian School, for changes in the equilibrium rate of interest (if we still permit ourselves under these circumstances to think of an equilibrium rate existing at any given moment) are as follows, arranged in the approximate order of increasing " physicalness ": "psychology", i.e. waves of optimism and pessimism; investment changes induced by changes in income or consumption as postulated in the different variants of the acceleration principle (including that of Kaldor); inventions and innovations and the forces giving rise to the " bunching " of innovational investment as described by Schumpeter; " lumpiness " of investment due to the durability and indivisibility of capital instruments together with the asymmetry in the operation of the accelerator, the replacement waves and " echo effects " which follow from the fact that capital goods are durable; speaking of bunching and lumpiness of capital investment we cannot forget in the world in which we live the most powerful external factor causing intense concentration (and hence instability) of investment, namely, wars and preparation for wars.

All these factors have been used, singly or in combination, to explain the business cycle. But in all these theories, although they are no longer purely monetary, monetary factors enter more or less importantly—and not only in the trivial sense that everything that happens in a money economy (as distinguished from barter) wears a monetary garb.

The theories which use the various " building blocks " just mentioned vary greatly not only in content but also as to the degree of formal refinement.

Let me first say a word on the latter aspect. The earlier theories have relied on verbal analysis and rough estimates of magnitudes. Since the pioneering article of Frisch, " Propagation Problems and Impulse Problems in Dynamic Economics ",[1] Lundberg's celebrated *Studies in the Theory of Economic Expansion*, and especially since the formal marriage of multiplier and acceleration principle (who earlier lived together under different names in illdefined relationship), a great change has come over business cycle theorizing. The theory has been formalized in complete endogenous sequence models using difference and differential equations. The earlier models were linear but soon non-linear models with "floors", "ceilings", "asymmetries", "stochastic variables", and "exogenous shocks" were added. Not only mathematical blueprints but full-blown econometric models relating to individual countries or even to the whole world with constants and parameters statistically evaluated are pouring from single scholars' studies and statistical laboratories like automobiles from the assembly line.

This surely is a very interesting development and this type of approach is undoubtedly worth trying and perfecting. But there can be hardly a doubt any more that so far the results have been most disappointing. The multiplicity of more or less inconsistent models, many of them based on broadly plausible assumptions and, if of the econometric type, fitting the data from which they are derived fairly well, but none of them standing up to the test of extrapolation beyond the period from which the data were taken—this is a spectacle that is not calculated to inspire confidence.

But let me return to the substantive question concerning the role of monetary forces in the cycle. It would seem to be a valid generalization that purely monetary explanations have become increasingly unpopular and although most current theories are mixed in the sense that monetary and real factors interact, the monetary factor has been more and more deemphasized and relegated to a merely passive or permissive role.

Let me consider, as an example, Hicks' classic *Contribution*

---

[1] *Economic Essays in Honour of Gustav Cassel*, London, 1933.

to the Theory of the Trade Cycle—the most elegant and most carefully elaborated specimen of a great variety of similar systems.

His principal model runs almost entirely in " real " terms: Consumption expenditure is a function of *real* income; investment a function of the rate of change in *real* income; there is a physical ceiling which may or may not be hit and, owing to the *physical* impossibility of using up durable capital faster than it wears out, the accelerator is weaker on the downgrade than on the upgrade. Wages are supposed to be perfectly rigid and so are prices (with minor qualifications).

In the basic model money plays a purely passive role; monetary circulation automatically expands during the upswing and automatically contracts during the downswing of the cycle.[1] Money is a mere veil or rather a tricot (as Mises used to put it[2] which faithfully reflects without distortion the contours of the economic body and all its changes.

Although Hicks regards the " real " model as the heart of his theory and the latter as an adequate picture of reality, he is too much of a realist to rely entirely on the " real " part of his theory for the explanation of actual cyclical experience. In the last two chapters of his book he introduces the " monetary factors " as a very active element and thus modifies his theory more drastically than appears on the surface or than he himself seems to admit. But let me spend a few more minutes on the " real " models.

---

[1] Monetary complications are, however, invoked to explain one feature of actual cyclical experience which in Hicks' opinion cannot be accounted for by his "real" model. He thinks that after the downturn the contraction of output usually proceeds faster than the multiplier-acceleration mechanism would lead one to expect. So he introduces as an intensifier what Pigou many years ago (in his *Industrial Fluctuations*, 1926, which to this day has kept remarkably fresh) called the detonation of bankruptcies and business failures into which the upswing explodes. For this concession to realism Hicks was promptly rebuked by Kaldor who believes that also this particular feature of the cycle can be explained by the "real" mechanism.

[2] Needless to say Mises did not accept the view that money was a mere tricot.

Although in these models money plays no active role in the sense that no deliberate inflationary measures, or rising prices, falling interest rates or lowered credit standards are required to explain a cyclical upswing—nor the opposite of all this to account for the depression phase—money is nevertheless essential because the upswing could not proceed unless the supply of money were elastic in the sense that either M or V increased without sharp rises in the interest rates.[1] If there is not sufficient scope for V to expand the monetary authorities must permit the necessary expansion in M; if V can expand it is sufficient that they refrain from counteracting the increase in V by contracting M.

The downturn is brought about entirely by the " real " mechanism and during the downswing the role of money is even less important than in the upswing; for while the monetary authorities can always stop or slow down an expansion they can do nothing or very little to soften a contraction (although they could presumably intensify it). When the " real " forces " decree a contraction", MV shrinks inexorably and if monetary policy prevents M from shrinking (or expands it) the result is simply an offsetting drop in V.

There can be hardly a doubt that this account greatly underestimates the importance of monetary factors in producing the major cyclical swings of actual experience. What is open to question is the degree of distortion of the true picture. While I realize that many of those who have put forward real models of the cycle would be ready to admit that their picture of the cycle is liable to be changed somewhat by the operation of monetary factors, I still believe that modern theory has tended grossly to underestimate the importance of the monetary factors. Not only in the field of business cycles, but in other areas as well alleged stubborn " structural " and " real " instabilities and impediments to necessary adjustment have been overemphasized and over-

---

[1] It is true there has been a strong tendency to discount the importance of the interest rate but it has hardly gone so far as to deny that sharply rising rates would act as a brake on the expansion.

estimated at the expense of monetary factors and the closely related element of price and wage rigidity. This is a matter of great importance which has farreaching policy implications.[1]

§ 5.   MONETARY FACTORS IN DEPRESSIONS

The operation of monetary forces is especially conspicuous in depressions. But the seeds of depression are sown during the boom and they are not entirely of " real " origin.

Let me enumerate a few instances in which monetary factors have notoriously greatly intensified depressions although perhaps not brought them about.

The Great Depression of the 1930's in the U.S. was made much more severe than it would otherwise have been by the wholesale destruction, through bankruptcies, of banks and bank money. It is surely not an essential feature of the real cycle that the banking system should collapse during the depression. The same thing happened in several other countries and the breakdown of the gold standard, the liquidation of the gold exchange standard, and the international scramble for liquidity is essentially the same monetary process on the international level.

It is gratifying to see a prominent champion of the " real " cycle theory like Professor Hicks himself emphatically stressing the basically monetary nature of the Great Depression thereby flatly rejecting " real " explanations of the events of the 1930's, his multiplier-acceleration theory, as well as the " secular stagnation " thesis.

Let me quote the relevant passage hidden away in a footnote:

" I do not see that there is any adequate reason to suppose that the *real* boom of 1927–9 was at all an exceptional boom; if the accelerator mechanism, and nothing else, had been at work, it should not have been followed by an exceptional slump.

---

[1] Thus it was necessary to "rediscover monetary policy." See Prof. Ellis' celebrated article "The Rediscovery of Money ". The same felicitous phrase was used independently by Prof. M. A. Heilperin.

But the slump impinged upon a monetary situation which was quite exceptionally unstable. The main cause of this instability was not the purely superficial speculative over-expansion which had occurred in New York in 1928–9; its roots went much further back. The monetary system of the world had never adjusted itself at all fully to the change in the level of money incomes which took place during and after the war of 1914–18; it was trying to manage with a gold supply, which was in terms of wage-units extremely inadequate. Difficulties in the postwar adjustment of exchange rates (combined with the vast changes which the war had produced in the creditor-debtor position of important countries) had caused the consequential weakness to be particularly concentrated in certain places; particular central banks, as for instance the Bank of England and the Reichsbank, were therefore particularly incapable of performing their usual function as ' lenders of last resort '."[1]

This explanation of the Great Slump has long been propounded by continental European economists, notably by the late Charles Rist, but has not found many supporters among Anglo-American economists.

Two general observations are called for. First, it should be stressed that price rigidity, which is in practice primarily wage rigidity, is an essential prerequisite of any monetary explanation. This remark must, however, not be interpreted to mean that everything would be put right and cyclical instability could be banished by introducing wage flexibility. The problem is much more complicated, because of the existence of fixed contracts and possible adverse dynamic and expectational repercussions of a perfectly flexible wage and price system.

Second, it is well known that throughout the 19th century the British monetary system operated on a very narrow gold reserve. This narrowness of the monetary base made for a jerky credit policy, because it forced the Bank of England to react sharply to slight cash drains. Thus it contributed to monetary instability

---

[1] *Loc. cit.*, p. 163. This explanation does not quite fit the American case. It cannot well be said that the monetary (gold) base of the U.S. economy was too narrow even though the dollar was later devalued in terms of gold. The speculative orgies of the late 1920's were not as superficial as Hicks thinks; they surely contributed much to the collapse of the banking system.

throughout the 19th century.[1] The growing wage rigidity in the 20th century made that system unworkable.

It is well known, although often forgotten, that monetary mismanagement, namely, the revaluation of sterling after the first world war, without the necessary wage adjustments, was responsible for the semi-stagnation of the British economy during the 1920's.[2]

The Great Depression of the 1870's offers many parallels with that of the 1930's. It too was greatly intensified by monetary factors, both in the U.S. and in Europe. In the U.S. large budget surpluses followed the deficits during the Civil War and the premium on gold was gradually reduced from 57 percent in 1865 to zero in 1879,[3] the terminal year of the depression—a situation which in many respects resembles the British position in the 1920's. True, the general economic background—19th century U.S. vs. 20th century Britain—is entirely different, but the difference in the surrounding conditions makes the similarity of the outcome all the more remarkable and serves to support the hypothesis that the monetary factors were in both cases of decisive importance.

These are conspicuous and notorious cases in which depressions have been intensified by monetary factors. Similar though less conspicuous and serious monetary disturbances entailing credit contraction, pessimistic expectations and inducement to increase liquidity (reduction in V) can be found in practically every but the mildest depression.

---

[1] On all this and for references to the contemporary literature see especially VINER, *Studies in the Theory of International Trade*, chapter V.

[2] This outcome was correctly foretold by KEYNES in his pamphlet *The Economic Consequences of Mr. Churchill*, 1925.

As Prof. HAYEK has pointed out (*Monetary Nationalism and International Stability*, London, 1937, p. 44) Keynes' warning was based on orthodox teaching. A hundred years ago (1821) Ricardo in a letter to Wheatley said, "I never should advise a government to restore a currency, which was depreciated 30 per cent to par., I should recommend . . . that the currency should be fixed at the depreciated value." (Ricardo, Sraffa edition, Vol. IX, p. 73). Under 20th century conditions of wage rigidity, most economists would say that a 10 per cent over-valuation is too much to be dealt with by deflation rather than by devaluation of the currency.

[3] See R. FELS, "American Business Cycles 1865-79", in *American Economic Review*, June 1951, pp. 325-349.

§ 6.   MONETARY FACTORS DURING BUSINESS CYCLE UPSWINGS

While it is, thus, easy to point to instances in which depressions have been greatly intensified by monetary factors and policies during the depression and while, following Pigou and Hicks, we may venture the generalization that in many less conspicuous cases than those mentioned the severity of depressions has been enhanced by monetary repercussions of financial crises, the role of monetary factors in the upswing and boom phase of the cycle is much more controversial and difficult to assess.

I take it that hardly anyone would defend nowadays the proposition, and I certainly would not do so myself, that the tapering-off of the upswing and the subsequent depression could be avoided either by keeping M, or MV (in some sense) or some general price level constant. Hence the failure of money or monetary policy to conform to any simple rule cannot be held responsible for the fact that booms do not last forever and are always followed by depressions. But from the fact that it is difficult or impossible to discover a monetary rule which, if observed during the upswing, would guarantee perpetual prosperity, it does not follow that the behaviour of money or monetary policy during the upswing cannot greatly contribute to the severity of the following contraction.

The length and severity of depressions depend partly on the magnitude of the " real " maladjustment which developed during the preceding boom and partly on the aggravating monetary and credit factors already mentioned—the scramble for liquidity by financial institutions as well as by others, destruction of bank money by bank failures, and similar events on the international level.

While monetary arrangements and policies during the upswing probably cannot entirely prevent the emergence of real maladjustments—except perhaps by preventing the upswing itself—imprudent monetary policies surely can aggravate them; moreover, the financial crises which frequently mark the downturn of the cycle and the monetary and financial complications during the depression are partly the consequence of monetary forces and policies operating during the preceding expansion.

The term " real maladjustment " must not be interpreted in a narrow, exclusive sense.[1] There are alternative types of such maladjustments and I do not wish to suggest that there is a presumption that every boom breeds the same kind of trouble. Let me mention only two or three types.

The Harrod-Hicks theory (envisaged also by other writers) that when an expansion runs head on into a full employment ceiling (which need not be a rigid barrier but may be a flexible bottleneck zone) induced investments will collapse,[2] describes one kind of real maladjustment.

Another type of maladjustment is the one described by Schumpeter. It can be characterized as a temporary exhaustion of investment opportunities in the particular area in which the boom was concentrated. The chances that there should be a *general* and *chronic* dearth of investment outlets for current savings (as distinguished from a temporary one in a particular area) are so remote and *sub specie historiae* so far-fetched that we can ignore them.[3]

While these real maladjustments are closely tied up with growth

---

[1] In the economic literature it is closely associated with F. A. Hayek's theory of the cycle. However, the "real maladjustment" which Hayek describes, "over extension of the period of production" (the concept is not easy to define in operational term) is only one kind of maladjustment out of a multitude of possibilities, and not the most likely or most easily ascertainable one.

[2] In other words, "capital widening" comes to an end and since "capital deepening" cannot quickly take up the slack, aggregate investment is bound to fall and a depression ensues.

[3] This does not, however, alter that fact that in every severe depression we experience a revival in lay and expert circles alike of the theory that most if not all depressions are the consequence of a chronic lack of investment opportunities—only to be given up during the following upswing and replaced in the minds of many by the opposite point of view to the effect that we have at last conquered the business cycle and entered the "new" era of perpetual prosperity. This illustrates the "Konjunkturgebundenheit" of economic thinking and can be claimed as supporting evidence by those economists who stress the importance of the "psychological" factor in the generation of the business cycle. In recent years Prof. W. A. Jöhr has dwelt upon the "psychological factor" in his monumental volume on Business Cycles.

and expansion itself and are most difficult to diagnose and to avoid (except by preventing the expansion itself) most upswings are characterized in varying degrees by excesses which at least *post-festum* appear unnecessary, undesirable and avoidable, even though the line which separates them from the maladjustments mentioned earlier cannot always be drawn neatly at the time when things are going well.

What I mean are speculative excesses in the real as well as in the financial sphere: overoptimistic overproduction in particular lines of industry and overbuilding, speculative land booms and speculative overinvestment in inventories,[1] and in the financial sphere, excessive speculation on the stock exchanges.

It is mainly in this area that money and monetary policy become important during the upswing. These " unhealthy " developments are not possible, or at least not possible on the large and disturbing scale on which they actually occur, without excessive credit expansion. It is, of course, often difficult to diagnose such developments when they occur and a most difficult task of monetary policy to prevent inflationary excesses without endangering expansion itself; no easy rule such as stabilizing some general price level will be sufficient. It is nevertheless a fact, I believe, that these things do happen in every major upswing and that they breed financial upheavals and revulsions which then greatly contribute to the severity of the succeeding deflation and depression.

§ 7.   THE COMPARATIVE IMPORTANCE OF MONETARY AND REAL
FACTORS IN THE CYCLE

My general conclusion is that monetary factors and policies play an important role in generating economic instability. A large part of modern cycle theory has unduly neglected monetary

---

[1] I suspect that the "non-speculative" inventory cycle based on a multiplier acceleration mechanism (analyzed in masterly fashion in Metzler's celebrated articles) is only a small part of the real story and that inventory cycles without price speculation and monetary stimuli (elements which play no part in Metzler's theory) would be mild and uninteresting affairs.

factors and overplayed the " real " factors, although most proponents of " real " theories of the cycle find it necessary to bring in monetary factors as modifying elements at some stage before applying their theories to the cycle of the real world.

Let me now raise the quantitative question: Suppose the various destabilizing monetary complications which I have enumerated could be avoided by institutional reforms and skilful monetary policy; would that damp down the cycle drastically or would it not make much difference? In other words, is the " real " cycle without the so-called "complications" really a very serious problem?

This is, of course, an extremely complicated question. I cannot hope in the course of one lecture to formulate it with all the care and precision which it requires, let alone to give a well-documented answer.

But let me make bold to suggest tentative answers to some subdivisions of the main query.

If the wholesale destruction of bank money during depressions through bank failures, runs on banks, lack of confidence in the financial institutions as well as analogous phenomena in the international sphere could be avoided—a modest minimum program of monetary reform—catastrophic slumps as in the 1930's would be eliminated. Avoidance of mistakes such as in the revaluation of the Pound after the first world war and a modest policy of monetary expansion (I am speaking now of monetary policy, not of fiscal policy, i.e. the creation of counter cyclical budget deficit in a depression) would make prolonged periods of semi-stagnation like that of the British economy in the 1920's extremely unlikely.

If, in addition to this, inflationary and speculative excesses during cyclical expansions were prevented and a mild counter cyclical budget policy adopted, cyclical instability would be damped down to moderate proportions. In other words, the " real " cycle without the monetary " complications " (comprehensively defined) is, in my judgment, a rather mild affair.

What are the chances that the " monetary complications " will in fact be avoided henceforth? I think that a majority of economists would agree that the chances are good as far as anti-depression policy is concerned. Runaway deflation, like in the 1930's, is, I believe, out of the question everywhere, even in the most capitalistic countries. More than that, as far as anti-depression policy is concerned, there is certainly more danger in most countries of too soon and too much rather than of too late and too little. Does that mean that we have reached the millenium of economic stability? Now, as far as employment is concerned, there is probably little chance anywhere of prolonged mass unemployment due to a deficiency of effective demand. True, this does not exclude unemployment due to a lack of cooperating factors. But dislocations where that happens on a large scale are exceedingly rare.[1]

§ 8. SECULAR INFLATION

But for other dimensions of economic stability than employment, for example, for price stability, the outlook is definitely not so good. The low tolerance for unemployment, the strong inclination to suspect an incipient major depression in every slight actual or imagined dip in economic activity, the high propensity to

---

[1] Such conditions existed after the war in war-ravaged countries due to a lack of raw materials, machinery, and transportation. The spectre of that kind of unemployment arose in some countries such as in Britain during severe balance of payments crises; but it never came to pass. Some theorists have played with the idea that this kind of unemployment exists *chronically* (!) in disguised form in underdeveloped countries. It is based on the assumption of constant coefficients of production, that is to say that capital and labor can be combined only in one or two fixed proportions (rectangular or at least angular production functions). Capital is scarce, hence much labor must remain unemployed. The assumption that such conditions should exist in the long run not for particular narrowly defined industrial processes but for industry as a whole or broad subdivisions, seems to me unrealistic to the point of being preposterous. It must be pointed out, however, that this same phantastic assumption underlies the famous Harrod-Domar model of long run economic growth.

These theories constitute other extreme examples of the modern propensity to overemphasize real factors and to look for real, in this case literally physical rigidities, instead of for monetary factors, price and wage rigidities and the like (For an able criticism of the Harrod-Domar model see L. B. YEAGER, "Some Questions about Growth Economics," in *American Economic Review*, March, 1954).

apply anti-depression measures—all that coupled with the powerful urge to invest and develop, the constant pressure of organized labor for higher wages and, in some countries, of organized agriculture for higher prices, makes for secular, intermittent or continuous, creeping or galloping inflation.

Continuous galloping inflation is found in some underdeveloped countries—Chile is perhaps the most extreme recent example. There can be no doubt that it retards growth (through lowering the allocative efficiency of the economy and discouraging saving) even if acute depressive reactions can be avoided.

In the advanced industrial countries secular inflation threatens in the form of a creeping and intermittent rise in prices. That is to say, prices rise over the long pull at an *average* rate of a few percent per annum, not steadily but in waves, periods of rapidly rising prices being interrupted by shorter periods of stable or even slightly falling prices. This is an insidious process which is not easy to diagnose and on the consequences of which there is little agreement between economists, at least so long as the average price rise is not more than, say, 2–3% a year.

I am not going to speculate about the average annual speed and time shape at which secular inflation will begin to have serious consequences. I shall instead discuss one aspect of the causal mechanism which brings about this condition and one of its consequences on the international level.

As Bronfenbrenner[1] points out, there are two different explanations of the tendency in the industrial countries of the West towards secular creeping inflation. The one school blames the pressure groups of organized labor and organized agriculture; the other blames monetary policy which has become lax under the influence of the Keynesian thinking of our time. According to the first, the price level is gradually pushed up by rising wages; according to the other view, it is pulled up by monetary policy.

Money plays, of course, its role in both schemes. Labor unions could not push the price level up unless monetary policy gave way.

---

[1] "Some Neglected Implications of Secular Inflation," in *Post-Keynesian Economics* (1954).

It should also be observed that it is not necessary that labor be organized in one huge bloc (as it actually is in some countries) and force up the whole wage level in one big push. For the inflationary mechanism to work, it is a sufficient condition that big chunks of wages be forced up here and there by some of the large unions. The forces of competition and actions of other unions can then be relied upon rapidly to generalize these increases. Pull and push always interact once the upward movement has started. Thus the difference between the two schools seems to degenerate into one of the hen and egg variety.

But there remains an important operational difference. Although both schools agree that despite union pressure on wages the price level could be held, if monetary policy stood firm (as it had to under the gold standard), the pressure group school asserts (or implies) that if monetary policy does stand firm, wages (or some wages) will be pushed up anyway. As a consequence unemployment will appear and monetary authorities are then confronted with the dilemma either to " create " a certain amount of unemployment or to tolerate at least from time to time a rise in the price level.

The other school takes a more optimistic position. According to them there is no such dilemma. If the monetary authorities stand firm wages will not rise or will rise only a little. A small amount of unemployment or the mere threat of unemployment will sufficiently persuade the unions to desist from wage demands in excess of the gradual increase in over-all labor productivity.

Given the fact that the tolerance for unemployment in our time is low, the difference of opinion between the two schools thus reduces to one's estimate of the power and policy of labor unions and employer reactions. Obviously much depends also on public opinion and government policy.

I am inclined to side on this issue with the pessimists.[1] But this

---

[1] Bronfenbrenner too (*op. cit.*) is on the pessimistic side and so is the Dean of American "labor economists", S. H. Slichter. The optimistic view is represented by members of the "Chicago School". See e.g. MILTON FRIEDMAN, "Some Comments on the Significance of Labor Unions for Economic Policy" in *The Impact of the Union*, New York, 1951, and W. K. MORTON, "Trade Unionism, Full Employment, and Inflation", *American Economic Review*, March, 1950.

is certainly a question on which it would be unwise to take a dogmatic position. The power and policies of labor unions as well as the behaviour of employers, reactions of public opinion and government policy differ from country to country and although the trend has been everywhere in the free world in the direction of increased union power towards a "laboristic society" (Slichter), this trend obviously depends on political and social forces whose future course cannot be foreseen. The economist has certainly no special expert qualifications for making such prophecies.

§ 9.   INSTABILITY OF THE INTERNATIONAL BALANCE OF PAYMENTS

I now come to my last topic which dramatically illustrates the modern tendency to look for deep-seated structural defects and to see stubborn real stumbling blocks to the maintenance of stable equilibrium where in reality faulty monetary policies and the rigidity of certain key prices provide a perfectly satisfactory explanation for the existing disequilibrium or instability.

While in a closed economy with a unified monetary and banking system, free mobility of funds and a fair degree of mobility of labor, a secular inflation of 2–3% per year may not have deleterious effects for quite some time, at least not clearly visible ones, in the actual world, consisting as it does of different countries with different monetary systems and policies, little or no mobility of capital funds and labor between them, even a small deviation in the rate of inflation between different countries must almost immediately lead to balance of payments disequilibria.

What holds of differences in the degree of secular inflation is, of course, also true of deviations in timing and magnitude of cyclical and other short run expansions and contractions. Analytically it is, moreover, only the other side of exactly the same problem, if the disequilibrium in the balance of payments has been caused initially by a shift in international demand (however brought about). In that case the persistence of the disequilibrium can be said to be due to the failure of the monetary mechanism to bring about an *equilibrating* divergency between the rate of expansion in the surplus country and that in the deficit country,[1] while in the cases mentioned before the disequilibrium in the balance of payments was caused by the appearance of a *disequilibrating* divergence of the same sort.

But let me concentrate on the chronic case, because it illustrates most clearly the point I wish to make, namely, the contemporary propensity to overemphasize " real " factors and to neglect monetary factors and institutional rigidities.

There is to-day much more agreement than there was a few years ago on the proposition that the basic reason for the chronic (continuous or intermittent) balance of payments deficit, *alias* " Dollarshortage," from which many countries are suffering is to be found in the fact that the deficit countries have, for a variety of reasons, a higher " propensity to inflate " than the surplus countries. (It should be stressed, however, that it is grossly misleading to speak of a shortage of the U.S. Dollar only. The same shortage applies just as much to the Canadian Dollar, Mexican Peso, Venezualian Bolivar, Swiss Franc, more recently also to the German Mark, Dutch Guilder and other currencies which are more or less freely convertible into U.S. Dollars).

The reasons for a high propensity to inflate are, of course, many. Some are of an "ideological", "political", and " social " nature, others are deeply rooted in the recent or more distant historical development of a country; still others are very "real". It is, for example, easy to understand why for some time after the war it was almost impossible for war-torn and ravaged countries to restrain inflation (of the " open " or " repressed " variety); moreover, it stands to reason that countries with a low tolerance for unemployment, an elaborate social welfare establishment, exhorbitant rates of direct taxation, agressive trade unions, will constantly strain against the leash; similarly, it is not surprising

---

[1] The equilibrating mechanism can be of the gold standard type (stable exchanges, expansion in the surplus countries and contraction in the deficit countries) or it can use the technique of flexible exchanges under which no expansion and contraction in the local currency circulation is necessary. Complicatons caused by price and wage rigidities and consequential changes in employment or by speculative movements of capital cannot be discussed here.

at all that poor and backward countries when they wake up and set their minds to develop in a hurry and to catch up with the more developed countries, are continuously tempted to overspend their meagre resources and to live beyond their means.

With such a wealth of explanatory material available which offers unlimited opportunities for bringing into play "propensities", "asymetries",[1] " demonstration effects " and many other gadgets dear to the heart of the economic theorist, it is difficult to understand why anyone should find it necessary to fall back on such implausible and farfetched hypotheses as the sudden appearance in the fourth decade of the 20th century of stubborn real inelasticities of international demand (of whole continents and a great variety of countries) or on the equally bizarre theory that, again beginning with the third or fourth decade of our century, balances of payments (and terms of trade) must turn inexorably in favor of the most rapidly progressing countries.

§ 10.   SUMMARY AND CONCLUDING REMARKS

My main conclusion is: Monetary factors comprehensively defined bear a heavy share of responsibility for short run economic instability—for the ordinary business cycle (again comprehensively defined) as well as for the instability and chronic disequilibria in the balances of payments.

By " monetary factors " I do not merely mean active policies of inflation or deflation—the latter having become almost inconceivable since the Great Depression and the rise of Keynesian thinking —but also monetary repercussions of financial crises which frequently mark the upper turning point of the cycle or occur during the downswing—irrespective of whether the downturn itself can or cannot be attributed to monetary factors. For example, the collapse of the American banking system in the 1930's, the downfall of the gold standard, the ensuing sudden liquidation of

---

[1] See e.g. C. KINDLEBERGER, *L'asymétrie de la balance des paiements*, "Revue Economique", 1954, p. 166-89.

the gold exchange standard, withdrawal of international credits, hot money flows and the general scramble for liquidity—all these and similar events on the national and international level are monetary factors. If these things could be avoided, catastrophies like the Great Depression would be impossible and other cycles would be mitigated.

If we define the concept "monetary factor" somewhat more comprehensively so as to include as its effects that part of existing instability which would disappear in the event that monetary policy succeeded (in addition to preventing the monetary disturbances mentioned above) in imparting a mildly anticyclical pattern to the supply of money and credit—monetary factors would be responsible for a still larger share in economic instability. In other words, the amplitude of the cycle would be sharply reduced if monetary factors in that comprehensive sense became inoperative (which would require, of course, acts of commission as well as of omission on the part of the monetary authorities).

This does, however, by no means imply that non-monetary factors are of no importance.

First of all, the monetary factors operate in an environment or impinge on a system which possesses certain non-monetary features that make the system respond to the monetary forces as it does. One could easily imagine an economic system in which the monetary factors would not produce large swings in output and employment but only fluctuations in prices, which would be a much less serious matter. If, for example, deflation did not breed pessimism and inflation did not produce exaggerated optimism,[1] if in addition wages and prices were flexible and there were no large fixed monetary contracts, the effects of monetary instability on aggregate output and employment would be much smaller than they are in the real world.

The "monetary" factor, the "psychological" factor and the "rigidity" factor are complementary in the strict sense of the word and reinforce each other. The resulting instability is their joint

---

[1] Prolonged and too rapid inflation may, of course, produce pessimistic reactions.

product and it is therefore quite legitimate to attribute to each of these factors a substantial share of the existing economic instability in such a way that the sum of their (alternative) shares greatly exceeds the total.[1]

Second, I do not wish to discount completely—for short run purposes—fixity of capital coefficient as postulated by the acceleration principle—although even in the short run the capital-output ratio (and labor-output ratio) is not as rigid as many modern business cycle models assume.[2] Nor would I ignore the multiplier. But the acceleration principle plus multiplier, unless combined with and reinforced by monetary factors, psychology and rigidities would hardly produce more than mild and inconsequential fluctuations. All these factors together bring it about that our economic system is subject to cumulative, self-reinforcing processes of expansion and contraction.

Third, there are autonomous changes in aggregate expenditure, especially the concentrations followed later by slumps of investments demand (including demand for consumer durables) caused by technological innovations and above all by wars and preparations for war. These " real factors " obviously do contribute their share to economic instability. But in my judgment it is mainly in their role as starters, intensifiers and interrupters of cumulative processes that they do their destabilizing work. That is to say, the " propagation problem " is more important than the " impulse problem ". And in the propagation mechanism, the way in which the economy responds to outside impulses, the monetary factor plays a decisive role.

One important reason for this hypothetical evaluation is the historical experience that modern economies frequently take

---

[1] This has been pointed out many years ago by A. C. PIGOU in his *Industrial Fluctuations*, 2nd ed., London, 1929.

In Part I, Chapter 22 He says: "It is possible that more than one factor may be a dominant cause of fluctuations in the sense that, if it were removed, the amplitude of these fluctuations would be reduced to insignificant proportions". (See *op. cit.*, Table of Contents, p. XIIII.)

[2] To assume that it is rigid in the long run or subject only to autonomous changes (due to technological innovations) and not to equilibrating adjustments seems to me hopelessly unrealistic.

terrific impulses and shocks in their stride while on other occasions they seem to react strongly to modest shocks. Recent history offers numerous examples. Let me mention the transition from peace to war and the transition from war to peace, the latter entailing a tremendous sudden drop in government expenditures; another example is the reconstruction of war-torn countries—such as Italy, Germany, Austria—and the subsequent levelling out of these economies into a more normal course of development. These shocks, which were absorbed with surprising ease, were certainly incomparably more severe than those that are supposed to have started the Great Depression.

I conclude that the response mechanism is more important than the severity of the external shocks and in the response mechanism monetary factors play a most important role.

APPENDIX

THE PIGOU EFFECT ONCE MORE[1]

I

The Pigou effect continues to draw comments.[2] Much of the discussion seems, however, to suffer from an unfortunate mixing of different levels of abstraction and from an unnecessary and historically incorrect interpretation of the theorem as a more or less rigid and exclusive policy recommendation.[3]

I do not know of any modern writer among the adherents of the Pigou effect who has argued that antidepression policy should consist entirely or primarily of making wages and prices flexible by relying on the Pigou effect, that is, on the rise of the real value of cash balances brought about by falling prices to stimulate sufficient expenditure, to relieve a situation of general unemployment. Surely the author of *Industrial Fluctuations* himself is miles away from recommending such a policy.[4]

Let us not forget in what doctrinal situation and for what purposes Pigou enunciated the "wealth-saving relation" (to use Professor Metzler's apt description of the Pigou effect). It was designed as a refutation of the post-Keynesian secular stagnation thesis,[5] which is based on the Keynesian notion of an under-employment *equilibrium* under *competitive* conditions in the labor

---

[1] Reprinted from Journal of Political Economy, June 1952.

[2] The latest comments are A. H. Hansen's interesting note, "The Pigovian Effect", this *Journal*, December, 1951, and L. A. Metzler's admirable article, "Wealth, Saving and the Rate of Interest", this *Journal*, April, 1951. See also the revised version of Don Patinkin's well-known paper, "Price Flexibility and Full Employment", in *Readings in Monetary Theory* (Philadelphia: Blakiston, 1951).

[3] This criticism does not apply to the contribution of Professor Metzler, who remains throughout his paper within the confines of his abstract theoretical model.

[4] See, especially, chap. xi on "Wage Policy" in Part II of *Industrial Fluctuations*. In the Preface to his *Lapses from Full Employment*, Professor Pigou goes out of his way " to say clearly " that he is *not* " in favour of attacking the problem of unemployment by manipulating wages rather than by manipulating demand " (p. v). The two essays, "The Classical Stationary State" (*Economic Journal*, LIII [1943], 343–51) and "Economic Progress in a Stable Environment" (*Economica*, XIV [new ser., 1947], 180–90, now reprinted in *Readings in Monetary Theory*), where the Pigou effect was formally introduced, are frankly and severely abstract and theoretical; the author eschews any direct policy implications and even disclaims, overmodestly in my opinion, any relevance of his model for the real world.

[5] I say "post-Keynesian" because it is not quite clear whether Keynes himself really believed in the secular stagnation thesis as an actual condition rather than a future contingency. It would be easy to quote from *The General Theory* passages where he accepts it along with others which point in the opposite direction.

market, that is, with flexible wages. In the heydays of Keynesianism it was believed that the possibility of a competitive under-employment equilibrium can be proved for the static Keynesian model. This implies, as Pigou points out—referring to Professor Hansen's presentation of the theory in *Fiscal Policy and Business Cycles*—that the argument

> is conducted on the level of abstraction where perfect homogeneity and mobility of labor are assumed, so that "full employment" signifies a state of things in which everybody seeking employment at the ruling (uniform) rate of wages is able to obtain it. It does not have the esoteric meaning, which is given to it in much current writing, where full employment is allowed to prevail alongside of large masses of "frictional unemployment". In this article also I shall stand on that level of abstraction.[1]

The ideal, static conditions under which the Pigou effect has been formulated, assuming away as they do disturbances caused by unfavourable expectations, immobility of labor, bottlenecks, the dead weight of fixed money contracts, are thus of the Keynesians' own choosing. Let us also remember that in the static, Keynesian world with competitive, flexible wages, full employment will be effectively maintained even without the operation of the Pigou effect, except in the extreme cases where either the liquidity preference is infinitely elastic at a positive interest rate or the marginal efficiency of capital is entirely inelastic with respect to the interest rate. Barring these extremes, full employment will be assured, as Keynes himself realized, by virtue of the "Keynes effect", that is, through a fall in the interest rate. The Pigou effect need be called upon to bring about full employment only in the extreme cases just mentioned whose actual occurrence in a static world is highly questionable. It thus effectively removes the narrow remaining basis of what has often been hailed as Keynes's greatest achievement, *viz.*, the demonstration of the possibility of a static, competitive underemployment equilibrium. (This claim does, by the way, decidedly less than justice to Keynes. But any theory which throws doubt upon the feasibility of a well-functioning free-price system seems to be sure of enthusiastic welcome.)

It is not surprising, therefore, that the Keynesians find it advisable to leave the static Keynesian world, which in its simplicity and transparency hardly offers any hiding place, and to seek refuge in the jungle of institutional and dynamic complications in which the real world abounds.

II

Hansen calls attention to the fact that in the real world cyclical fluctuations in output and employment are closely paralleled by fluctuations in the price level. Hence the Pigou effect actually operates as an expansionary factor only during the downswing of the business cycle and possibly contributes something to stopping "the deflation and the decline in output and employment." But it "could never of itself restore the economy to full employment" because as soon as employment and output pass the lower turning point, "prices and

---

[1] " The Classical Stationary State", *op. cit.*, p. 343.

wages will cease falling, and the real value of (money) assets will cease rising".[1]

That prices do in fact move with the business cycle (apart from occasional short lags or leads at the turning points) is not open to doubt, and hence actual cyclical upswings cannot be explained in terms of a continuing upward shift of the expenditure function caused by a sustained rise in the real value of cash and government bonds. I do not know, however, of any economist who has put forward such a theory of cyclical expansion. It surely is completely alien to Pigou's thinking.

But in the static Keynesian model world, wages and prices would behave differently: If there was "thoroughgoing competition" (Pigou) among wage-earners, the (uniform) wage rate as well as prices would go on falling right up to the point of full employment.[2] Why does the real world not correspond to the Keynesian model? Evidently a combination of circumstances is responsible. First, wages (and certain prices) were never very flexible, even before the emergence of powerful trade-unions made wage rates almost completely rigid in the downward direction.[3] Moreover, unions not only make wages rigid downward but tend to push them up even if there is still a good deal of unemployment.

Second, even if wages were very flexible, immobility of labor, that is the, existence of noncompeting groups[4] as well as material and equipment shortages in particular fields, would result in the rise of certain prices as soon as aggregate effective demand expands. There is almost always the important agricultural bottleneck where employment is well maintained even in depressions and where, precisely because there is little slack in the form of unemployment, prices can be expected to rise soon after demand begins to increase. As the expansion proceeds, full employment is reached in other branches of the economy, and the number and importance of bottlenecks increases. But so long as there is unemployment elsewhere, under competitive conditions (flexible wages and prices), the price rise in the fully employed sectors (bottleneck areas) may be only relative to prices in those fields where there is still unemployment, and where, hence, prices are still falling. In other words, the price *level* may still fall or remain unchanged.

Admittedly that is not the typical picture of a cyclical upswing. In the cycle of the real world the price *level* starts rising either when or soon after output and employment have turned upward. But that proves nothing against

---

[1] *Op. cit.*, p. 535.

[2] If we assume constant marginal cost, prices and wages would fall at the same rate, and the real wage remain constant. If marginal costs rise, prices would fall less fast than wages, and real wages would decline.

[3] I cannot agree with Hansen when he denies that " frictions preventing further wage declines so long as any unemployment remains " have anything to do with the fact that prices rise during cyclical upswings, even if there still exisits a lot of unemployment. Wage rigidity is not the whole story, but it is surely an important part of the story. Hansen says: " Improved expectations will raise prices and wages in the most perfectly flexible markets " (*op. cit.*, p. 535). I cannot see how expectations could raise wages in a perfect labor market so long as there is much involuntary unemployment.

[4] I assume competition among the members of each noncompeting group.

the Pigou effect and the proposition that a Keynesian underemployment equilibrium is impossible without rigidity. First, the price behaviour which we observe in the real world is largely due to rigidities. Second, if the economy has passed the lower turning point and a cumulative process of expansion gets under way and proceeds in the familiar fashion financed by a more rapid turnover of money and by new bank loans, the Pigou effect is no longer needed "to restore the economy to full employment". Nobody claimed that it was needed except under the extreme conditions of the static Keynesian system. Third, even sectional (involuntary) unemployment (unemployment in "depressed areas" as distinguished from general or wide-spread unemployment) is incompatible with *competitive* equilibrium.[1]

If unemployment persists in isolated pockets, with demand for the products in question being inelastic and workers unable or unwilling to move elsewhere, wages may have to fall to intolerable levels, if full employment is to be re-stored. We could not rely, in that case, on the Pigou effect to eliminate unemployment; but an increase in aggregate money demand would not help either. The analytic equivalence of the two types of policy still exists.

III

Let us take a few more steps away from the static model into the jungles of the real world. We have dropped the assumption of a homogeneous, mobile labor force. The real world is also complicated by the existence of fixed money contracts and by the fact that price declines may give rise to adverse expectations. For these two reasons it would be foolish to rely en-tirely on price and wage deflation to cure a depression through the Pigou effect. To repeat, I do not know of any writer who has recommended that kind of policy.

It does not follow, however, either that wage and price rigidity is unim-portant or desirable or that the wealth-saving relationship is of no conse-quence in the real world.

Surely a certain flexibility of *relative* wages and prices is desirable. And in a general depression changes in relative wages and prices will mainly have to assume the form of differentiated wage and prices reductions. If there is unemployment and excess capacity everywhere, one would hardly want to recommend that wage and price reductions in some lines must be compen-sated by wage and price increases elsewhere so as to keep the wage and price level unchanged. It should be easy, however, to prevent, by means of mone-tary and fiscal methods of expansion, an intensification of a general deflation resulting from such a policy of differentiated wage and price reductions.

Moreover, I find it hard to believe that there do not exist important cases in which investment in certain lines (*e.g.*, in the building trade) or consump-tion of particular commodites can be significantly stimulated by cost and

---

[1] Needless to say, I do not wish to minimize the seriousness of such conditions or to recommend that nothing except making wages flexible should be done about them.

price reductions without offsetting changes elsewhere. Since it is clearly possible to cripple or damage an industry by excessive wage demands or choke demand for particular commodities by exorbitant prices, the opposite must be possible too. I conclude that flexibility of relative prices is desirable not only from the point of view of correct allocation of resources but also as a possible stimulant of aggregate expenditure.[1]

The importance of the wealth-saving relation goes beyond the case usually designated by the Pigou effect, *viz.*, beyond the effect of an increase in the real value of cash balances and government bonds due to falling prices. Suppose the quantity of money is increased by tax reductions or government transfer payments, government expenditures remaining unchanged and the resulting deficit being financed by borrowing from the central bank or simply by printing money.[2] The wealth-saving theorem tells us that, apart from the operation of the Keynes effect (through the rate of interest), consumption and investment expenditure will increase when the quantity of money grows. I find it difficult to believe that this might not be so.

There is, furthermore, the possibility that the secular growth of real (per capita) wealth may gradually push up the consumption function, and thus, counteract the effect of rising income on the level of saving.

My guess is that the Pigou effect does not play an important role in the actual cycle mechanism. On this I entirely agree with Hansen. But it does dispose effectively of the secular stagnation hypothesis, also in a cycle-ridden world (not only within the static Keynesian model world). In the actual cycle-ridden world the secular stagnation thesis amounts to saying that even at the top of the boom there is no approach to full employment because of a secular insufficiency of effective demand.[3] Let me illustrate what I mean by

---

[1] That there are relations between relative prices and changes in relative prices, on the one hand, and changes in aggregate demand, on the other, has been increasingly recognized in recent years. But no comprehensive theory of this relation has yet been developed. See, however, the article by G. Ackley and Daniel B. Suits, " Relative Price Changes and Aggregate Consumer Demand " (*American Economic Review*, Vol. XL [December, 1950]), for a promising beginning and some references to the literature.

[2] Open-market operations are different, because they result merely in a substitution of one type of asset for another; and public works (increase in government spending) result, of course, directly in increased demand for goods and services.

[3] I do not think that it would be correct to represent the secular stagnation thesis as merely saying that the cycle plays around a less-than-full-employment trend. For the trend (average rate of output over the cycle) cannot help being below the full-employment level, because it is impossible to imagine that the overfull employment that may exist during part of the boom can be anywhere near the same order of magnitude as the unemployment during the depression. (By " overfull employment " I mean here a situation in which people work temporarily longer hours than they are really prepared to work, or take a job although they would rather stay at home, because, say, of patriotic appeals or because they are under a money illusion or something like that.) If I understand him right, Professor Higgins reaches the same conclusion in his interesting paper, " Concepts and Criteria of Secular Stagnation", in *Income, Employment, and Public Policy: Essays in Honor of Alvin H. Hansen* (New York, 1948).

applying it to Hicks's theory.[1] Hicks's "Equilibrium line" (the "E-line" in his Diagrams 12 and 13, pp. 97 and 121, *op. cit.*) cannot be an equilibrium line except with rigid wages and prices. If wages were flexible, the trend value of real cash balances would grow (prices would fall more in depressions and rise less in prosperity periods), and Hicks's equilibrium ("E-line") would be pushed up the full-employment level ("F-line"). As far as I can see, the rest of Hicks's theory would not be affected in any way by this amendment. A similar argument applies to similar (nonlinear) models as, for example, those of Goodwin and Harrod.[2]

IV

I should like to end my note with a few comments on Metzler's most interesting article. His thesis is this: A theory which accepts the wealth-saving relation differs from the orthodox classical position as exemplified by Ricardo, because the equilibrium rate of interest is no longer determined exclusively by "real" conditions. Metzler tries to show that, if the wealth-saving relation is accepted, certain types of changes in the quantity of money must be assumed to alter the rate of interest permanently. Specifically, if the quantity of money is increased by the central bank's buying securities in the open market, the equilibrium, full-employment rate of interest is reduced.

This somewhat unexpected conclusion follows from three premises: (1) open-market purchases of securities reduce the real value of privately held wealth; (2) this leads, according to the Pigou effect, to an increase in the supply of saving; while (3) there is no reason to believe that the demand for saving (investment) is affected. Hence saving and investment come into equilibrium at a lower rate of interest than before.[3]

Let us examine these three premises. Initially, open-market purchases cause a change in the composition of privately held wealth: the stock of securities (common stock which stands for real wealth) is reduced while the

---

[1] *A Contribution to the Theory of the Trade Cycle* (London, 1950), *passim*.

[2] I realize that serious difficulties remain, inasmuch as it is hard to reconcile even cyclical (short-run) unemployment with a fully flexible wage and price system. No adequate discussion of that problem is, of course, possible in this note. But it may be suggested that the simplest, though not the only, solution seems to be the assumption that wages and prices, although flexible in a somewhat longer run, are rigid in the short run. It must be emphasized, however, that this does not imply that cyclical (short-run) fluctuations in aggregate output could be eliminated (they may not even be reduced) simply by somehow making wages and prices flexible in the short run.

[3] It is interesting to observe that after the long Keynesian interlude we are back at the old classical position which was so vehemently attacked by Keynes: saving and investment are again equated by the rate of interest. True, the mechanism is not exactly the same as it used to be, the argument has become more sophisticated, and the wealth-saving relation has been added. But let me repeat the reminder: The wealth-saving relation has to be called upon only in extreme cases which may rarely be realized in practice.

stock of money increases. But since the increase in the quantity of money drives up prices, the real value of money falls again, and the result is a reduction of total private wealth. Within the Metzlerian model there seems to me no reason to doubt that this is correctly deduced. The second premise is a clear consequence of the saving-wealth relation. Professor Duesenberry has convinced me that the third premise, which I was at first inclined to question, is valid: Since Metzler evidently assumes that aggregate private income remains unchanged (the government, by lowering taxes or transfer payments, feeds back into the private income stream the dividends on the securities which it has acquired),[1] there seems to be no plausible reason why the inducement to invest should have changed one way or the other.

It thus seems that Metzler has proved his thesis: Certain monetary policies do, indeed, tend to affect the equilibrium rate of interest. I do not believe, however, that from a classical standpoint this should be regarded as a disturbing or heretical conclusion. For, as Metzler himself points out, even thoroughly "classical" writers found it necessary to qualify their contention that, broadly speaking, the rate of interest is determined by "real" conditions. For example, if credit inflation changes the income distribution in such a way that the community's propensity to save increases, the real equilibrium rate of interest will fall.[2] I imagine that Ricardo himself would have accepted that proposition.

Metzler's case seems to be exactly analogous. He assumes that open-market operations produce a change in the wealth distribution in favor of an economic unit, the government, which has a different behaviour pattern than the rest (i.e., does not save less when its wealth increases). Hence the over-all propensity to consume is changed.

I am sure that Metzler will agree that his model, although undoubtedly an improvement over the original Keynesian model, is still much too drastically simplified a picture of the real world to warrant the deduction of practical conclusions with respect to such complex questions as the one under consideration. He surely does not wish to recommend inflationary open-market purchases (or a capital levy in kind which, as he points out, is strictly analogous to open-market purchases inasmuch as it too reduces private wealth—without inflation at that!) in order to stimulate saving, to bring down the rate of interest, and to accelerate economic growth.

I hasten to add that these remarks are not meant to cast aspersion on Metzler's essay. The great theoretical value of the article is beyond question, but it seems to lie in the most elegant method of analysis and the exemplary clarity of exposition rather than in its concrete results with respect to the influence of monetary or other policies on the rate of interest.

---

[1] If he assumed that the government used the dividends for its own purposes and thus reduced private incomes, he could not be sure that private savings would increase; the reduction in private income would tend to reduce savings and thus offset the increase induced by the reduction of wealth.

[2] Much more important, I am sure, are dynamic changes as envisaged by Schumpeter. If by inflationary credit expansion Schumpeterian innovators are enabled to carry out their projects and to squeeze out or force into action lethargic, static producers, profound and lasting changes may be wrought.

NAME INDEX TO PARTS I AND II

SUBJECT INDEX TO PARTS I AND II

NAME AND SUBJECT INDEX TO PART III

Printed in the United States
by Baker & Taylor Publisher Services